RENAISSANCE DRAMA
New Series XXVIII   1997

Renaissance Drama

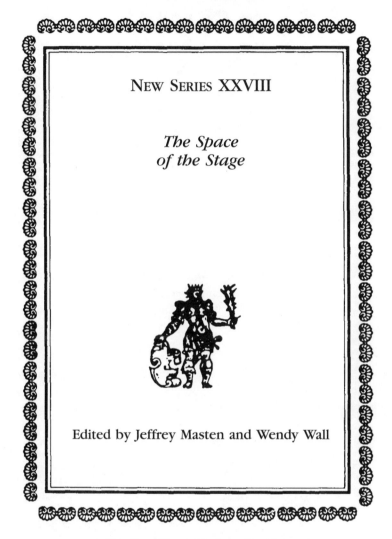

New Series XXVIII

*The Space
of the Stage*

Edited by Jeffrey Masten and Wendy Wall

Northwestern University Press

EVANSTON 1999

Contents

Editors' Preface   vii

Information for Contributors   ix

GARRETT A. SULLIVAN JR.   *Space, Measurement, and Stalking Tamburlaine*   3

CRYSTAL BARTOLOVICH   *Putting* Tamburlaine *on a (Cognitive) Map*   29

ROSEMARY KEGL   *"[W]rapping Togas over Elizabethan Garb": Tabloid Shakespeare at the 1934 Chicago World's Fair*   73

MICHAEL NEILL   *"Material Flames": The Space of Mercantile Fantasy in John Fletcher's* The Island Princess   99

JUDITH HABER   *"My Body Bestow upon My Women": The Space of the Feminine in* The Duchess of Malfi   133

HENRY S. TURNER   King Lear *Without: The Heath*   161

FIONA MCNEILL   *Gynocentric London Spaces: (Re)Locating Masterless Women in Early Stuart Drama*   195

WILLIAM N. WEST   *The Idea of a Theater: Humanist Ideology and the Imaginary Stage in Early Modern Europe*   245

Notes on Contributors   289

Editors' Preface

THIS IS A YEAR of transition for *Renaissance Drama*. With this issue, Mary Beth Rose ends her impressive twelve-year tenure as editor, and the journal moves from the Renaissance Center at the Newberry Library to the English Department at Northwestern University, where we will be co-editing it. We are pleased that Mary Beth Rose will continue to serve on the Editorial Board.

We hope that the readers of *Renaissance Drama* will join us in thanking Professor Rose for the magnificent guidance she has provided the journal for the past twelve years, a period that has seen momentous changes in the study of Renaissance dramatic literature and theatrical practice. While always maintaining *Renaissance Drama*'s reputation as a site for serious intellectual inquiry, Professor Rose has encouraged scholarly work that engages in creative new ways of interpreting dramatic texts, and has allowed the journal to be a venue where critical questions about drama and culture are debated. In this project, as in many of her endeavors, Mary Beth Rose has provided innovative and responsible leadership for the journal and for the field from which it takes its name—forging scholarly communities and reminding us all of the potential liveliness and energy of our discipline. She has set a very high standard, one that we as the journal's next editors hope to emulate.

We attempt to do so in this special issue of *Renaissance Drama* devoted to "The Space of the Stage." We hope through this rubric to gesture both toward an interest, in recent years, in the place of the theaters especially within early modern English culture (as our alluding to Steven Mullaney's *The Place of the Stage* should suggest), but also toward the way in which questions of the cognition and epistemology of space have increasingly energized the discussion of literature and performance. The essays gathered here draw especially from recent critical attention to early modern mapping, geography, and material practices in the early modern theater.

The plurality of enterprises and wide-ranging inquiries contained within "The Space of the Stage" demonstrate, we believe, the productiveness of this category—its ability to frame a rethinking of something as small (and seemingly contained) as a line of iambic pentameter or as large (and theoretically vexed) as the terrain of global capitalism. Noticing ways in which metaphors of space as well as real civic and household spaces helped to constitute early modern grammars of gender and sexuality, several essays in this volume also make clear the significance of space for ongoing critical projects in feminism and queer theory. These essays as well take up the question of the (literal) space of a number of stages: the bare early modern stage and its implications for thinking a theory of playing space and representing it in print; the appropriation of the early modern playing space through its reconstruction in a twentieth-century World's Fair. These essays join in making space strikingly legible as textual feature and mental construct, alerting us in the process to some guiding assumptions of theatrical practice, literary interpretation, and historical research. Since it figures prominently in modern critical attempts to understand Renaissance texts and practices, it is perhaps inevitable that the space of literary criticism becomes an object of inquiry here as well.

Jeffrey Masten and Wendy Wall
Guest Editors

Information for Contributors

A N ANNUAL and interdisciplinary publication, *Renaissance Drama* invites submissions that investigate traditional canons of drama as well as the significance of performance, broadly construed, to early modern culture. We particularly welcome essays that examine the impact of new forms of interpretation on the study of Renaissance plays, theater, and performance. There are no fixed chronological or geographical limits.

Renaissance Drama conforms to the stylistic conventions outlined in the most recent MLA Style Manual. Scholars preparing manuscripts for submission should refer to this book. Manuscripts should be submitted in triplicate; those accompanied by a stamped, self-addressed envelope will be returned. Submissions and inquiries regarding future volumes should be addressed to *Renaissance Drama,* c/o Professors Jeffrey Masten and Wendy Wall, Department of English, Northwestern University, Evanston, IL 60208, USA.

RENAISSANCE DRAMA

New Series XXVIII   1997

Space, Measurement, and Stalking Tamburlaine

GARRETT A. SULLIVAN JR.

I N HIS ACCOUNT of the events of 1603, which he dubs "The Wonderfull Yeare," Thomas Dekker famously refers to "Death [which] (like a Spanish Leagar, or rather like stalking *Tamberlaine*) hath pitcht his tents . . . in the sinfully-polluted Suburbes" (44). Dekker's "Death" takes the form of the plague. His association of the suburbs with the origins of plague is a commonplace one, as commonplace as figuring the suburbs as "sinfully-polluted." Even the spatial trope upon which the metaphor depends— the walled city of London threatened by its corrupt environs—is familiar. However, the scene from Marlowe's *Tamburlaine the Great, Part 1* that Dekker alludes to describes the siege of another walled city, Damascus, by Tamburlaine and his army. The pitched tents of Dekker's metaphor evoke a practice of Tamburlaine's, depicted here by a messenger to the Soldan of Egypt, that signifies his intentions toward the occupants of the city he besieges:

> The first day when he pitcheth down his tents,
> White is their hue, and on his silver crest
> A snowy feather spangled white he bears,
> To signify the mildness of his mind,
> That satiate with spoil refuseth blood.
> But when Aurora mounts the second time
> As red as scarlet is his furniture;
> Then must his kindled wrath be quench'd with blood,

3

> Not sparing any that can manage arms.
> But, if these threats move not submission,
> Black are his colors, black pavilion;
> His spear, his shield, his horse, his armor, plumes,
> And jetty feathers menace death and hell;
> Without respect of sex, degree, or age,
> He razeth all his foes with fire and sword.
>
> (4.1.49-63)

Having expected external aid, the Damascene city fathers have waited until Tamburlaine's "tents have now been altered / With terrors to the last and cruell'st hue" (5.1.7-8). At this point, they send out the city's virgins in the hopes of convincing Tamburlaine to be merciful, but to no avail. Tamburlaine asserts that the Egyptians "know my customs are as peremptory / As wrathful planets, death, or destiny" (5.1.127-28). In a formulation echoed by Dekker, Tamburlaine says that on his sword "sits imperious Death, / Keeping his circuit by the slicing edge" (5.1.111-12). Tamburlaine stalks outside the city walls of Damascus, promising in the name of his "customs" to destroy all those within.

Most immediately, Death's circuit is the path traced by Tamburlaine's sword as he wields it against the hapless Damascenes. In addition, Death is compared to a justice of the peace making his "circuit" through the city and exercising judgment. In the name of peremptory customs, Death— Tamburlaine's sword—condemns the actions of the "proud Egyptians" (5.1.121). This act of judgment, the keeping of a circuit, would also seem to involve the traversing of a measured area. Contemporary meanings of "circuit" define it as "[t]he line, real or imaginary, described in going round any area; the distance round" (*OED* 1a) or "[t]he space enclosed by a given circumference or boundary; area, extent, tract" (*OED* 2a). However, insofar as Tamburlaine has of yet neither fought the Damascenes nor entered their city, the "keeping" of the circuit is actually his measuring of it for the first time. Imperious Death, in the form of Tamburlaine's weapon, both measures and judges the Egyptians, tracing with Tamburlaine a circuit of the city.

Of course Tamburlaine's justice is highly equivocal, his measurements taken in the service of intransigent and ruthless ambition. Moreover, throughout the play Tamburlaine's "customs" are pursued at the expense of conflicting ones that particularize the regions that Tamburlaine invades. In general, custom and customary measures operate as principles of sociospatial definition that, in certain arenas of Elizabethan culture, are under siege. We can see this through a discussion of the measurement of land, a topic that not only illuminates aspects of the logic of *Tamburlaine the Great, Part 1,* but that offers us a way of understanding sociospatial transformations that were occurring in Elizabethan England. *Tamburlaine, Part 1* symbolically responds to the Elizabethan production of national statutory measures that pose a threat to customary measures and the regional forms of self-identification from which they are inseparable; the play represents the production of a coercive form of nationhood that emerges out of the near-universal imposition of Tamburlaine's custom. It also reveals the contestatory nature of disparate early modern spaces while complicating conceptions of space adduced by both literary critics and social theorists.

Arguably the most important modern theorist of space, Henri Lefebvre has written powerfully about the technocratic and capitalist domination of space in the twentieth century.[1] Describing what will eventually follow from the Renaissance rediscovery of perspective, Lefebvre states in *The Production of Space* that "[t]he history of space will begin at the point where anthropological factors lose their supremacy and end with the advent of a production of space which is expressly industrial in nature—a space in which reproducibility, repetition and the reproduction of social relationships are deliberately given precedence over works, over natural reproduction, over nature itself and over natural time" (119–20). Consequently, for Lefebvre the West has indeed witnessed the end of the history of space, for "reproducibility, repetition and the reproduction of social relationships" characterize the spatiality of the twentieth century. There are, however, still traces of an "anthropological" spatiality—a spatiality in which practice and architecture are organized in accordance not with a rationalized plan but in terms of the symbolic—to be located within the capitalist spatial order identified by Lefebvre. Their place and significance can be made clear through the rehearsal of a vocabulary that Lefebvre introduces early in his book.

Lefebvre distinguishes among three kinds of space: *spatial practice* "embodies a close association . . . between daily reality (daily routine) and urban reality (the routes and networks which link up the places set aside for work, 'private' life and leisure)"; in *representations of space* we encounter "conceptualized space, the space of scientists, planners, urbanists, technocratic subdividers and social engineers"—the space of the grid; and *representational space* is "space as directly *lived* through its associated images and symbols, and hence the space of 'inhabitants' and 'users' " (38–39). Vestiges of an "anthropological" spatiality are to be located in representational space—that is, in those spaces, like those of church or home, that are imbued with a symbolic meaning. However, representational space is "the dominated—and hence passively experienced—space which the imagination seeks to change and appropriate" (Lefebvre 39). Capitalist spatial practice, the daily routines that structure and are structured by the "routes and networks" linking up disparate spaces, reduces specific locales suffused with either traditional or innovative symbolic meanings to, at best, sites of attenuated and untheorized opposition. That is, home may be where the heart is, but the meaning with which home is imbued only exists as a relic of an anthropological spatiality or as evidence of the imaginative reconceptualization of one tiny segment of a dominant spatial order (or as both).

For Lefebvre, then, the symbolic ("representational space") offers scant resistance to the spatiality of capitalism, instantiated in and reproduced by spatial practices that structure everyday life in a way that works to ensure that capitalism will perpetuate itself. It is important to underscore the fact that this analysis assumes and depends upon the hegemony of a capitalist sociospatial order. I note this for the obvious reason that in the late sixteenth century such an order was at most emergent. What, then, does Lefebvre have to offer a student of early modern culture and drama? To answer this question, consider the spatial model offered up by Steven Mullaney. *The Place of the Stage* has defined for a generation of critics the social and spatial "place" of the theater, not to mention relations between the worlds on different sides of the city wall; its emphasis is on the liberties, those mostly suburban sites of license where the playhouses thrived alongside brothels and bear-baiting arenas. For Mullaney, social location and spatial location are mutually defining; that is, both spatially and socially the theater is marginal, on the periphery.[2] Mullaney shows that at least some of London's citizens believed that the theaters, if not theatricality itself, posed a threat to the city. Following Dekker, he asserts that, "[l]ike a plague or a stalking Tamburlaine, theatricality subjected the city. It was a plague in its own right, contaminating morals and manners when it did not, in its pathological alliance, contaminate the flesh itself. It infected the body politic" (50). For Mullaney, echoing the arguments of antitheatricalists and city fathers, a stalking Tamburlaine who metaphorizes both moral plague and theatricality does in fact invade London. However, an "invasion" like this one requires that the city come to the suburbs to be infected, for the site of theatricality that Mullaney dwells on is the fixed suburban stage. Thus, the spread through London of theatricality necessitates seeing the suburbs not merely as the staging ground for an invading force but also as a site of social exchanges between those from both sides of the wall, as a space not antagonistic to but imbricated in the life of the city.[3] This means that the spatial trope upon which Mullaney's analysis is built defines only one way among several of representing sociospatial relations in early modern London. Mullaney's London is a representational space, the coherence of which is challenged by spatial practice.

If Lefebvre's spatial taxonomy allows us to complicate Mullaney's conception of London, his focus on the spatiality of a fully developed capitalism means that he pays little attention to the early modern period. In this regard, Lefebvre's "anthropological" spatiality fails to capture the complexity of sociospatial relations in early modern England; his analysis can only imperfectly illuminate the spatial order of a capitalism that is nascent at best. While he discusses Florence's architectural development to produce a cogent account of the "transition from a representational space ([the city's layout as embodying] an image of the world) to a [city rebuilt in terms of a] representation of space, namely perspective" (119), the period of transition comes less sharply into focus than does what is left behind (a vital "anthropological" spatiality) and what is to follow (the spatial order ushered in and suggested by perspective). That is, perspective seems less one early modern technology among many, each with different ideological and conceptual underpinnings and implications, than it does a clear harbinger, if not "usherer in," of the capitalist spatial order to come.

The problem with talking about the late sixteenth century in terms of nascent capitalism (or, for that matter, as early modern) is that it not only privileges what is to come, it also encourages us to read the period in terms of what follows (as if "capitalist" or "modern" were transparent categories in the first place). My aim in the next section of this essay is both to talk about sixteenth-century developments that are necessary preconditions to a capitalist spatiality and to insist that the implications of those developments should not simply be construed in terms of that spatiality. In this case, preconditions to a capitalist spatiality take the form of changes in the nature of measurement, but such changes were contested, and the meanings of measurement were multiple; these preconditions obviously did not recognize themselves as such, and they had effects and resonances quite alien to the imperatives of the spatial order that was eventually to follow.

Marlowe wrote during a period in which the monarchy was engaged in standardizing measurement to a remarkable degree. Between 1582 and 1602, Elizabeth created not only standards for troy and avoirdupois weights, but also capacity measure standards (Zupko 86-93). In 1593 the mile was standardized in a statute (35 Elizabeth I c 6 1592/3) designed to restrict building in London's suburbs. Such efforts may seem from our perspective simply to entail the banishment of imprecision in favor of uniformity and accuracy, but it is worth considering the way in which, in the case of the mile, a measure emerging in response to the problem of London's growth aspired to become the measure of the nation. It is certainly true that the statute mile was only "adopted gradually throughout the kingdom, the adoption being nearly complete by the end of the eighteenth century, but only becoming of universal application through the all-encompassing Act of 1824 (5 George IV c 74)" (Connor 70). However, the eventual effect of that adoption was to impose London's mile on the entire country. This statutory measure was to become both the measure of the nation and the means by which the nation was measured.

But what of the measures that statutes were supposed to replace? In addressing this question, it is worth keeping in mind the following assertion: "Every measure as a social institution is an expression of a particular configuration of human relations and may well throw light upon these relations. . . . The increasing standardization of measures through time is an excellent indicator of one of the most powerful . . . historic processes—the process of the waxing unity of mankind" (Kula 101). The waxing unity that Witold Kula refers to comes here at the expense of regional measures and, thus, of "particular configuration[s] of human relations." Moreover, as M. Bloch states, "The persistence of measures is closely bound up with the questions of communal memory" (qtd. in Kula 111) and thus with communal identity. The gradual eradication of customary measures contributes to and registers "the waxing unity of mankind" at the expense of regional forms of affiliation and identification.

What exactly is meant by custom here? A useful definition is offered in a text devoted to the maintenance of London's customs: "a Custome is applyed to the commoditie of some one prouince, circuite or citie, and grounded upon a speciall reason of conueniencie or comoditie, for those persons or place where it is obserued" (*A Breefe Discourse* 6–7). While the writer's emphasis throughout is on the city and its customary law, there is obviously a broader application, for customs exist as "the principall ioyntes and uerie sinowes of all good corporations and fellowships, and [are] also the mainteiners of a sacred unitie and natural amitie betweene the husband and his wife, the parentes & their children" (*A Breefe Discourse* 4). Custom is the frame upon which "all good corporations and fellowships" are built; crucially, it defines particular spaces (anything from household to "prouince, circuite or citie") in terms of the activities peculiar to each space, thereby existing at the intersection of topography or architecture and social practice. Of course, custom cannot be summed up in customary measures. Instead, such measures need to be read not as evidence of pre-empirical imprecision, but, again, as partly constitutive of an identity, whether it be regional, civic, or even manorial. Statute measures are created to enable exchanges across regions, but customary measures attest to the irreducibility of a specific region.

A case in point is the acre, as we can see by drawing on the work of Andrew McRae. McRae talks of the way in which "measures derived from traditional agricultural practices within a region" inculcate notions of land that link it both to labor methods and to local identity. "[T]he dimensions of the acre originally had a customary quality, derived from the quantity of land a yoke of oxen could plough in a day, while the statutory definition, which dates from the thirteenth century, was based on a standard common-field rectangular plot of four by forty perches or rods" (184).[4] While the statute acre was obviously not an Elizabethan innovation, regional differences in the length of a perch meant that for centuries English communities were far from standardization. However, what happens starting in the second half of the sixteenth century is that surveying works to regularize local measures. As McRae puts it, "the techniques and terminology of the surveyors profoundly altered appreciations of the conventional unit of land quantification. Through the imposition of a national empirical standard, acceptance of local particularity gave way to a representation of land as a commodity easily accessible and transferable within a market economy" (186). Thanks to surveying, the statute becomes the flag-bearer for "a national empirical standard." More is at stake than the fate of a regional measure; "local particularity" can include a whole host of land-based labor

practices that in a predominantly agrarian society are primary determinants
of identity. (Equally important but tangential here is the fact that surveys
often reallocated the land in ways detrimental to tenants.) No wonder John
Norden, even in an apology for surveying, depicts a farmer who complains
that those who have had their land surveyed "are abridged of such liberties
as they have long used in Mannors; and customes are altred, broken, and
sometimes peruerted or taken away by [the surveyor's] meanes" (2-3).[5]

Norden's farmer suggests that surveyors act unjustly in violating custom;
in doing so, he also reveals the extent to which measurement is a site of
cultural contestation, one with implications for the figuration of land- and
region-based conceptions of identity. The yoking of justice and measurement is hardly an idle one, for there is a venerable tradition linking the two,
manifested in the familiar image of blind Justice with her scales. As Kula has
argued, "Very early . . . we find that 'the just measure' becomes symbolic of
justice in general. Practices bound up with man's attitude to measurement
assume the character of a symbolic expression of many elements of popular
'social philosophy' " (9). But where does the "justness" of the measure
reside? An obvious answer would seem to recommend itself—"justness"
is to be found in general adherence to a standardized measure, in the
production of uniformity in accordance with, say, statutes demarcating the
size of bushel bags. However, we have seen that standardization poses problems for at least one conception of justice, and ethical behavior mandated
by "popular 'social philosophy' " further complicates such a seemingly
transparent connection between justice and measurement. Consider this
passage from the New Testament: "Give, and it shall be given unto you;
good measure, pressed down, and shaken together, and running over, shall
men give into your bosom. For with the same measure that ye mete withal
it shall be measured to you again" (Luke 6:38). The final sentence offers
a Christian model that inverts Hammurabi's code and an Old Testament
ethic—justice not as retribution (an eye for an eye), but as reciprocity
(what you give is what you get). Notice, however, that the measure given by
and to the generous Christian does not conform to but exceeds that which
one might expect from literal adherence to statutory regulation—"good
measure" means that the sack is overflowing, its contents "pressed down,
and shaken together, and running over." Moreover, the passage from Luke,
with its metaphorical insistence on the interpenetration of measurement
and ethics, suggests that measurement and the exchanges predicated upon

it exist as a way in which social relations articulate themselves; Christian values and prescribed behaviors are expressed in terms of "good measure."

While the passage from Luke reveals something important about one version of the "just measure"—its justice resides not in *any* but in a *particular* use of a standard measure—my emphasis is on statutory land measures and the way in which they strive to produce complete uniformity of measurement. Moreover, as the example from Norden shows, such uniformity was sometimes understood to be corrosive of justice. Another way of depicting the relationship among surveying, justice, and measurement is to be found in William Folkingham's *Feudigraphia: The Synopsis of or Epitome of Surveying Methodized.* Folkingham declaims as follows: "Take away Number, Weight, Measure, you exile Iustice, and reduce and haile-vp from Hell the olde and odious Chaos of Confusion. Priuate Intelligencers, intimating (by their roaued [i.e., conjectural] Aymes at Quantities and Qualities) vnder-hand and sinister informations, abuse the Lessor & wrong the Lessee, where the iust and iudicious Feudigrapher . . . duly and discreetly obseruing all particulars incident to the Plot, certifies a true Relation" (A3r).[6] Again we see the yoking of "true" measurement and justice, but what should be underscored here is that the "Number, Weight, [and] Measure" Folkingham advocates are those of McRae's "national empirical standard." That is, he is thinking primarily of the figures generated by the surveyor. While Folkingham claims that producing a "true Relation" works for the good of both tenant and landlord—it leaves no room for "Priuate Intelligencers" to traffic in false information—surveyors were routinely loathed because the figures they produced were, as Norden's farmer says above, abusive of the customary. For Folkingham, then, justice and the "true Relation" inhere in measurements that were widely seen as being taken at the expense of traditional agrarian practice. Moreover, measurement of the land exists here as the process by which the land is brought to order, for measurement leads to the banishment of chaos. It is worth considering the political overtones of the phrase "Chaos of Confusion"; Folkingham's bombastic rhetoric suggests that more is at issue than the production of reliable figures. For Folkingham, surveying does at the estate level what it was designed to do in English attempts to survey Ireland—it imposes order on a landscape dominated by customary practices that are denigrated as chaotic if not dangerous.[7]

What has to occur for measurement to become seemingly divorced from ethics, for it to have an (at least mostly) instrumental relationship to social practice? That is, what has to happen to make measurements what they are today?[8] Examples that I have already adduced represent early strokes in the severing of connections between measurement and (one conception of) justice. For instance, once the acre is divorced from traditional agrarian practice, it begins to take on an instrumental identity, one in which it is generally construed in terms of exchange-value rather than use-value. Put crudely, the standardization of measurement benefits more those who sell or trade land than it does those who work it. Standardization makes possible a notion of land as fungible, as a marketable commodity rather than that which it had traditionally been seen as—a social site central to a moral economy.[9] Standardization also enables the eventual production of representations of space, the urban planner's or the land developer's grid. That is, from standardization it is only a few short conceptual steps to the capitalist spatiality analyzed by Lefebvre, a spatiality in which the symbolic meanings of land (land as representational space: "space as directly *lived* through its associated images and symbols, and hence the space of 'inhabitants' and 'users' ") exist in a dominated relationship to land's status as a commodified and frangible form parceled out in units of uniform acres.[10]

But this is not to say that the short steps were hastily taken. Short conceptually, yes, but long historically, and not steps that, in the late sixteenth or early seventeenth century, would have had an air of inevitability about them. If the grid necessary to Lefebvre's representations of space requires standardized measurement, that does not mean that standardization instantly produced the grid. More pointedly, what standardization did produce may seem alien from the perspective of the grid and the rationalist logic that it undergirds and that undergirds it. A case in point is Folkingham's standardization-driven retooling of the traditional association of measurement and justice. Folkingham's "Number, Weight, [and] Measure" represent and enable a reconfiguration of land-based social relations. If this is justice, it adheres neither in an understanding of land as a locus of social (or customary) practice, nor, more broadly, in the notion that "with the same measure that ye mete withal it shall be measured to you again"; instead, justice only requires producing "accurate" measurements and then shaping land management in accordance with them (through, for instance, the banishment of "Priuate Intelligencers"). Again, Folkingham gestures toward measurement as we know it, the measurement of capitalist spatiality, characterized by faith placed in numbers and the truth claims they underwrite. At the same time, his invocation of Justice and Chaos attests to how differently it means to take land measurements in the early seventeenth and late twentieth centuries. More importantly, this discussion of the relationship between measurement and custom in early modern England both makes clear the degree to which the former is a contested category and shows us that the taking of measurements often registered as the violent subduing of local imperatives—as, that is, an act of conquest.

By now connections between my discussion of measurement and *Tamburlaine, Part 1* will have suggested themselves. As we have seen, Tamburlaine's assault on Damascus goes hand in hand with an act of measurement—his sword's tracing of a circuit of the city. While this is a metaphorical measuring, it gestures toward a literal act of surveying. In the early modern period surveying preceded and enabled a siege such as Tamburlaine's. Nick de Somogyi has recently pointed out in relation to *Tamburlaine* that "[t]he same geometric constructions necessary to survey a town are those required to open up a breach in its defences" (101). De Somogyi's analysis makes clear the interrelations between surveying and military conquest. For a martial leader like Tamburlaine, the measurement of Damascus would be a prerequisite for subduing it. At the same time, Tamburlaine's measurements are taken in the name of his "custom," which is mentioned three times in relation to the ritual of the tents (see 5.1.13, 67, 127). His execution of "justice" involves the imposition of his peremptory customs on the areas he subdues.

We should notice that what Tamburlaine means by "custom" is different from what our anonymous advocate of London's traditional practice meant by it. Tamburlaine's custom is "[a] habitual or usual practice; common way of acting" (*OED* 1a). For Tamburlaine, then, insistence on his customs entails the conquering of the spaces he encounters in accordance with his habitual practice. While this is clear enough, it is worth pointing out that "custom" in the sense of habit can be construed in terms of Pierre Bourdieu's description of *habitus*: "an acquired system of generative schemes" or "an infinite capacity for generating products—thoughts, perceptions, expressions and actions—whose limits are set by the historically and socially situated conditions of its production" (55). Custom as habit is a point of intersection between the individual subject and the social whole. While behaviors dictated by custom are presumably less varied than many others produced out of the subject's habitus, "habit" has its limits "set by the historically and socially situated conditions of its production," conditions that structure but need not narrowly determine individual behavior. This means that custom as habit can be seen as continuous with and structured in accordance with the definitions of custom we encountered above: custom as traditional practice and as a principle of sociospatial demarcation. In Tamburlaine's case, however, "custom" reverses the relationship between social practice and individual habit, for his custom constitutes the arbitrary imposition onto others of personal practices elevated by him to the level of higher imperative. At first glance, Tamburlaine's insistence on and near-deference to his custom may seem to suggest that it exists as something larger than himself, as a set of inviolable norms that govern his actions: "my customs are as peremptory / As wrathful planets, death, or destiny." That is, when Tamburlaine appeals to his "custom," he seemingly gestures toward a higher force or principle, like death or destiny; he cannot spare the Damascene virgins because he is an agent of his custom. Of course, Tamburlaine is the one who has invested his custom with the weight of authority. For him to appeal to and insist upon it as an unyielding code of behavior is finally to do no more than to insist upon adherence to his own desires as formalized in "custom."

The installation of Tamburlaine's custom is concomitant with the installation of a spatiality. This view is confirmed by Tamburlaine's famous description of his plan to (re)map the world:

> I will confute those blind geographers
> That make a triple region in the world,
> Excluding regions which I mean to trace
> And with this pen [i.e., his sword] reduce them to a map,
> Calling the provinces, cities, and towns
> After my name and thine, Zenocrate.
> Here at Damascus will I make the point
> That shall begin the perpendicular.
>
> (4.4.73–80)

While earlier we saw Tamburlaine's sword metaphorized as "imperious Death, / Keeping his circuit," here it is a pen that "trace[s]" neglected regions and "reduce[s] them to a map." In following his sword, Tamburlaine will rename existing "provinces, cities, and towns." His act of measurement—the surveying of these regions—goes hand in hand with conquest, as is made abundantly clear by his plan to name these newly mapped spaces after himself and his lover. However, these actions are to be performed in the service of "reducing" regions to a map. This is usually glossed as the mere recording of these regions in map form—in Stephen Greenblatt's words, here we see "the reduction of the universe to the coordinates of a map" (195)—but we should approach the notion of reduction more carefully.[11] Marlowe's hero is to produce an abstract spatiality in his own name and image. As his "custom" finally reigns in Damascus, so it will in the regions of the world excluded by the "blind geographers," but only as a result of measurement and conquest, both undertaken in the service of the imposition of Tamburlaine's worldview.

My point is simple: this spatiality, which reduces all regions in accordance with the tyranny of Tamburlaine's ambitions, is produced as, and out of, a violence done to the geographical spaces and customs "measured" (not only surveyed, but also judged and subdued) by Marlowe's indefatigable warrior. In thinking about this, one could turn to recent critical work that has provocatively linked *Tamburlaine* to early modern imperialism and international commerce (e.g., Bartels, Mead, Wilson) and connect the production of such a spatiality to English fantasies involving the "reduction" of the world to a map made in the nation's image. However, I want to consider this spatiality in light not of international but domestic space. Insofar as it denies the incommensurability of disparate regions, the specificity of Kula's "particular configuration[s] of human relations," Tamburlaine's spatiality is reminiscent of the English statutory measures that threaten customary ones. Tamburlaine "trace[s]" with his sword—that is, measures, surveys, judges—"provinces, cities, and towns" in order to make them his by naming them, thereby reducing these disparate cultural spaces to manifestations of his own authority and the devouring spatiality that underwrites it. By doing throughout the play what he says from the outset that he will do—"be a terror to the world, / Measuring the limits of his empery / By east and west" (1.2.39–40)—Tamburlaine installs a spatiality that elevates *his* custom above all others. The connection can be drawn between Tamburlaine's efforts and the only gradually realized effects of the statute mile, which, as we have seen, eradicates the customary in the name of a homogenizing national measure produced by the Crown. More broadly, Tamburlaine's martial endeavors can be considered as a symbolic response to, if not a symbolic version of, Elizabethan attempts to produce a national standard at the expense of customary measures. (Of course, this response is played out internationally, across the far-flung regions

Tamburlaine conquers. However, it is hardly unusual in early modern drama for national concerns to be displaced onto foreign lands. Moreover, it is my contention that *Tamburlaine* is not interested in, for instance, Persian customs per se, but in Persia's status as a region subdued by Tamburlaine. Marlowe's geographic specificity, as evidenced by his oft-noted use of Ortelius's atlas, is not incompatible with the production of exotic regions which serve as the arena for the exploration of Anglocentric issues.) Put differently, through its representation of Tamburlaine the play exaggerates the Crown's efforts by offering us a refracted and coercive vision of nation-formation, a version of "national" unity achieved through the eradication of local difference.

The installation of Tamburlaine's custom as a geospatial category occurs upon his first appearance. Zenocrate and Tamburlaine come on stage together, the former as the latter's prisoner. In her first speech, Zenocrate describes herself as

> a silly maid,
> Who, traveling with these Median lords
> To Memphis, from my uncle's country of Media,
> Where all my youth I have been governed,
> Have pass'd the army of the mighty Turk,
> Bearing his privy signet and his hand
> To safe conduct us thorough [*sic*] Africa.
>
> (1.2.10–16)

In addition to providing biographical details, Zenocrate outlines her itinerary in a way that makes plain the perils attendant upon traveling across countries that exist in a complex and often hostile relation to one another. Nevertheless, Zenocrate and her companions have both respected and managed such perils, as is attested to by her attainment of the Turk's signet. Magnetes, one of the Median lords, confirms this, stating that, "since we have arriv'd in Scythia, / Besides rich presents from the puissant Cham, / We have his highness' letters to command / Aid and assistance if we stand in need" (1.2.17–20). The overriding sense one has at this moment is of the necessity of respecting the cultural claims of those whose borders one crosses or armies one passes. That is, Marlowe produces at this point a variegated cultural landscape, thereby gesturing toward a multiplicity of "customs," each specific to a people and/or region. In light of this, the nature of Tamburlaine's assertion of his authority, made in response to Magnetes, is crucial: "But now you see these letters and commands / Are countermanded by a greater man, / And through my provinces you must expect / Letters of conduct from my mightiness" (1.2.21-24). In anticipation of his later assertion that he would name "provinces, cities, and towns" after himself, Tamburlaine claims Scythian provinces as his own, inaugurating himself as controller of safe passage through the territories in which he steals. It is only fifteen lines later that he announces his ambition to "[m]easur[e] the limits of his empery / By east and west," an ambition of a piece with his usurpation of provincial authority. The crucial point is that we witness here the first installation of a spatiality brought into being by Tamburlainian fiat. The accounts of Zenocrate and Magnetes hardly suggest geographical space as abstraction or vacancy. Instead, we see that space homogenized by Tamburlaine's assertions of ownership. For Tamburlaine, to measure the world is to lay claim to it and to transform it into a reflection of himself, judging unworthy those who resist the imperatives of his colonizing spatiality.

Most of the rest of *Tamburlaine, Part 1* is taken up with the successful imposition of Tamburlaine's authority, associated with his conquest of far-flung regions. The play is saturated with the language of measurement, as in Tamburlaine's desire to "measure every wand'ring planet's course" (2.7.23) or in his question to Zenocrate, "Think you I weigh this treasure more than you?" (1.2.84). Unsurprisingly, the play also repeatedly concerns itself with the traversing of geographical space, which is almost invariably associated with Tamburlaine's conquest of it. For instance, when Tamburlaine boasts that Zenocrate "shalt be drawn amidst the frozen pools / And scale the icy mountains' lofty tops" (1.2.99-100), her ascent functions as evidence of the projected extension of his authority to even the most distant peaks. A hyperborean landscape is evoked, but only as it is to be subjugated to Tamburlaine. It should be clear by now, also, that the traversing of space can also be linked to acts of measurement. We can see this without knowing that "to scale" can mean not only to ascend, but "to weigh as in scales" (*OED* 2 fig. A) (a kind of measurement that brings us back to the execution of justice, as in the case of Angelo, the Duke's "corrupt deputy [who is] scaled" in *Measure for Measure* [3.1.255-56]). For Tamburlaine, the crossing of geographical space always entails the intersecting processes of measurement and subjugation. In this case, Zenocrate's projected safe passage, the description of which follows closely on the heels of her thwarted journey to Egypt, would attest to the successful completion of those processes and reveal the extent to which Tamburlaine has laid claim to even the mountaintops as his provinces.

Although Zenocrate's trip to the peaks is never taken, Tamburlaine's status as monarch of all he surveys is secure at play's end. Moreover, little resistance is offered throughout to the extension of his spatiality. While he is fought by figures such as Mycetes, Cosroe, and Bajazeth, they are not spokespersons for an alternative spatiality; in fact, they are sometimes actively involved in the promulgation of Tamburlaine's spatiality, as in Menaphon's depiction of the Scythian shepherd to an approving Cosroe as one "In every part proportioned like the man / Should make the world subdued to Tamburlaine" (2.1.29–30). Tamburlaine's physical proportions are linked to his successful conquests. To Menaphon and Cosroe, then, he is both subduer (or measurer) of the world and "the measure of all men"—the yardstick against which other warriors measure themselves and fall short. (This last point is suggested by Menaphon's murky syntax, which asserts that Tamburlaine alone is the one "proportioned" to act like Tamburlaine.) The imposition of a homogenizing spatiality goes hand in hand with the installation of Tamburlaine as a martial ideal.

One must stress, however, that Tamburlaine exists as a *martial* ideal, and that the spatiality associated with him is an emphatically military one. In this regard, the context of the play's interrogation of the meanings of measurement is different from the historical context suggested by my examination of the Elizabethan introduction of statutory measures. And yet, these contexts are not mutually exclusive, as was made clear by the earlier linkage of de Somogyi's and my analyses of Tamburlaine's deadly measurement of Damascus. What I am most interested in now, however, is resistance to this martial ethos and the spatiality aligned with it. Such resistance is to be found in the response of Zenocrate to the siege with which we began discussion of this play.

Glimpses of the customary imperatives that Tamburlaine suppresses are, intriguingly enough, articulated by his lover after Tamburlaine begins his assault on Damascus. In response to Tamburlaine's characteristically unempathetic question, "[W]hy art thou so sad?," Zenocrate answers, "My lord, to see my father's town besieg'd, / The country wasted where myself was born, / How can it but afflict my very soul?" Then she pleads that Tamburlaine "raise [his] siege from fair Damascus' walls / And with my father take a friendly truce" (4.4.61–70). It is in response to this request that Tamburlaine vows not to spare Damascus but to name "provinces, cities, and towns" after the two of them. Zenocrate foregrounds the particularity of this walled city, linking it to both her father and herself. Moreover, the "friendly truce" she encourages Tamburlaine to make might necessitate his acknowledging the integrity of Damascus's (and presumably Egypt's) authority and borders. Such a truce also evokes Zenocrate's thwarted attempt to travel to Egypt and the painstaking negotiation of competing authorities and spaces that accompanied that attempt. As we have seen, Tamburlaine denies such authorities, transforming all geographical spaces into his provinces. Moreover, Tamburlaine's plan to rename certain locations after Zenocrate entails not merely his intention to commemorate his love for her but also his attempt to obliterate her identity as an Egyptian. He offers her new territories for old, but the old are ones that ground her identity, and Tamburlaine's assault on them "afflict[s her] very soul."

The particularity of this walled city is further adumbrated in Zenocrate's lamenting response to Damascus's fall:

> Wretched Zenocrate, that livest to see
> Damascus' walls dy'd with Egyptian blood,
> Thy father's subjects and thy countrymen;
> Thy streets strowed with dissevered joints of men
> And wounded bodies gasping yet for life;
> But most accurs'd, to see the sun-bright troop
> Of heavenly virgins and unspotted maids,
> Whose looks might make the angry god of arms
> To break his sword and mildly treat of love,
> On horsemen's lances to be hoisted up
> And guiltlessly endure a cruel death.
>   (5.1.319–29)

Critics have often seen Tamburlaine's siege of Damascus as a moment where audience identification with the ruthless leader is strained, if not ruptured. This is also a moment where an alternative to the spatiality promulgated by Tamburlaine is offered. More precisely, the assault on Damascus both represents a customary civic spatiality—Damascus as representational space—and makes apparent the costs of the bulldozing spatiality associated with Tamburlaine. Zenocrate's intense emotional engagement with this city is made clear through her use of the possessive pronoun; the city is defined in terms of her father's subjects, her countrymen, her streets—or does "thy" refer in this last case to the city itself? This ambiguity suggests the fusion of Zenocrate with the city, the extent to which she understands its fate to be her own.

The fate of the "sun-bright troop / Of heavenly virgins" is also crucial here. As Lisa Hopkins has pointed out, Tamburlaine "kills the innocent—his slaughter of the virgins of Damascus is of course an act of violence directed against those considered most holy by the Christian religion" (8). The chastity of these virgins can also be metaphorically linked with the integrity of the city that they plead with Tamburlaine for the sparing of. The association of the chaste woman with a besieged fortress is a Renaissance commonplace, as in Spenser's depiction of Una as a "fort assayle[d]" by Sans Loy, or Shakespeare's of Lucrece as a "never-conquer'd fort" before Tarquin's rape and as a "blemish'd fort" afterward (*Faerie Queene* bk. 1, canto 6, stanza 5, line 3; "Lucrece" 482, 1175). In short, Damascus functions as what Lefebvre has called a representational space, an "anthropological" space imbued with powerful symbolic and cultural associations. The destruction of Damascus evokes both the rape of the virgins and the obliteration of a culture whose integrity and organicism are symbolically suggested by the spatial trope of the city wall. Thus, the city offers both an alternative and resistance to the leveling spatiality of Tamburlaine. Moreover, its strong association with Zenocrate marks it as a locus of identity and as a site of customary practice.[12]

However, in *Tamburlaine, Part 1* representations of a resistant spatiality coincide with or follow upon that spatiality's obliteration. Moreover, Zenocrate's grief over the destruction of Damascus subsides in the face of her love for Tamburlaine; in her final line of the play, Zenocrate stresses that not to want to marry Tamburlaine would be for her to "forget [her]self" (5.1.500). This is a telling formulation of her desire for her soon-to-be husband. According to the *OED*, to forget oneself is "[t]o lose remembrance of one's own station, position, or character; to lose sight of the requirements of dignity, propriety, or decorum; to behave unbecomingly."[13] While "forgetting oneself" may seem from our perspective little more than a momentary deviation from one's "usual" behavior, in the early modern period more is at issue. The self that is forgotten is constituted relationally, in terms of the subject's place in a social network. That is, in this period before the predominance of ideologies of unique individuality, to forget oneself would entail becoming dislodged from a social network constitutive of one's identity. "Forgetting oneself," then, had implications far greater than is suggested by our sense of it as a momentary subjective lapse; the trope can describe the reformulation of one's identity in a way that involves the eradication of a previous social identity. This makes clear the significance of Zenocrate's final line. After having earlier witnessed an assault on the spaces and people not merely associated with but largely determinate of her identity—Damascus: her father's subjects, her countrymen, her streets—Zenocrate here reimagines herself in a way that suggests her identity exists only in relation to Tamburlaine. Thus, to forget herself at play's end would be for her to forget him. This underscores the fact that, over the course of the play, "Tamburlaine colonises the stage and everything on it" (Sales 53). His conquest of the world has been mirrored by his conquest of Zenocrate, the success of which is made manifest in her forgetting of herself (as an Egyptian), an act that enables her final claim that she will never forget herself (as Tamburlaine's lover).[14]

Tamburlaine the Great, Part 1 ends with marriage and with Tamburlaine "tak[ing] truce with all the world" (5.1.529). This truce does not promise what the aforementioned truce with Damascus might have, however—the acknowledgment of the sovereignty and particularity of specific regions. Instead, we are told that Tamburlaine's loyal followers are to be rewarded through the allocation of the lands he has conquered; he tells them to "Mount up your royal places of estate, / Environed with troops of noblemen, / And there make laws to rule your provinces" (5.1.525–27). This utterance both echoes Tamburlaine's earlier claim to Scythian provinces, a claim he has since made good on, and returns us to the topic of custom—in this case, customary law. In relation to debates over James I's plans for unifying Britain, Claire McEachern has identified important questions raised by the unification issue: "Is a local law a cultural practice, to be modified in and through use even to the extent of its eventual disappearance, or an ineradicable legal mark of local autonomy? Quaint or stubborn? Tourist attraction or intransigent cultural difference? If it yields to a general law, at what point does it do so, and if it does, what, then, remains its force? Part of the problem with defining the customary at this historical juncture is that the English themselves were elusive" (160). Tamburlaine, however, has no doubts: the regions he has conquered are his to allocate, and customary laws are to be ignored in the name of laws his followers generate to rule provinces identified as belonging to them. Certainly there are echoes here of the abuses perpetrated by estate surveyors, who were believed to (re-)measure lands in the name of acquisitive landlords and at the expense of custom. Most important, though, is that the rule of law described here extends the spatiality that we have seen associated with Tamburlaine from his first appearance on stage. That is, law, like the statute measure or Tamburlaine's custom, is to be imposed on a region in a way that violates and/or ignores that region's traditional identity, an identity intertwined with local practice. Tamburlaine may "take truce with all the world," but even in peacetime that world is to remain subject to his colonizing spatiality.

This essay has shown not only how an argument that pays particular attention to the category of space can illuminate Marlowe's play, but also how close analysis undertaken in terms of that category can help us isolate assumptions undergirding early modern cultural practice. I want to conclude by returning to the image of a "stalking *Tamberlaine*." To stalk: "To walk with stiff, high, measured steps, like a long-legged bird. Usually with disparaging notion, implying haughtiness, sullenness, indifference to one's surroundings, or the like" (*OED* 4). Stalking: "Walking with great strides" (*OED* 2). A 1607 example of the latter asks, "Haue you never seene a stalking-stamping Player." Measured steps, indifference to one's surround-ings, a player walking with great strides: the spatiality that I have identified with Tamburlaine's acts of colonization intersects with that of the blank stage, across which Tamburlaine stalked in a fashion that historians and critics have routinely identified as innovative and influential. Andrew Gurr alludes as follows to *Tamburlaine*'s role in the transition from a theater dominated by comedians to one dominated by tragedians: "What is clear is that the role of the clown in adult company plays had diminished markedly in value as plays began to offer more scope for the tragic actors. . . . Both [Will] Kemp and [Robert] Armin claimed descent from [celebrated clown, Richard] Tarlton, but between 1580 and 1600 the inheritance had dropped sharply in value. *[Edward] Alleyn's Tamburlaine now bestrode the stage*" (88–89; emphasis added). This bestriding (or stalking) also marks a change in audience address and the spatiality concomitant with it, as Robert Weimann's work makes plain; while clowns were associated with the *platea,* and thus regularly engaged in direct exchange with the audience, tragedians inhabited the *locus,* an illusionistic space separated from non-illusionistic engagement with the audience. The stage space that Tamburlaine produces with his measured steps is sealed off, measured out by his imperious stride.

Such a space is also measured out in measured language—language that is "uniform in movement; metrical, rhythmical" (*measurable, OED* 5), the kind of language associated not only with late sixteenth-century endeavors to reform English, but also with *Tamburlaine, Part 1* itself. In his prologue (1–6), Marlowe tells the playgoer or reader that his aim is to

> From jigging veins of rhyming mother wits,
> And such conceits as clownage keeps in pay,
> . . . lead you to the stately tents of war,
> Where you shall hear the Scythian Tamburlaine
> Threat'ning the world with high astounding terms
> And scourging kingdoms with his conquering sword.

As Alleyn's bestriding Tamburlaine represents a spatiality concomitant with the passage of clowns from the stage, Marlowe's "high astounding terms" expel clownage and "jigging veins of rhyming mother wits," taking us to the "stately tents of war" from which Tamburlaine measured out justice against the Damascenes. Critics commonly refer to the significance of this prologue, reading it in terms both of the arrival on the popular stage of blank verse, which attested to the ascendance of the University Wits (Leech 42; Hunter 35), and of Tamburlaine's powerful, performative rhetoric. As David Daiches has influentially put it, "[Tamburlaine's] action . . . involves his way of talking, and indeed we might almost say that in view of the way it is put [in the prologue] language and action are actually equated: threatening with words and scourging with swords are parallel and even equivalent activities" (78–79). In this sense, the measured language of Tamburlaine coincides with both the actor's measured strides and the character's measurement of the lands he conquers. In addition, the immediate and extensive influence of the play (see Levin, Berek) makes clear that Tamburlaine conquered his audience. Dekker's image of a Tamburlaine stalking the suburbs takes much of its force from the fact that the character so successfully stalked the suburban stage. In at least the theater, Tamburlaine's "custom" did for a time prevail.

These final comments are designed not merely to isolate briefly some of the other multiple and intersecting ways in which measures and measurement can mean, but also to trace connections between disparate spaces, from that of the blank stage to those of the lands conquered by Marlowe's hero. They are also meant to reveal the thoroughgoingness of Marlowe's ambition; his desire to colonize both theatrical language and stage space finds its corollary in Tamburlaine's need to "[m]easur[e] the limits of his empery / By east and west." At the same time, reading Tamburlaine's (and Marlowe's) ambition in terms of the history of the stage reminds us that the spatiality he promulgates is primarily a dramatic one, specific to the stage. That it bears some resemblance to Lefebvre's representations of space, or that it seems a troubling symbolic version of the spatiality hinted at by the Elizabethan standardization of measurement, suggests crucial intersections between disparate sociospatial arenas, but such resemblances must not lead us to produce a narrow or homogenized conception of early modern space, to confuse spatial representations with spatial practice. If drama, Marlovian or otherwise, infected the culture of early modern England, the disease spread not because theatricality stalked its way inside the city walls, but because the city integrated the theater and theatrical representation into both its social life and its spatial practice.

Notes

I would like to thank Patrick Cheney, Linda Woodbridge, and the readers for *Renaissance Drama* for their helpful feedback on earlier drafts of this essay.

1. For discussions of space, measurement, and custom that overlap in places with what follows, see Sullivan.

2. I should point out, however, that Mullaney would agree with Peter Stallybrass and Allon White when they assert that "what is *socially* peripheral is so frequently *symbolically* central" (5).

3. As Karen Newman asserts in a review of Mullaney's book, "Stow and the social history of early modern England . . . [suggest] not so much . . . the liberty and license of London's margins, as they [do] their vigorous incorporation into the emphatically market economy, if not the walls, of the city" (502). Mullaney has also described London as "a *ceremonial* city. It was shaped . . . by the varied rites of initiation, celebration, and exclusion through which a ceremonial social order defined, maintained, and manifested itself, in time and in space" (10). To see London as a "ceremonial city" is to focus only on the symbolic and not on shifting spatial practice; an emphasis on the latter would make, for instance, the suburbs less marginal sites of license than of growing industry (McMullan 28). That is, there is a disjunction between the symbolic meanings ascribed to the suburbs—as sites that, through their symbolic production (via rituals of demarcation and exclusion) as "the outside," help purify and clarify the boundaries of the city proper (I am invoking the work of Mary Douglas here)—and the fact that in crucial material ways the suburbs (and the theater itself) are integrated into the life of the city, into its spatial practice.

4. McRae echoes the following assertion by Kula: "Land measures vary, depending on the quality and type of soil, the location (level or slope), and the chief crop grown on it. The name of a particular geometric area unit may long have remained the same . . . but the

actual area specified may have changed over time and certainly varied at any particular time between provinces and villages, or even among farmsteads within particular villages" (35).

5. For more on surveying and some of its implications in this period, see Sullivan.

6. Compare Edward Worsop, also writing about surveying, in 1582: "True measure is not extremitie, but good justice" (qtd. in McRae 187).

7. On surveying in relation to English attempts to subdue the Irish, see Jones and Stallybrass.

8. It should be pointed out that the separation of measurement from ethics is in itself an ethical operation masquerading as a value-neutral one. That measurement has come to be seen as ethically neutral under capitalism only reveals another of the ways in which capitalism has triumphed.

9. On land as the locus of a moral economy, see McRae; Sullivan.

10. Of course I am not arguing that without standardization the land market would not have been possible; the aftermath of Henry VIII's expropriation of the monasteries would put the lie to such an assertion. What I am proposing is that standardization of measurement is a necessary but not sufficient cause of the gradual and general reworking of the meaning of land. There are complex ideological factors that need to come into play for the meanings suggested by measurement's standardization to outstrip traditional conceptualizations of land. McRae does a fine job of isolating many of those factors.

11. This reading is both indebted to and deviates from Greenblatt's influential explication of the spatial logic of the Tamburlaine plays. As Greenblatt puts it, "In *Tamburlaine* Marlowe contrives to efface all [regional and cultural] differences, as if to insist upon the essential meaninglessness of theatrical space, the vacancy that is the dark side of its power to imitate any place. This vacancy—quite literally, this absence of scenery—is the equivalent in the medium of the theater to the secularization of space, the abolition of qualitative up and down, . . . the equivalent then to the reduction of the universe to the coordinates of a map. . . . Space is transformed into an abstraction, then fed to the appetitive machine [i.e., Tamburlaine]" (195–96). I am arguing that what is for Greenblatt a spatial *precondition* for Tamburlaine's actions is actually the *result* of them. That is, Tamburlaine works to produce the space, in conjunction with his customs, that Greenblatt sees as underwriting and enabling his efforts.

12. It is worth thinking about this discussion of the siege of Damascus in relation to both Dekker's "stalking *Tamberlaine*" passage and Mullaney's unpacking of Dekker's plague metaphor. In implicitly comparing Damascus to London besieged by sin and plague, Dekker develops Marlowe's depiction of the walled city as representational space—that is, in each case one encounters an assault on a space whose putative organicism is figured by the trope of the wall, which provides that space with symbolic coherence. The integrity and supposedly self-identificatory and self-contained nature of civic culture are gestured toward through this trope. However, when Mullaney relates Dekker's metaphor to the spread in the sixteenth and seventeenth centuries of a plague-like theatricality, he slides not only from representation to "real life," but from representational space to the spatial practice of which theatergoing, as well as various other forms of civic theatricality, is a part. Moreover, as I've suggested, he does so in a way that elides the crucial distinction between the meanings with which spaces are imbued and the series of everyday practices that structure and are structured by disparate spaces. The passage of playgoers from outside to inside (or vice versa) can be metaphorized as (and even be a literal agent of) the spread of plague, but such passage should also be read

in terms of, in Lefebvre's terms, "the routes and networks which link up the places set aside for work, 'private' life and leisure"—of spatial practice and the vision of civic life and identity that it offers.

13. This is actually the most relevant of four overlapping meanings, the others of which are as follows: "a. To omit care for oneself; . . . c. To lose one's way; d. To lose consciousness."

14. It might be more precise to say that Zenocrate does not forget her Egyptian identity but has its terms redefined for her by (and in the terms of) Tamburlaine. The Soldan bemoans "the loss of Egypt and [his] crown" only to have Tamburlaine "render all into [the Soldan's] hands, / And add more strength to [his] dominions" (5.1.444–48). This is followed by what Simon Shepherd has defined as "the patriarchal arrangement of property marriage . . . that structures the final scene" (187). That is, the Soldan gives away his daughter, but only after Tamburlaine has spared his life and reinvested him with (both paternal and royal) authority. The marriage is a ritual that seemingly confirms Zenocrate's Egyptian identity—a ritual like the one that motivated her original truncated journey—but only after Tamburlaine has permitted to continue to exist the Egypt we have seen him come close to destroying. Tamburlaine's sparing of Egypt is merely the obverse of his colonizing of it.

Works Cited

Anonymous. *A Breefe Discourse, Declaring and Approving the Necessarie and Inviolable Maintenance of the Laudable Customs of London.* London: Henrie Middleton for Rafe Newberie, 1584.

Bartels, Emily C. *Spectacles of Strangeness: Imperialism, Alienation, and Marlowe.* Philadelphia: U of Pennsylvania P, 1993.

Berek, Peter. "*Tamburlaine*'s Weak Sons: Imitation as Interpretation before 1593." *Renaissance Drama* ns 13 (1982): 55–82.

Bourdieu, Pierre. *The Logic of Practice.* Trans. Richard Nice. Stanford: Stanford UP, 1990.

Connor, R. D. *The Weights and Measures of England.* London: HMSO, 1987.

Daiches, David. "Language and Action in Marlowe's *Tamburlaine.*" *Modern Critical Views: Christopher Marlowe.* Ed. Harold Bloom. New York: Chelsea House, 1986. 77–96.

Dekker, Thomas. *The Wonderfull Yeare, 1603.* London: The Bodley Head Quartos, 1924.

de Somogyi, Nick. "Marlowe's Maps of War." *Christopher Marlowe and English Renaissance Culture.* Ed. Darryll Grantley and Peter Roberts. Aldershot: Scolar, 1996. 96–109.

Douglas, Mary. *Purity and Danger: An Analysis of Concepts of Pollution and Taboo.* Middlesex: Pelican, 1970.

Folkingham, William. *Feudigraphia: The Synopsis of or Epitome of Surveying Methodized.* London: Richard Moore, 1610.

Greenblatt, Stephen. *Renaissance Self-Fashioning: From More to Shakespeare.* Chicago: U of Chicago P, 1980.

Gurr, Andrew. *The Shakespearean Stage, 1574–1642.* 3rd ed. Cambridge: Cambridge UP, 1992.

Hopkins, Lisa. " 'Dead Shepherd, Now I Find Thy Saw of Might': *Tamburlaine* and Pastoral." *Research Opportunities in Renaissance Drama* 35 (1996): 1–16.

Hunter, G. K. "The Beginnings of Elizabethan Drama: Revolution and Continuity." *Renaissance Drama* ns 17 (1986): 29–52.

Jones, Ann R., and Peter Stallybrass. "Dismantling Irena: The Sexualizing of Ireland in Early Modern England." *Nationalisms and Sexualities.* Ed. Andrew Parker et al. New York: Routledge, 1992. 157–71.

Kula, Witold. *Measures and Men.* Trans. R. Szreter. Princeton: Princeton UP, 1986.

Leech, Clifford. *Christopher Marlowe: Poet for the Stage.* Ed. Anne Lancashire. New York: AMS, 1986.

Lefebvre, Henri. *The Production of Space.* Trans. Donald Nicholson-Smith. Oxford: Blackwell, 1991.

Levin, Richard. "The Contemporary Perception of Marlowe's Tamburlaine." *Medieval and Renaissance Drama in England* 1 (1984): 51–70.

Marlowe, Christopher. *Tamburlaine the Great, Parts 1 and 2.* Ed. John D. Jump. Lincoln: U of Nebraska P, 1967.

McEachern, Claire. *The Poetics of English Nationhood, 1590–1612.* Cambridge: Cambridge UP, 1996.

McMullan, John L. *The Canting Crew: London's Criminal Underworld, 1550–1700.* New Brunswick: Rutgers UP, 1984.

McRae, Andrew. *God Speed the Plough: The Representation of Agrarian England, 1550–1660.* Cambridge: Cambridge UP, 1996.

Mead, Stephen X. "Marlowe's *Tamburlaine* and the Idea of Empire." *Works and Days* 7.2 (1989): 91–103.

Mullaney, Steven. *The Place of the Stage: License, Play, and Power in Renaissance England.* Chicago: U of Chicago P, 1988.

Newman, Karen. Review of Steven Mullaney, *The Place of the Stage. Shakespeare Quarterly* 39 (1988): 501–03.

Norden, John. *The Surveyors Dialogue.* London: Hugh Astley, 1607.

Sales, Roger. *Christopher Marlowe.* New York: St. Martin's, 1991.

Shakespeare, William. "Lucrece." *The Poems.* Ed. F. T. Prince. 1961. London: Routledge, 1990.

———. *Measure for Measure.* Ed. J. W. Lever. 1965. London: Routledge, 1992.

Shepherd, Simon. *Marlowe and the Politics of Elizabethan Theatre.* New York: St. Martin's, 1986.

Spenser, Edmund. *The Faerie Queene.* Ed. Thomas P. Roche with C. Patrick O'Donnell Jr. London: Penguin, 1978.

Stallybrass, Peter, and Allon White. *The Politics and Poetics of Transgression.* Ithaca: Cornell UP, 1986.

Sullivan, Garrett A., Jr. *The Drama of Landscape: Land, Property and Social Relations on the Early Modern Stage.* Stanford: Stanford UP, 1998.

Weimann, Robert. *Shakespeare and the Popular Tradition in the Theater: Studies in the Social Dimension of Dramatic Form and Function.* Ed. Robert Schwartz. Baltimore: Johns Hopkins UP, 1978.

Wilson, Richard. "Visible Bullets: Tamburlaine the Great and Ivan the Terrible." *ELH* 62 (1995): 47–68.

Zupko, Ronald Edward. *British Weights and Measures: A History from Antiquity to the Seventeenth Century.* Madison: U of Wisconsin P, 1977.

Putting Tamburlaine
on a (Cognitive) Map

CRYSTAL BARTOLOVICH

No justice . . . seems possible or thinkable without the principle of some *responsibility,* beyond all living present, within that which disjoins the living present, before the ghosts of those who are not yet born or who are already dead, be they victims of wars, political or other kinds of violence, nationalist, racist, colonialist, sexist, or other kinds of exterminations, victims of the oppressions of capitalist imperialism or any of the forms of totalitarianism. Without this *non-contemporaneity with itself of the living present* . . . what sense would there be to ask the question "where?" "where tomorrow?" "whither?"

—Derrida, *Specters of Marx*

I T IS A COMMONPLACE of early modern studies that the appearance of Christopher Marlowe's drama on the public stage marks a decisive break with the past. A range of current discourses on Marlowe assert his ruptural force; for example, the *Norton Anthology* offers undergraduates this rapt description of *Tamburlaine*'s verse: "The English theater had heard nothing like this before" ("Christopher Marlowe" 793). For scholars, Harry Levin provides a similar assessment: "[I]n a period which already boasted its Sidney and Spenser but had still to achieve its preeminence in dramatic poetry, Marlowe was a born playwright. It was for him to discover that dominant mode, to explore and chart and extend its potentialities" (8). Supporting such views, Marlowe and his work seem to have captured an unusual degree of attention (approving and disapproving) of fellow playwrights and other period commentators as well as later critics, from Ben Jonson's (perhaps ambivalent) celebration of "Marlowes mighty line" to Swinburne's assertion that Marlowe was "the greatest discoverer, the most daring and inspired pioneer, in all of our poetic literature."[1] In particular, *Tamburlaine, Parts 1 and 2*—Marlowe's pair of plays that trace the career of a fourteenth-century (1336?-1405) Mongol emperor who rose from humble origins to the position of the mightiest conqueror of his time—appear to have been spectacularly successful in the late Elizabethan period; they were performed often and much imitated, as well as referred to

29

and commented upon (along with Marlowe's purportedly scandalous life) even after tastes of playgoers changed.[2] Building upon a foundation laid by the significant impression made by both Marlowe and his plays in their own (immediate) time, late twentieth-century criticism recognizes, as an editor of a recent collection of essays claims, that "Marlowe's contribution to literature is at once so original and the course of his career so difficult to chart that he never fails to challenge, for good or ill, the imagination of reader and playgoer" (Friedenreich ix). In light of its apparent impact, past and present, *Tamburlaine* seems to offer an especially compelling site in which to explore the work of cultural production, both in the late Elizabethan period and our own.

To do so, we must detail what Marlowe's remarkable "contribution" and "challenge" consist of and situate them in the conditions of their current as well as early modern emergence and reception, a task that is rendered somewhat more plausible in the case of *Tamburlaine* than most early modern plays because of the relatively large number of responses extant.[3] Although none of the early modern responses remark on the novelty of Marlowe's plays per se, they often suggest that there was something arresting and/or unsettling about them. In 1628 George Wither contends, for example, that Tamburlaine's bombast might "strike hearers dead with admiration," which implies—through the negative charge of "dead"—both that the hearers were rapt and that the observer is unsettled by this (qtd. in Richard Levin 54). Like Wither's, most of the early modern responses assert the *power* of the plays, attributing it to their spectacle (including the stylized and emphatic performances the scripts seemed to elicit), their rhetoric, and the dramatically displayed rise of Tamburlaine from obscure origins to world dominion (along with the concomitant fall of the various rulers he conquered). Richard Levin has collected many of these period responses and concludes that most of them "emphasize some aspect of Tamburlaine's power and success" (63) as conveyed through the apparent power and success of the plays' language, particularly their rhetoric and the effect of their still novel use of "pure Iambick verse" on the public stage (Hall qtd. by Levin 53). The much-remarked formal attributes of the plays were bound up, it seems, with long-recalled "sights of power," suggesting that the rupture signaled by *Tamburlaine* is, perhaps, more than aesthetic (and, thus, that the aesthetic might not be neatly separable from the political).[4]

Along with the rhetorical effects and political themes which preoccupied the earliest commentators, recent scholarly criticism has shown a marked tendency to focus explicitly and specifically on the *spatial* aspects of the plays, situating them in the disruptions and uncertainties of an era in which not only was the "New World" still really new to Europe, but enclosure, cartographic knowledge, and trade were expanding as well.[5] Although a 1924 essay on *Tamburlaine,* "Marlowe's Map," is the classic study of Marlowe's geography, its author, Ethel Seaton (who establishes that Ortelius's *Theatrum Orbis Terrarum* served as a source for the geographical references in *Part 2*), is largely indifferent to the question that has captivated *Tamburlaine* critics in the past two decades: *why* Marlowe seems to be obsessed with geography. From Stephen Greenblatt's insistence that *Tamburlaine* embodies "the acquisitive energy of English merchants, entrepreneurs, and adventurers, promoters alike of trading companies and theatrical companies" (*Self-Fashioning* 194) to Richard Wilson's location of this "acquisitive energy" very specifically in the activities of the Muscovy Company to which Marlowe was linked by family ties, recent critics have read *Tamburlaine* as a tale of English desire for expansion of trade and territory. Emily Bartels, for example, situates the play with English travel narrative, Stephen Mead associates it with its "idea of Empire," and James Shapiro argues that Shakespeare's echoes of Marlowe in *Henry V* can be attributed to *Tamburlaine*'s force as an "Armada play." Thomas Cartelli sees Marlowe as writing with an eye to English designs on the New World, while Nick de Somogyi sees him as interested in the use of maps in war reportage emergent at the time. Furthermore, the plays' spatial interests have sometimes been seen as imbricated with domestic social disruption and aspiration, such as in Mark Burnett's essay linking *Tamburlaine* to the worries of early modern elites over the social problems they labeled "vagrancy" and wandering.[6] Indeed, on the spatial and social preoccupations of *Tamburlaine,* at least, there seems to be at the current moment something like that ordinarily elusive state: a scholarly consensus.[7] What we are to make of the sociospatial preoccupation (on the part of both Marlowe's plays *and* their most recent critics) is less certain, however, since the extant criticism focuses resolutely on the "early modern"—as opposed to current—significance of it.

Rather than simply situating *Tamburlaine* in the remote past, then, a time kept safely and thoroughly distant from the concerns and problems of late modernity, I want to examine what (critical preoccupation with) the "spaces" of *Tamburlaine* might suggest about spatial (and social) crisis in the present, even as I continue to explore their "early modern" import. Unless we assume that the themes and practices that obsess current scholarly production are *wholly* autonomous and accidental (which I do not), we must open the question of whether recent criticism of Marlowe tells us as much (if not more) about the present than about the past.[8] Hence, I will argue here, first of all, that Marlowe's *Tamburlaine* presents us with an example of an early modern figuration of what Marx called "primitive accumulation"—the ruthless establishment of the conditions of possibility for capitalism—and that the disproportionate sense of rupture, unease and fascination that the plays have elicited can be attributed, at least in part, to this figuration.[9] But I will argue at the same time that current critical concern with space in Marlowe's plays has both registered and mystified this figuration by speaking of space in ways that tie it to processes of primitive accumulation—colonialism, trade expansion, vagrancy due to dispossession, and so on—while rejecting, neglecting, or undertheorizing Marxist concepts, and situating the violence of an (unnamed) primitive accumulation in the remote reaches of the past rather than tracking its palpable presence in the here and now. The "spatial turn" in current criticism of *Tamburlaine* is, then, I suggest, a *symptom* that reveals, in spite of its resolute refusal to take up current concerns, a heightened sensitivity to spatial crisis under conditions of *late* capitalism, and also, it seems to me, a disavowed recognition that primitive accumulation continues into the present moment as capitalism (with)draws sectors, areas, and aspects of existence into and from its active sphere. If I am right about this, we won't be able to understand what Greenblatt has described as the "historical matrix" of *Tamburlaine* unless we consider it in terms of primitive accumulation explicitly, including the possibility of its continued violence.[10]

To show that *Tamburlaine* figures an "uncompleted project" of primitive accumulation,[11] I must first say a few words about the dominant spatial conditions—usually catalogued under the sign of "globalization"—in which recent critics have produced the spatially interested ruminations on *Tamburlaine* I describe above, and then establish their relation to the spatial condition in which Marlowe's plays emerged. "Globalization" is typically defined as the tendency of flows of capital, commodities, information, and so on to interconnect far-flung places—across the boundaries of nation-states—as distance is eroded by technological innovations, from jet aircraft to the Internet.[12] Since the mid-1970s, journalists, corporate CEOs, politicians, academics, and grassroots organizers have used this term with increasing frequency and have attributed a variety of ills and benefits to its processes, from escalating levels of inequality (local and global) to higher "productivity."[13] When capitalism is examined historically, however, it becomes possible to see not only that not every aspect of "globalization" is as new as the term itself, but also that, in any case, the aspiration to, or fantasy of, globalization, even in the current moment, often exceeds its actually existing condition.

As Paul Smith has cautioned: "Capitalism now claims an isochronic command over the space of the globe as well as territorial control over all its economic processes. Yet in material terms the globe is marked by differentiations in time and space that belie such simultaneity and integration" (18). Furthermore, neither the claims of global reach nor the differentiations are new; to the contrary, they have characterized every regime of capital accumulation to some extent. For this reason, David Harvey has insisted that we understand "globalization" *not* as a specifically current "condition," but rather as a "process" which emerges *with* capitalism, as an effect of its contradictions, and which is, thus, of very long standing:

Certainly from 1492 onwards, and even before, the globalization process of capitalism was well under way. And it has never ceased to be of profound importance to capitalism's dynamic. . . . Without the possibilities inherent in geographical expansion, spatial reorganization, and uneven geographical development, capitalism would long ago have ceased to function as a politico-economic system. The perpetual turning to "a spatial fix" to capitalism's contradictions has created a global historical geography of capital accumulation whose character needs to be well understood. (2)

Although, for Harvey, this expanded historical horizon of globalization does not "preclude saying that the process has . . . entered into a radically new stage," he nonetheless adamantly maintains that failing to historicize "globalization" adequately is just as problematical as failing to pay attention to the "spatial" aspects of capital in the first place, since strategies of resistance are dependent upon proper spatiohistorical understanding (2). In any case, distinguishing a "*new* stage" requires that we take stock of it in relation to the past—including the "past" that survives in the "present"—

including the cultural forms that continue to resonate powerfully as part of what Raymond Williams calls a "selective tradition" (115).[14]

To these ends, I'd like to supplement the usual question asked by critics when they wield Marxist concepts (what can Marxism do for *Tamburlaine*?) with another question: what can *Tamburlaine* do for Marxism *now*? Attention to the past in the present raised by such a question is necessary because capitalism develops *unevenly* (as Harvey suggests in the quotation above)—which is to say (1) it emerges and reproduces itself in relation to other modes of production in any given social formation, and (2) it develops at different rates and to different degrees within as well as among sectors, regions, and states.[15] Because of its uneven development, which is also—as Trotsky emphasized—a *combined* development (i.e., all the parts of the global system—capitalist and noncapitalist—exert pressures on each other), "past" and "present" are always cohabiting in any social formation, however precariously. With an eye to such uneven development, Richard McIntyre has suggested that one of its implications for the analysis of the global economy is the understanding that "there is no end to 'primitive accumulation' as long as capitalism survive[s]" (80). Not only does capitalism originally assert itself among (and continue to interact with) noncapitalist forces, but "*within* capitalist production itself there is a recurrent pattern of uneven development associated with technical change, the evolution of new productive sectors and retardation of old ones, concentration of capital, and so on" (85; emphasis added).[16] In such a world, if *Tamburlaine* is assumed by many recent critics to comment upon the social and spatial disruptions of "its" time, this criticism itself may well reveal something about our own spatial and social crises, which are effects of the ongoing unevenness of capital's expansion.

For Marx, the primary work of primitive accumulation is the production of the enabling inequality of capitalism (the division between owners and non-owners of the means of production)—principally, in the first instance, through the dispossession of the bulk of a local population from land so that, in order to live, their descendants will be required to sell their labor-power. The ongoing work of primitive accumulation still demands this particular dispossession (in, for example, the continuing erosion of the peasantry and/or the transformation of usufruct to systems of private property), but, now that capital is globally dominant, primitive accumulation exacts other costs as well when capital moves around the globe in search of the most highly exploitable labor, leaving formerly "developed" areas in decay. In all its forms, old and new, primitive accumulation relies, of necessity, upon extra-economic coercion—explicit forms of repression and violence, such as laws regulating wages and population flows across state borders as well as police surveillance and management—because market mechanisms are inadequate to its goals; in addition, it is multiple in its effects, from erosion of unions and well-remunerated employment, to "homelessness" and social dislocation. Since its processes are slow, uneven, and untidy, it is characterized by severe crises of labor supply and demand, which give rise (for example) in early modern England to an ample, vehement, and alarmed literature of moral outrage about its effects—on the part of both those who advocated a hasty return to the ostensible order and benevolence of earlier social relations, and the advocates of accelerated embrace of the new.[17] It is remarkable how uncannily familiar this literature can sound to a reader inhabiting the putative new world order. In 1538, for example, the "powre Artyfycer" John Bayker wrote to Henry VIII to bring to his king's attention what he saw as a deplorable state of the kingdom: "I have beyne in the most payrte off the cytys and greyt townes in england; I have allso gone thorowe many lytyll townes and vylygys: but alasse yt dyd pety my hert, to se in evyry place so many monyments wer that howsess and habytatyons hayth beyne and nowe nothynge but bayr walls standynge" (Tawney and Power 2: 303). A walk through North Philadelphia, Southcentral Los Angeles, Flint, Michigan, or any of the other abandoned inner cities or industrial towns, would give one a similar experience, a jolt of recognition.[18]

Similarly, the numerous early modern complaints against the "infynytt numbers of the wicked wandrynge Idell people of the land" which flowed from the pens of elites and their organic intellectuals find a contemporary analogue in demonization of the "homeless," along with welfare "reform" (with its reinstitution of the workhouse logic in "workfare" and its inten-sified stigmatization of poverty), as well as anti-panhandling legislation.[19] Such extra-economic forms of regulation are called upon precisely because the market cannot regulate people it has excluded. In both early modern and current moments, the victims of massive socioeconomic reorganiza-tion are punished twice over: first in their exclusion from the means of production, and then by legislation and social policies which blame them for being so excluded. What the similarities of current strategies and effects of capital accumulation with those of its past should indicate is not, of course, that there is no difference between the crises of the sixteenth and the late twentieth centuries (manifestly not the case), but rather that, just as the establishment of the conditions of possibility for capitalism produced widespread misery and social dislocation, so too does each attempt to establish the conditions most favorable to capital's continued existence on an expanding scale, exploding the myth of unilinear and homogenous capitalist "progress."[20]

What might a play such as *Tamburlaine* (and its criticism) tell us about this process? By the 1580s, the elements of what would become capitalism had gathered enough force to render visible the detrimental as well as the "progressive" aspects of capitalism, if not yet a systematic understanding of how it worked. At such a moment, *Tamburlaine* taps into and helps generate a "worldview"—literally a way of seeing the world, and the interaction of its parts—appropriate to changing conditions. Most interestingly, it does so because of (rather than in spite of) its reliance on a story that featured, from the perspective of a London audience in the late Elizabethan period, an "outsider" who lived long ago. Although an identificatory response on the part of this audience may appear to be simply a misrecognition, it participates in one of the fundamental practices of emergent modernity, a process that Anthony Giddens has called "disembedding"—the " 'lifting out' of social relations from local contexts of interaction and their restructuring across infinite spans of time-space" (21). In the early modern period, the rise of the joint-stock companies, along with the expansion of market participation, brought a growing percentage of the English population into direct implication in global trade and colonization schemes, weaving the fates of personal fortunes into the international market just as the fate of London as a city (and through it, England as a state) already was.[21] In such a world, "disembedding" is a more complex process than a loss of *gemeinschaft* (face-to-face community), because it involves the weaving of the distant and alien into the fabric of the local and familiar. In 1589, for example, John Lyly observed that "trafficke and travell hath woven the nature of all Nations into ours, and made this land like Arras, full of devise."[22] Just as Lyly's "Arras" metaphor proposes, Giddens argues that "what happens [in a process of disembedding] is not simply that localized influences are driven away into the more impersonalized relations of abstract systems. Instead, the very tissue of spatial experience alters, conjoining proximity and distance in ways that have few close parallels in prior ages" (140). He elaborates on this point in his description of the dynamic of "globalization," which he defines as "the intensification of worldwide social relations which link distant localities in such a way that local happenings are shaped by events occurring many miles away and vice versa. This is a dialectical process because such local happenings may move in an obverse direction from the very distanciated relations that shape them. Local transformation is as much a part of globalisation as the lateral extension of social connections across time and space" (64). "Disembedding," thus, provides a way of theorizing the relation of the "local" and "global" such that the local is not seen as merely collapsing before a tidal wave of external pressures, but rather as integrating "alien" elements into its "own" framework, and, in turn, exerting "external" pressures of its own.[23] It is this process we can see at work in *Tamburlaine*'s particular deployment of temporal and spatial otherness, as well as in the current critical assessment of the plays' spaces.

Indeed, questions of spatial and temporal "disembeddedness"—and therefore "globalization"—are raised emphatically by *Tamburlaine*'s appearance on the public stage and in the bookshops of late Elizabethan London. Although current critics have found it a simple matter to read *Tamburlaine* as a transparent allegorical representation of England's own ambitions, and, thus, to link the plays with English colonialism, trade, and competition with European rivals for global position (the "global" aspects of primitive accumulation), I would like to allow the plays to remain more opaque, and foreground for a moment the significance of relying on *imports* (as English playwrights regularly did) to (presumably) tell their "own" story. What in the world would interest London playgoers and readers in the life of a fourteenth-century Mongol conqueror so much that Marlowe's plays about him would be woven profoundly into social memory until the middle of the seventeenth century?[24] After all, not only was a fourteenth-century Mongol literally alien and distant, temporally and spatially, from the Londoners of Marlowe's day, but his story came to England mediated through Continental European texts, such as Pedro Mexia's 1542 biographical sketch, which George Whetstone translated into English in 1586. When Marlowe tapped into such material, he participated in a long history of English reliance upon the East (via Continental intermediaries) as a source of cultural- and exchange-value. According to Simon Shepherd, "there was a fashion for plays about Turks (and other Islamic nations) in late Elizabethan drama" (141).[25] Like spices, silk, and other riches, images and stories of the East were woven into "English" society, and made to participate in local semiotic and political economies which transformed them. These orientalist discourses, however grotesque, always carried with them a reminder, by their very presence, of the "other" inhabiting the here and now that rendered England comprehensible to itself, and, on another level, pointed to the extent to which material life as the English knew it was underwritten by various importations—inoculating against the identity crisis that could be provoked by such a process even as it was (or, rather, by) demonizing and romanticizing the "other."

Of course, popular cultural forms previously and now, too, rely on such displacements, offering imaginary solutions to real social contradictions via detours through space stations (*Star Trek: Deep Space 9*), or ancient Greece (*Xena, Warrior Princess*), but in spite of the persistence of this strategy, why a *particular* displacement engages an audience at a particular time is nonetheless open to historical investigation. In the case of *Tamburlaine*, one possible explanation for its appeal *as an import* is quite straightforward: it marked an *inheritance* of a project from "the East." Jeffrey Knapp has argued (discussing works other than *Tamburlaine*) that a persistent logic of westward movement of civilization underwrites England's own colonial aspirations in the New World, particularly in its competition with Spain throughout the early modern period. From this perspective, the historical accounts of Eastern conquerors *are* England's history (and destiny). Knapp cites a 1524 Spanish text that tracks the itinerary of "dominion" from Asia through Persia, Chaldea, Egypt, Greece, Italy, and France, at long last to arrive in Spain (40). According to Knapp, English elites were aware of their own position at the edge of the Ptolemaic world (the new world of the old "East"), as well as of being both a previously conquered people *and* having the prophecy of Brute yet to realize (as Geoffrey of Monmouth rendered it: "a race of kings will be born there from your stock and the round circle of the whole earth will be subject to them" [qtd. in Knapp 42]). The explosion of the Ptolemaic map makes the appeal of *Tamburlaine* in England comprehensible, with "England" itself cast into the conqueror's role, taking on what it saw as a still to-be-completed project from the past as "civilization" moved "westward," and made a claim on what the colonial propagandist Richard Hakluyt described as "those temperate and fertile partes of America, which . . . seeme to offer themselves unto us, stretching nearer unto her Maiesties Dominions, than to any other part of Europe" (*Divers* [1]r). In such a world, England's obscurity in the 1580s—like that of the young Tamburlaine—might then, too, be prologue to world dominion.

From this perspective, it may be especially significant that the Tamburlaine story seems to have come to England most immediately from Spain.[26] As Hakluyt put it, following a logic of manifest destiny in the *Divers Voyages* (1582): "When I consider that there is a time for all men, and see the Portingales to be out of date & that the nakedness of the Spaniards, and their long hidden secrets are nowe at length espied. . . . I conceive great hope, that the time approcheth and nowe is, that we of England may share and part stakes (if we will ourselves) both with the Spaniard and the Portingale in part of America, and other regions as yet undiscovered" ([1]r). Not only *would* England supplant Spain and Portugal, but it already *has* merely by desiring to do so, because this is the first step toward accepting its destiny. The curious formulation "approcheth and nowe is" captures well the implication of so much of Hakluyt's prose: what could be already is, "if we will ourselves." In Hakluyt's case, the "disembedded" temporality is even more complex than that outlined by Knapp: the English (ostensibly) inherit a project initiated elsewhere and beforehand that becomes a goal for a future imaginatively mastered in the present.

As any reader of *Tamburlaine* knows, the future anterior might also be described as the informing grammatical structure of its eponymous hero, who declares that " . . . 'will' and 'shall' best fitteth Tamburlaine, / Whose smiling stars gives him assured hope / Of martial triumph ere he meet his foes" (*Part 1* 3.3.41–43). His "words are oracles" that anticipate his actual material conquests (*Part 1* 3.3.102). The work of a totalizing spatio-temporal imaginary in effecting material conquest is continuously proposed and reinforced. Indeed, Tamburlaine's power (and his empire) literally grow to fit his rhetoric. Long before he has any definite conquests to back it up, Tamburlaine's speeches "import" him a "Lord" to others, such that the proleptic effect of language itself is imbricated with the play's imperial theme (*Part 1* 1.2.33). While the details of specific figures, or the delicate flow of enjambment, would not necessarily register in any emphatic way on a viewing audience of the period, the sense that Tamburlaine's words "work"—open up a space for—deeds, certainly could.[27] They signal a process in motion, a process which is left incomplete at the end of *Part 2,* when the dying Tamburlaine muses, while gazing on a map, "and shall I die, and this unconquered?" as he bequeaths the task of (specifically New World) conquest ("a world of ground / . . . westward from the midst of Cancer's line") to successors (5.3.146). The ongoing *project* of conquest is larger than even Tamburlaine, and is left behind by him to be inherited.

Hakluyt seems to see England as the inheritor of just such a project of conquest. Indeed, although I would not suggest that there is any direct influence of Marlowe on Hakluyt, or vice versa, the similarities in their discourse can be striking. While Marlowe's plays assert "from the East unto the furthest West / Shall Tamburlaine extend his puissant arm" and "win the world at last" (*Part 1* 3.3.246–47, 260), Hakluyt envisions a similar (and similarly phantasmatic at the time) triumphant global reach for Elizabethan England: "[S]o in this most famous and peerless government of Her most Excellent Majesty, her subjects, in compassing the vast globe of the world more than once, have excelled all the nations and people of the earth" (*Voyages* 33). In addition, Hakluyt details in his volumes an itinerary that rivals Tamburlaine's. At the end of his life, Marlowe's Mongol emperor can boast "here I began to march towards Persia, / Along Armenia and the Caspian Sea" (*Part 2* 5.3.126–27), and he defeats (and incorporates the land of) a king who came "from Soria with seventy thousand strong. Ta'en from Aleppo, Soldino, Tripoli, / And so unto my city of Damasco" (*Part 2* 3.1.58–60); Hakluyt's merchants and explorers not only retrace these steps, but exceed them: "[W]hich of the kings of this land before Her Majesty, had their banners ever seen in the Caspian Sea? Which of them hath ever dealt with the Emperor of Persia, as her Majesty hath done, and obtained for her merchants large and loving privileges? Who ever found English Consuls and agents at Tripolis in Syria, at Aleppo, at Babylon, at Basra, and which is more, whoever heard of Englishmen at Goa before now?" (*Voyages* 33). The shared expansive historical trajectory, geographical idiom, and future anterior grammatical mode in which ambition is depicted in both Hakluyt's and Marlowe's projects situate "England" as the inheritor of a disembedded world-historical force originating "outside" and "before" itself, making claims on the "distant" and the "past" as part of its "own" project, while at the same time wrenching a desired future into the present in the form of "will."

Hakluyt does so for England directly and explicitly, while Marlowe's *Tamburlaine* plays are more indirect. That the plays are meant to comment on England's present is urged, however, by a peculiar and striking "disembedding," a dissonance between the ostensible historical situation of Tamburlaine's speeches and their geographical frame of reference, as we have already seen in the discussion of the map scene at the conclusion of *Part 2*. Specifically, while the Mongol emperor whose life is depicted in the plays built his world empire in the fourteenth century, he is able to refer to places, such as the Americas, even though they would have been entirely unknown (and, of course, unconquered) by him, as the "old" and "new" worlds would not encounter each other for another century. In addition, for London audiences watching this play in the late Elizabethan period, certain geographical markers would signify quite differently than they possibly could for the historical figures conjured up before them: the "furthest West," for example, meant something very different in the time of the historical Tamburlaine, when the "British Shore" Tamburlaine imagines there would have been the referent of such a phrase, and not the Americas, which captivate the English in the time of the emergence of Marlowe's plays (see *Part 1* 3.3.244-60). This gap or slippage between the plays' geography and temporality permits *Tamburlaine* to become for Elizabethan audiences a figuration of their *own* particular predicament of "disembedding" and "globalization" at a time of primitive accumulation of capitalism, and thus helps render these forces available for ideological processing. Specifically, the display of Tamburlaine's violence and ruthlessness *transferred into their own temporal and spatial imaginary* provides a means for audiences to come to terms with the violent activities advocated by the organic intellectuals of primitive accumulation, such as Hakluyt, in which the English themselves are caught up, both at home and abroad. Tamburlaine's ability to speak out his bombast in English, and in the familiar person of actors such as Edward Alleyn, further reinforces the acceptance of Tamburlaine's past as prologue to England's present.[28]

Marlowe's extensive use of geographical references, mapping imagery, and actual maps in production is particularly significant in this respect, in part because the period of the most intensive performance and publication of *Tamburlaine* (roughly 1587-1606) coincides with the publication of a number of English texts that assert mastery of local and global spaces—not only Hakluyt's *Principal Navigations* (1598-1600), but also numerous atlases, chorographies, navigational treatises, and surveying manuals, as Richard Helgerson and John Gillies, among many others, have extensively documented.[29] At a moment when many such texts aspired to situate readers in *time* as well as *space*—Hakluyt, for example, endeavors to establish a historical record of England's efforts in exploration and trade as well as a data bank of geographical information—Marlowe's plays can be seen to fulfill an especially crucial role in ideological restructuring for its contemporary viewers by situating them in relation to a historical and spatial narrative that provides an explanatory framework for their own world. Marlowe appears to have derived much of his geographical knowledge from Ortelius, for whom "the reading of Histories doth both seeme much more pleasant, and in deed so it is, when the Mappe being layed before our eyes, we may behold things done, or places where they were done, as if they were at this time present and in doing" ("To the Reader" n.p.). Since the printer's note (1590) to the *Tamburlaine* plays describes them as "Histories," we might imagine that not only the map, which is finally displayed at the end of *Part 2,* but the whole dense network of geographical references which characterize both the plays—especially since it describes a world coeval with early modern viewers—are meant to help bring the past to life just as Ortelius suggests: that is, not only to make the past vivid to a viewer, but also, in some sense, to make it *current*: "as if . . . at this time present and in doing." While the import of the passage in Ortelius's epistle to the reader is directed toward rendering the past comprehensible to the present—by bringing it to the present—the effect of mapping in *Tamburlaine* is even more complex, suggesting that the future belongs to its temporality as well: what "will" and "shall" be done.

The first explicit mapping passage of *Tamburlaine, Part 1* works along these lines. Attempting to explain why he can show even the father of his wife no mercy as he sets about the task of conquering the world, Tamburlaine declares:

> Zenocrate, were Egypt Jove's own land,
> Yet would I with my sword make Jove to stoop.
> I will confute those blind geographers
> That make a triple region of the world,
> Excluding regions which I mean to trace,
> And with this pen reduce them to a map,
> Calling the provinces, cities, and towns
> After my name and thine, Zenocrate.
> Here at Damascus will I make the point
> That shall begin the perpendicular.
>
> (4.4.71–80)

Space is depicted here as an effect of the future anterior, and, thus, as contingently organized by historical forces (figured by Tamburlaine's "pen" [sword]). Tamburlaine rejects both divine ("Jove") and traditional cartographic authority ("geographers") and grounds this deterritorializing activity in the power of his (apparently secularizing and modernizing) violence alone. Whether the "blind geographers" to whom Tamburlaine refers are producers of T/O or Ptolemaic maps, each of which would include only Asia, Africa, and Europe as the "known world," *he* must *imagine* the "excluded regions" as he invents them with his actions. This gesture also draws the audience directly into the mapping process as the "excluded regions" refer to *their* spatial conditions, emphatically not those of the historical Tamburlaine. If maps, as Ortelius claimed, can make the past seem as if "present and in doing," *Tamburlaine*'s map here invites such a practice in a quite literal way. In *Part 1,* the emphasis is on the restriction of the old maps from which Tamburlaine declares he must break free, just as early modern cartographers were doing. Changing spatial relations, however, are also changing social relations, as Tamburlaine's own speech makes explicit, in its claim on the power to rename and transform social units such as "provinces, cities, and towns." Mapping here not only signifies the literal process of spatial representation in a world of changing spatial relations, but also figures broader processes of rupture and change from one sociopolitical organization of the world to another brought into existence by global forces, which in Marlowe's plays bear the proper name "Tamburlaine." Tamburlaine's "tracing" explicitly involves violence on the ground, struggles over territory and conditions of existence, which only later will be documented on a map. Mapping, thus, means in these plays nothing less than the material processes of "history" itself.

Implicating early modern viewers in this ongoing historical process, the map that appears on stage at the conclusion of *Part 2* must have been relatively recent—perhaps even one of Ortelius's own—if the actor playing Tamburlaine is to be able to gesture to the "whole world" of the Americas that are still "unconquered." On display, right before their very eyes, early modern subjects are offered a view of *their* world as if it were Tamburlaine's, which, in turn, encourages them to treat Tamburlaine's project as their own. In this way, maps become the site in *Tamburlaine* not just for the comprehension, but the *making* of history. What is "present and in doing" is not only the performance of a "history" understood as "the past," but rather a continued performance of history in the space of their own now, a process "Tamburlaine" putatively initiates and which English viewers must participate in if the spatial referents of the plays are to make sense, which they do only in relation to the spatial imaginary inculcated by texts such as Hakluyt's. This is the work of temporal/spatial disembedding in Marlowe's plays, which bring them in line with Hakluyt's colonial propaganda of the same period.

However, in spite of a shared scope of geographical imaginary in Hakluyt's and Marlowe's works, as well as shared reliance on the future anterior as temporal mode, in one crucial respect, the world Marlowe describes in *Tamburlaine* and Hakluyt's worldview are radically different. Marlowe conjures up an endless string of violent military conquests and a system of tributary kings united in what seems to be a sort of imperial confederacy under Tamburlaine, who is the primary dynamic force in the play and is readily identifiable as its center. Hakluyt presents us instead with a collection of narratives and stories contributed over a vast tract of time by numerous merchants and explorers, none of whom is dominant. The "English Nation" is the only identifiable "center" of Hakluyt's "merchant epic," for which commerce, not a demonstration of superior military prowess, is the primary dynamic force.[30] There is plenty of violence in Hakluyt's texts, of course, but it is directed more to the opening up of world markets and access to resources and labor than to glory or power for any individual conqueror, even if residual appeals to such archaic notions continue to appear as part of the violence of primitive accumulation itself. Whereas Tamburlaine draws together and orders the fragments of the world in the power of his person, only the continually reinforced power of exchange-relations connects the fragments of Hakluyt's incipiently mercantile-colonial world. Immanuel Wallerstein sees this shift from military to mercantile conquest as one of the defining moments of capitalist modernity, which is characterized by an *economic* interlinking and interdependence of spaces that operate in relative autonomy from the bureaucratic apparatuses that characterized the ancient world systems.[31] One of the effects of this shift is that—rather than power and agency being easily situated in a single powerful individual, such as Tamburlaine—the organizing power structure for the interlinked areas is far more diffuse and unlocalized, even though it operates in the interests of only a minority of the populations linked. Such a shift does not occur overnight; and, of course, capitalism even now deploys military might when economic coercion fails. However, Wallerstein is pointing to the difference in logics of coercion and fundamental forces, and argues that capitalist modernity tends toward global linkages that are, in the first instance, economic.

In spite of *Tamburlaine*'s seemingly resolute avoidance of these overt "economic" themes, much of the recent criticism of *Tamburlaine* focuses precisely on them: the "acquisitive energy" of merchants (Greenblatt), the travails of the Muscovy Company (Wilson), the aspiration of English elites for Eastern trade (Bartels) or New World colonies (Cartelli). The question arises, then, of how it happens that so many recent critics (including myself) see *Tamburlaine* as most concerned with issues that it nowhere explicitly takes up. Tamburlaine's sole engagement with trade (which is barely mentioned at all in the plays), after all, is to disrupt it. Early on, for example, Meander denounces him as a "Sturdy Scythian thief, / That robs [the] merchants of Persepolis / Trading by land unto the Western Isles" (*Part 1* 1.1.36–38). As Mark Burnett and Tom Cartelli have shown, to the extent that the economic enters the plays at all, Tamburlaine is associated with *delegitimated* economic activity, such as theft. These critics observe the social-climbing aspect of Tamburlaine's rise to power, and note the repeated association of Tamburlaine and his fellows with vagrancy by his enemies (who all have established "high" social positions). They link these aspects of the plays to the discourse of vagrancy circulating in early modern England, a discourse that is inextricably allied with specifically economic concerns, as well as threats of social disorder. It is through this subtheme of the plays, it would seem, that an explicitly economic discourse enters them and makes it possible to recode Tamburlaine's violent acquisitive energy as mercantile rather than merely military. Yet usually these two "readings" are kept distinct and offered as *alternatives*.[32] Rather than keeping them separate, however, I suggest that both readings are available to critics because the plays are attempting to point us toward a *connection* between the two processes: the "local" social and economic disruptions are negotiated under conditions established in part by "global" forces.

So, while the *Tamburlaine* plays at first glance might seem to be absolutely devoid of any discernible "economic" content—and thoroughly allied with the earlier "world empire" formation to boot—when we yoke together the theme of concern in the play for the "vagrant" and "thief"—which echoes the concerns of early modern English social and economic discourses—with the broad spatial imaginary of Tamburlaine's conquest, we can see not only an opening for late Elizabethan socioeconomic conditions to enter the experience of playgoers, but also an exploration of how these "local" socioeconomic problems are part of a world system. Specifically, Tamburlaine is depicted as both conqueror and vagrant because the *systemic force* he figures produces both effects: the processes of primitive accumulation, as Marx puts it, "conquered the field" so that capitalism can come into the world (*Capital* 895); in the process, it (necessarily) dispossesses the peasantry and initiates an economic struggle "which has the globe as its battlefield" (*Capital* 915). The vagrancy theme, belonging to the viewer's time, links up with the spatial imaginary of the play, also of the early modern viewer's time, imbricating the social and the spatial as well as the past and present. "Local" and "present" conditions are thus situated in and among far broader historical and geographical processes.

One period response in particular, I think, indicates a way in which the more explicit "global" aspects of the plays link up with the perceived "local" (and "economic") effects of primitive accumulation. In 1629, a volume was published that reports a newly instituted practice in the handling of Bridewell (workhouse) prisoners. The unfortunate "masterless men" and other displaced persons from the countryside found themselves yoked to carts that they had to "draw like Horses" as they set about their appointed public works tasks of street cleaning and trash removal, under the watchful eye of beadles and crowds. Here is how the text describes the popular reception of this practice: "as they passe the people scoffing say, / Holla, ye pampred Jades of Asia" (R. M. qtd. in Richard Levin 60). The last line is, of course, a reference to *Tamburlaine, Part 2,* where conquered kings are hitched to a chariot and so taunted by Tamburlaine as they draw him from battle to battle. One possible interpretation of this remarkable citation is that "the people" takes onto itself here a *Tamburlaine-like* position in relation to the Bridewell prisoners by repeating his line, an identification that participates in a social dynamic that Peter Stallybrass and Allon White have called "displaced abjection," the violent abuse and "demoniz[ation of] weaker, not stronger, social groups" (19).[33] In this reading, "the people" attempt to secure their relatively better-off position by actively engaging in the marginalization of the prisoners, and, thus (regressively), help maintain the status quo of a "high" and "low" binarization of society. That they do so by way of identification with an ostensibly spatially and historically remote figure also suggests, however, that Marlowe's plays somehow were legible as stories about, or at least applicable to, "local" conditions of existence.

Indeed, if we draw on the "global" as well as the "local" themes of the play, the crowd's response can be seen as moving in some interesting directions that point us toward an identification of "Tamburlaine" as the figuration of an absent, alien, unrepresentable global force that bridles the prisoners and crowd alike, driving them all on—or at least renders such a figuration thinkable.[34] In other words, because the historical personage "Tamburlaine" is unmistakably the direct agent of the conquered kings' subjection in the plays, the association of him with early modern conditions of existence inserts the prisoners (perhaps unconsciously on the crowd's part) into a narrative that simultaneously removes them from sole responsibility for their lot and looks elsewhere for the cause of their subjection. This is a matter of some consequence since, as Marshall Berman has observed, in the first phase of modernity "people are just beginning to experience modern life; they hardly know what hit them. They grope, desperately and half blindly, for an adequate vocabulary; they have little or no sense of a modern public or community within which their fears and hopes can be shared" (17). Berman is not an early modernist and offers no archival evidence for this observation, but the historical record, as it happens, does suggest that the early modern period was marked by a widespread sense of social upheaval, whose cause and cure were difficult to ascertain. Keith Wrightson describes it thus:

Agricultural improvement and agrarian distress, increased production and wide-spread deprivation, undoubted prosperity and equally striking impoverishment: in all these ways contemporaries identified the paradoxical symptoms of a changing socio-economic environment. Of change they were undoubtedly aware, though they found it difficult, in the midst of the process of change and lacking the statistical information to inform their analysis, to explore in any depth either the course or the causes of the developments which forced themselves upon their attention. (122)

Laws were passed against both "vagrancy" and "depopulation" throughout the sixteenth century and into the seventeenth, suggesting an incertitude, or ambivalence, about how government should respond to changing conditions. That there were no "Tamburlaines" around upon which to pin all the blame for the disorienting and troubling social changes appears to have been very vexing. The crowd's response to the Bridewell prisoners, even if overtly malicious, might also be seen in its context as the implicit expression of a desire to find a definite cause for the inexplicable and bewildering.

Social problems were regularly depicted in the early modern period as impossible to localize and particularize because so spread out and enormous. The displaced poor were often described as a huge, anonymous, and virulent force—"Infynatt numbers of . . . wicked wandrynge Idell people"—responsible for the "spoyle and confusion of the land," and capable of endless deception: "they will change both name and habytt and comonly go ynto other sheers [shires] so as no man shall knowe them" (Tawney and Power 2:341, 344). On the other side of the great divide, elites were starting to seem to be a more dispersed and anonymous dominating force as well. In the middle of the sixteenth century, Robert Crowley suggested that changing social conditions made it difficult for the poor to get their bearings, or resist their scattered foe: "Oh good maisters, what shuld I cal you? You that have no name, you that have so many occupacions and trads that ther is no on name mete for you! You ungentle gentlemen! You churles chikens, I say! Geve me leve to make answere for the pore ideotes over whom ye triumphe" (Tawney and Power 3:58). Such men, Crowley suggests, appear to the "pore" as "Men without conscience. . . . Yea, men that live as thoughe there were no God at all! . . . men that would leave nothyng for others; men that would be alone on the earth; men that bee never satisfied. Cormerauntes, gredye gulles; yea, men that would eate up menne, women and chyldren" (Tawney and Power 3:57). Like Tamburlaine in the eyes of his enemies, these men refuse their settled identity in a community through the pursuit of personal gain by whatever means presents itself as most advantageous; they disrupt local social relations, and destruction follows, destruction that depopulates, eats up, destroys, as it concentrates the possessions of the many into the hands of "gredye gulles" alone. Furthermore, both Tamburlaine and Crowley's protocapitalists act without discrimination or remorse, considering ethical niceties or tender emotion entirely superfluous to the act of accumulation. The difference between the two, of course, is that in Crowley's polemic a single Tamburlaine is replaced by a collectivity producing a "Tamburlaine-effect"—a *class* of exploiters. Unable to localize in a single individual the forces causing the changes around them and through them, the "crowd" makes a connection between *effects* in the case of the *Tamburlaine*-inspired taunt in their encounter with the Bridewell prisoners, which, willy-nilly, identifies a class relation in the latter case.

At the end of the chapter in *Capital* in which Marx outlines the mechanisms by which the peasants were separated from the means of production (land) in England in the early modern period, he, too, emphasizes the overwhelming and indiscriminate (from the perspective of older social and economic norms) violence of primitive accumulation activities, including,

the spoliation of the Church's property, the fraudulent alienation of the state domains, the theft of the common lands, the usurpation of feudal and clan property and its transformation into modern private property under circumstances of ruthless terrorism, all these things were just so many idyllic methods of primitive accumulation. They conquered the field for capitalist agriculture, incorporated the soil into capital, and created for the urban industries the necessary supplies of free and rightless proletarians. (895)

Not only the poorest of the poor were losers in this process, but also some of the richest of the rich: the clerics who lost landholdings and other sources of wealth at the dissolution, and some lay landholders, not all of whom thrived in the new, competitive conditions of emergent agrarian capital. Primitive accumulation, in this respect as so many others, was a very Tamburlaine-like process, violently transforming for better or worse the conditions of existence of everyone in its path, across the social scale.[35] At such a moment, *Tamburlaine* provides a striking image of a systemic force operating socially and spatially, locally and globally, at once, in ways that would seem all too familiar to any early modern peoples living through the throes of primitive accumulation.

Among these familiar forces, the very people who found their way into workhouses were constantly assessed in terms of global politics by authors of colonial and mercantile propaganda in the period. Whether the elites, in response to a perceived threat, dreamed of transplantation ("we may plant on that main the offals of our people"), or of lowering unemployment ("if vent may be, we shall set our subjects in work . . . more worth to our people besides the gain of the merchant, than Christchurch, Bridewell, the Savoy, and all the hospitals of England"), the early modern colonial theorists made explicit and frequent reference to the link between control of global markets and the control of the unpropertied population at home.[36] The fate of the "poorest [s]he in England," then, was already seen by elites as bound up in a global economy of which most people may have been only dimly aware. Every time elites equated "rogues" with foreign enemies, or imagined them as pawns of extra-national political and economic strategies, they connect them to a set of global relations.[37] This unprecedented global spatial relation, an effect of the delinking of peasants from the land in tandem with new attempts at colonial dispossession and market expansion, set the unpropertied and propertied alike in an entirely new relation to the space of "England." It is this new relation that is worked out (among others) in *Tamburlaine*'s continuous evocations of "the whole world," a vast, unimaginable totality, in which other places are constantly shown to have material effects in "local" spaces, irreducibly imbricating them.

Tamburlaine's alienness as a figure and a text, when brought to bear on a "local" situation—as in the taunting of the Bridewell prisoners—suggests that "the people," like Lyly, have some vestigial (or potential) understanding that in their world the "elsewhere" and "before" are materially imbricated with their "here" and "now."

Hence, of the many critical attempts to explain the cultural work performed by texts such as *Tamburlaine* at such a time, I have found none better than one that has eluded the notice of scholars of Elizabethan literature—at least in relation to the early modern period. *Tamburlaine,* it seems to me, can be no better characterized than as an effect of an artistic quest for "forms that inscribe a new sense of the absent global colonial system on the very syntax of poetic language itself, a new play of absence and presence that at its most simplified will be haunted by the exotic and be tattooed with foreign place names, and at its most intense will involve the invention of remarkable new languages and forms" (Jameson, *Postmodernism* 411). *Tamburlaine* is emphatically haunted by "foreign place names." One cannot read even a few lines of the plays without meeting up with an expansive geographical catalogue. And these "foreign place names" are effects of a properly unrepresentable totality, not only because Tamburlaine's world does not yet (and never does fully) exist, nor because large parts of the globe are still terra incognita for Marlowe's audience in the 1590s, nor even because the world of the putative speaker does not coincide with the moment in which it was presumably spoken, but rather because "the world"—being a set of increasingly vast and complex relations, always in flux—can nowhere appear in its totality; we only know it as an effect of these relations. This gap between representation and the unrepresentability of totality is marked by *Tamburlaine*'s "remarkable new languages and forms" (including the mighty line and lofty rhetoric for which Marlowe was so well known in his time and our own) developed perhaps to direct an audience toward some sense of an elusive global social whole even more powerful and overwhelming than the plays' language.

Despite its seeming appropriateness, however, the reference to "the absent global colonial system" and "remarkable new languages and forms" quoted above was not written to describe *Tamburlaine* or any other early modern text, but rather was written by a self-proclaimed theorist of postmodernity, Fredric Jameson, in the course of a discussion of what he calls "cognitive mapping," or the (potential) ability of postmodern subjects to situate themselves in "the totality of class relations on a global . . . scale" (*Postmodernism* 416); *Tamburlaine* is thus distant from the archive the passage seeks to address.[38] Indeed, Jameson explicitly has in mind cultural artifacts and practices for which Marlowe's work would be several centuries antecedent. A typical critical gesture at this point would be to claim that Marlowe somehow "anticipates" forms that will mature only later; however, I think a rather different dynamic is at work: the latter forms conjure up from the past an uncompleted "spatial" and social project, initiated with primitive accumulation and marked in the violence and energy of *Tamburlaine* as well as in its spaces and form.

In his reassessment of the temporality of revolutionary struggle in the early 1930s, Ernst Bloch suggested that Marxism must take a more nuanced perspective of "non-synchronous elements" in relation to proletarian revolution and proposes what he calls a "multi-spatial and multi-temporal dialectics" to do so (37). Marxist theorists must still sort out the costume-drama dross that confuses historical situations as Marx suggests in the "Eighteenth Brumaire," but, Bloch argues, they must *also* be attentive to historical elements in the present that "continue to be effective" not as mere citations, but as living forces (37).[39] Thus, although Bloch situates revolutionary priority with the proletarian "synchronous contradiction" with capitalism, he nonetheless insists that an "additional revolutionary force" can obtain if "the incomplete wealth of the past" (or "nonsynchronous contradictions") with capitalism are brought into *proper* contention with it. In part, Bloch urges this course for reasons of practical politics; he begins from the proposition that "not all people exist in the same Now," and argues that a Marxist appeal to the actual conditions of existence of youth, peasants, and the petite bourgeoisie, among others, requires a recognition of the "past" (or, in the case of youth, "future") at work in the present in the material lived experience of these groups (23).[40] Bloch, then, rejects the view that all elements of the past are necessarily "regressive." Rather, he suggests that "past" historical elements (via their "living" representatives) can become part of a liberatory project as long as they are transcoded for current conditions: "the task is to extrapolate the elements of the non-synchronous contradictions which are capable of antipathy and transformation, that is, those hostile to capitalism and homeless in it, and to refit them to function in a different context" (36). Such transcoding, of course, can also be undertaken for regressive purposes, as Nazi uses of the past demonstrated, Bloch notes. Thus one needs to be aware of the "past" in the present both to safeguard against its regressive forms and uses, as well as to transcode it for liberatory purposes when possible.

Though Jameson relies on Bloch for his formulation of history in *The Political Unconscious* (in this respect, according to his own distinctions, rendering it "modernist"), he sees the "postmodern" condition as having closed up the temporal unevenness that characterized earlier moments in capitalism's development:

[T]he postmodern must be characterized as a situation in which the survival, the residue, the holdover, the archaic, has finally been swept away without a trace. . . . Everything is now organized and planned; nature has been triumphantly blotted out, along with peasants, petit-bourgeois commerce, handicraft, feudal aristocracies and imperial bureaucracies. Ours is a more homogeneously modernized condition; we no longer are encumbered with the embarrassment of non-simultaneities and non-synchronicities. Everything has reached the same hour on the great clock of development or rationalization (at least from the perspective of the "West"). (*Postmodernism* 309–10)

Cognitive mapping, with its primarily *spatial* rather than temporal emphasis, then, becomes the focus of his theorization of resistance to the postmodern condition. There are, however, other ways of imagining the (post)modern, available in Jameson's own work. Indeed, much of what Jameson has to say on the subject of postmodern space can be reconnected with his previous work on "time" even though he has not himself made these connections.

Analogy is always perilous, but I will put forth a very limited one here just the same, because I think it reminds us that Jameson's theorizations of both time and space are meant to be deployed strategically. Physics tells us that light can be seen to work as a particle or a wave, depending upon how you look at it, and for what purpose. History, too, according to Jameson, can be viewed from what seem to be "two apparently inconsistent accounts": "metasynchronicity," which emphasizes "the co-existence of various synchronic systems or modes of production" at any given moment, or "systemic transformation," which produces a linear trajectory of successive modes (*Political* 97). Hence, when Jameson outlines a "linear" progression of stages of capital, each of which is characterized by a space peculiar to it, "the result of discontinuous expansion of quantum leaps in the enlargement of capital, in the latter's penetration and colonization of hitherto uncommodified areas" (*Postmodernism* 410), we are to understand this production of tidy domains as a theoretical abstraction, which must be "preserved and canceled all at once" (*Political* 98). In attempting to theorize postmodernism in its specificity, Jameson abstracts "other times" from its periodicity. However, because I am interested in testing for the persistence of other times in the current moment, I must examine it historically, that is, from the other perspective Jameson identifies— "metasynchronicity"—rather than the abstract "systemic transformation" emphasis he himself chooses in discussing postmodernism.

As part of this project, I have examined *Tamburlaine* as a cognitive map in ways that Jameson has reserved for his work on cultural forms produced since the 1970s alone. From this gesture, two "temporal" critiques of Jameson's formulation of cognitive mapping follow. First of all, I question the notion that cognitive maps were less necessary earlier in the history of capitalism than now.[41] Second, I am doubtful that any cognitive map that only accounts for postmodernity, as abstractly distinguished by Jameson, could possibly provide the basis for an analysis of contemporary capitalism in any actually existing site. As I have argued above, capitalism can engage in its necessary accumulative drive *only* unevenly, both locally and globally. If postmodernism abolishes such unevenness, it must abolish capitalism as well. Once we accept unevenness as a theoretical and historical necessity of capitalism, we must always seek out the past at work in the present in order to examine its effects.[42] A reading of *Tamburlaine* as a "cognitive map," then, contributes not only to a better understanding of these plays and their historical situation, but also to a refinement (or re-inflection) of "cognitive mapping" as a general project. Specifically, if "cognitive mapping" is a means by which individual subjects might come to a collective understanding of the disorienting complexity of capitalist globalization, and if globalization has a long history, so, too, must cognitive mapping. At the very least, the temporality of "cognitive mapping" deserves as much attention as the "spatial" aspects that have hitherto preoccupied Jameson in his discussion of it. Testing out this possibility, I have proposed that the spatial imaginary of the *Tamburlaine* plays be viewed as a figuration of an "uncompleted project" of primitive accumulation, and that this figuration accounts for their early modern impact as well as the current critical interest in their spaces (at a time of new crises for capitalist globalization), even though in most other respects the plays are now culturally alien.

Indeed, their alienness reinforces their point—today as in the early modern period—by indicating the imbrication of the "alien" in what we tend to think of as a distinct here and now, but in which the absent ("elsewhere" and "before") often play a greater role than we are willing to admit. Hence, it is not Tamburlaine's local heroic displays of self-fashioning and conquest in a succession of victories over rivals in personal combat that invite viewers to engage in the process of cognitive mapping in Jameson's sense. The specific mechanism at work in these main plot elements (related to, but more narrowly focused than, cognitive mapping) is closer to what Stallybrass and White have called the "carnivalesque," a process in which "the low troubles the high" as part of the production of social meaning in a particular cultural context.[43] Displays of the high/low "binary extremism" in *Tamburlaine* depend upon and ripple out onto the already extant play of binaries in the dominant cultural order, and become part of the pool of cultural meanings through which social relations are played out. "Cognitive mapping" brings this local idiom toward an understanding of the global social "totality" that structures it, and of which it is part.

Thus it is significant to his potential effectiveness as a figuration of primitive accumulation—with an ability to help insert individual subjects imaginatively in a global social totality—that Tamburlaine is not only a prince of "high astounding terms" (*Part 1* Prologue.5) and individual lofty deeds, but also a prince (in aspiration) of the whole world. "We will triumph over all the world" (*Part 1* 1.2.173), declares Tamburlaine in various terms throughout the plays. He is described by enemies as the "Tyrant of the world" (*Part 2* 5.3.55) and defeats troops that are believed to be "enow to win the world" (*Part 2* 3.1.44). Period responses seem to be quite aware of this aspect of the plays. In *Selimus* (c. 1592), one of the numerous imitations of *Tamburlaine* that emerged in the wake of its popularity, another fallen emperor compares his fate to *Tamburlaine*'s Bajazeth, who was forced "to be a spectacle to all the world" (qtd. in Richard Levin 58). The English traveler and writer Thomas Coryat, too, was struck by the global scope of Tamburlaine's triumph, which is "published over the whole world" (qtd. in Richard Levin 59). Such assumptions of global reach are implicit in numerous observations about Tamburlaine's "mightiness," the effect of which is his being remembered as "the Terror of that age" and for rendering Bajazeth into a "Spectacle unto that Age" (qtd. in Richard Levin 62, 59). "Tamburlaine," "the world," and "the age" seem to have often been thought simultaneously, which made Marlowe's plays a potentially useful site to think about "England" and "the world" (space) as well as "the age" (time), and, more importantly, for viewers or readers to subjectively situate themselves in relation to the process of their production, an activity invited by the familiar (coeval) aspects of the plays' geography, and their invocation of local social problems, such as vagrancy. Thus, in its depiction of a huge, overwhelming force that determines the fates of multitudes, connecting them in mutual subjection, however far separated in space, *Tamburlaine*'s surface content, which is geographically, historically, and even formally distant from the everyday lives of its viewers and readers in the late Elizabethan period, nevertheless appeals to their "experience" of primitive accumulation, and offers the lesson that the conditions of possibility for everyday lives of locally situated subjects are partly generated elsewhere (whether in the decisions of "local" landowners or of wool factors on the Continent). In its reliance on estranged labor and ever-expanding (geographically as well as in scale) production, capital is profoundly de-localizing in its effects.

Hence, it is not surprising that not only *Tamburlaine,* but also the urgent polemic of early modern merchants and their organic intellectuals is "tatooed with foreign place names," to borrow Jameson's phrase. In a mid-sixteenth-century argument for dying cloth in England rather than shipping it into the Continent for this purpose, William Cholmeley imagines the links tying the "littell corner of the earth" called England with a vast topography via an extensive merchants' network, as he attempts to persuade his readers that finishing cloth in England will not depress local wool production, since cloth was already a necessary component of trade in the world system:

[W]ith what wyll the Italyans pass beyound them into Turky, Constantinople, Alexandria, and other farre contreys and cyties, to fetche sylkis, spyces, drugges, jewellis, currantes, gallis, malmesey . . . golde, and suche lyke, but with cloth? yea, with English cloth. . . . Wherwith wyll the Easterlyngis, Russlande, Sweaneland, Pomerland, Toterlande, and suche other farre contreys passynge to Rye and Revell that waye eastwarde; as masts, waynescote, hemp, pytche, tarre, ashes, wax, flex, copper, yron, and corne, which commeth so plentuously oute of Pollande? but even with Englyshe cloth. Wherwithall wyll the Spaniardis and Portugalles traffycke into Calicute, into Affrica, Barbaria, Nova Hispania, into the yles of Canarya, into Perew, Brasilia, and manye dyverse ilandis and contreys, to fetch sugar, spices, wodd, brassell . . . golde, and other commodities? even with Englyshe cloth. . . . Wherwithall woulde the cold and large contreys of Doutchlande, Almayne, and Hungarye cloth themselves, and consume the commodities which they make, as fustians and many other, if they shulde not have oure Englyshe cloth? (Tawney and Power 3: 139)

Cholmeley's world, like Lyly's, is one in which trade and travel turn the world itself into a weave, rendering the constituent parts far more dependent and integrated than a focus on polities and "home markets" alone would suggest. Because "disembedding" both preserves and transforms the "local," the cloth remains "English" even as it moves through the world. However, as it travels (along with much else besides), what "English" designates is necessarily unsettled and ever-changing, since relations are effected that alter the social conditions in the narrow geographical space labeled "England" as the cloth (among other things) circulates. In such a world, not only the merchant and his factors, but the small boy who tended the flocks, the shearers, the weavers, the porters, and so on were all implicated in the world system, as were the countless others on whom they depended to be clothed, shod, fed, and housed. Numerous elsewheres were "in" the local for all of these people, even if they had never left the shire of their birth, and even if they had never seen a map, or heard of Hakluyt.

The *Tamburlaine* plays can be viewed as cognitive maps to the extent that they indicate this globalized local, and render it imaginable as an effect of the set of processes that would come to be called primitive accumulation, even though such a term did not yet exist. The appearance of such a pedagogic cultural form is not surprising given its conditions of emergence: although no more than one-eighth of the rural population had ever been landless prior to the mid-sixteenth century, between 1570 and 1640 the percentage of English peasants who were forced into waged-labor rose to forty; by 1688 the majority (fifty-six percent) were laborers.[44] As primitive accumulation set the stage for capitalist exploitation by separating direct producers from the means of production in this way, disrupting long-established social relations in the process, a figure such as Tamburlaine, depicted as a massive "outside" force undermining all local autonomy and settled relations, could resonate powerfully. Even the structure of the plays reinforces such a reading; all of *Part 1* and much of *Part 2* unfolds in such a way that "high" characters are introduced for whom Tamburlaine is a marginal—and geographically distant—irritant: their local objectives and interests are emphatically directed elsewhere. In each case, however, Tamburlaine displaces their local narratives such that not only does he bring the "high" characters "low," but, in the process, he short-circuits some ongoing local narrative trajectory. Repeatedly, Tamburlaine is depicted as a force that disrupts categories of (geographical) center and margin, local and global as well as (socially) high and low. For example, *Part 1* opens with the depiction of intrigue in the Persian court, as the brother of the sitting king plots to usurp the throne. Compared to this struggle between the brothers, Tamburlaine at first seems entirely peripheral as a threat— a small-time bandit ("paltry Scythian") who can be put into place by a relatively insignificant (by the grandiose standards of the play) military detachment (a thousand horse). This implied marginality is reinforced by the absence of Tamburlaine from the first scene, which takes place in the Persian court where Tamburlaine's only presence is as a name. However, for the audience, who knows from the prologue, if not from prior knowledge of the story, that Tamburlaine is about to begin his career of "scourging kingdoms with his conquering sword" on the backs of these very kings and their people, the first scene cannot but seem steeped in dramatic irony, heightening the power of the form. The structuring of the action in this way demonstrates that the seemingly distant and peripheral can have profound and long-lasting local effects, especially for viewers living in a world where "disembedding" and "re-embedding" are becoming part of an everyday dynamic.

This is a demonstration that the *Tamburlaine* plays provide again and again. When act 3 of *Part 1* opens, the "high and mighty" Bajazeth is the main focus of our attention on stage, and his attention is devoted primarily to the siege of Constantinople, not the seemingly distant threat of a leader of a pack of "eastern thieves" (3.1.2). And like *Part 1, Part 2* opens up with a scene in which Tamburlaine appears only as a signifier, which has no embodied presence until scene 3. As Tamburlaine goes about his task of turning the world upside down, reducing kings to the status of beasts, or even lowly inanimate objects, he also disrupts the lives of numerous ordinary people, to whom he had been previously peripheral (if evident at all). He is, especially in *Part 1,* a force that seemingly comes out of nowhere, but has emphatic and far-reaching social effects, as in the case of the virgins of Damascus, who come out to beg mercy for their city but are instead taught by Tamburlaine to see "imperious Death" sitting at the end of a spear for themselves and all the rest of the townspeople as well (5.1.111). For commoner and king alike, Tamburlaine determines the "given" conditions in which life and death are transacted.[45] Indeed, his wide-ranging impact is intensified by being visited on several occasions on every inhabitant of resistant cities, such as Damascus in *Part 1* and Babylon in *Part 2,* where every "man, woman and child" (5.1.168) is killed by Tamburlaine's soldiers, much as Robert Crowley's protocapitalists "eate up menne, women and chyldren" in the English countryside.

At once heroic and terrifying, awe-inspiring and repulsive, vital and destructive, Tamburlaine not only embodies the novel acquisitive energies of certain *individuals* in the late Elizabethan period, or the threat posed by the dispossessed, as many critics have already suggested, but also the huge, dynamic, relentless *systemic* movement of primitive accumulation. It is crucial to this figuration that no single individual or group in the play is able to capture or destroy Tamburlaine; only an ineffable, unlocalizable force like that from which he claims to have derived his own power can lay him low: "something . . . but I know not what" (*Part 2* 5.2.218). In his uncertainty, viewers can confront their own, and perhaps be in a position to see (human) agency where before they have seen only chaos or "nature" at work. The potential for such a recognition lends a special power to the map scene at the end of *Part 2* of *Tamburlaine,* which is very much about the process of "reproduction"—and disavowal. As the dying conqueror calls upon his sons to finish his work for him, Tamburlaine seems to assume that though the work of conquest is incomplete, the work of explicit, violent mapping is over:

> Give me a map. Then let me see how much
> Is left for me to conquer all the world,
> That these my boys may finish all my wants.
> > *One brings a map*
> Here I began to march towards Persia.
> > (*Part 2* 5.3.123–26)

From here Tamburlaine recounts his exploits for 19 lines, before drawing his sons attention to the task he has set for them. In these lines, Tamburlaine relies on the past tense as he recounts his martial itinerary. He makes the map speak the violence that engendered it as he "traces" his now swordless fingers across a page whose inscriptions remind us of the demarcations made earlier on the places encountered with a sword, a past that lives into the present as documented on the map and as lived in actually existing social relations of the conquered in relation to the conqueror (manifested most dramatically in the presence of the bridled former kings on stage at that very moment). As a document, the map, rather than a restraint to be rejected (as Tamburlaine asserts in *Part 1*), has become reified and naturalized: an ostensibly stable site both for the operation of memory and planning for the future. Tamburlaine no longer emphasizes his (or his sons') deterritorializing force, but instead, being invested in a certain version of the landscape he has already traced out, situates his empire in an putatively fixed world. He thus entices his sons with a narrative of "New World" wealth in a West that he does not claim they will have to compose themselves:

> Look here, my boys, see what a world of ground
> Lies Westward from the midst of Cancer's line,
> Unto the rising of this earthly globe,
> Whereas the sun, declining from our sight,
> Begins the day with our antipodes.
> And shall I die, and this unconquered?
> Lo here, my sons, are all the golden mines,
> Inestimable drugs and precious stones.
>   (*Part 2* 5.3.145–52)

The unsettling deterritorializing force that Tamburlaine had earlier unleashed is contained here. This map even already represents land "which never was descried" (*Part 2* 5.3.155), whereas earlier he claimed to need to imagine excluded regions. To consolidate his own rule, and that of his progeny, he must rule space and betray a contradiction in the imperial project, which requires mapping, an ongoing process, and also attempts to stabilize a particular set of power relations in a map "document."

The difference between this "map" scene and the "mapping" scene in *Part 1* discussed earlier reveals a dilemma for emergent capital (or any other systemic change) as well. Primitive accumulation, as the set of social, political, economic, and cultural forces that undermine precapitalist formations and thus open the way for capitalism, *is* a form of deterritorialization and conquest. Once capitalism becomes the dominant mode in a given social formation, however, its mission is reproduction as well as expansion. Thus it develops an interest in reification of the deterritorializing energies that brought it into being, though it (contradictorily) continues to rely upon deterritorializing energies to (re)open regions and domains to itself (the ongoing work of primitive accumulation). In addition to this contradiction, capital is faced with the problem that, once the transformational energy that brings it into being is released, it can be used for other ends. If Tamburlaine can conjure up "all the world" to inspire the desire to conquer it, others perhaps can imagine "all the world" in order to free themselves of "Tamburlaine" and his legacy via a "globalization from below."[46] This is an alternative uncompleted project with which the end of *Tamburlaine* leaves its viewers and readers: an uncompleted project of resistance to capital-emergent wherever and whenever it may be. This uncompleted project is represented less by Callapine's dispersed army than in a debt to the real-life counterparts of the defeated multitudes of innocents in the play: the towns and lives destroyed by "Tamburlaine" in his Eastern or Western, medieval or modern forms.[47] Such a reading of *Tamburlaine* participates in Bloch's proposal that we recognize in the "uncompleted projects" of the past liberatory elements that can still be turned against capital in a progressive fashion in the present. Thus, I have particularly emphasized how the invocation of *Tamburlaine* in the response to the Bridewell prisoners on the streets of London in the early seventeenth century hints at the availability of material for a potentially liberatory "cognitive mapping" in Marlowe's plays, which might serve us even now, even if the recorded response of "the people" participates most directly in a repressive regime in its immediate moment.

Through a reformulation of "cognitive mapping" via Bloch, I have provided what I hope is a more complex approach to the "temporality" of cultural forms and their criticism, which opens the possibility for an ongoing political use-value for *Tamburlaine* in its criticism, a possibility that most criticism closes off just as resolutely as Tamburlaine attempts to conjure away the ongoing process of mapping (History) by turning to a reified map. For example, Stephen Greenblatt's *Renaissance Self-Fashioning* (1980)— a text that helped make "spatial" analysis of the early modern fashionable through its reference to travel narrative—opens its chapter on Marlowe with an excerpt from an evocative account of a visit by the merchant John Seacoll to "a town of . . . Negroes" in 1586. At the approach of the Europeans, the inhabitants of the village flee, giving the merchant and seamen time to see the sights at their leisure. After admiring the cleanliness of the streets and the cunning architecture of the village, Seacoll abruptly reports "our men at their departure set the town on fire, and it was burnt . . . in a quarter of an hour" (qtd. in Greenblatt, *Self-Fashioning* 193). Noting that the passage "serves as a reminder of what *until recently* was called one of the glorious achievements of Renaissance civilization" (193; emphasis added), Greenblatt observes, "What is most striking is the casual unexplained violence" (194). He concludes his remarks on the Seacoll narrative by claiming that Marlowe's *Tamburlaine* offers "a meditation on the roots" of the behavior of the English mariners in Seacoll's account, and that "if we want to understand the historical matrix of Marlowe's achievement, the analogue to Tamburlaine's restlessness, aesthetic sensitivity, appetite, and violence, we might look . . . at the acquisitive energies of English merchants, entrepreneurs, and adventurers, promoters alike of trading companies and theatrical companies" (194). Apparently, "we" now find the "casual violence" of this "acquisitive energy" alien and shocking, having "recently" learned not to read accounts of market expansion and its attendant violent social upheaval as heroic.

However, it seems that such shock is reserved only for atrocities committed centuries ago, since, at the very moment that Greenblatt was writing, the planet was in the throes of a paroxysm of violent restructuring of capitalism which left behind effects of "casual violence" and decimation-at-departure as astonishing and disturbing as anything Seacoll describes. Here is one such account from a site not so very many miles down the coast highway from Berkeley, where Greenblatt wrote his book:

As the Los Angeles economy in the 1970s was "unplugged" from the American industrial heartland and rewired to East Asia, non-Anglo workers have borne the brunt of adaptation and sacrifice. The 1978–82 wave of factory closings in the wake of Japanese import penetration and recession, which shuttered ten of the twelve largest non-aerospace plants in Southern California and displaced 75,000 blue-collar workers, erased the ephemeral gains won by blue-collar blacks between 1965 and 1975. Where local warehouses and factories did not succumb to Asian competition, they fled instead to the new industrial parks in the South Bay, northern Orange county or the Inland Empire—321 firms since 1971. An investigating committee of the California Legislature in 1982 confirmed the resulting economic destruction in Southcentral neighborhoods: unemployment rising by nearly 50 per cent since the early 1970s while community purchasing power fell by a third. (Davis 304–5)

What followed in the wake of this devastation was not "economic development" of any kind, but rather an escalation of violence: the well-advertised militarization of the Los Angeles Police Department, whose chief at the time regularly referred to Southcentral as "Vietnam" and treated the neighborhood and its inhabitants accordingly.[48] Mike Davis's *City of Quartz* bears witness to this *ongoing* violence wrought by the inescapably uneven development of capital, for which underdevelopment and laying waste are regular features, which cannot be isolated in the distant past, as if they were unfortunate but temporary "growing pains" for capitalism in its earliest moments.

Thus, I have argued in this essay that the "historical matrix" (to borrow Greenblatt's phrase) of *Tamburlaine* is incomprehensible without attention to this ongoing process.[49] Any "historical matrix" includes the past that continues to haunt the present, and the present conditions that haunt the way we read the remnants of the past. To understand *Tamburlaine* in the here and now, we need to include an interrogation of the themes that interest its current critics, and wonder why it seems to speak to those critics more emphatically in some ways than others. To fail to do so is to mystify history (understood as an ongoing process), rather than to illuminate it, as Greenblatt's "cultural poetics" purports to do (*Learning to Curse* ch. 8). Globalization and primitive accumulation are ongoing processes that extend back to the moment of the emergence of capital (and Marlowe's *Tamburlaine)*. Is it so very surprising that in the current moment of particular cataclysm and crisis for capitalism, catalogued under the sign of "globalization" and characterized by dislocations and violence visited upon populations throughout the globe—even in U.S. universities—that critics might revisit *Tamburlaine* in terms of its spaces and its violence?[50] To explode the mystificatory relegation of this violence to the past, we need to examine the criticism in *its* conditions of emergence, even as we examine *Tamburlaine* in its originary conditions of emergence, which by no means exhausts its significatory force.

Notes

1. For a selection of these responses, see Maclure. The Swinburne passage cited here comes from Maclure 184; the Jonson observation comes from his memorial poem for Shakespeare's First Quarto, here cited from the *Riverside Shakespeare* 65.

2. *Tamburlaine (Parts 1 and 2* together) was first published in 1590, with references to previous performance on its title page ("sundrie times shewed upon Stages in the Citie of London"), and we have records of its having been staged throughout the 1590s and into the next century, with at least twenty-two performances of one or the other of the parts in 1594–95 alone, as recorded by Henslowe. Reissues of the 1590 print edition appeared in 1593, 1597, 1605, and 1606. As this performance and publication history attest, the plays were highly successful. Even when the *Tamburlaine* plays were nearly ten years old, they were still among the biggest box office draws performed by the Admiral's Men at the Rose (see discussion in Chambers 146–49, as well as Jump's introduction to the Regents' edition). In addition, their success seems to have spurred many imitations, from the now obscure *Selimus* to Shakespeare's *Henry V.* At the very least, we can be confident that within the London scene it was a relatively well known text, if not at first hand, then by reputation. On the early modern responses to *Tamburlaine,* see Richard Levin. Many of the references Levin collects indicate a shift in taste (commenting critically on both the acting style invited by the plays, and their bombastic rhetoric), which does not seem to have abated the power of the plays in the imagination of Londoners. On shifting taste, also see Shawcross, which

attributes the continuation of references to Marlowe after his plays ceased to be performed to their having entered the public sphere more generally and thus being similar to "our contemporary remarks about E.T. or Mr. Spock (even if we have seen neither movie nor television show)" (66). What both of these authors suggest is that Marlowe's plays exceed the moment of their performance as theatrical texts, and take on a life of their own in the broader culture of early modern London.

3. According to Richard Levin, "a great many responses to *Tamburlaine* have come down to us, more than for any other play of the period" (51).

4. In this respect, my essay can be read as an extended response to Stephen Greenblatt's anti-Marxism in essays such as "Towards a Poetics of Culture" (*Learning to Curse* 146-60), which asserts the existence of an independent aesthetic realm and defends capitalism as a "complex historical movement" against the (ostensible) reductiveness of Marxists (Jameson is obliged by him to serve as a metonym) who transform it into a "unitary demonic principle" (151). It is simply not the case that Marxists (or even Jameson) see capital as a "unitary demonic principle"; to the contrary, Marxists see capital precisely as a "complex historical movement" (as Greenblatt acknowledges that they do "in principle" but not "in practice"—see 151) that nonetheless (and ineluctably) forecloses its ability to actualize the most liberatory, equitable, and humane potentialities for which it opens the way because of the limits imposed by its relations of production. However, since capitalist ideologists do an excellent job of praising capitalism, Jameson, as most Marxists, sees his task as engaging in its *critique* as his most immediate and urgent task; this does not mean that such critics do not understand history "complexly," as I hope to demonstrate in this essay. On "sights of power" and their relation to rhetoric in the plays, see Thurn.

5. The literature on early modern spatial imaginaries and practices is now enormous; see, for example, Fuller; Gillies; Helgerson; Knapp; and McRae.

6. Also see Cartelli, *Marlowe, Shakespeare* ch. 3; and Sales. Simon Shepherd has a rather different "social" interpretation, concerning the role of fathers, on and off stage.

7. Of course not every article published on *Tamburlaine* in the past twenty years is concerned primarily with spatial matters, nor is this spatial interest, where it does appear, confined to studies of Marlowe, being part of a larger "spatial turn" (see Soja) in several disciplines. Nevertheless, there *has* been a striking tendency—after Greenblatt's *Renaissance Self-Fashioning*—to read *Tamburlaine* spatially. Even in essays not specifically concerned with tracking spatializing force and implications, Marlowe's spatial concerns are often now taken for granted, as when, for example, Marjorie Garber observes that the "drama of the word" with which she is concerned in her reading "is played out in *Tamburlaine* with special reference to the Koran and the conqueror's map of the world" (301). I am interested in exploring what about Marlowe's *Tamburlaine* might render it a particularly attractive site for spatial investigation in the context of this general turn toward preoccupation with space.

8. Although we regularly identify historically contingent reasons for the critical and editorial preoccupations of earlier moments (as, for example, in Margreta de Grazia's work on the editors of Shakespeare), such a historicizing gaze is rarely directed to our own critical production. I am simply here making an observation that seems easy to make about earlier critics, and extending it to our own critical practice. I follow here Michel de Certeau: "[N]o

thought or reading is capable of effacing the specificity of the place, the origin of my speech, or the area in which I am researching. This mark is indelible" (56).

9. I am using "figuration" here in Fredric Jameson's sense of the ability of cultural forms to render available to tangible experience abstractions, such as "class," which would otherwise elude us. See *Signatures of the Visible* 37–38. On primitive accumulation, see Marx, *Capital* chs. 26–33; and Halpern. My own view of primitive accumulation differs from Halpern's in that he tends to localize its processes in England, whereas I focus on its operation in what was already (to my mind) a "world system." In Marxism, this divide between the (generally, more European-oriented) "orthodox" group, which includes, most influentially, Robert Brenner and, most emphatically, Ellen Wood, and the "world systems" and "dependency theory" proponents of various stripes is a long-standing and heated one because of its implications for how to understand global inequality now as well as in the past. There are problems with aspects of "world systems" perspectives such as Immanuel Wallerstein's—e.g., a tendency toward economism and some shoehorning of historical details to fit theoretical models, among others—but for all of its problems, theorists keep returning to the "world system" perspective because of the promise it holds out of coming to an understanding of global relations which does not limit itself to interactions between ostensibly intact and coherent societies. Barrie Axford provides a good summary of critiques of world systems theory in *The Global System* chs. 2, 3. Like Axford, I accept from Wallerstein the necessity of examining the world as a "system," though, as my argument shall show, I differ on the details of how this system works. Briefly, my position is that Wallerstein's "system" must be re-inflected through Giddens's emphasis on complex analyses of local/global power, and Axford's insistence on multiple determinations of the system, in order to move beyond some of the problems with economism and rigid differentiation between "center" and "periphery" with which Wallerstein's model has been identified.

10. "Historical matrix" is a term I borrow (and re-define) from a point Greenblatt makes about *Tamburlaine* in his influential chapter on Marlowe in *Renaissance Self-Fashioning*: "If we want to understand the historical matrix of Marlowe's achievement, the analogue to Tamburlaine's restlessness, aesthetic sensitivity, appetite, and violence, we might look not at the playwright's literary sources, not even at the relentless power-hunger of Tudor absolutism, but at the acquisitive energies of English merchants, entrepreneurs, and adventurers, promoters alike of trading companies and theatrical companies" (194).

11. "Uncompleted project" is a phrase I have borrowed from Ernst Bloch, which will be elaborated below.

12. See, for example, McGrew, who defines "globalization" as "the multiplicity of linkages and interconnections that transcend the nation-state (and by implication the societies) which make up the modern world system" (470).

13. There are helpful bibliographies in Axford, McGrew, and Paul Smith.

14. In the course of his discussion of the politics of history in *Marxism and Literature,* Williams explains "selective tradition" as follows: "What we have to see is not just 'a tradition' but a *selective tradition* . . . . From a whole possible area of past and present, in a particular culture, certain meanings and practices are selected out for emphasis and certain other meanings and practices are neglected or excluded. . . . It is a version of the past which is intended to connect with and ratify the present" (115–16).

15. See Richard McIntyre, "Theories of Uneven Development and Social Change."

16. For historical reasons, the effects of unevenness are, of course, global, and, indeed, often far more brutal outside of the arena of the "North" because of the already massive gap between the wealthiest states (twenty percent of global population), which—albeit unevenly—nevertheless control eighty-six percent of the world's wealth. See, for example, Amin.

17. For an excellent overview of this literature, see McRae.

18. The footage of the blocks and blocks of abandoned houses in Michael Moore's film about downsizing in the auto industry, *Roger and Me,* underscore this point very effectively.

19. The early modern passage is cited from a report of the Somerset justice of the peace Edward Hext in 1596 (Tawney and Power 2: 341). Hext is incensed, among other things, that it is difficult to convict petty thieves in the countryside because "simple Cuntryman and woman, lokynge no farther then ynto the losse of ther owne goods, are of opynyon that they wold not procure a mans death for all the goods yn the world," suggesting a certain sympathy—which belies the demonization of the "vagrants" by elites—among the "simple" country people, even though they suffered the most from theft, according to Hext.

20. In many sites around the globe, in Export Processing Zones (EPZs), extra-economic coercion regulates even those who are not excluded from the wage market (by forbidding union activity, for example, and suppressing any spontaneous dissent immediately and violently). These situations provide even more emphatic examples of a return to the premodern strategies of primitive accumulation in the late modern world. See ch. 3 of Barnet and Cavanagh's *Global Dreams* ("The Transformed Workplace") for some examples.

21. For historical accounts that emphasize the emergence of capitalism as a "global" phenomenon, see Braudel 352-58; Alan Smith 108-15; and, especially, Arrighi 174-213; also helpful are Scott; and Rabb 26-101.

22. That this state of affairs resulted from greed in Lyly's mind is perhaps suggested by this passage's appearance in the introductory matter to a dramatization of "Midas," which, in Lyly's version, depicts the king as not only begging to be freed of his ability to transform everything he touches into gold, but also renouncing his imperial ambitions.

23. Of course as the histories of colonization, the slave trade, and global uneven development illustrate, some "locals" exert pressures elsewhere more successfully than others; Giddens's point is not to discount such relations of power, but rather to insist that we understand them as *relations*: that we look at the work of integration, resistance, and counterpressure in each site to see why and how there are (net) global "winners" and "losers" in various locales, and according to what criteria.

24. See note 2 above, especially the reference to Shawcross.

25. On fascination with the East, also see Bartels, Raman, and Singh.

26. The importance of England's competition with Spain has been asserted in a number of studies of *Tamburlaine,* including Cartelli, "Marlowe and the New World," and also Shapiro.

27. As Theridamas, who had been talked into defecting from the Persian army into Tamburlaine's own, observes of Tamburlaine: "You see . . . what working words he hath. / But when you see his actions top his speech, / Your speech will stay or so extol his worth / As I shall be commended and excus'd / For turning my poor charge to his direction" (*Part 1* 2.3.25-29).

28. Of course this is a (necessary) stage convention, but *how*—specifically—conventions are deployed matters: what figures and countries are so represented; which, and when, this convention is altered (e.g., the deployment of "stage" languages to indicate alienness, as in the depiction of many "Irish" or "Welsh" characters, use of accents, intrusion of bits of a foreign tongue to establish the "foreignness" of the character, or an explanation given for why a character can speak English, and so on). From this perspective, given the broad range of options available to indicate "otherness" verbally, it is significant that Tamburlaine speaks English—at least in so far as the text indicates—"transparently."

29. See note 5 above.

30. For a discussion of Hakluyt's collections as "merchant epic," see Helgerson ch. 4; my position differs from Helgerson's, however, in that I see the forces that work to "form" the nation—being global—as simultaneously de-forming it. One of the most curious and contradictory aspects of relying on a "merchant epic" to inform nationhood is that such a text must depict the nation as irreducibly dependent on the not-self (for trade), even as it "defines" the self.

31. See, for example, Wallerstein's *The Modern World-System;* see also the comments on Wallerstein's work in note 9 above.

32. Cartelli, for example, describes his earlier and more recent discussions of the plays as follows: "In my own earlier work on *Tamburlaine* . . . I positioned Tamburlaine's radical exercise in social mobility in relation to the specifically English phenomenon of the masterless man, drawing support from the repeated representation of Tamburlaine and his cohorts in terms employed elsewhere in the period in descriptions of popular uprisings and rebellions. It now seems to me that Tamburlaine may also be modeling the exploits of another kind of masterless man, particularly, the opportunistic conquests of the conquistador, and doing so at least in part to suggest what similarly motivated 'pryvat men' of England might do for themselves by operating outside the pale of officially constituted constraints and controls" ("Marlowe and the New World" 114).

33. Stallybrass and White's full passage reads: "Carnival often violently abuses and demonizes weaker, not stronger, social groups—women, ethnic and religious minorities, those who 'don't belong,' in a process of displaced abjection."

34. As Roger Sales points out (52), it is impossible to know from the available evidence whether any irony was intended (that is, whether the crowd is mocking the prisoners, their keepers, or both). And, of course, it is impossible to know whether this event ever happened at all. For purposes of my argument, it is sufficient that "R. M." (*Micrologia*'s author) thought it *could* have happened.

35. On the effects of primitive accumulation on different groups, see Lachmann.

36. Both of the quotations are from Hakluyt, *Voyages* 211, 213; see also Knorr.

37. As Edward Hext complained of "wandarynge . . . people" in 1596: "they are so myche strength unto the enymey" (Tawney and Power 2: 344).

38. Jameson's term "cognitive mapping" derives from Kevin Lynch's study of how individuals negotiate urban spaces and what makes some cities easier to find one's way around in than others, transcoded into an Althusserian problematic: "I have always been struck by the way Lynch's conception of city experience—its dialectic between the here and now of immediate perception and the imaginative or imaginary sense of the city as an absent

totality—presents something like the spatial analogue of Althusser's great formulation of ideology itself, as 'the Imaginary representation of the subject's relation to his or her Real condition of existence' " (*Postmodernism* 415). Lynch argues that the ability to find one's way around a city is determined by the ease with which it enables one to carry around in one's head a "map" of the whole, into which a current position can be inserted at any time. Any elements of the environment, such as landmarks, natural or built, and a grid system for streets, can assist this, while lack of these aids make a city more bewildering. For Jameson, the "positioning" most pertinent to his Marxist problematic is not restricted to either the urban or the spatial, but is the relation of a subject to global capitalism. In the essay that he has called "the only full-dress analysis of cognitive mapping at work in a cultural artifact that I have myself succeeded in completing" (*Postmodernism* 416), Jameson emphasizes the importance of studying popular cultural forms for evidence of cognitive mapping—however unlikely they may seem to harbor such possibilities at first glance—since they offer a "mode of experience that is more visceral and existential than the absent certainties of Marxian Social Science" (*Signatures* 37). Because cultural forms are complex, and the conditions under which they are produced riddled with contradictions, part of their meaning might lead in the direction of a utopian imaginary even if the work is otherwise regressive and commercial. Through the experience of such latent possibilities, Jameson asserts, "we . . . begin to sense the abstract truth of class through the tangible medium of daily life in vivid and experiential ways" (*Signatures* 38).

39. Contrast Marx, in the "Eighteenth Brumaire": "[J]ust when they appear to be engaged in the revolutionary transformation of themselves and their material surroundings, in the creation of something which does not yet exist, precisely in such epochs of revolutionary crisis they timidly conjure up the spirits of the past to help them; they borrow their names, slogans and costumes so as to stage the new world-historical scene in this venerable disguise and borrowed language" (146).

40. As a secondary gain, a rigorous study of "uneven times" can help address the problem identified by Johannes Fabian in *Time and the Other,* which critiques the tendency of Western anthropology to define some cultures as living in the "modern" world but not others. Since all social formations, according to a theory of "combined and uneven development," are the effects of relations between several modes of production, global and local, all social formations are "backward" and "progressive" at the same time, and one can study how the effects of each formation affect all the others for better or worse as well, enabling a complex "development theory," capable of a non-homogenizing view of the world system, or any of its parts, which pays attention to local circumstances as part of a "world system." This is only possible, of course, if one does not use one time as the measure of all the others. See Althusser and Balibar ch. 4.

41. Stephen Best and Douglas Kellner (188–92) have critiqued Jameson's privileging of space over time as well. It is not the case, of course, that Jameson thinks there was no confusion over actually existing social relations in previous moments; rather, he thinks that the pace and intensity of this confusion increases with the rate of circulation of information, people, and so forth: "[T]his alarming disjunction point between the body and its built environment—which is to the initial bewilderment of the older modernism as the velocities of spacecraft to those of the automobile—can itself stand as the symbol and analogon of

that even sharper dilemma which is the incapacity of our minds, at least at present, to map the great global multinational and decentered communicational network in which we find ourselves caught up" (*Postmodernism* 44). But, of course, with rocket ships (to follow the metaphor) also come Geographic Information Systems (GIS).

42. According to Stuart Hall, "We used to think at an earlier stage, that if one could simply identify the logic of capital, that it would gradually engross everything in the world into a kind of replica of itself, everywhere; that all particularity would disappear. . . . But the more we understand about the development of capital itself, the more we understand that that is only part of the story. That alongside that drive to commodify everything, which is certainly one part of its logic, is another critical part of its logic which works in and through specificity" (29-30). Jameson sometimes appears to attribute to postmodernism precisely the kind of "singular, unitary logic" that Hall here calls into question, though this is not the same as the "unitary demonic principle" Greenblatt accuses it of being (*Learning to Curse* 151) since Jameson attributes "positive" as well as "negative" attributes to it. See Jameson, *Postmodernism* 47.

43. "Cultures 'think themselves,' " Stallybrass and White argue, "in the most immediate and affective ways through the combined symbolisms of . . . four hierarchies: psychic forms, the human body, geographical space and the social order" (3). The "high" produces itself by identification and rejection of a "low" in each of these domains, whose symbolic systems reinforce each other, but "what is excluded at the overt level of identity-formation is productive of new objects of desire" (25).

44. See Lachmann 16-17. My analysis of the significance and cause of these figures differs significantly from his, as he is invested in England as a unit, in which capitalist relations emerged "internally."

45. I am *not* suggesting that in actually existing conditions "outside" the play that there was no "agency" (promoting or resisting capital) or that the successful emergence of capital as it happened was inevitable. What Tamburlaine figures in his omnipresent and "leveling" effect is not that everyone was *equally* affected by primitive accumulation, but rather than everyone was inserted into (and participated in the production of) radically changed conditions of existence—though not, of course, all in the same way.

46. On processes of "globalization from below" today, see Brecher and Costello.

47. As Walter Benjamin puts it in the "Theses on the Philosophy of History": "The past carries with it a temporal index by which it is referred to redemption. There is a secret agreement between past generations and the present one. Our coming was expected on earth. Like every generation that preceded us, we have weak Messianic power, a power to which the past has a claim" (*Illuminations* 254). Refer also to the passage from Derrida that serves as the epigraph for this essay (xix).

48. See Davis's "The Hammer and the Rock" in *City of Quartz*. Of course the description of Southcentral Los Angeles as "Vietnam" raises questions of the politics of space and time similar to those raised by Marlowe's own text. The displacement here—the transformation of the "war against poverty" into the "war against crime" in terms of the (ghost of a) "war against communism"—indicates not just a residual playing out of cold war politics on a "Third World" within the "First," but also the disciplining of the world's populations, in widely distant sites, to the effects of capitalist accumulation's advances and retreats. I would, thus, change

the emphasis in Davis's passage here in one respect; because of his focus on, and sympathy for, U.S. workers, he neglects to bring into his critique the plight of workers in Asia and in other sites around the world who, too, bear the brunt of capital's discipline (this is not true of Davis's work as a whole, which takes up elsewhere, for example, the plight of migrant workers from Mexico and further south).

49. Of course *Tamburlaine* as a play can be "read" in multiple ways; my point here is that the *historical situation*—or "matrix"—of literary and other texts includes their moments of reading as well as their moment of writing.

50. Bill Readings has suggested that the decline of the humanities in the university, with all the attendant downsizings and turns to casual labor that have followed in its wake, can be attributed at least in part to a globalizing economy, which lessens, or at least disrupts, the character of the "national culture" that it was the work of the humanities to inculcate. Without this task to justify itself (however implicitly), the humanities are left without their traditional mission and therefore without their historically recognized claim of value to a larger community.

Works Cited

Althusser, Louis, and Etienne Balibar. *Reading* Capital. Trans. Ben Brewster. London: NLB, 1970.

Amin, Samir. *Capitalism in the Age of Globalization.* London: Zed, 1997.

Arrighi, Giovanni. *The Long Twentieth Century.* London: Verso, 1994.

Axford, Barrie. *The Global System: Economics, Politics and Culture.* New York: St. Martin's, 1995.

Barnet, Richard, and John Cavanagh. *Global Dreams: Imperial Corporations and the New World Order.* New York: Touchstone, 1994.

Bartels, Emily. *Spectacles of Strangeness: Imperialism, Alienation, and Marlowe.* Philadelphia: U of Pennsylvania P, 1993.

Benjamin, Walter. "Theses on the Philosophy of History." *Illuminations.* Trans. Harry Zohn. New York: Schoken, 1969. 253-64.

Berman, Marshall. *All That Is Solid Melts into Air.* New York: Penguin, 1988.

Best, Steven, and Douglas Kellner. *Postmodern Theory: Critical Interrogations.* New York: Guilford, 1991.

Bloch, Ernst. "Nonsynchronism and the Obligation to Its Dialectics." Trans. Mark Ritter. *New German Critique* 11 (1977): 22-38.

Braudel, Fernand. *The Perspective of the World.* Trans. Sian Reynolds. Cambridge: Harper & Row, 1984.

Brecher, Jeremy, and Tim Costello. *Global Village or Global Pillage.* Boston: South End, 1994.

Brenner, Robert. "The Origins of Capitalist Development: A Critique of Neo-Smithian Marxism." *New Left Review* 104 (1977): 25-92.

Burnett, Mark Thornton. "Tamburlaine: An Elizabethan Vagabond." *Criticism* 33.1 (1991): 31-47.

Cartelli, Thomas. "Marlowe and the New World." Grantley and Roberts 110-18.

——. *Marlowe, Shakespeare and the Economy of Theatrical Experience*. Philadelphia: U of Pennsylvania P, 1991.

Certeau, Michel de. *The Writing of History*. Trans. Tom Conley. New York: Columbia UP, 1988.

Chambers, E. K. *The Elizabethan Stage*. Vol. 2. Oxford: Clarendon, 1923.

"Christopher Marlowe." *Norton Anthology of English Literature*. 5th ed. New York: Norton, 1986. 1:792-93.

Davis, Mike. *City of Quartz*. New York: Vintage, 1992.

de Grazia, Margreta. *Shakespeare Verbatim*. Oxford: Clarendon-Oxford UP, 1991.

de Somogyi, Nick. "Marlowe's Maps of War." Grantley and Roberts 96-109.

Derrida, Jacques. *Specters of Marx*. Trans. Peggy Kamuf. New York: Routledge, 1994.

Fabian, Johannes. *Time and the Other*. New York: Columbia UP, 1983.

Friedenreich, Kenneth, et al., eds. *"A Poet and a Filthy Play-maker": New Essays on Christopher Marlowe*. New York: AMS, 1988.

Fuller, Mary. *Voyages in Print*. Cambridge: Cambridge UP, 1995.

Garber, Marjorie. " 'Here's Nothing Writ': Scribe, Script, and Circumspection in Marlowe's Plays." *Theatre Journal* 36.3 (1984): 301-20.

Giddens, Anthony. *The Consequences of Modernity*. Stanford: Stanford UP, 1990.

Gillies, John. *Shakespeare and the Geography of Difference*. Cambridge: Cambridge UP, 1994.

Grantley, Darryll, and Peter Roberts, eds. *Christopher Marlowe and English Renaissance Drama*. Aldershot: Scholar, 1996.

Greenblatt, Stephen. *Learning to Curse*. New York: Routledge, 1990.

——. *Renaissance Self-Fashioning: From More to Shakespeare*. Chicago: U of Chicago P, 1980.

Hakluyt, Richard. *Divers Voyages*. London: Thomas Woodcocke, 1582.

——. *Voyages and Discoveries*. Ed. Jack Beeching. London: Penguin, 1972.

Hall, Stuart. "The Local and the Global: Globalization and Ethnicity." *Culture, Globalization and the World System*. Ed. Anthony D. King. London: Macmillan, 1991. 19-39.

Halpern, Richard. *The Poetics of Primitive Accumulation*. Ithaca: Cornell UP, 1991.

Harvey, David. "Globalization in Question." *Rethinking Marxism* 8.4 (1995): 1-16.

Helgerson, Richard. *Forms of Nationhood*. Chicago: U of Chicago P, 1992.

Jameson, Fredric. *The Political Unconscious: Narrative as a Socially Symbolic Act*. Ithaca: Cornell UP, 1981.

——. *Postmodernism*. Durham: Duke UP, 1991.

——. *Signatures of the Visible*. New York: Routledge, 1990.

Knapp, Jeffrey. *An Empire Nowhere*. Berkeley: U of California P, 1992.

Knorr, Klaus. *British Colonial Theories, 1570-1850*. Toronto: U of Toronto P, 1968.

Lachmann, Richard. *From Manor to Market*. Madison: U of Wisconsin P, 1987.

Levin, Harry. *The Overreacher*. Cambridge: Harvard UP, 1952.

Levin, Richard. "The Contemporary Perception of Marlowe's Tamburlaine." *Medieval and Renaissance Drama in England* 1 (1984): 51-70.

Lyly, John. "Midas." *Complete Works of John Lyly*. Vol. 3. Ed. R. Warwick Bond. London: Oxford UP, 1902. 113-62.

Lynch, Kevin. *The Image of the City*. Cambridge: MIT P, 1960.

Maclure, Millar. *Marlowe: The Critical Heritage, 1588-1896.* London: Routledge, 1979.

Marlowe, Christopher. *Tamburlaine the Great, Parts 1 and 2.* Ed. John D. Jump. Lincoln: U of Nebraska P, 1967.

Marx, Karl. *Capital.* Vol. 1. Trans. Ben Fowkes. London: Penguin, 1976.

———. "The Eighteenth Brumaire of Louis Bonaparte." *Surveys from Exile.* Ed. David Fernbach. Trans. Ben Fowkes. Harmondsworth: Penguin, 1973.

McGrew, Anthony. "A Global Society." *Modernity: An Introduction to Modern Societies.* Ed. Stuart Hall et al. Cambridge: Blackwell, 1996. 467-503.

McIntyre, Richard. "Theories of Uneven Development and Social Change." *Rethinking Marxism* 5.3 (1992): 75-105.

McRae, Andrew. *God Speed the Plough: The Representation of Agrarian England, 1550-1660.* New York: Cambridge UP, 1996.

Mead, Stephen X. "Marlowe's *Tamburlaine* and The Idea of Empire." *Works and Days* 7.2 (1989): 91-103.

Ortelius, Abraham. *Theatrum Orbis Terrarum.* Antwerp, 1570. London, 1606.

Rabb, Theodore. *Enterprise and Empire.* Cambridge: Harvard UP, 1967.

Raman, Shankar. "Imaginary Islands: Staging the East." *Renaissance Drama* ns 26 (1995): 131-61.

Readings, Bill. *The University in Ruins.* Cambridge: Harvard UP, 1996.

Sales, Roger. *Christopher Marlowe.* New York: St. Martin's, 1991.

Scott, William Robert. *The Constitution and Finance of English, Scottish and Irish Joint-Stock Companies to 1720.* 3 vols. Gloucester: Peter Smith, 1968.

Seaton, Ethel. "Marlowe's Map." *Essays and Studies* 10 (1924): 13-35.

Shakespeare, William. *The Riverside Shakespeare.* Ed. G. Blakemore Evans. Boston: Houghton Mifflin, 1974.

Shapiro, James. "Revisiting Tamburlaine: *Henry V* as Shakespeare's Belated Armada Play." *Criticism* 31.4 (1989): 351-66.

Shawcross, John. "Signs of the Times: Christopher Marlowe's Decline in the Seventeenth Century." Friedenreich 63-71.

Shepherd, Simon. *Marlowe and the Politics of Elizabethan Theatre.* New York: St. Martin's, 1986.

Singh, Jyotsna. *Colonial Narratives/Cultural Dialogues.* London: Routledge, 1996.

Smith, Alan. *Creating a World Economy.* Boulder: Westview, 1991.

Smith, Paul. *Millennial Dreams.* London: Verso, 1997.

Soja, Edward. *Postmodern Geographies.* London: Verso, 1989.

Stallybrass, Peter, and Allon White. *The Politics and Poetics of Transgression.* Ithaca: Cornell UP, 1986.

Tawney, R. H., and Eileen Power. *Tudor Economic Documents.* 3 vols. London: Longmans, 1935.

Thurn, David. "Sights of Power in *Tamburlaine.*" *English Literary Renaissance* 19.1 (1989): 3-21.

Wallerstein, Immanuel. *The Modern World-System: Capitalist Agriculture and the Origins of the European World-Economy in the Sixteenth Century.* New York: Academic, 1974.

Williams, Raymond. *Marxism and Literature*. Oxford: Oxford UP, 1977.

Wilson, Richard. "Visible Bullets: Tamburlaine the Great and Ivan the Terrible." *ELH* 62.1 (1995): 47–68.

Wood, Ellen Meiksins. *The Pristine Culture of Capitalism*. London: Verso, 1991.

Wrightson, Keith. *English Society: 1580–1680*. New Brunswick: Rutgers UP, 1982.

"[W]rapping Togas over Elizabethan Garb": Tabloid Shakespeare at the 1934 Chicago World's Fair

ROSEMARY KEGL

The [Elizabethan] actors wore, for the most part, the dress of their own time. The audience saw nothing incongruous in Agamemnon appearing in doublet and hose, though the Roman plays were marked by the wearing of togas over the contemporary dress. A vivid sense of present life, rather than an archaeological faithfulness, was the result.

—Thomas Wood Stevens, *The Globe Theatre*

ON DECEMBER 4, 1934, almost two months after the closing of the Chicago World's Fair, William E. Vogelback, president of the Merrie England exhibit, explained how he had convinced the fair's organizers that the second year of their Century of Progress Exposition should include an exhibit variously entitled the English Village, Old England, and Merrie England. His application had promised a "village built on high standards" that would have an "atmosphere of dignity, peace, quiet and repose, and have no exhibits, side-shows, nor entertainment which could be regarded as offensive to good taste and decency."[1] In Vogelback's account, Merrie England was remarkably successful in creating that atmosphere. Reminiscing about the village's magical effect on otherwise unruly fairgoers, he claimed that

[h]oodlums seldom came into the Village, and when they did, they looked uncomfortable and seemed unable to determine what to do with themselves. On days when 15 or 20 thousand people visited us, we never experienced the slightest trouble. On children's day, when hundreds of thousands of children were let loose, they damaged other concessions in a ruthless fashion—but when they came into the English Village they were as well behaved as at a Sunday School class. On the closing night, hoodlums tore up most of the villages, but we experienced practically no damage whatsoever.[2]

73

Vogelback's befuddled hoodlums are "uncomfortable" and "unable to determine what to do with themselves" in part because they literally have
no place in the Merrie England of his memory. That English Village, as
newspaper reporters rhapsodized in 1934, was the " 'class draw' of the
World's Fair," presenting "programs of the standard that one expects in the
concert hall." Among those programs were forty-minute productions of
Shakespeare's plays, staged in the fair's reconstructed Globe Theater. Under
the general direction of Thomas Wood Stevens, the Merrie England Players
offered performances at 2, 3, 4, 5, 7:30, 8:30, and 9:30 p.m. every day.
Their repertoire, to which new plays were added throughout the summer
and early autumn, included *All's Well That Ends Well, As You Like It,
The Comedy of Errors, Julius Caesar, King Lear, Macbeth, A Midsummer
Night's Dream, The Taming of the Shrew,* Marlowe's *Doctor Faustus,* and
Shaw's *The Dark Lady.*[3]

According to the exhibit's officers, over 1.5 million fairgoers entered
Merrie England during the five months of the 1934 World's Fair. Over
400,000 of those who entered Merrie England attended performances
at the Globe, including Max Reinhardt, who attended the village's production of *A Midsummer Night's Dream* while pausing, between trains,
on his way to direct his own version of the play in Hollywood, and Sam
Wanamaker, who visited Merrie England with his father and who later
credited the 1934 Chicago World's Fair with providing one childhood
inspiration for his adult involvement in efforts to reconstruct Shakespeare's
Globe Theater on the Bankside in England. Although Vogelback eventually
admitted that exhibit officers and newspaper accounts had overstated
the popularity of the Globe productions during the theater's first two
months in operation, he insisted that, beginning at the end of July, the
plays consistently drew full houses and that, during the final day of the fair,
crowds lined up for several blocks and waited up to four hours to see a
single performance.[4]

I became interested in the Century of Progress Exposition a number
of years ago, after reading Graham Holderness's 1986 interview with Sam
Wanamaker.[5] The interview is organized around Holderness's attempt to
sort through the intellectual and political effects of bardolatry. Holderness
describes the elaborate dedication ceremony that marked the 1936 relocation of the Chicago Globe Theater to Dallas, during which "Stratford
earth and water from Avon were sprinkled reverently across the stage." He
then asks whether Wanamaker's experience of Shakespeare at the 1934

Chicago World's Fair wasn't "more a matter of American bardolatry than of Renaissance popular theater." Wanamaker responds:

My encounter with the Chicago reconstruction was in fact at a time when I was most conscious of my working-class culture: my father was unemployed because of a strike, consequent on his attempts to build a union, and my first experience of Shakespeare was in that context. The experience produced no contradiction and was not at all bardolatrous. . . . I had no interest in Shakespeare, but inherited a taste for the theatre from my father who used to take me to the Yiddish Theatre. I went to the World's Fair: and found there a free spectacle—English morris-dancing and Queen Elizabeth and her courtiers. From there one entered the theatre. I have no interest in the bardolatry: the quasi-religious ceremony and reverential verbiage seem to me ludicrous. The source material itself is so incredibly rich that people are still mining it, still digging and discovering. . . . And of course the Globes that were reconstructed in America bore no resemblance to the real thing!

Wanamaker emphasizes, as an integral part of his initial experience of Shakespeare's plays, the village spectacle through which fairgoers would travel before entering the theater. The spectacle that Wanamaker encountered might have been impressive, but it was not free. In a fair whose adult admission fee was 50 cents, entrance to Merrie England cost an extra 25 cents; entrance to the Globe Theater cost yet another 25 cents and, later in the summer, 35 cents so that the increasingly lucrative Globe productions could help to subsidize the salaries of performers such as Ruth Pryor and her Chicago-based ballet company, who danced on the village green for those who had already paid their fair admission and their admission to Merrie England. Throughout the five months of the 1934 season, the village also offered its paying customers, at no additional charge, madrigal singers; Elizabethan pageants; a Punch and Judy show; a strolling gypsy; a trained bear act; jugglers; morris dancing; a mummer's play; a demonstration of Houdini's magic; acrobats; horses, dogs, and clowns from the Royal English Circus; and a boomerang-maker whose police dog, Olga, climbed up and down ladders that were propped against the Red Lion restaurant and the Globe Theater.[6]

I realize that I am quibbling about the details of a memory that had been in the making for over fifty years when Wanamaker spoke with Holderness. And yet the forgotten fee is, like the remembered spectacle, very much in keeping with Wanamaker's definition of popular theater—an accessible public space that is continuous with its patrons' daily lives:

The early theatre with its open stage, and before it the platform in the inn-yard or the booth-stage in the street, offered an accessible event available to all: a show like the circus or other forms of popular street-entertainment. We have lost the popular public theatre through these changes in theatrical architecture.

Wanamaker adds that the reconstructed Globe in England "will make the *theatre* (not only Shakespeare) once again popular, public and accessible: the working class man will feel less constrained and inhibited there than in the plush, enclosed space of a bourgeois theatre."[7] It is with this definition of the popular in mind that he fends off Holderness's charge of bardolatry. Wanamaker's experience of Shakespeare at the 1934 Chicago World's Fair was "not at all bardolatrous" because it "produced no contradiction" between Shakespeare, on the one hand, and Yiddish Theater, his father's union organizing, and his own identification with working-class culture, on the other.

Whatever the merits of Wanamaker's argument, it is worth noting that he does answer a slightly different question from the one that Holderness posed. He was not asked to balance bardolatry against popular theater, but to balance American bardolatry against Renaissance popular theater. This shift in terms is in itself hardly surprising. Wanamaker and Holderness speak at cross-purposes throughout most of the interview. Although both men would agree that they share a common commitment to the left, they differ by profession, by generation, by national tradition, and by temperament in their political impulses and in their definition of the popular. I find Wanamaker's shift in terms intriguing less for what it tells us about his more general tendency to misconstrue Holderness than for what it tells us about his very particular understanding of historicism. When Wanamaker evades the temporal and geographical specificity of Holderness's question, he is asserting the explanatory power of a historicist sensibility whose texture is most evident in the concluding section of the interview. In their final exchange, Holderness and Wanamaker discuss the experience of being a tourist. Holderness suggests that the modern tourist resembles the medieval pilgrim; the former visits a sacred national site and returns with a souvenir, the latter visits a sacred religious site and returns with a relic. Wanamaker responds:

Anyone who visits another place is a tourist: why denigrate that? To visit a place or site for its historical associations is to acquire an experience. To visit the ruins of an important historical centre is to acquire an experience. To visit a replica or reconstruction is not quite the same, yet such places can acquire the patina of the original. St. Paul's Cathedral is a reconstruction; Southwark Cathedral a nineteenth-century building incorporating a few blocks of stone from the original. The new stones acquired the patina of what they'd replaced: and a reconstructed Globe, genuinely and carefully researched, and constructed with fidelity to the known facts, will absorb the spirit of the original theatre. People who come to it—whether in superficial curiosity, reverential love, or deep appreciation—will experience something of the past. If they take an object away with them—a photograph, a model, a figure—it will serve as a link with the experience, and act as an enrichment. There's nothing wrong with that.[8]

Wanamaker's faith in the transformative power of architectural verisimilitude is tempered with his equally strong conviction that a reconstructed Globe, however scrupulous its designers' attention to historical detail, will always provide the modern tourist intent on visiting Shakespeare's stage with, at best, an asymptotic approach to their destination. The reconstruction will "absorb the spirit of the original theatre"; people who visit it will "experience *something* of the past" (emphasis added). In Wanamaker's account, experiencing "something of the past" does seem to be one step removed from acquiring "an experience" at sites with "historical associations" or at the "ruins of an important historical centre." Yet Wanamaker is fairly casual in spelling out the distinctions among these various forms of tourism. His attention is fixed much more firmly on the fact that each location—historical sites, ruins, and replicas—offers even the most unsuspecting of its visitors some sort of engagement with the past. It is this turn to history that fascinates Wanamaker. His tourist purchases a souvenir that recalls neither Shakespeare's Globe nor its modern reconstruction but what it felt like to begin to close—however briefly and however imperfectly—the distance between the two. This is not to say that the accuracy of the reconstruction is irrelevant—"And of course the Globes that were reconstructed in America bore no resemblance to the real thing!" Architectural verisimilitude might not be able to guarantee direct access to Shakespeare's stage, but "fidelity to the known facts" does increase the likelihood that visitors will experience the pleasures of a historicist sensibility. Wanamaker's historicism goes hand in hand with his definition of a popular theater. If the Globe reconstruction "will make the *theatre* (not only Shakespeare) once again popular, public and accessible," it will also make the turn to history (not only the turn to Shakespeare's stage) once again popular, public, and accessible.

I have spent the last several paragraphs outlining Wanamaker's claims not because I defer to his worldview but because his response to Holderness reinforces my sense that bardolatry is something of a red herring—an analytical category that is far too general to be useful and that, at the same time, is not as generally applicable as Holderness suggests. This essay discusses the spatial properties of the 1934 Chicago World's Fair and of its reconstructed Globe. Bardolatry sheds very little light on the quirky decision to include Shakespeare and the Globe Theater in the topography of a fair that was devoted more generally to recent advances in science and technology. Nor does it help us to understand the commitment to architectural verisimilitude that Wanamaker shares with the businessmen, educators, and theater directors who constructed and marketed the Chicago Globe. I consider, instead, what the historicist sensibilities that inform these spatial phenomena might tell us not only about the fair and its Globe Theater, but also about the contradictions inherent in late nineteenth- and early twentieth-century "Elizabethan" staging. In the final few pages of the essay, I return to Wanamaker's remarks and ask how the convergence of historicism and Shakespeare's stage might help us to analyze the impulse to historicize that is so prevalent in late twentieth-century Shakespeare studies.

Even allowing for the odd disjunctions that tend to characterize world fairs, it was by no means inevitable that either Merrie England or plays performed in a reconstructed Globe Theater would find a home—rhetorical or topographical—in a fair whose customers were encouraged to believe that the progress of science would allow them to "outdistance anything of the past." Chicago's World Fair was presided over by Rufus Cutler Dawes, who at the time of his death in 1940 was the president of the Museum of Science and Industry and who had been on that museum's board since its inception only a few years before the fair began. More commonly known as the Century of Progress Exposition, the fair announced as its goal "to convey to the public an understanding of the nature and significance of scientific discoveries and of the changes in living conditions brought about by their application in industry." To this end, organizers began to promote the fair by contracting with Williams & Wilkins to publish, between the autumn of 1931 and the early months of 1933, a "series of small books on scientific subjects, with the object of arousing a wider interest in science and scientific achievements." These books were to be "popularly and non-technically styled for general reading"—of about twenty-five to thirty thousand words in length, illustrated, and written in "simple understandable English." During the fair, organizers offered the Hall of Science a central location within the fairgrounds and within their promotional material. The hall's exhibits alternated between display space that illustrated the "nature of important discoveries in the realm of pure science and the methods by which they were made," and display space that was purchased by "great leaders of American Industry" who advertised the products made possible by those discoveries. In the two years before the opening of the World's Fair and in the months between its 1933 and 1934 incarnations, fair organizers published a weekly promotional magazine called *Progress.* There they narrated the production of their own "Master Drama"—the Century of Progress Exposition—often by referring with excruciating detail to the scientific discoveries and industrial applications that made its staging possible.[9]

Fair organizers were clear that this pervasive emphasis on science and industry would rightly overshadow the arts:

> If 2,300 years ago the people of Athens had held a centennial celebration, they might have recorded achievements in architecture, sculpture, dramatic art, and perhaps athletics. . . .
>
> The past century, and particularly the last half of it, has emphasized control by man of the forces of nature to his own uses. In the last one hundred years, man has made more progress in adjusting himself to a comfortable relation to his physical world than in all the centuries that have preceded it. . . . Distance in communication has been annihilated, distance in transportation almost conquered and voices may be heard through the air around the world.[10]

Understandably hard-pressed to explain the rationale for locating Merrie England and its Globe Theater within the preceding century of scientific progress, guidebooks and newspaper articles tended to focus on the fair's ability to manipulate spatial and temporal distance. In *So You're Going to Merrie England,* Clara E. Laughlin writes that "if traveling by rockets ever becomes feasible, it will not make possible such hundred league steps as we're taking this summer at Chicago. For instance, you may have just left Tunisia when you stroll into Merrie England!" Laughlin's remarks are in keeping with 1934 promotional material that promised visitors to the fair's cluster of foreign villages a "tour of the world in a single day." One reporter notes that "[t]he world is concentrated in a few acres. This is the way to travel! You traverse not only space but time. You cross the Atlantic in the time it takes to smoke a cigar and you find yourself in an American colonial village."[11]

The ability to surpass the speed of rockets not yet invented or to reproduce the journey of English colonists "in the time it takes to smoke a cigar" does seem to be something of a promotional afterthought. And yet, however strained this connection to science and technology might be, the desire to restructure conventional spatial and temporal relations actually figured quite prominently in the fair organizers' persistent efforts to include foreign villages in their Century of Progress. In 1952 Lenox R. Lohr, president of Chicago's Museum of Science and Industry and former general manager of the Century of Progress Exposition, revisited the Chicago World's Fair in his case study in fair management, recalling that "[h]igh hope of foreign participation—with exotic exhibits . . . and old world buildings reproduced on the shores of Lake Michigan loomed large in the early plans of A Century of Progress." The countries invited to participate were generally skeptical of a fair topography that would locate foreign villages in close proximity to the contemporary Chicago skyline and to the futuristic buildings that served as Century of Progress's architectural signature. Immersed in an economic depression, and wary of an "Old World theme" through which foreign countries, "living in a dead past," would provide a backdrop to the scientific innovations of the United States, foreign government officials eventually offered to send delegates to the Hall of Science but were reluctant to subsidize the anachronistic villages that Lohr found so compelling. In the end, the vision of Lohr and his fellow organizers prevailed. A series of foreign villages, most of which were built and operated as concessions by local businessmen, allowed the fair to present, in Lohr's words, a "more foreign and exotic appearance than it probably would have had if foreign countries had come in in the usual way with large and dignified buildings." Five villages were constructed for the 1933 World's Fair; the financial success of two—the Belgian Village and the Streets of Paris—led to their reappearance in the 1934 fair and to the construction of several new villages, including Merrie England.[12]

Vogelback recalled that when he applied to include Merrie England among the foreign villages in 1934, Shakespeare was not his most promising gambit. His advisors had warned him against offering Shakespearean productions in his village. They reminded him that Shakespeare had not been successful at the Chicago Civic Theater and would certainly be "out of place" in a World's Fair.[13] Instead, they suggested that Gilbert and Sullivan,

English music hall vaudeville, or single acts from classical plays would be more appropriate. In spite of this advice, Vogelback hired Thomas Wood Stevens to oversee the reconstruction of the Globe and to produce its abbreviated Shakespeare plays. Stevens directed Merrie England's architects, Holabird and Root, to follow a combination of the Visscher and Hollar illustrations of the Globe and the original contracts for the Fortune Theater. In keeping with early twentieth-century speculations about the Globe, the fair's theater was octagonal and included, as playing spaces, an inner stage, a middle stage, an outer stage, and an upper balcony. In keeping with World Fair building codes, it included a blue star-studded ceiling and walls with mansard roofs in order to convey the effect of an open-air theater.[14]

The technical tour de force required to satisfy Stevens's quest for architectural verisimilitude might have made good copy in the pages of *Progress*. And yet, although Merrie England was eventually billed as "the land of Shakespeare and Dickens" and although the Globe was eventually accorded advertising space alongside Riley's English Toffee in a list of village shops and restaurants, Shakespeare and his reconstructed Globe Theater were relatively inconspicuous when fair organizers initially set about publicizing the construction of their English Village. Instead, Sulgrave Manor, the English home of George Washington's parents (which seems never to have appeared in Merrie England) promised to be "one of the most conspicuous features of the show." Additional reports focused on plans to construct the Cheshire Cheese Inn, described as host to the conversational skills of Samuel Johnson and James Boswell; Charles Dickens's Old Curiosity Shop; the cottage of Robert Burns; Haddon Hall, the English home of John Harvard, founder of Harvard University; and the cottage of Ann Hathaway. In descriptions of Hathaway's cottage, Shakespeare either appeared in a parenthetical phrase or remained an absent but understood contributor to the cottage's romance.[15]

If Shakespeare had been a risky addition to Vogelback's application and almost absent in early publicity about Merrie England, he and his theater eventually figured prominently in newspaper accounts of what the *New Yorker* called the midway's shift from "fan dance" to "folk dances." When Vogelback promised the fair organizers "good taste and decency," he was offering them quite specifically an alternative to Sally Rand's well-attended fan dances, to the midway's popular nightclubs and floor shows, and to the controversial "Live Models" exhibit, in which women posed within reconstructions of famous paintings. Merrie England became one exhibit in a new Street of Villages that was constructed in 1934 on the fair's midway, where, in one newspaper reporter's words, "a year ago, Sally Rand flaunted her saucy fans, and furtive male visitors slunk in to preview other dazzling charms." Rand had left the fair after two well-publicized arrests for indecent exposure in 1933, and the remaining cabaret shows had been relegated to a "strip of beach on Northerly Island." Although Vogelback applied unsuccessfully to introduce bare-fisted boxing and cockfighting to Merrie England and although in August he added a Cockspur Lane and Limehouse district to the exhibit's attractions, Merrie England marketed itself throughout the summer and early autumn as "not Sally Rand," even offering among its regular sources of entertainment, a small and scantily-clad monkey named Jimmie whose talents included conducting a fan dance.[16]

The *Chicago Sunday Tribune* announced the Globe's opening by remarking that the 1933 fair had been "a carnival of cabaret shows, but it was singularly lacking in the higher forms of theatrical arts." The *British American* characterized the Globe's inaugural production of *The Taming of the Shrew* as "the first serious drama ever given at the Century of Progress." The *Chicago Loop News* wrote that the "Fair, an otherwise gloriously glorified carnival, redeems itself in its Shakespearean productions." By the end of June, the *Chicago Journal of Commerce* pronounced the Globe Theater as lucrative a concession as Sally Rand had been the year before. A headline in the July edition of the *Chicagoan* announced, "The Bard goes Tabloid, Shakespeare Outdraws the Fan Dances and Peep Shows."[17] During that same month, Eleanor Roosevelt arrived in Chicago to inaugurate a series of five radio shows on NBC and decided to broadcast her first program from the fair's reconstructed Globe Theater. The debates about decency, profit, corporate responsibility, and artistic freedom that had persisted well beyond Rand's arrests dovetailed nicely with Roosevelt's national agenda. "From the setting of an Elizabethan theater," one skeptical reporter commented, "the stronghold of license more than 300 years ago, Mrs. Eleanor Roosevelt last night hailed as a distinct advance in the campaign for decency in motion pictures voluntary censorship on the part of the industry." Roosevelt denounced the movies' "tendency to glorify the racketeer and criminal, or at least to make him appear a sympathetic character" and urged the motion picture industry to "use its tremendous power" for the "improvement of the country."[18]

Although the Globe Theater's box office undoubtedly benefited from this burst of publicity, Stevens and Marc T. Nielson, general manager of the fair's Globe Productions, seem to have largely ignored the local and national debates about decency with which Roosevelt and Vogelback were preoccupied. Instead, they emphasized the historical accuracy of Merrie England's reconstructed Globe:

Here we have for the first time a real Elizabethan stage and a practical entire theater such as was used in Shakespeare's day. The so-called Elizabethan methods have always been makeshift. . . . But now, for once, an Elizabethan stage is being built that will permit us to give short, carefully worked-out versions of Shakespeare— not individual scenes or acts, but versions so constructed that they will present the highlights and motifs of the essential characters presented. We shall at last be able to present Shakespeare in the Elizabethan method and in a theater especially designed for that purpose.[19]

Stevens oversaw the construction of a stage that was "not a picture frame for scenery but a platform projecting into the pit." That stage allowed "the Elizabethan method" to supersede the makeshift "so-called Elizabethan methods" with which earlier directors, working with less realistic reproductions, were forced to content themselves. The fair's "Elizabethan" stage techniques emphasized the continuous flow of performance—a continuity that was not interrupted by pauses between acts or scenes, by the distractions of elaborate scenery, or by "call boys coming out and holding up, in lieu of scenery, signs reading 'This is a Forest' or 'This is a Queen's Chamber.'"[20]

Stevens promised that he would offer "plays exactly as Shakespeare gave them." In the same breath, he announced that he would produce those plays in a miniature Globe that seated only four hundred spectators; that combined in one structure, by his own count, the architectural traits of at least three versions of Shakespeare's theater; and that, however envious he might have been of William Poel's ability to substitute a "quick-eared choir boy" for a "temperamental actress," featured women among the actors in its forty-minute productions.[21] Stevens's double-edged turn to history—a scrupulous attention to historical detail on the one hand, a careless disregard for that detail on the other—would have secured the reconstructed Globe a comfortable niche in Merrie England. When guidebooks and newspaper articles billed Merrie England as a "picture of that great age of England" or as offering the "atmosphere of old England," it was not always clear to what great age or to which Old England they were referring. Vogelback explained to his 1934 audience that the exhibit's organizers decided that a contemporary English hamlet would demand "too much explanation to an average American" and opted, instead, for the presumably more familiar "composite village" that would span "Norman to comparatively modern [times]" with an Elizabethan focus. And the same reporters and publicists who boasted that the village included "exact reproduction[s]," based on "long and careful study" of the "original buildings" and furnished with "authentic pieces and antiquities of great rarity and value," insisted upon labeling the reproduction of Allington Castle the Tower of London.[22] The eventual prominence of Shakespeare and the Globe Theater within the village did nothing to alter the temporal and topographical confusion through which Merrie England's visitors journeyed into the past. When a replica of the home that Shakespeare purchased in 1611 opened at the fair, its "historical accuracy" was said to derive from its being "furnished as nearly as possible in the style of Shakespeare's Day" with the "material and furnishing used in the days of Queen Elizabeth." An ad for the "Replica of the Globe Theatre" featured interlocking illustrations of Henry VIII and of the Globe where, the text explained, "Shakespeare's great plays were produced and where the great playwright himself appeared before the footlights." The back cover of the Cheshire Cheese menu depicted Shakespeare and Samuel Johnson, united in their common gaze at a steaming pot of food.[23]

The village's double-edged turn to history—its attempt to attract an audience both through its precise fidelity to historical detail and through its sleight-of-hand presentation of a "composite" past—gives equal time to two promotional imperatives at the Century of Progress: the practical application, including the educational benefits, of technological expertise (in this case the expertise of the architect and archaeologist), and the perceived continuity between past and present that made credible the fair's narrative of our nation's "remote European origins."[24] Stevens's double-edged turn to history bears a formal resemblance to the temporal and topographical logic of Merrie England, but I suspect that he is responding to a set of imperatives more closely linked to the spatial properties of the reconstructed Globe and the critical properties of late nineteenth- and early twentieth-century "Elizabethan" staging.

Merrie England's publicists emphasized that Stevens and his assistant, B. Iden Payne, had worked with William Poel, who, in Stevens's words, initiated the "modern use of the original stage forms." Like Nielson, Poel "had long thought that something should be done to make Shakespeare more generally enjoyed by all classes of society."[25] By 1934, Poel had been advocating the use of Elizabethan stage techniques for over half of the fair's century of progress. "Some people have called me an archaeologist," Poel wrote in 1913, "but I am not. I am really a modernist. My original aim was just to find out some means of acting Shakespeare naturally and appealingly from the full text as in a modern drama. I found that for this the platform stage was necessary and also some suggestion of the spirit and manners of the time." Poel learned quickly that even when theater managers allowed him to construct a platform stage, they generally required that the platform be inserted within the theater's existing proscenium arches. Under these conditions, Poel was able to offer platform productions that employed "Elizabethan" theatrical practices—bringing spectators closer to the stage, training actors to speak rapidly and with "Elizabethan" pitch and cadence, eliminating the modern use of props and scenery, and playing without interruptions between scenes or acts—but audiences were inevitably one additional theatrical step removed from experiencing the "spirit and manners of the time." In 1895, Poel established the Elizabethan Stage Society in order to revive "the masterpieces of the Elizabethan dramatists upon the stage for which they were written, so as to represent them as nearly as possible under the conditions existing at the time of their first production— that is to say, with only those stage appliances and accessories which were usually employed during the Elizabethan period." In 1900 Poel attempted to generate support for a Globe Theater reconstruction in London. Although he failed, his effort to "perpetuate for the benefit of posterity the kind of stage with which Shakespeare was so long and intimately associated" was the logical extension of the Society's work.[26]

Poel was well aware that his project, even under the best of circumstances, demanded a delicate and perhaps unattainable balance. He hoped that his use of "Elizabethan" stage techniques would convey to contemporary audiences the vitality of a drama that was neither designed for nor suited to modern staging. And yet he recognized that contemporary audiences, unaccustomed to the theatrical practices associated with Shakespeare's platform stage, entered the theater with a very different set of expectations than their Elizabethan counterparts. In the spring of 1916, Stevens, who was then chairing the drama department at the Carnegie Institute of Technology, invited Poel to coach his students in "Elizabethan" stage techniques. When Poel returned to the United States later that year, he agreed to direct productions of the *Poetaster* in Pittsburgh and Detroit. Stephen Allard wrote in the *Theatre Arts Magazine* that "[i]nstead of trying to reconstruct the outward semblance, the architectural detail, [Poel] set himself the task of finding what it was in the Elizabethan drama that could hold a crowd of 'groundlings' absorbed for two solid hours. He had long ago mastered the scholarly side of the subject, and he knew that mere fidelity to detail could not hold either a seventeenth-century or a twentieth-century audience. He sought the solution in the *manner* of the performance, in the *spirit* with which the director 'put over' the play." Poel's stage experiments more generally received predictably mixed responses. The same man who was accused of employing a "form of representation which appeals only to the dilettante and the enthusiast" convinced George Bernard Shaw that the Society's "method of presenting an Elizabethan play is not only the right method for that particular sort of play, but that any play performed on a platform amidst the audience gets closer home to its hearers than when it is presented as a picture framed by a proscenium."[27]

Performances in the fair's Globe Theater would not escape the tensions inherent in Poel's project. In memoirs published over forty years after the closing of the 1934 World's Fair, Stevens's assistant, B. Iden Payne, discusses his experiments with "modified Elizabethan staging" at the Carnegie Institute, whose drama department he chaired after Stevens's resignation in 1925; at the 1934 Chicago World's Fair; at Stratford in the years following the Chicago fair; and at the San Diego National Theater Festival where the 1934 Globe was eventually housed. Recalling audiences that laugh louder, applaud longer, and enjoy better these "Elizabethan" productions without elaborate modern stage devices, Payne is convinced that "Shakespeare for a modern audience can be a living experience if both the limitations and the advantages of the Elizabethan theatre are observed." And yet, having worked briefly with Poel in England, he acknowledges that "to those who have not experienced the extraordinary fluidity of an Elizabethan stage, its physical limitations seem restrictive. To confine a production to it can appear, as Poel's *Measure for Measure* first did to me, a somewhat pedantic archaism." Payne remembers that, as he grew more accustomed to the spatial properties of the platform stage, he became acutely aware that scholars' descriptions of Shakespeare's theater were speculative at best. He argued for what he considered to be a more measured engagement with the past in which "what are widely regarded as the main elements of an average Elizabethan stage structure" would serve as the "basis for the production of Shakespeare's plays." Payne hoped that his "modified Elizabethan staging" would correct for Poel's tendency to overestimate both the adaptability of modern audiences and the accomplishments of modern scholarship. Payne's modified Elizabethan stages observed two essential theatrical practices—swift and continuous performances, uninterrupted by breaks between acts or scenes, and the strategic use of what he called the playing "zones" of an upper stage, an inner "discovery" stage, and a lower stage divided into the foreground, middle, and two sides.[28] Although Payne's memoirs depict Stevens as unwilling, or unable, fully to endorse modified Elizabethan staging during his tenure as the first chair of the Carnegie drama department and as manager of Chicago's Goodman Theater, Stevens redeemed himself with his "hypothetical" reconstruction of the Globe. Payne writes, "The enthusiastic response of audiences— even of those casually sampling attractions in the carnival atmosphere of world's fairs that also boasted a nudist colony and a midget circus—once more confirmed my faith in the style of staging I had chosen."[29]

The enthusiastic audiences in Payne's memoirs find their counterpart in newspaper accounts of the Chicago Globe's opening night. Vogelback invited Chicagoans who were prominent in industry, politics, and the arts to visit Merrie England and to attend the theater's inaugural performance of *The Taming of the Shrew.* One critic reported:

For the first time in my play going I have heard—and helped—an audience roar with laughter at a Shakespearean play. . . .

Mr. Stevens' young people seemed to have forgotten all the trappings, and traditions and impediments which classicism has thrown on the bard. They jumped upon the uncurtained bandstand type of stage and began to play Shakespeare as if they had never learned that he was an awesome and sacred master. They acted as if their playwright was just another George M. Cohan. And the net result was a production as swift, pointed, shrewd and unendingly funny as if it had been written by Mr. Cohan himself. . . .

What was, however, most astonishing was the fact that while watching this educational and historically minded performance in the quaint replica of an Elizabethan theater, I forgot entirely that it was anything but a rip-roaring altogether funny play; which is proof, I take it, that Mr. Stevens' Shakespeare is at once Queen Elizabeth's and ours.[30]

Another reviewer confirmed that producing the plays in their "original environment" created an unmistakably contemporary American event:

Seated on a front row bench, I nearly had the comic servant Grumio dropped into my lap by a lusty kick from his swaggering master, Petruchio. . . . It was almost as exciting as Jack Dempsey's collapse into the ringside typewriters in the famous fracas with Firpo. . . . And when the leg of mutton and the tableware began to fly around, in the final scene of the shrew's subjugation, I buttoned up my overcoat and prepared to dodge foul balls. . . .[31]

And yet another reporter added that "several actors nearly followed Petruchio's boot into a front row critic's lap, whereupon the critic's wife, being an actress and also something of a pitcher, popped it right back on the stage where it belonged."[32] These reporters consistently cast themselves— and their fellow prominent Chicagoans—as spectacles for their readers, for fellow theatergoers, and for one another. Their prominence in the audience recalls Patrick Kirwin's productions of abbreviated Shakespeare plays at the 1912 English Village in London—productions about which Major O. S. F. Keating, general manager of the Chicago Merrie England exhibit, spoke with enthusiasm over twenty years later. Kirwin had hired actors to impersonate supposedly authentic, unruly Renaissance audiences and then had been criticized by Poel for presenting an audience spectacle so compelling that it distracted theatergoers from Shakespeare's plays.[33]

Poel might have questioned Kirwin's methods, but both Poel and Stevens were familiar with the promotional benefits of the sort of spectacle that the reporters depict or that captured Wanamaker's imagination as a child. In December 1895 the Elizabethan Stage Society demonstrated its stage techniques in a well-publicized production of the *Comedy of Errors* at the hall of Gray's Inn, where, three hundred years earlier, the play had been performed as an after-supper interlude. In the play's 1895 incarnation, audience members occupied the places of the original playgoers at the hall's long tables. After listening to the Queen's Prayer and Elizabethan music, they were entertained by actors who entered through the hall doors and who performed without an elevated stage and without pausing between scenes or acts.[34] Stevens brought to Merrie England his varied theatrical experience not only as a playwright, as the founder and director of the first university drama program, and as the manager of Chicago's Goodman Theater, but also as the prolific author and apparently tireless director of pageants—including the Centennial Pageant of the Rensselaer Polytechnic Institute; the Historical Pageant of Florida; the Pageant and Masque of St. Louis; the Historical Pageant of the Dunes; the National Red Cross Pageant; the Pageant of the Hidden Treasures of Earth, presented by the Chamber of Commerce of Pittsburgh to celebrate the dedication of the Pittsburgh Station Bureau of Mines; and the Pageant and Masque of the Nations in Wilmerding, whose first scene was entitled "The Invention of the Air Brake."[35] Similar pageants were well-funded and well-attended attractions at the fair—traits that might very well have commanded the attention of village organizers, who were already nervous about the marketability of Shakespeare's plays.[36]

However gratified fair organizers may have been by newspaper accounts of the Globe's spectacular inaugural performance, those accounts would have been somewhat less gratifying to readers who were interested in the textual properties of the abbreviated *The Taming of the Shrew.* Throughout the summer and early autumn, reporters continued to offer very few dètails about the abbreviated plays, but interested readers were able to begin to assemble a growing collection of tabloid Shakespeare. *The Taming of the Shrew* and the fair's remaining seven Shakespeare plays were printed and distributed by Samuel French between 1934 and 1937 "for the use of amateur groups which may not have at hand the facilities for giving the complete text." The Globe's thirty-six-minute inaugural performance was typical of the abbreviated fair productions. The plays were reduced both through a series of scene-by-scene, line-by-line deletions and through the elimination of large sections of the plays: the fair's production of *A Midsummer Night's Dream* was confined to the interlude, and its forty-five-minute *Julius Caesar* ended after Marc Antony's speech at Caesar's funeral. The eight texts published by French seem to be the result of several shared editorial impulses—including the reduction or elimination of subplots; of extended metaphors; and of dialogues, monologues, or plot devices that identified the plays' preoccupations as early modern. *The Taming of the Shrew* omitted the framing device of Christopher Sly and ended, on the evening of Kate and Petruchio's marriage, with Petruchio's lesson on how best to "kill a wife with kindness" (4.1.8). The rivalry among Hortensio, Lucentio, and Gremio was diminished, and Lucentio and Hortensio's simultaneous courtship of Bianca eliminated. Extended metaphors and classical references were condensed, as were references to the suitors' fiscal, familial, and geographical credentials; Baptista's criteria as he selects the proper husband for each of his daughters; and the unsettling consequences, for fathers and masters, of Tranio's disguise.[37] These deletions make a certain kind of sense, especially given that fair organizers had predicted that their audiences would be unfamiliar with Shakespeare's plays. And yet if fair organizers worried that the audiences' inexperience with Shakespeare's texts might impede their ability to understand the intricate plotting, the rhetorical properties, and the literary and social contexts of the plays, they were presumably much more confident that the same audiences would be able to overcome their inexperience with Shakespeare's platform stage.

It should be clear by now that I have arrived, by way of the abbreviated Merrie England productions, at yet one more version of what I characterized earlier as a double-edged turn to history—in this instance, a scrupulous attention to the techniques associated with Shakespeare's platform stage, coupled with a disregard for the early modern literary and social contexts of the plays produced on that stage. Initially I had focused my remarks more narrowly on the "Elizabethan" stage techniques that followed from Stevens's commitment to architectural verisimilitude—his claim to offer "plays exactly as Shakespeare gave them" in a theater that was considerably smaller than Shakespeare's Globe, that combined in one building three successive early modern amphitheaters, and that abandoned the early modern practice of training boys to play women's roles. It is worth returning to that emphasis on stage techniques because Stevens's double-edged turn to history elevates into aesthetic policy what is otherwise a persistent dilemma for "Elizabethan" staging, a dilemma that the opening night reports elide and that neither Poel nor fair organizers could hope to resolve: too little attention to the spatial properties of the stage for which Shakespeare's plays were written guarantees that theatergoers will respond to the plays as pedantic archaisms, too much attention to the spatial properties of a platform stage with which modern audiences are unfamiliar guarantees that theatergoers will respond to the productions as pedantic archaisms. Stevens's aesthetic is summed up best when he remarks on the Elizabethan tolerance for anachronism:

The [Elizabethan] actors wore, for the most part, the dress of their own time. The audience saw nothing incongruous in Agamemnon appearing in doublet and hose, though the Roman plays were marked by the wearing of togas over the contemporary dress. A vivid sense of present life, rather than an archaeological faithfulness, was the result.[38]

These remarks are most explicitly a rejection of the Victorian practice of attending more carefully to the historical setting of the plays than to the historical details of their sixteenth- and seventeenth-century productions. But they are also an endorsement of the pleasures of Elizabethan anachronism. The staging of temporal distance as a layering of costumes, like the double-edged turn to history that characterizes Stevens's "Elizabethan" productions, finds its energy precisely by making past and present synchronic. Both are equally visible to the audience—Shakespeare is, quite literally, "at once Queen Elizabeth's and ours"—and the presumed effect of this double-vision is not incongruity but clarity. Stevens's aesthetic is more generally compatible with abbreviated productions that foreground the plays' early modern theatrical contexts and yet disregard their early modern literary and social contexts. As even my thumbnail sketch of the careers of Poel and Payne suggests, Stevens's aesthetic is just one in a series of possible accommodations to the difficulties inherent in late nineteenth- and early twentieth-century experiments in "Elizabethan" staging. But it is an accommodation that is peculiarly suited to a fair whose foreign villages were designed, by virtue of their proximity to the contemporary Chicago skyline and the exposition's futuristic architecture, to underscore temporal distance and technological progress precisely through the pleasures of anachronism.

I conclude with a deceptively simple question: what do late twentieth-century Shakespeare scholars hope to explain when our own turn to history involves a turn to Shakespeare's stage? However intriguing the quirky role of the Globe Theater in a Century of Progress Exposition might be, it is the connection between historicism and Shakespeare's stage that first interested me in the abbreviated productions at the Chicago World's Fair and that has continued to sustain my interest in this project. The 1934 Globe reconstruction was an experiment in the potentially transformative power of "Elizabethan" staging; the limitations of that experiment were certainly apparent, even to its participants. Although they differed on what they would hope to find in the past—Shakespeare's intent, performances based on the collaborative work of the theater, accurate versions of the plays—they agreed that they were whittling away at a historical distance that would never entirely be overcome. Earlier in this essay I described the asymptotic approach to the past that characterized Wanamaker's historicism. Poel and fair organizers tended to assume less that the past can be approached but never encountered, than that the past—given the contingencies of historical evidence, theatrical performance, and audience response—can only be encountered in fitful and unpredictable leaps of recognition. No recipe for proper staging is able to sustain these encounters between modern audience and early modern theater or even the certainty that, however compelling an individual theatergoer's experience might have been, these encounters actually occurred. And yet if Payne and Stevens were willing to acknowledge the difficulties inherent in their engagement with the past, they were no more willing than Poel had been to forfeit "Elizabethan" staging altogether. Modifications and aestheticization aside, they continued to share with Poel a general conviction that a faithful reconstruction of Shakespeare's platform stage would help to narrow the gap between contemporary audiences and early modern plays.

We might not share their faith—or Wanamaker's—in architectural verisimilitude, but I would suggest that the literary critic's turn, however systematic or incidental, to the properties of Shakespeare's stage provides a common faultline along which we can distinguish the various historicist sensibilities that define late twentieth-century Shakespeare studies. It would be fair to say that literary criticism centered on Shakespeare has been characterized for a good number of years by a strong historicizing impulse. It also would be fair to say that it sometimes has been difficult to tease out the methodological assumptions about literature and history that underpin even the most influential of this work. This might sound like a slightly outmoded complaint, directed at new historicism and better suited to the mid-1980s. Yet I am concerned not with the shortcomings of new historicism but with what have been, for literary critics, its most enduring and productive legacies in Shakespeare studies—the range of legitimate objects of analysis, the respectability of linking literary texts to larger cultural and political forces, and the insistence that thinking about literature might reasonably entail thinking about history. These legacies have become second nature and no longer require a great deal of justification. This is not to say that literary critics have been particularly reluctant to outline the methodological assumptions that underpin their work, but simply that historicism tends to be something of a methodological silent partner—its contributions assumed but seldom explicitly discussed. And, at the same time, the range of objects and the range of cultural and political forces under scrutiny often make it difficult to locate a common faultline along which we might distinguish the various historicisms that coexist within our more general impulse to historicize. In other words, at the very moment that the impulse to historicize has become so prevalent in Shakespeare studies, the motivations, variations, and implications of that impulse have become correspondingly elusive. I find the literary critic's turn to Shakespeare's stage telling not only because it is a moment when we understand ourselves to be involved in a historical project, but also because it is a moment when we understand ourselves to be involved in a project whose historicism demands scholarship that extends beyond the boundaries of literary texts. Working along this common faultline does not suggest that we should restrict the range of objects or social forces that fall within Shakespeare studies, but it does help us to make legible the historicist sensibilities that continue to reconfigure how we describe what properly belongs within our purview, and the academic and non-academic audiences for whom and to whom our contemporary historicisms hope to speak.

Notes

The quotation in the title is from Claudia Cassidy, *Chicago Journal of Commerce* (4 June 1934).

1. "Outline for Address by William E Vogelback, President, Merrie England, On the Occasion of the Testimonial Dinner to Mr. and Mrs. William E. Vogelback by the Cordon Club of Chicago" (4 December 1934, manuscript located in the Chicago Historical Society), 1.

2. "Outline" 4.

3. For quotations see, in order of citation, Lloyd Lewis, *Chicago Daily News* (23 August 1934), and Glenn Dillard Gunn, *Chicago Herald and Examiner* (4 June 1934). The schedule of the village's Globe performances is listed in several promotional articles and guidebooks, including *Highlights of the Educational Exhibits, Chicago World's Fair, Compiled for School Teacher Conductors for Student Tours, September–October, 1934* (Chicago: Century of Progress Exposition, 1934), 26. Here, and in the remaining endnotes, all newspaper articles are cited from scrapbooks that are located in the Chicago Historical Society. *Progress,* the fair's promotional magazine, is located in the Newberry Library.

4. The Chicago Globe seated four hundred people; the attendance figures initially cited in newspaper reports and by fair promoters imply virtually full houses at all productions. For information about attendance at Merrie England and at the Globe Theater, see Charles Collins, "*As You Like It* is Pleasing in Short," *Chicago Daily Tribune* (2 July 1934); *Chicago Daily News* (1 September 1934); *Chicago Daily Times* (14 August 1934); Lenox R. Lohr, *Fair Management: The Story of a Century of Progress Exposition* (Chicago: Cuneo, 1952), 176; Vogelback, "Outline" 3, 5; and Vogelback, "Globe Theatre—A Rambling Account" (1950, manuscript located in the Chicago Historical Society), 4. Lohr reasserts Vogelback's account, describing a "continuous line stretched from the box office into the narrow street" (*Fair Management* 176). For references to Max Reinhardt's visit to the Chicago Globe, see Vogelback, "Globe Theatre" 4, and "Outline" 3. Reinhardt first produced *A Midsummer Night's Dream* in 1905; he revived the play throughout Europe for almost thirty years before producing it in six cities (including Hollywood) across the United States in 1934 and as a Hollywood film in 1935 (J. L. Styan, *Max Reinhardt* [Cambridge: Cambridge UP, 1982], 54). Two years after visiting the Century of Progress Exposition, Wanamaker joined Chicago's Goodman Theater School and, one year later, performed in abbreviated Shakespeare plays in

a reconstructed Globe at the Great Lakes Festival in Cleveland, Ohio. After over thirty years of acting on the stage and in movies produced in Britain and in the United States, he became involved in the Globe reconstruction project that would preoccupy him until his death in 1993 (Barry Day, *This Wooden 'O': Shakespeare's Globe Reborn: Achieving an American's Dream* [London: Oberon Books, 1996; reprint, New York: Limelight Editions, 1998], 25, 45–46).

5. *The Shakespeare Myth*, ed. Graham Holderness (Manchester: Manchester UP, 1988); these passages quoted in this paragraph appear on 21–22.

6. For information about admission fees, see *Chicago American* (13 July 1934); Claudia Cass, *Chicago Journal of Commerce* (31 May 1934); *Chicago Journal of Commerce* (31 August 1934); *Progress* 2: 35 (31 August 1932), 1; Freida Louise Stein, *World's Fair Time Saver and Guide* (Chicago, 1934). For information about the village spectacle, see *Chicago Daily News* (8 May 1934, 26 May 1934, 28 July 1934, and 13 September 1934); *Chicago Journal of Commerce* (19 June 1934, and 20 June 1934); *Chicago Loop News* (10 June 1934); *Highlights of the Educational Exhibits* 22–23; Robert Pollack, *Chicago Sunday Times* (29 July 1934); Julius Rosenthal, *Chicago Daily Times* (7 September 1934); " 'Round an' About the World's Fair," *Chicago Sunday Times* (9 September 1934); Vogelback, "Outline" 3–4.

7. Holderness, ed., *Shakespeare Myth* 21.

8. Holderness, ed., *Shakespeare Myth* 22–23.

9. For quotations see, in order of citation, *Progress* 1: 10 (3 June 1931), 2; *Progress* 1: 1 (1 April 1931), 2; *Progress* 1: 2 (8 April 1931), 2; ibid.; ibid. ; *Progress* 2: 1 (6 January 1932), 2; ibid. I take the term "Master Drama" from "Chicago Stages Master Drama," *Progress* 2: 41 (12 October 1932), 2. A typical installment of *Progress* might mix its reports on new exhibits and new sources of civic and financial support with an article outlining how engineers tested the safety of "curves of various radii from 30 feet to 700 feet" in order to determine the safest "width of the high speed thoroughway to be constructed" for the Greyhound buses that would operate within the fairgrounds (*Progress* 2: 37 [14 September 1932], 3). See also Rufus Cutler Dawes, *Report of the President of a Century of Progress to the Board of Trustees, March 14, 1936* (Chicago: Century of Progress, 1936), and *Rufus Cutler Dawes, 1867–1940,* memorial from Board of Trustees of a Century of Progress, at special meeting held 15 March 1940 (located in the Newberry Library).

10. *Progress* 1: 7 (13 May 1931), 2.

11. For quotations see, in order of citation, Clara E Laughlin, *So You're Going to Merrie England* (Chicago: Colortext, 1934), 1; *Urbana Illinois Courier* (11 May 1934); *Chicago Herald and Examiner* (27 May 1934).

12. For the fair organizers' attempts to interest foreign governments in the villages, see "A Century of Progress Chicago International Exposition of 1933: A Statement of its Plan and Purposes and of the Relation of States and Foreign Governments to Them" (located in the Chicago Historical Society), 9; Lohr, *Fair Management* 153–58; and *Progress* 2: 1 (6 January 1932), 2. See Lohr, *Fair Management* 153, 155, 155, and 157 for quotations.

13. Vogelback, "Globe Theatre" 2–3, and "Outline" 2. For quotation see "Globe Theatre" 2.

14. *Chicago Daily News* (8 May 1934); *Chicago Herald and Examiner* (5 May 1934); Laughlin, *So You're Going to Merrie England* 18; Lloyd Lewis, "Stage Whispers," *Chicago*

Daily News (9 May 1934); Thomas Wood Stevens, *The Globe Theatre* (Chicago: Colortext, 1934); Vogelback, "Globe Theatre" 2–3; Vogelback, "Outline" 2.

15. For examples of the advertisements and brochures that fairgoers eventually received, see the archives of the Chicago Historical Society and the Newberry Library. For examples of the initial publicity, see "Europe Will Be Brought to Your Doorstep in 1934," *Progress* 4: 2 (15 January 1934), 1; Malcolm McDowell, *Chicago Daily News* (23 December 1933); *Official Guide Book of the Fair, 1933, With 1934 Supplement* (Chicago: Century of Progress, Cuneo, 1934), 146. For quotations see, in order of citation, an advertisement from the *Chicago Daily News* (26 May 1934), and McDowell.

16. For a discussion of Rand's arrests and the larger debates about decency, see *A Century of Nudity* (Chicago, 1933, located in the Chicago Historical Society); Lohr, *Fair Management* 170, 222–23; "Out of Town," *New Yorker* (23 June 1934). The *Pensacola Journal* (1 June 1934) discusses Rand's saucy fans, her furtive male visitors, and the eventual containment of the cabaret shows to Northerly Island. Jess Krueger, *Chicago American* (30 May 1934), discusses Vogelback's application to include bare-fisted boxing and cockfighting. Lloyd Lewis, "Shakespeare Proves a Sensational Side-Show 'Hot Spot,'" *Chicago Daily News* (4 June 1934), and Julius Rosenthal, "Around the World with the Times: Dignified and Highbrow Merrie England Going Hey-Hey!" *Chicago Daily Times* (24 August 1934), and "Finding Fun at the Fair," *Chicago Daily Times* (28 August 1934) discuss the village's Cockspur Lane/Limehouse district. *Chicago Daily News* (21 August 1934) describes Jimmie's performances in Merrie England. Gail Borden compares Merrie England's Ruth Pryor dancers to their fair competition: "It is more than a relief to see a 'village' show at the Fair in which the dancing girls had on a few clothes. But Ruth Pryor and her lassies have more charm draped than do the multitude of nudies here and there. Maybe it's because they can dance" (*Chicago Daily Times* [7 August 1934]).

17. For quotations see, in order of citation, "Shakespeare as Side Show for New Exposition: Old English Village to Give Classic Dramas in Elizabethan Style," *Chicago Sunday Tribune* (20 May 1934); "Fair Visitors to Get Real Shakespeare Super Plays: Thomas Wood Stevens to Direct Authentic Drama in Merrie England," *British American* (19 May 1934); Henry J. Lazarus, "Footlight Parade," *Chicago Loop News* (7 June 1934), 4. The *Chicago Journal of Commerce* described the financial success of the Globe in its 27 June 1934 issue. The July 1934 *Chicagoan* article was written by William S. Boyden.

18. For descriptions of Roosevelt's visit, see Vogelback, "Outline" 5; *Chicago Daily Times* (10 July 1934); *Chicago Daily Tribune* (10 July 1934). The reporter's response is from the *Tribune* article; Roosevelt is quoted in the *Times* article.

19. *Chicago Herald and Examiner* (5 May 1934).

20. For quotations see, in order of citation, Stevens, *The Globe Theatre* 3, and Lloyd Lewis, "Stage Whispers," *Chicago Daily News* (9 May 1934).

21. Stevens discusses the three versions of Shakespeare's stage and Poel's use of boy actors in *Globe Theatre* 3, 7. The quotations are from, in order of citation, Lloyd Lewis, "Stage Whispers," *Chicago Daily News* (9 May 1934), and *Globe Theatre* 7.

22. For quotations about Merrie England, see *Official Guide Book of the World's Fair of 1934* (Chicago: Century of Progress International Exposition, Cuneo, 1934), 120–21, and *Highlights of the Educational Exhibits* 22. Vogelback's remarks are in his "Outline" 1. See

also his "Globe Theatre" 1. The *Christian Science Monitor* (23 May 1934) comments on the pervasive confusion between Allington Castle and the Tower of London. For the accuracy of Merrie England's reproductions, see also *Chicago Daily News* (19 May 1934); *Chicago Sunday Tribune* (6 May 1934); and Malcolm McDowell, *Chicago Daily News* (23 December 1933).

23. For quotations about Shakespeare's home, see *Chicago Daily News* (23 June 1934). See also *Official Guide Book* 120-21. The advertisement for the replica Globe (*Chicago Journal of Commerce* [7 June 1934]) and the Cheshire Cheese menu are located in the Chicago Historical Society.

24. *Chicago Daily News* (23 May 1934).

25. For quotations see, in order of citation, Stevens, *Globe Theatre* 9, and *Chicago Daily News* (15 September 1934).

26. For information about Poel's theatrical experiments, see Stevens, *Globe Theatre* 7-8; William Poel, *Monthly Letters* (London: T. Werner Laurie, 1929) and *Shakespeare in the Theater* (London: Sidgwick & Jackson, 1913); Robert Speaight, *William Poel and the Elizabethan Revival* (Melbourne: Heinemann, 1954). For quotations see, in order of citation, *Daily Chronicle* (3 September 1913), qtd. in Speaight, *William Poel* 90; Poel, *Shakespeare in the Theater* 203-04, 228.

27. Speaight (*William Poel,* 225-26) discusses Poel's visits to the Carnegie Institute of Technology. Allard's remarks in *Theatre Arts Magazine* (November 1916): 24-26, are quoted in Speaight 226; Poel's critic on 103; and Shaw on 116.

28. Ben Iden Payne, *A Life in a Wooden O: Memoirs of the Theatre* (New Haven: Yale UP, 1977), 159, 162-64, 189-90. For Payne's depictions of audience responses to his modified Elizabethan staging, see 171, 174-76, 181-84, 187, 189. For quotations see, in order of citation, 184-85, 189, 159, 159. Payne brought photographs of productions in which he had made use of modified Elizabethan staging to England in the summer of 1934 when he visited Poel a few months before the latter's death (184).

29. For Stevens's supposed reluctance to use Elizabethan staging, see Payne, *A Life* 151-52, 156. For quotations see, in order of citation, 187,189.

30. Lloyd Lewis, "The Theatre," *Chicago Daily News* (28 May 1934).

31. Charles Collins, "Shakespeare Done at Fair is Roaring Fun: *Taming of the Shrew* Played with Elizabethan Gusto," *Chicago Daily Tribune* (28 May 1934).

32. Claudia Cassidy, "On the Aisle: Stellar Petruchio Tops Rollicking Inaugural Performance in Old Globe Theatre at the Fair," *Chicago Journal of Commerce* (28 May 1934).

33. For Kirwin's English Village productions, and Poel's response, see Marion F. O'Connor, "Theatre of the Empire: 'Shakespeare's England' at Earl's Court, 1912," *Shakespeare Reproduced: The Text in History and Ideology,* eds. Jean E. Howard and Marion F. O'Connor (New York: Methuen, 1987), 86-91. Keating's response to Kirwin is discussed in "So You're Going," *News* (May 1934).

34. Speaight, *William Poel* 109-11.

35. Copies of pageants that Stevens produced between 1913 and 1934 are available in the Newberry Library Archives (see Thomas Wood Stevens, *Miscellaneous Writings* and *Plays and Pageants*). The program for the September 1934 Four-Nation Celebration advertised Stevens as "America's foremost mass-dramatist."

36. For descriptions of the fair's most elaborate pageant—a pageant honoring advances in transportation—see *Official Guide Book of the Fair* 46–48, and *Progress* 2: 46 (16 November 1932), 1.

37. *Globe Theatre Versions: The Taming of the Shrew*, ed. Thomas Wood Stevens (Chicago: Samuel French, 1937). Quotations are from, in order of appearance, *Taming of the Shrew*, ed. Stevens, prefatory "Note," and *The Riverside Shakespeare*, ed. G. Blakemore Evans (Boston: Houghton Mifflin, 1974). The Newberry Library has a partial collection of the eight Merrie England Shakespeare plays published by French. The Folger Shakespeare Library has a complete collection of the eight Merrie England plays and of four additional abbreviated plays (*Hamlet, Romeo and Juliet, The Tempest*, and *Twelfth Night*), also published by French, that were produced in Chicago's Studebaker Theatre and at the San Diego and Dallas Expositions, where the Chicago Globe was relocated after the closing of the Century of Progress. French's *Taming of the Shrew* includes both its thirty-six-minute Century of Progress text and its fifty-five-minute San Diego and Dallas text.

38. Stevens, *Globe Theatre* 10.

"Material Flames":
The Space of Mercantile Fantasy in
John Fletcher's The Island Princess

MICHAEL NEILL

And his opportunity sat veiled by his side like an Eastern bride waiting to be uncovered by the hand of the master.

—Joseph Conrad, *Lord Jim*

I. "The Scene India"

WHEN THE LORD Chamberlain's Men constructed, from the dismantled timbers of London's first permanent playhouse, the edifice that was to become the most celebrated of early modern theaters, they chose for it a name even more universal and absolute than that of its predecessor: "The Theatre" now became "The Globe" itself, in a transformation that wittily exemplified the motto supposedly emblazoned on the trade sign of the new house: *Totus mundus agit histrionem.* More was involved in the choice of name, however, than a playful inversion of the ancient *theatrum mundi* trope: the term "globe," after all, was a recent borrowing from French, closely associated with the revolutionary achievements of Renaissance cartography; not found in English before the mid-sixteenth century, it was linked from the beginning with the revolutionary conceptualization of terrestrial space produced by Martin Behaim's construction of the first cartographic globe at Nuremberg in 1492 (*OED n.* 1–3). Thus the icon of "Hercules and his load" hanging above the entrance to the Globe (*Hamlet* 2.2.345)[1] drew attention to the role of the Shakespeare's theater as an engine for reimagining the world: a space where, as the Swiss traveler Thomas Platter observed, a people not much given to travel could vicariously experience the wonder of unfamiliar places;[2] and an arena, therefore, in which dreams of geographic mastery—of national consolidation and expansion, of discovery, conquest, and mercantile splendor—could be played out.

99

Over the last two decades, work on plays as diverse as Marlowe's *Tamburlaine* and *The Jew of Malta,* Heywood's *Fair Maid of the West,* Shakespeare's Roman and English histories, *Othello, The Merchant of Venice, Cymbeline,* and above all *The Tempest,* has made us familiar with the ideological dimensions of the various geographic fantasies that inhabited the space of the stage.[3] In all of this busy historicization, however, very little attention has been paid to the writing of the most popular of all Jacobean playwrights, John Fletcher, Shakespeare's successor as principal dramatist to the King's Men. This is perhaps because Fletcher's reputation as an essentially frivolous theatrical opportunist, an "entertainer to the Jacobean gentry" whose espousal of courtly values helped to father the so-called Caroline "decadence," has (despite the new historicism's professed canonical skepticism) continued to deflect serious critical attention from his work. Yet it would be surprising if someone as close to the centers of London intellectual and political life as the well-connected Fletcher should have remained indifferent to the geographic excitements that infused the work of his contemporaries; and toward the end of his career Fletcher attempted his own imaginative penetration of the regions of mercantile and colonial adventure in two plays that were to enjoy significant popularity throughout the century. Evidently designed as companion pieces, the pair were written for the King's Men within a short time of one another— *The Island Princess* having its first recorded performance at Court on 26 December 1621, while *The Sea-Voyage,* produced in collaboration with Fletcher's own successor, Philip Massinger, was licensed for the stage on 22 June 1622.

The respective settings of these plays link them to the two principal sites of early imperial enterprise in what Donne called the "Indias of spice and mine"—the worlds of American plantation, and of East Indian commercial expansion; and they exhibit a common preoccupation with the ideal of temperance, that ruling theme of early English imperial discourse.[4] Of the two, *The Sea-Voyage* has attracted slightly more attention—probably because of its relation to Shakespeare's *Tempest,* on which (as Dryden was the first to observe)[5] it is openly parasitic. Rather as Fletcher's early comedy *The Woman's Prize; or The Tamer Tamed* (?1607–08) appropriated the central character of *The Taming of the Shrew* to make its own spirited contribution to the debate on gender, so this satirical romance revisits the exotic territory of *The Tempest* to engage in a witty critique of colonial propaganda. If *The Sea-Voyage,* in its oblique, allusive fashion, offers itself

as an anticolonial document, *The Island Princess* complements that position by fostering the vision of a purely mercantile empire, untainted by the
greed and appropriative violence of plantation. Set in the Moluccan Spice
Islands during the early period of sixteenth-century Portuguese commercial domination, it makes no direct reference to English enterprise in the
region; yet it is a work that makes complete sense only in the context of
the long-running propagandist debate associated with that enterprise. This
was a debate in which concepts of national identity were systematically
attached to the pursuit of particular commercial objectives; and it was a
debate that had developed a particularly fierce edge in the second decade
of the seventeenth century as a result of the deteriorating fortunes of the
English East India Company in the increasingly vicious struggle with their
Dutch counterparts for control of the lucrative spice trade. Performed in
the ideologically charged atmosphere of the Court, where pro- and anti-
Dutch facations competed for influence, while proponents of Western
planting vied with the advocates of Eastern commerce, and supporters of
mercantile expansion tilted with the champions of a closed economy, *The
Island Princess* can hardly have seemed as innocent a fantasy as it is likely
to appear to most modern readers; while even in its public performances
it must have capitalized on popular fascination with exotic marvels to turn
the stage into a space of glamorous transformation in which the crude and
often brutal realities of oriental commerce were metamorphosed into a
dream of chivalric heroism and erotic conquest, vicariously transporting
its audience to a scene of projected national triumph. The play's romantic
fable, as I hope to show, is only superficially escapist; and it would be
a great mistake to see either the romance plot or the theatrical display
that embellishes it as simple distractions from the politics of trade. Instead
the courtship and conquest of the Moluccan princess Quisara by the Portuguese hero Armusia can be read as giving a distinctively mercantile twist
to a familiar gendered trope of territorial penetration and possession, while
the spectacular firings of the town of Ternata in act 2 and of the fort and
palace of Tidore in act 5 appropriate a recurrent nightmare of East Indian
voyaging to create a theatrical emblem of the moral and technological
superiority, by means of which English mercantile enterprise proposed to
stamp its authority on the world.

Recent work by Gordon McMullan and Shankar Raman has gone some
way toward restoring *The Island Princess* and *The Sea-Voyage* to their
proper context of early imperial enterprise to which they belong.[6] In

the course of his welcome attempt to rescue Fletcher's drama from the depoliticized world of aristocratic fantasy to which it has traditionally been relegated, McMullan explores the dramatist's interest in the discourse of colonial plantation. His reading of the two plays is skewed, however, by the same Atlantic bias that characterizes a great deal of writing on the literature of early modern imperialism; for he insists upon reading both as contributions to the debate surrounding Virginia Company activities in the New World. This makes some sense in the case of *The Sea-Voyage,* where the shipwrecked passengers include the merchant Lamure, who plans to lay out his usurious wealth "To buy new lands and lordships in new Countreys" (1.1.11),[7] and the foolish courtiers Morillat and Franville, who dream of colonial enrichment in those "most fertile Islands, / Where we had promises of all things" (3.1.89–90). These colonial fantasies are set against the unhappy fate of the castaways who inhabit the actual islands where the play is set, "industrious Portugals" who have been driven "From their plantations in the Happy Islands" (5.2.96–7) by the fathers of the play's pirate-heroes, Albert and Raymond. But even here there is actually very little in the play to warrant McMullan's confident assumption of a specifically "American" location; indeed Fletcher takes almost as much care as Shakespeare to divorce his "desart [*sic*] Islands" from any identifiable New World setting.[8] Where Shakespeare's lone islander, Caliban, has at least an anagrammatic relation to the natives of the Caribbean, the Amazons of Fletcher's play prove to be no more than shipwrecked Portuguese ladies who have adopted the habit and customs of its reputed, but long-vanished indigenes. This odd effacement of the native population might seem like a recognizable strategy of colonial mystification, were it not for the fact that, at the ending of the play, far from desiring plantation of this new territory, Fletcher's Portuguese and French alike are (like Prospero) eager to "return / To [their] several homes" leaving the islands quite unmarked by their passing (5.4.114–15). There can be no equivalent here of Prospero's civilizing mission. The play's island is merely an exotic stage on which to play out domestic issues: if the colonial economy intrudes on this fantastic space it is only as the source of "cursed Gold" (1.4.87), the "fatall muck" (5.2.140) which infects the denizens of the islands with the distempered greed that drives them to piracy, mutual betrayal, and ultimately to the brink of cannibalism. In this sense *The Sea-Voyage* belongs with the strain of anticolonial propaganda that includes Samuel Daniel's poem "To Prince Henrie," with its scornful attacks on the moral and economic corruptions of

New World pelf and its appeal to Christian conscience against the colonial "inheritance of violence."

By contrast with the deliberate geographic vagueness of *The Sea-Voyage, The Island Princess* is assigned to a quite specific East Indian location. If this play bears any of the "clear traces of the American experience" claimed for it by McMullan, it is only, I would argue, by way of negative reflection; and to discount its highly particularized setting is to dehistoricize it in an important way. It is easy to forget, in the light of subsequent Atlantic history, that the main thrust of English expansion in the sixteenth century had been toward the East, which still bulked more largely on the English imaginative horizon than the New World;[9] and there were, as we shall see, good reasons why English audiences in the early 1620s should have felt a quite immediate interest in the world of East Indian merchanting. Shankar Raman's essay returns the play squarely to this historical setting (143), reading it in the light of Hakluyt's *Principall Navigations* (1589), with its account of Drake's triumphant progress through the East Indian archipelago. For Raman, the play is a meditation on Portuguese decline and English opportunity in which Fletcher "looks at his object, the (hi)story of the Portuguese conquest of the Moluccas, with the present knowledge of England's exclusion from the Indies. . . . resurrect[ing], in the names of these known yet faraway places, England's past in the Moluccas"(139). But, while nostalgia for Drake's successes is certainly a recurrent theme in accounts of English voyaging in the region, the English in 1621 hardly saw themselves as *excluded* from the East Indies, where the East India Company had operated a number of successful trading factories since 1603. The company was, it is true, approaching the climax of a prolonged struggle for commercial dominance with its Dutch counterpart; but, although the Dutch had by now established a clear strategic advantage, the likely outcome of this rivalry was by no means as clear as it would be only eighteen months later in the wake of the disastrous setback to English fortunes produced by the so-called Massacre of Amboyna in February 1623.

To understand the history of this confrontation—and thereby gain a better sense of what precisely was at stake in the performance of Fletcher's play—we need to turn not to the *Principall Navigations* itself but to Samuel Purchas's sequel, *Hakluytus Posthumus or Purchas his Pilgrimes,* a work that provides the most detailed contemporary commentary on the gathering East Indian crisis.[10] Although the *Pilgrimes* was not published until early 1625, substantial portions of it had already circulated in

pamphlet form; and its author (apart from what he had inherited from
Hakluyt) must have been collecting material for his monumental folio
for some years. Indeed the main East Indian section (pt. 1, bks. 3–5)
seems to have been assembled by 1622, within a few months of the court
performance of *The Island Princess*.[11] Perhaps the most striking difference
between the *Pilgrimes* and its predecessor is the prominence it gives to
this material, which is placed at the beginning, in the immediate wake of
Purchas's philosophic introduction on the theological and moral justifica-
tions of voyaging and merchant enterprise.[12] There was a solid practical
reason for this priority: Purchas was working under the direct patronage
of the East India Company, which granted him the substantial sum of one
hundred pounds for his work;[13] and in consequence, for all its scholarly
and philosophical pretensions, the *Pilgrimes* has to be seen as (at least in
part) a work of company propaganda.[14] Like Fletcher's play, moreover, it
seems to have been aimed in the first instance at a court audience, being
dedicated to Charles, Prince of Wales (soon to be Charles I), a substantial
shareholder in the East India Company,[15] who would have been among
the audience for the court performance of *The Island Princess*.

Of course the ambitions of Purchas's book, which presents itself as nothing less than "*a History of the World in Sea Voyages and Lande Travels
by Englishmen and others,*" extend well beyond any local propagandistic
purpose. As the iconography of its frontispiece suggests, its enshrines a
vision of the English nation as the Chosen People, the role of whose
navigational prowess is to foster the spread of God's word, the unification of
all peoples, and ultimately the accomplishment of the millennial destiny of
humankind. The elaborately engraved frontispece displays a portrait of the
author poised between representations of the Eastern and Western hemi-
spheres, balancing them as carefully as it balances the competing claims of
conquest and trade with the motto "*Tam Marte quam Mercurio: Soldiors
and Marchants the Worlds two eyes to see it selfe.*" But the text makes
it plain the compiler was more impressed by the benefits of merchanting
than of colonization—a preference fully in accord with the prominence
given to eastward voyaging over westward discovery and plantation. From
a perspective that invites the reader to treat all voyages as allegorical or
anagogical performances of holy pilgrimage,[16] it is the merchant rather
than the soldier or the colonist who emerges as the truest type of the
Christian pilgrim, since peaceable commerce, in Purchas's vision, is best
equipped to foster a harmonious and godly unification of humankind. It can

do so because its friendly material intercourse reconciles the conflicting claims of that "universall tenure in the Universe," which is the God-given birthright of all humanity with the "proprietie in . . . peculiar possessions" that sets the bounds of habitation and possession for nations and individuals alike.[17]

The *Pilgrimes* is framed by a lengthy opening chapter (occupying over a third of bk. 1), entitled "A Large Treatise of King Salomons Navie," which uses the voyage to Ophir to vindicate English mercantile ambition. This story is carefully chosen: for if Jason's search for the Golden Fleece was the legend most frequently invoked as the type of New World adventure, then Solomon's quest for the fabulous wealth of Ophir was the foundational myth of eastward navigation. Thus later in the *Pilgrimes* we find John Davis, who visited Sumatra in 1599 and again in 1604, identifying the wealthy kingdom of "Achen" (Aceh) with the goal of Solomon's fleet.[18] For Purchas the Old Testament story serves to demonstrate that "Merchandising and Sea trade" (unlike the wars of colonial conquest eschewed by the wise Solomon)[19] are "[ap]proved by God's law," because they have the capacity to make "the whole World as one body of Mankind" united in faith and amity.[20] Merchant enterprise promises to link

Solomon and Hiram together, and both with Ophir; the West with the East, and [joining] the remotest . . . parts of the world . . . in one common band of humanity (and why not also of Christianity?) Sidon and Sion, Jew and Gentile, Christian and Ethnike. . . . And this also we hope shall one day be the true Ophirian navigation, when Ophir shall come unto Jerusalem as Jerusalem then went unto Ophir. Meanwhile we see a harmony in this sea-trade, and as it were the consent of other creatures to this consent of the reasonable, united by navigation, howsoever by rites, languages, customs, and countries separated.[21]

If James liked to see himself as the second Solomon, the monarchs of East India unite in Purchas's imagination as the Hiram of this providential union.

"King Salomons Navie" ushers in a brief history of navigation from ancient times concluding with the circumnavigations of Magellan, Drake, Cavendish, de Noort, Spilbergen, and Schouten.[22] This is followed by three books chronicling English voyages to the East Indies. Part of the importance of the Drake and Cavendish sections is that (along with the fabulous journeys of Bishop Sighelm and Sir John Mandeville) they help to provide a heroic genealogy for English activity in the Spice Islands, predating the monopolistic claims of the Dutch, whom Purchas clearly sees as the

principal obstacle to the providential fulfillment of England's mercantile
destiny.[23] Even before the first decade of the seventeenth century was
over the Dutch had succeeded the Spanish and Portuguese as the principal
European power in the East Indian archipelago; and in the second decade,
as the Vereenigde Oostindische Compagnie sought to establish a complete
monopoly of the lucrative spice and pepper trade, English ambition had
been answered by growing Dutch ruthlessness, often issuing in open
hostilities.[24]

Responding to this situation, Purchas edited his material with a conscious eye to the predicament of the East India Company in its conflict
with these better established European rivals. Sometimes going out of his
way to secure versions that placed the Dutch in the most unflattering light
possible,[25] he annotated his documents with numerous marginalia drawing
attention to their overweening "pride," "spite," perfidy, and "cruelty," to
their brutal treatment of the East Indians, and to the doubtful legality of
their monopolistic practice,[26] urging his readers to "note that the Hollanders can shew no right to the Ilands, but Jus in armis."[27] So virulent
were these aspersions that Purchas, no doubt mindful of vaunted Dutch
influence at Court[28] and the legacy of popular sympathy for Holland, felt
the need to preface his book with an apologetic "Note touching the Dutch,"
disclaiming any "hatred to that Nation" as a whole, and insisting that his
shafts were aimed only at the abuses of individual "Dutch Zelots."

Dutch enmity was not the only cause of East India Company anxiety,
however; for at home its interests were challenged by the skeptical criticisms of influential opponents who believed that the luxury trade in spice
and pepper could only serve to diminish the store of national wealth—
especially since the company had secured a controversial exemption from
the law prohibiting the export of bullion.[29] Such were the arguments ad-
vanced by pamphleteers like Robert Kayll in *The Trades Increase* (1615)—
its title playing sardonically on the name of Sir Henry Middleton's ill-
fated flagship in the catastrophic voyage of 1611. Kayll's attack provoked
fierce legal reprisals from the company,[30] and triggered a campaign by
company apologists, notably Sir Dudley Digges in *The Defence of Trade*
(London, 1615), who denounces Kayll's work as an ill-informed "invective . . . against the East-Indian Trade" (1). Digges's arguments, demonstrating that the company's activities actually resulted in a substantial surplus
of imported over exported bullion, were taken up again and elaborated
by Thomas Mun in a series of sophisticated pamphlets published in the

1620s, one of which, the combative *Discourse of Trade from England unto the East Indies; Answering to divers Objections which are usually made against the same* (1621), Purchas selected to conclude his section on voyaging in the East Indian archipelago.[31] His reason for placing it in this decisive position is clear enough: the debate had been rejoined in the 1620s precisely because things had gone so badly for the company in the years since Kayll's attack. Profits, which—despite the disastrous outcome of some voyages—had averaged 155 percent in the period 1601–12, declined to 87 percent in the years 1613–23; and from 1615 onward they came under particularly acute threat as conflict with the Dutch escalated in the Spice Islands of Banda and the Moluccas. By mid-1621 things had come to such a pass that the company faced proposals for dissolution.[32]

In this context, Fletcher's decision to locate his new play in the Moluccas can hardly have been an innocent choice. From the time of its first voyage, the company had cast envious eyes on the clove and nutmeg islands of Ternata and Tidore, whose historic rivalry (as Fletcher's play reminds us) competing European powers had long exploited to their own advantage. Here the English endeavored to capitalize on favorable local memories of Drake's visit, in the course of which the King of Ternata had allegedly made an offer to put his kingdom under Elizabeth's protection.[33] However, despite some early flickers of interest on the part of the present king, who was suspicious of Dutch designs,[34] the company found it impossible to gain a foothold in the Moluccas, and instead concentrated its efforts on the adjacent islands of the Banda group, notably Pooloway (Pulo Ai) and Poolaroon (Pula Run), which in 1616 formally surrendered sovereignty to the English Crown.[35] Here the English apparently succeeded in ingratiating themselves with the islanders by persuading them that "our Nation . . . desired not to usurpe, and bring them in subjection, or bondage, as the Hollanders and other Nations [had] formerly."[36] Banda, however, was to prove, in Purchas's words, "almost the bane, and as it were the Trojane Horse to our Indian Ilium, whence an Iliade of miseries and mischiefs . . . issued to that Societie whereby their wonted gaines [were] suspended."[37] For here too their position was fiercely disputed by the Dutch, who claimed absolute rights both through the alleged suzerainty of the King of Ternate (by now their puppet), and also on the basis of a separate treaty concluded with the Bandanese themselves in 1609.[38] Regular attacks on English shipping, destruction of goods and property, and the maltreatment and public humiliation of English prisoners ensued, leading to a state resembling open warfare by mid-1619, when the principal English factor at Pula Run wrote to his superiors in Bantam complaining of the "intolerable pride and tyranny, that the Hollander useth in these parts upon us both, in bodies, and name . . . [and] the great outrage and infamy they have offered us . . . both in disgraceful speeches to our king and nation, and in their barbarous tyranny they have used to our weak forces, being captivated by them."[39]

In July of that year, after extensive negotiations, the rival companies signed a treaty of alliance agreeing to a division of the spoils of trade. But although this treaty substantially favored the Dutch, their commanders generally ignored its provisions except to levy English assistance against the Portuguese and recalcitrant indigenes. "They saw," as a company pamphleteer expressed it, "[that] they could not make their reckoning to any purpose unless they utterly drave the English out of the trade of those parts; thereby to have the whole and sole traffic of the commodities . . . and so to make the price at their pleasure, sufficient to maintain and promote their conquests."[40] Attacks on English shipping and factories therefore continued unabated; and in February 1620 the Dutch captured and burned the town of Lantore (Lonthor), where "Master Randall and other two English standing by the Companies goods were taken and stripped to their skins, bound, beaten, thrown over the town wall; and carried aboard the general, and put in chains."[41] Then in October 1620 a Dutch fleet overran the last Bandanese factory of the English company at Pula Run and commenced a genocidal slaughter of the Bandanese hosts. Throughout 1620 and 1621 merchants who had suffered losses at the hands of the Dutch since the signing of the treaty petitioned the king and Privy Council for redress; and in late 1621 the company, "imploring the Privy Council to observe how the Dutch have broken the treaty," dispatched two commissioners, its deputy-governor, Morris Abbott, and Sir Dudley Digges, to treat with the authorities in the Hague.[42] These negotiations finally broke down in early February 1622, and within a year the company's enterprise in the Spice Islands would be effectually snuffed out by the brutal *coup de main* against the Amboyna factory—an outrage still unredressed at the time of the Second Dutch War, when Dryden staged its atrocities as part of a new propaganda campaign against Holland.

Such, then, was the charged context in which Fletcher's Moluccan drama was played before King James—a context that no doubt helped to preserve its popularity into the Restoration, where it was among the more frequently performed and adapted of Fletcher's plays. At first sight, it is true, *The Island Princess* seems distinguished mainly by the care with which (in striking contrast to Middleton's nearly contemporary *Game at Chess,* for example) it appears to distance itself from current politics. The plot, based (sometimes very closely, but with a number of highly significant departures) upon Le Seigneur de Bellan's novella *L'histoire de Ruis Dias, et de Quixaire, Princess des Moloques* (1615), derives ultimately from a history of early Portuguese enterprise in the archipelago, Bartolome Leonando de Argensola's *Conquista de las Islas Molucas* (1609), a work which Fletcher may have known at first hand. Concerned primarily with the erotic rivalry of a pair of gallant Portuguese soldiers for the hand of the Tidorian princess Quisara, de Bellan's novella seems as unconcerned with national rivalries as it is indifferent to the material realities of the spice trade. Nevertheless, as I hope to show, there are ways in which the piece is particularly well attuned to promoting court enthusiasm for East Indian adventure. While there were still intermittent hostilities between English and Portuguese in the East Indies, these were completely overshadowed by the fierce contest with the Dutch; and it is possible to detect a certain identificatory nostalgia for Portuguese adventure in the *Pilgrimes,* in whose vision (as James Boon puts it) "[i]f Portugal had been the Prophet of the arts of Navigation, Britain was to be the Savior" (*Other Tribes, Other Scribes* 157). By locating his action in the era of Portuguese dominance, the dramatist could at once protect himself against the Dutch faction in Court (whose hostility even Purchas would attempt to beg off), and offer a pattern for the triumph of English mercantile adventure.

II. "A recompense so rich"

The plot of Fletcher's play centers on competition for the hand of Quisara, Princess of Tidore, among a group of Portuguese and East Indian suitors, including the neighboring rulers of Bakam, Siana, and Ternata, the Portuguese Captain Ruy Dias, and their newly arrived countryman, the "noble and daring" Armusia. In a radical departure from de Bellan's novel, Armusia takes the place of the young Tidorian aristocrat, Salama, as the hero of the piece. In de Bellan it is Salama who rescues the captive King of Tidore, confounds his Portuguese rivals, wins the love of Quixaire, and shortly afterward succeeds to her brother's throne; in Fletcher these feats are transferred to Armusia, except that the narrative concludes not with the hero's assumption of the Tidorian throne but with the religious conversion of the royal house. Having previously sought to persuade her lover to "change your religion, / And be of one belief with me" (4.5.34-35), Quisara is so moved by the steadfastness of his faith in the face of torture and martyrdom that she elects to "embrace [his] faith . . . [and] fortune" (5.2.121). Her gesture in turn leaves her brother too "half persuaded . . . to be a Christian" (5.5.66), and the play ends with the King's proclaiming a "peace" that resembles a fulfilment of Purchas's millenarian vision: "No more guns now, nor hates, but joys and triumphs, / And universal gladness fly about us" (5.5.90-91).[43]

As McMullan observes, Fletcher's alteration of the plot, by displacing a native with a foreign husband, transforms the meaning of the story, and gives a distinctively colonial twist to its sexual politics. Indeed McMullan reads the play's romantic ending with its "thoroughgoing sexual and fa-milial infiltration of Moluccan culture by the Portuguese" as a conscious refashioning of the classic narrative of "colonial intermarriage" (224) and "appropriation through 'legitimate' inheritance" (230)—the wedding of the Algonquin princess Pocahontas to the Virginia planter John Rolfe. But there is, I think, no necessary reason why contemporaries should have understood the Quisara plot in quite this way. The feminzation of exotic territory, as Louis Montrose has taught us, was a recurrent feature of early modern colonialist discourse;[44] and one might argue that in its own time the power of the Pocahontas story itself was less that of an originary New World myth than of an exceptionally vivid literalization of a pervasive colonial trope—that of European voyager or colonist as predestined husband come to claim the feminized body of the land. This, though seemingly best fitted, by its underlying quibble on "husbandry," to the agricultural projects of Irish or Virginian plantation, was in practice just as readily mobilized in the service of Guianese gold-hunting, or East Indian merchanting. *Connubium*, as James Boon points out, was the necessary complement of *commercium*, in a perpetuated alliance of kings such as Purchas dreamed of in the East Indies. For Boon, "Purchas's symbology of East/West reciprocal relations remained incomplete and therefore transi-tory" precisely because of the absence of this connubial ideal: "the marriage of Thames and Ganges . . . was not even imagined" (*Other Tribes, Other Scribes* 176). In point of fact, however, the trope of marriage is widespread in the *Pilgrimes,* where it is deployed not merely in reference to the "virgin" territory of Virginia, but as a way of figuring mercantile desire in East India.

Always implicit in this trope, and part of its strategic attractiveness, is the idea of the colonial "husband" as appointed guardian of his bride's honor, bound to defend it against the violent assaults of less temperate rivals. Thus, just as Purchas will justify the expropriation of American territory by claiming that "Virginia was violently ravished by her own ruder natives," so he represents the Dutch conquest of Banda as an assault upon "a rich and beautiful bride [who] was once envied to English Arms, and seemeth by the cries on both sides, to have been lately ravished from her new Husband, unwarned, unarmed, I know not whither by greater force or fraud."[45] Humphrey Fitzherbert similarly figures the loss of Pula Run as a species of rape, whose dishonor the East India Company is bound to restore:

Poolaroon (in imitation of her sisters, the other islands) is turned Dutch. There was in her neither pleasure nor profit, yet the ambitious King Coen hath made a conquest of her chastity. The civil law denieth a violent rape to be incontinency, because although the body be forced, the mind may yet be free. Recall her again and right this uncivil outrage by your wise and civil censure.[46]

Half a century later Dryden would make use of the same version of the trope in *Amboyna,* where the Dutch usurpation of English commercial privilege is figured in Young Harman's rape of the Ysabinda, the newly acquired Amboynese bride of the heroic English factor, Gabriel Towerson—whose marriage is fittingly described as his "golden day" (3.3 p. 47).[47]

In Fitzherbert, if the principal Dutch commander is cast as the usurping "King Coen," the island of Amboyna itself is represented as "Queen" of the Spice Islands:

Amboyne sitteth as Queen between the isles of Banda and the Moluccas; she is beautified with the fruits of several Factories, and dearly beloved of the Dutch . . . . Neptune is her darling, and entertained in her very bosom.[48]

A passage such as this is sufficient to alert us to the subdued quibble in the very title of *The Island Princess*; where Fletcher's romance differs from the *Pilgrimes,* however, is that it appears to render the trope literal in its identification of the rich territory of Tidore with the body of its princess, Quisara.[49]

From the beginning Fletcher's Portuguese imagine their national enterprise in erotically charged language that will have sounded wholly familiar

to English ears: Pyniero celebrates his country's natural propensity to
"bring . . . forth / Stirring unweary souls to seek adventures" (1.3.6–8); and
the hint of sexual excitement in *stirring* is taken up in his fantasy of exotic
territories that willingly open themselves to the exploitative embrace of
their discoverers:[50]

Where time is, and the sun gives light, brave countrymen, our names are known,
new worlds *disclose* their *riches,* their *beauties,* and their *prides*[51] to our *embraces.*
And we the first of nations find these wonders. (1.3.9–11; emphasis added)

And the newly arrived Armusia evokes the landscape in a rapturous display
of the rhetorical technique known as *enargeia* or *evidentia*[52] that instinc-
tively assimilates the "beauties" of Moluccan women with the "riches"
of an earthly "Paradise," "[w]here every wind that rises blows perfumes"
(1.3.17–20). Transformed by his autoptic vision, the stage becomes a *locus
amoenus* whose seductive welcome recalls the sensual delights of Ralegh's
Guiana:[53]

> We are arrived among the Blessed Islands,
> Where every wind that tides blows perfumes,
> And every breath of air is like an incense:
> The treasure of the sun dwells here, each tree,
> As if it envied the old Paradise,
> Strives to bring forth immortal fruit; the spices
> Renewing nature.
> .   .   .   .
> The very rivers as we float along
> Throw up their pearls, curl their heads to court us;
> The bowels of the earth swell with the births
> Of thousand unknown gems, and thousand riches;
> Nothing that bears a life, but brings a treasure.
>   (1.3.16–31)

In the context of such images, the love-plot of *The Island Princess*—with
its triangular contest among Quisara's native suitors, the established foreign
commander (and "ruler" of the princess's affections) Ruy Dias, and the
gallant newcomer, Armusia—asks to be read as a struggle for control of
the islands's material resources.[54] Indeed Pyniero goads his uncle, Ruy
Dias, by describing Armusia's successful courtship of Quisara precisely
as if it were a mercantile success: Armusia "has ended his market before
you be up . . . and tied the bargain, / Dealt like a man indeed, stood not

demurring, / But clapped close to the cause" (2.6.63–66); and the repeated stress on Armusia's tactical weakness as "a stranger," "a gentleman scarce landed, / Scarce eating of the air here, not acquainted" (2.6.64, 80, 70–71) emphasizes how this struggle mirrors the shifting and uneasy relationship between native East Indians, the established Dutch company, and their intrusive English rivals.[55]

The loose correspondence between English-Dutch rivalry and the erotic competition of Fletcher's Portuguese factions is complicated, however, by the displacement of some of their alleged characteristics onto the villainous Governor of Ternata—a displacement that reveals something of the deeply conflicted nature of English attitudes toward the Hollanders. In a significant departure from de Bellan, Fletcher expands the role given to the King of Tidore's traditional enemy, the King of Ternata, transforming him from rivalrous prince to Machiavellian villain, and renaming him "Governor"—a title surely calculated to remind viewers of Ternata's current subservience to Dutch power, and so to suggest a congruence between his political ambitions and the machinations of the Hollanders. Unlike the virtuous Armusia, who specifically declines to "force" the affections of Quisara (2.6.163), the Governor is presented as a would-be rapist whose capture of Quisara's brother puts him in a position to "take her" with "a compelled or forced affection" (1.1.80–81); and just as East India Company propaganda denigrated the Dutch as ambitious "usurpers" of both English rights and East Indian authority,[56] so the legitimacy of the Governor's power will be denounced by the King of Tidore at the end of the play: "His island we shall seize into our hands, / His father and himself have both *usurped* it" (5.5.79; emphasis added). At the same time the King's award of the Governor's town and castle to Pyniero comes near to legitimizing another reading of a familiar colonial sort, according to which their "heathen policy" (5.1.50) exposes the recalcitrant natives as usurpers of their own territories, which they are thereby bound to surrender to the invader— this potentially awkward implication is however kept in check by the final installation of the King of Tidore as sovereign ruler of both islands.

Fletcher's use of rival groups of Portuguese to reflect the competition of Dutch and English merchant interests is likely to confuse modern readers, but would have been readily licensed by the way in which the English (much as they may have resented the East Indian propensity to confuse the two nations)[57] habitually conceived of their relation with the Dutch as a species of emulous brotherhood, founded in their long history of alliance against Catholic Spain. Thus the Bantam factor, Edmund Scott, declared of the Hollanders that "though we were mortal enemies in our trade, in all other matters we were friends, and would have lived and died one for the other."[58] In *The Island Princess,* Armusia's courtship of Quisara provokes the mortal enmity of Ruy Dias, who denounces him (in language that echoes Dutch resentment of English intruders) as "that new thing, that stranger, / That flag stuck up to rob me of mine honor" (3.1.43-44). Ruy Dias duly conspires with his nephew Pyniero to have his rival "taken off" (3.1.62), and then provokes a duel that drives Armusia into wry reflection on their sibling rivalry: "strange dearth of enemies, / When we seek foes among our selves" (4.3.10-11). Yet, like Scott's mercantile competitors, they prove ready enough to live and die for one another when the machinations of the Governor unite the various Moluccan forces against the foreigners; and Armusia ends the play with a gracious acknowledgment of the "brave Ruy Dias" to whom he owes "my life, my wife and honour" (5.5.85-87).

If the rival Portuguese factions are joined by this common determination to resist the "villanies" of their East Indian enemies in their plot "to blow us with a vengeance out o'th'Islands" (5.1.8-11), they are at the same time set apart by the very different attitudes that condition their relationships with the native population. Pyniero's opening speech urges his guards to keep "Their vigilant eyes fixed on these Islanders. / They are a false and desperate people, when they find / The least occasion open to encouragement, / Cruel and crafty souls, believe me Gentlemen" (1.1.3-6). Armusia, by contrast, discovers in them a people "brave too, civil mannered, / Proportioned like the Masters of great minds" (1.3.33-34). Much later, as he faces martyrdom for his refusal to change religion, Armusia will himself denounce the Moluccans as "base malicious people" (5.5.32); but only to apologize a few lines later "for I was once angrie, / And out of that might utter some distemper" (5.5.72-73).

Pyniero's suspicion of East Indian craft and duplicity was, of course, by no means alien to English discourse about the region: Edmund Scott, for example, exhibits an almost paranoid obsession with the "subtleties," "villainies," "treasons," and habitual "dissembling" of the Javans. Nevertheless, it became increasingly important to the self-justification of English ambitions that they should represent themselves as sympathetic friends to the natives, in contrast to the overweening Hollanders with their "intolerable pride and tyranny."[59] English sympathy and Dutch tyranny, as company propaganda had it, flowed naturally from the different designs of the two nations—the English desiring friendly commerce, where the Dutch sought conquest and control. Thus the 1624 East India Company pamphlet, *A True Relation of the Vnivst, Crvell, and Barbarovs Proceedings against the English at Amboyna* boasts of

the different end and design of the English and Dutch Companies. . . . The English being subjects of a peaceable Prince, that hath enough of his own, and is therewith content, without affecting of new acquests; have aimed at nothing in their East-India trade, but a lawful and competent gain by commerce and traffic with the people of those parts.

Even when sovereignty was ceded by a local ruler to enable them to protect their trade, the company insisted, they would strive to respect and preserve local law, custom, and privilege, while

[o]n the other side, the Netherlanders, from the beginning of their trade in the Indies, not contented with the ordinary course of a fair and free commerce, invaded divers islands, took some forts, built others, and labored nothing more, than the conquests of Countries, and the acquiring of new dominions.[60]

In this context it is, I think, significant that whereas Ruy Dias and his nephew Pyniero are represented as captains of the military garrison, Armusia's appears to be a civilian role—a contrast that is given considerable symbolic weight when he and his companions achieve the feat of which their complacent soldier-rivals prove incapable, and effect the rescue of the King of Tidore by donning "habits like to merchants" in order to penetrate the enemy's stronghold (1.3.242).

In 2.2 Armusia and his followers enter "like merchants, armed underneath" to reflect on the success with which "policy" has prepared the way for "manly force" (16–17):

Suspectless have I travelled all the town through, and in this merchants shape won much acquaintance, surveyed each strength and place that may befriend us, viewed all his magazines, got perfect knowledge of where the prison is, and what power guards it . . . . No man suspecting what I am but merchant. (2.2.10–14, 44)

Then, in the following scene the "merchants house" they have occupied becomes the instrument for firing the Governor's adjacent magazine and castle, so enabling Armusia's successful raid upon the prison. One way of reading this piece of action (which Fletcher embroidered upon de Bellan's rather bare plot) is as a fable of mercantile chivalry, designed (like the Belmont plot in Shakespeare's *Merchant of Venice*/Venus) to put a gloss of nobility and romance upon the base world of commerce, and thereby to answer the play's own carefully posed question about the limits of honorable behavior.[61] Act 1 opens with a discussion of East Indian manners in which Pyniero and Christophero express puzzlement at the King of Tidore's recreations, wondering how such "base pleasures, / As tugging at an oare, or skill in steerage" can possibly "become Princes" (1.1.16-18). Pyniero comments:

> Base breedings love base pleasure;
> They take as much delight in a Baratto,
> A little scurvy boat, to row her titely,
> And have the art to turn and wind her nimbly,
> Think it as noble too, though it be slavish,
> And a dull labour that declines a Gentleman:
> As we Portugals, or the Spaniards do in riding,
> In managing a great horse which is princely,
> The French in courtship, or the dancing English
> In carrying a fair presence.
>
> (1.1.18-27)

In act 2, however, the King's "little scurvy boat" will have its counterpart in the vessel that ensures Armusia's "prosperous passage" to and from Ternata on the pretended merchant adventure whose "purchase" he claims in such strikingly materialist language:

> there is reward above my action too by millions:
> A recompense so rich and glorious,
> I durst not dream it mine.
> .   .   .   .
> It was her open promise to that man
> That durst redeem ye; beauty set me on,
> And fortune crowns me fair, if she receive me.
>
> (2.6.141-57)

"Well," confesses Pyniero, "he's a brave fellow, and . . . has deserved her *richly*" (188; emphasis added). Thus Armusia's rescue of the King is figured as a piece of consciously commercial enterprise, but one that reveals the inherent honor and bravery of its chivalrous factor. This is a trade that ennobles rather than degrades—a trade moreover that is squarely identified with the honor of the nation that pursues it, as Pyniero makes clear when he summons his uncle to Armusia's aid:

Now to make those believe, that held you backward and an ill instrument, you are a gentleman, an honest man, and you dare love your nation, dare stick to virtue though she be oppressed . . . now redeem and vindicate your honour. (5.1.58-64)

In this way *The Island Princess* seems well calculated to serve the purposes of a company whose propaganda sought to identify its own mercantile interests with the honor and "fame of the English nation" (Scott, *Exact Discourse* I3v). At the same time, however, the play runs the danger of disclosing the more aggressive designs that were typically entangled with mercantile voyaging. Indeed one might argue that Armusia's stratagem against the Ternatans rather awkwardly confirms the charges levied against the Portuguese by their Governor. Assuming the mantle of a pagan prophet,[62] he seeks to turn the King of Tidore against the intruders with a remarkable piece of anticolonial invective. They first arrived, he claims, as abject suitors to their island hosts—

These men came hither as my vision tells me. Poor, weatherbeaten, almost lost, starved, feebled; their vessels like themselves, most miserable; made a long suit for traffic, and for comfort, to vent their children's toys,[63] cure their diseases.

—but, once established, they used their commercial foothold to prosecute their imperial ambitions:

> They had their suit, they landed, and too th'rate
> Grew rich and powerful, sucked the fat, and freedom
> Of this most blessed isle, taught her to tremble;
> Witness the castle here, the citadel,
> They have clapped upon the neck of your Tidore,
> This happy town, till that she knew these strangers.
> (4.1.44-54)[64]

However, the Governor's insistence that the Portuguese pursuit of "traffic" has simply served as a Trojan horse concealing their hegemonic ambitions is ironized by the fact that he is himself disguised at this point in the play, employing his priestly persona to penetrate the enemy's walls and to advance his own plot against Tidore.[65] Thus he masks his tyrannical designs in very much the way that the Dutch were supposed to have masked theirs by libeling the English—presenting them, according to the King of Ternata, as usurpers who "came not as peaceable merchants, but to dispossess us of our kingdoms."[66] The play's comic catastrophe is precipitated by an act of emblematic "discovery" in which Pyniero strips off the false prophet's "beard and hair" to demonstrate the fraudulence of his "holy shape" (5.5.52–62). At the same time Fletcher abbreviates his source-narrative in a fashion that conveniently blurs the awkward issues of royal succession and territorial power attached to the marriage of Quisara: since the King remains alive and firmly ensconced on the twin thrones of Ternata and Tidore, the Princess's betrothal to Armusia need stand for nothing more than the amity and "universal gladness" promised by the propagandists of commerce.

III. "More temperate lessons"

In converting de Bellan's novel into a narrative of miscegenation Fletcher established a convenient metaphor for the "band of humanity" by which Purchas's "Ophirian Navigation" would unite the peoples of the earth in mercantile bliss; but inevitably he also raised the specter of "degeneration," which is a persistent theme in the colonial discourse of the period—a specter whose presence becomes especially threatening when, following their initial betrothal, Quisara urges Armusia to change religions. The pages of *Purchas his Pilgrimes* are haunted by anxiety about Europeans who abandon their faith or "turn Moor"—the standard phrase suggesting that religious apostasy is actually imagined as a kind of "racial" transformation or degeneration.[67] Racial anxiety is a factor even in the source, where actual miscegenation is avoided. De Bellan takes pains to justify the infatuation of Quixaire's Portuguese suitors by reassuring his readers that they should not imagine the beauty of East Indian females as darkened by "une couleur basanée, ou tout à fait More-Couleur [a sun-burnt color, or entirely Moor-colored]," since the women are careful to keep out of the sun, and therefore remain (unlike their men) "extremement blanches [extremely fair]," while their hair (in a telling analogy) is "de la mesme couleur de l'or qu'on nous apporte de leurs contrées [the same color as the gold that is brought to us from their lands]."[68]

Early in *The Island Princess* Christophero is made to remark in similar terms on the Princess's admirable fairness:

The very sun I think, affects her sweetness,
And dares not as he does to all else, dye it
Into his tawny livery.

(1.1.60-62)

Here, however, the issue is not so easily erased, and Pyniero cynically implies that there is something unnatural about the Princess's "wear[ing] her complexion in a case," because if exposed to the sun's kisses it would so readily convert to a dusky hue: "let him but like it / A week or two, or three, she would look like a lion" (63-64). As it turns out, the crisis of act 4 will present Armusia with the illusion of just such a racialized metamorphosis: at the point when Quisara urges her lover to forsake his faith, her beauty is suddenly transformed in his eyes to a black ugliness that "looks like death itself" (4.5.104). The racial suggestiveness of this simile is confirmed in the following act, where a penitent Quisara recognizes in the fairness of Armusia's countenance a sign of the purity of his religion—

your faith, and your religion must be like ye,
They that can show you these, must be our mirrors;
When the streams flow clear and faire, what are the fountains?

(5.1.118-20)

A few lines later she will denounce her brother for what she describes as his "foul swart ingratitude" toward Armusia's "fair virtue"—a darkening of his moral self that has, she proclaims, "taken off thy sweetness . . . [and] turned thee Devil" (5.2.46-51).[69]

Color, religion, and virtue, then, are imagined in Fletcher's play as virtually interchangeable markers of difference; and, as we might expect from contemporary imperial and colonial discourse, "temperance" is the moral attribute that more than any other distinguishes the "manly" virtue of the hero. It raises him above the violent jealousy of Ruy Dias (4.3.28), and is prominent among the qualities that earn the love and admiration of Quisara and the King. It was, of course, by their superior temperance that Ralegh's English would distinguish themselves from their intemperate Spanish rivals, and infallibly earn the admiration and allegiance of the natives of Guiana; and "navigation" itself, Purchas would argue, was inherently linked to this virtue as "a school of sobriety and temperance"—for, though the sea's riches might sometimes "make men's minds sea-sick, wavering, inconstant, distempered and . . . subject to tempestuous temptations," yet the sea itself "holds them in good temper, and is a correction house to the most dissolute; but the Land makes them forget the sea and temperance altogether."[70] Typically, of course, the "sun-burnt" peoples of the tropics were supposed to be deficient in this cool quality. In Shakespeare's tragedy of imperial degeneration, for example, the "tawny" Cleopatra is the very embodiment of oriental intemperance—a woman who, according to her Roman detractors, causes the hero's heart to "renege . . . all temper" (*Anthony and Cleopatra* 1.1.8), and earns from him the bitter rebuke "Though you can guess what temperance should be, / You know not what it is" (3.13.122).

In *The Island Princess* Philo's opening denunciation of Antony's intemperate dotage has its equivalent in Pyniero's satiric incredulity at his uncle's passion for Quisara:

> that he
> That would drink nothing to depress the spirit,
> But milk and water, eat nothing but thin air
> To make his blood obedient, that this youth
> In spite of all his temperance, should tickle
> And have the love-mange on him.
>
> (1.1.103–08)

At the same time he sneers sarcastically at the hot-tempered King of Siana, one of Ruy Dias's local rivals, as "he that's wise and temperate" (1.1.57). As it turns out, however, temperance in *The Island Princess,* though it certainly establishes a clear hierarchy of virtue, proves not to be an absolute marker of distinction between Eastern vice and Western virtue. To the contrary, it is precisely their admiration for temperate behavior that raises Quisara and her royal brother above the "fierce . . . unfaithful" Governor, the intemperate East Indian princes, and the distempered populace of "barbarous slaves" (5.1.19). These are rulers fitted to belong to Purchas's imagined "panorama of legitimate monarch . . . with James I (or . . . Charles I) at its apostolic center" (Boon, *Other Tribes, Other Scribes* 158). The King impresses even his Moorish captors by his capacity to "look . . . temperately. . . . No wildness, no distempered touch upon him" (2.1.38–40); while his sister actively seeks to temper the wild extravagances of her court. Quisara's first entry is to calm her brawling East Indian suitors: urging them to "be tempered / Or . . . no more . . . my Servants" she proclaims that any man who hopes to win her "Must put his hasty rage off, and put on / A well confirmed, a temperate, and true valour" (1.3.116-17, 127-28). Disapproving of Ruy Dias's jealous distemper (3.3.127), she is ultimately won by Armusia's demonstrations of temperance to embrace his religion and the martyrdom it seems about to earn him:

> I have touched ye every way, tried ye most honest,
> Perfect, and good, chaste, blushing-chaste, and temperate,
> Valiant, without vainglory, modest, staid,
> No rage, or light affection ruling in you:
> Indeed the perfect school of worth I find ye,
> The temple of true honour.
>
> (5.2.111-16)

By the same token it is the violence and cruelty of the pretended "priest" which encourages Quisara's waiting-woman, Panura, to betray the disguised Governor to Pyniero: "Sure he's a cruel man," she declares, "methinks Religion / Should teach more temperate lessons" (5.4.27-28). If temperance is the quality that separates Christian from pagan worlds; it is nevertheless East Indian tractability to Western tempering that warrants Armusia's identification of these people as "civil mannered / Proportioned like the masters of great minds" (1.3.32-33).

IV. "Flames so imperious"

Closely related to the play's idealization of cool temperance is its elaborate troping of fire, which has a complex and slightly paradoxical valency. The flames that visibly ravage Fletcher's East Indian landscape are at once material and immaterial—effects of European technological power and figurations of the destructive power of inflamed passion. Fire is, from one point of view, the symbolic opposite of temperance—a signature of the uncontrolled barbarity associated with the island world of pagan sun-worship; yet it can also be used to discipline that barbarity as the sympathetic instrument of temperance. It stands for a passion that may briefly "distemper" the agents of mercantile empire and their native allies, but it can also stand for the trials that will help to perfect their temper, as steel is tempered in the swordsmith's furnace.

There is a small hint for this in the source, where the fires of Salama's diversionary arson in Ternata seem to be mirrored in the description of Peynere's passion for the princess as "le feu secret qu'il nourrissoit dans son coeur [the secret fire which he nourished in his heart]."[71] But in *The Island Princess,* whose plot elaborates de Bellan's cursory account of Salama's escapade into two climactic episodes of firing, flames both metaphoric and literal break out everywhere. The first of these involves Armusia's raid on Ternata (2.2–5), and the second Ruy Dias's and Pyniero's assault on the town and palace of Tidore (5.1–5), as well as the fiery torture that the Governor intends to impose on Armusia ("Make the fires ready" [5.2.104]). In the first, fire spreads through Ternata ("pox o'their paper-houses, how they . . . light like candles, how the roar still rises" [2.3.35–36]), menacing the governor's powder magazine (37–38), spreading to his seat of power ("The castle now begins to flame" [42]), sowing panic in the town (2.4–5), and threatening to consume its citizen's stock of "wealth" (2.3.60–61) with its "imperious" flames. In the second, the "fire-spitting" Portuguese bombardment of Tidore "push[es] down palaces, and toss[es] . . . little habitations like whelps" (5.3.2, 14–15), alternately enraging and terrifying the citizenry ("A vengeance fire'em . . . . Come, let's do anything to appease this thunder" [11, 33–34]).[72] Here the play seems to be responding to more immediate English experience of the East Indian world; for the danger of fire in the flimsily constructed towns of Java and the Spice Islands is a recurrent preoccupation in the East Indian section of *Purchas his Pilgrimes*—notably in Scott's *Exact Discourse,* where it acquires nightmare significance.[73] In the factor's anxious imagination fire figures primarily as a native weapon, a characteristic instrument of those "subtleties," "policies," and "treasons" by which the enemies of the English sought to undermine and destroy their trade. In the most terrifying of these episodes, a group of Javan and Chinese thieves, whom Scott punningly describes as "eight *firebrands* of hell," undermined the English factory from a neighboring house and, as they endeavored to burn their way through the floor, inadvertently set fire to the building, destroying quantities of goods and nearly setting off some barrels of gunpowder (*Exact Discourse* E–F4v). Taking their revenge for this fright with gloating exactitude, the English merchants turned their persecutors' own weapon back upon them, torturing them with fire, as if determined to prove themselves the masters of the very instrument with which their enemies threatened to destroy them.[74]

It is possible, I think, to trace a recollection of this reversal in *The Island Princess,* where Armusia, working from the cellar of his "merchants house next joining" (2.4.11), prepares for his raid on the King's prison cell by setting fire to the Governor's storehouse, "Where all his treasure lies, his arms, his women" (2.2.28). The striking parallels with the attack on Scott's storehouse are emphasized by the citizens' outrage at this "treason" of a "neighbour"; and in the bawdy dialogue of 2.4 there is a distinct suggestion that the Ternatans are burned with the fire of their own intemperance, as the Second Citizen seems to imply:

I have been burnt at both ends like a squib . . . . give me whole tuns of drink, whole cisterns; for I have four dozen of fine firebrands in my belly, I have more smoke in my mouth, then would bloat a hundred herrings.[75] Thy husband's happy, though he was roasted, and now he's basting of himself at all points; the clerk and he are cooling their pericraniums—Body o'me neighbours! there's fire in my codpiece. . . . I fry like a burnt marrow-bone . . . run wenches run . . . run as the fire were in your tails. (3–46)

This suggestion of vindictive symmetry is made even more apparent in the second episode, where "the *fire-brand*" prophecy of the disguised Governor, as it "fires" and fans the King's rage, seems to have literally ignited the flames now consuming the city (5.4.28). The efforts of the false prophet and his followers "blow [the strangers] with a vengeance out o'th'islands," and their attempt to sacrifice Armusia to "the fires" of torture, are then met with the fiery counterblast of gunpowder, through which (as in the case of Scott's burning of the Chinese "firebrand" Hinting) the intruders use fire to cast out fire: responding to the threat of Armusia's execution, Pyniero declares:

They dare as soon take fire and swallow it, take stakes and thrust into their tails for clysters. . . . I have physic in my hand for 'em shall give the goblins such a purge—

> . . . .
> Let [the fort] but spit fire finely . . .
> . . . .
> . . . [we'll send em] fine potatoes
> Roasted in gunpowder, such a banquet sir
> We'll prepare their unmannerly stomachs.
> (5.1.40–46, 69–77)

Again and again in the play these material flames are treated as though they were allegoric displays of the psychological states of those who produce them. Thus Ruy Dias, stung by jealousy at the "blaze" of Armusia's honor after his triumphal arson in Ternata (3.1.54), brags of the "fire" that burns in his own "brave thoughts" (4.3.31-34); and in the last act his followers similarly boast that they are "all on fire" for their incendiary assault on the recalcitrant Ternatans (5.1.80); while Panura accuses the disguised Governor of fanning the King's vindictive flames against Armusia and his compatriots: "he fires him on still, / And when he cools enrages him" (5.4.3-4). These are stock metaphors, of course, but they are given a special charge by the scenes that give such spectacular theatrical emphasis to the troping of fire.[76]

Flames do not simply express the firestorms of ungoverned passion, however. Just as fire is used on the literal level to overcome fire, so on the metaphoric level it is identified with emotional states to which, provided they are moderated by temperate self-control, the romantic plot completely endorses. Quisara, for example, blames Ruy Dias for his "cold" reluctance "fly like fire" to her brother's rescue (1.3.158); while Pyniero flatters the Princess herself as "the eye . . . From which all hearts take fire" (3.1.241-43); and Quisara's conversion to Christianity is imaged in a figure that imagines the bonfire of martyrdom ignited by the tinder of erotic passion—

> I feel a sparkle here,
> A lively spark that kindles my affection,
> And tells me it will rise to flames of glory.
> (5.2.122-24)

Even more strikingly, in a fashion reminiscent of the weird punning inspired by Scott's obsession with fire ("I thought I would burn him a little, for we were in the heat of our anger"),[77] Armusia envisages torching of the Governor's town as though it were the literal expression his fiery passion for the Princess:

> The fire I brought here with me shall do something
> Shall burst into material flames, and bright ones,
> That all the island shall stand wond'ring at it,
> As if they had been stricken with a comet:
> Powder is ready, and enough to work it,
> The match is left a-fire; all, all hushed, and locked close,
> No man suspecting what I am but merchant:
> An hour hence, my brave friends, look for the fury,
> The fire to light us to our honoured purpose.
> (2.2.38-47)

The literal flames that raze the East Indian towns of *The Island Princess* are, in the end, an instrument of a European technology which controls and manages its violent effects precisely as temperance controls, manages, and directs the fiery tempests of inward passion. But in the marvelously telling metamorphosis of love's fire into the "material flames" of Ternata, Fletcher's language discloses the links among sexual desire, mercantile greed, and imperial violence which the play's official ideology struggles in vain to suppress. More than one "discovery," then, will be made by what Armusia calls the "comely light" (2.3.54–55) of the burning towns: when "imperious" flames first "turn . . . to ashes" the objects of the Governor's "worship" (2.2.48–50), and then threaten to consume the "palace" and "temples" of Tidore to make way for Armusia's "monument" (5.5.38–39), they illuminate a scene of imperial desire.[78] It is the very scene on which is fixed the covetous gaze of what Purchas calls "the worlds two eyes to see itself"—the "soldiers and merchants" of his mercantilist vision. Like that vision it masks its violent appetencies with talk of "peace" and "universal gladness" instituted in a wedding that assert the "common band of humanity"; and it can do this the more effectively because of the mystifying effect of the historical displacements that, as I hope to have shown, conceal its role as instrument of nationalist propaganda in the trade war against the Dutch. In its celebration of heroic temperance as the providential instrument of Christian empire, we can glimpse the beginnings of that process by which the people whom Napoleon would dismiss as "a nation of shopkeepers" learned to clothe mercantile interest in the romance of a civilizing mission.

Notes

This paper was originally written for the "Theatre and Nation" Conference at Waterloo, Ontario in July 1997; it has since been revised in the light of Skankar Raman's "Imaginary Islands: Staging the East" (see note 6).

1. *The Riverside Shakespeare,* ed. G. Blakeman Evans (Boston: Houghton Mifflin, 1972).

2. Thomas Platter, *Travels in England,* trans. Clare Williams (London: Jonathan Cape, 1937), 170.

3. The literature on nationalist and colonial discourse in Shakespeare is by now extensive; but among the more important contributions are: Emily C. Bartels, *Spectacles of Strangeness: Imperialism, Alienation, and Marlowe* (Philadelphia: U of Pennsylvania P, 1993); John Gillies *Shakespeare and the Geography of Difference* (Cambridge: Cambridge UP, 1994); Stephen Greenblatt, *Marvelous Possessions* (Oxford: Oxford UP, 1991); Richard Helgerson, *Forms of Nationhood: The Elizabethan Writing of England* (Chicago: U of Chicago P, 1992); Margo Hendricks and Patricia Parker, *Women, "Races," and Writing in the Early Modern Period* (London: Routledge, 1994); Peter Hulme, *Colonial Encounters: Europe and the Native Caribbean, 1492-1797* (London: Methuen, 1986); Claire McEachern, *The Poetics of English*

Nationhood (Cambridge: Cambridge UP, 1996); Peter Womack, "Imagining Communities: Theatres and the English Nation in the Sixteenth Century," *Culture and History, 1350-1600,* ed. David Aers (London: Harvester, 1992), 91-145.

4. See, for example, Louis Montrose, "The Work of Gender in the Discourse of Discovery," *Representations* 33 (Winter 1991): 1-41; Jeffrey Knapp, "Distraction in *The Tempest,*" *An Empire Nowhere: England, America, and Literature from* Utopia *to* The Tempest (Berkeley: U of California P, 1992), ch. 6, 220-42; and John Gillies, "Shakespeare's Virginian Masque," *ELH* 53 (1986): 673-707.

5. See Dryden's prefatory epistle for the Dryden/Davenant adaptation of *The Tempest,* in *The Dramatic Works of John Dryden,* ed. George Saintsbury, 8 vols. (Edinburgh, 1882), 3: 106. All citations from Dryden are to this edition.

6. Gordon McMullan, *The Politics of Unease in the Plays of Beaumont and Fletcher* (Amherst: U of Massachusetts P, 1994); Shankar Raman, "Imaginary Islands: Staging the East," *Renaissance Drama* ns 26 (1995): 131-61.

7. Citations from Fletcher are to *The Dramatic Works in the Beaumont and Fletcher Cannon,* ed. Fredson Bowers, 10 vols. (Cambridge: Cambridge UP, 1966-96). In quoting from this and other old-spelling texts, I have modernized spelling and (where necessary) punctuation.

8. For further comment on the "otherworldliness" of both *The Tempest* and *The Sea-Voyage* see Knapp, *An Empire Nowhere* 241-42.

9. This was due in part to the continuing European anxiety about Islamic (and specifically Turkish) expansionism in the Mediterranean, and in part to the much greater rewards antici-pated from Eastern trade—which had, after all, provided the original motivation for Atlantic voyaging. Although the formation of the English East India Company in 1600 postdated that of the Virginia Company, it had important predecessors in the Muscovy and Levant Companies (1555, 1981), which had pioneered overland caravans to the Middle East and India, and which had already sent feelers into the Moluccas by the end of the century.

10. *Hakluytus Posthumus or Purchas his Pilgrimes,* 20 vols., 1625 (Glasgow: MacLehose, 1905-07).

11. Books 3-5 deal almost exclusively with events up to January 1621, but include a translation of a Dutch propaganda pamphlet published in 1622 and two English replies to it (bk. 5, ch. 12). Purchas took care, however, to insert an account of subsequent events, leading up to Amboyna in a later section (pt. 1, bk. 10, ch. 16).

12. Purchas formally divided his text into two equal parts, dealing with the "Old" and "New" Worlds—but since his "New World" includes China, Japan, and other formerly "unknown" parts of East Asia, the space devoted to America is relatively slight, amounting to about a quarter of the whole and consigned to the final section of the book

13. James A. Boon, *Other Tribes, Other Scribes: Symbolic Anthropology in the Compar-ative Study of Cultures, Histories, Religions and Texts* (Cambridge: Cambridge UP, 1982), 155-56.

14. McMullan also attributes a local orientation to the *Pilgrimes,* but (in line with the Atlantic bias of his approach to early modern expansionism) treats it as a work essentially con-cerned with New World plantation—a "lengthy commentary on the travels of the colonists" (199).

15. Philip Lawson, *The East India Company: A History* (London: Longman, 1993), 30.

16. Vol 1: pt. 1, bk. 1, ch. 1, sections 1, 2, 3, and ch. 2, section 1.

17. Vol 1: pt. 1, bk. 2, ch. 1, p. 10.

18. Vol 2: pt. 1, bk. 3, ch. 1, p. 322; cf. also Samuel Purchas, *Purchas his Pilgrimage* (1617), 696.

19. It is true that in the final part of the work, an angry response to the massacre of 1622, entitled "Virginia's Verger," Purchas offers a very different view of colonial expropriation, arguing that since "Virginia [has been] violently ravished by her own ruder natives," these "unnaturall Naturalls" have forfeited their rights to her soil by their "disloyall treason." Nevertheless "King Salomons Navie," in arguing for the superior morality of trade, enjoys the rhetorical advantage of setting an argumentative context that treats the property rights of infidels as (albeit inferior to the rights of Christians) fundamentally inalienable (1: 9-13, 38-45).

20. *Pilgrimes* 1: pt. 1, bk. 1, ch. 1, p. 10.

21. *Pilgrimes* 1, p. 56.

22. *Pilgrimes* 1: bk. 1, ch. 2 through bk. 2, ch. 5.

23. The insistence on English priority is a recurrent theme of company propaganda, and surfaces again in Dryden's *Amboyna* (1673), a lurid dramatization of the massacre, designed to inflame public opinion in favor of the Second Dutch War. Here the Dutch merchant, Van Herring, is made to confess that the English "were first discoverers of this isle, first traded hither, and showed us the way" (1.1 p. 15).

24. Friction with the Portuguese continued but on a much smaller scale, and mainly on the Indian subcontinent, so that Fletcher's romanticization of the period of Portuguese domination would not have seemed especially contentious—especially in court circles. For a lively and concise account of the struggle with the Dutch, see John Keay, *The Honourable Company: A History of the East India Company* (New York: Macmillan, 1991), ch. 2, "This Frothy Nation," pp. 24-51.

25. Purchas substituted, for example, a version of Edmund Scott's *Exact Discourse* that was much more fiercely hostile to the Dutch than the readily available pamphlet printed in 1606. Purchas's vision, in Boon's words, is of "a royal British order, [excluding both] Catholics and Dutch Protestants alike, which tied exotic courts to the monarch, over and above any companies, parliaments, or other forces of interest" (*Other Tribes, Other Scribes* 157)— though the *Pilgrimes* characteristically strives to elide together the interests of monarch, nation, and company.

26. See, eg., 2: pt. 1, bk. 3, ch. 1, p. 313; ch. 6, p. 535; 3: pt. 1, bk. 3, ch. 9, pp. 93, 108, 109; 3: bk. 4, ch. 1, p. 433; 4: pt. 1, bk. 4, ch. 15, p. 303; 4: bk. 5, ch. 3, pp. 510, 525, 527; 5: pt. 1, bk. 5, ch. 7, p. 8, ch. 9, pp. 90, 97, 100, ch. 10, p. 135; 6: pt. 1, bk. 5, ch. 12, p. 167, ch. 15, pp. 210, 223.

27. 5: pt. 1, bk. 5, ch. 9, p. 92.

28. Thomas Spurway, for example, recounts Dutch boasts after the conflict at Banda in 1617: "Also may it please your Worships to understand, that the Hollanders having beene by some of our people, told of their vile abuses done unto us, and that it will lie heavie upon them at home, being knowne; the better sort of them have replied, that they can make as good friends in the Court of England as you (the Honourable Companie our Employers) can" (*Pilgrimes* 4: 5.3 p. 531).

29. See Lawson, *East India Company* 20-23. This argument was pursued with special vigor because the company, finding little demand for English goods in the East, had secured a special dispensation to export bullion. See Lawson 22-23. Cf. also *Calendar of State Papers (Colonial)*, entries for 14 June 1621 (1022-25), esp. 1023: "Reasons to prove that the trade from England unto the East Indies doth not consume but rather increase the treasure of this kingdom."

30. In February 1615 the company persuaded the Archbishop of Canterbury to suppress the pamphlet; it then took advice from the Attorney General, in whose opinion Kayll had come close to treason, and considered Star Chamber proceedings; finally on 4 April, Kayll was summoned for questioning by the Privy Council and temporarily committed to the Fleet prison, from which he secured his release on 17 April: see John B. Hattendorf's introduction to Tobias Gentleman, *Englands Way to Win Wealth, and to Employ Ships and Marriners* (1614), with Robert Kayll, *The Trades Increase* (1615), and Edward Sharpe, *Britaine's Busse* (1615) (New York: Scholar's Facsimiles and Reprints, 1922), 15-16.

31. 5: pt. 1, bk. 5, ch. 17. In Purchas, Mun is introduced as "one of the Societie" (i.e., a member of the East India Company). On the effective propaganda war conducted by Digges and Mun, see Lawson, *The East India Company* 35-37.

32. See *Calendar of State Papers (Colonial)*, entries for 14 June 1621, 1025: "Reasons against dissolving the East India Joint Stock and deserting that trade, showing the loss the king and kingdom would sustain in doing so."

33. Richard Hakluyt, *Navigations,* 12 vols. (Edinburgh: MacLehose, 1903-05), 11: 125.

34. In 1605 the king wrote to James I, recalling his predecessor's dispatch of a "token of remembrance" to Queen Elizabeth, and feeling out the possibility of using the English as a counterbalance against the newly ascendant Dutch. In his letter the king accused the Dutch of having dishonestly persuaded him that the English "came not as peaceable Merchants, but to dispossess us of our kingdoms" (*Pilgrimes* 5: pt. 1, bk. 5, ch. 14, p. 191).

35. *Pilgrimes* 5: pt. 1, bk. 5, ch. 9, p. 87.

36. *Pilgrimes* 4: pt. 1, bk. 5, ch. 3, p. 511.

37. *Pilgrimes* 5: bk. 5, ch. 15, p. 193.

38. *Pilgrimes* 5: bk. 5, ch. 9, p. 106; ch. 12, pp. 147, 156-60.

39. *Pilgrimes* 5: bk. 5, ch. 9, p. 109.

40. *A True Relation of the Vnivst, Crvell, and Barbarovs Proceedings against the English at Amboyna . . . Also the copie of a Pamphlet, set forth first in Dutch . . . falsly entituled, A True Declaration of the Newes that came out of the East-Indies . . . which arrived at Texel in June, 1624. Together with an Answer to the same Pamphlet. By the English East-India Companie* (London, 1624), A4v. The author of this pamphlet claims that its publication has been delayed out of a desire to preserve "the ancient amity and good correspondence held between this Realm and the Netherlands" (A1), insisting that the company has at all times gone out of its way to respond peaceably to Dutch provocation: both before and after the 1619 treaty "the English Company from time to time contented themselves with informing His Majesty and his Honorable Privy Council with their grievances privately in writing, to the end that necessary relief and reparation might bee obtained, without publishing any thing to the world in print, thereby to stir up or breed ill blood between these nations which are otherwise tied in so many reciprocal obligations" (A2-A2v).

41. *Pilgrimes* 5: pt. 1, bk. 5, ch. 10, p. 133.

42. *Calendar of State Papers (Colonial),* entry 1180 for 1621.

43. Traces of Salama's assumption of the Tidorian throne remain in the Governor's hints that Armusia seeks the Princess's hand only because she is heir to the kingdom (41.63), and in Pyniero's wish that the children of Quisara and Armusia's union will be "Kings at least" (5.5.71).

44. See Parker, "Rhetorics of Property" (esp. 139-54), in *Literary Fat Ladies: Gender, Order, Rule* (London: Methuen, 1987); and Montrose, "The Work of Gender," *passim.*

45. *Pilgrimes* 19: pt. 2, bk. 9, ch. 20, p. 229; 5: pt. 1, bk. 5, ch. 15, p. 237.

46. "A pithie Decription of the chiefe Ilands of Banda and Moluccas, By Captaine Humphrey Fitz-herbert in a Letter to the Companie" (1621), in *Pilgrimes* 5: pt. 1, bk. 5, ch. 13; quotation from pp. 176-77.

47. *Amboyna* 4.2-3. Ysabinda's rape is oddly prefigured in the episode that Towerson perceives as a "heavy omen to my nuptials" (3.3 p. 53), in which Captain Middleton brings on an Englishwoman "all pale and weakly, and in tattered garments," who has been barbarously mistreated by the Hollanders: the parallel appears to invite a construal of Ysabinda's rape as an act of national violation.

48. *Pilgrimes* 5: pt. 1, bk. 5, ch. 13, p. 177.

49. For a reading of the play which explores how "reproductive [hetero]sexuality sustains the ideology of masculine colonial domination," see Mario DiGangi, *The Homoerotics of Early Modern Drama* (Cambridge: Cambridge UP, 1997), 155-60 (156).

50. On the trope of *opening, unfolding, dis-covering* (or "disclosing"), see Parker, *Fat Ladies,* 140-46.

51. The bawdy sense of *pride* as "sexual desire" is clearly involved here (*OED n* 11).

52. On the function of *enargeia/evidentia* as "a substitute for direct ocular experience for those who could not be present to see with their own eyes," see Parker, *Fat Ladies,* 38-40; Parker associates the technique with the role of the *nunitus* or messenger, but (as the Choruses to *Henry V* repeatedly remind us) it also is the principal means by which the theater typically works on the imagination of the audience to transform the abstract space of the stage into a "local habitation" for the exotic.

53. "[H]ere whole shires of fruitful grounds, lying now waste for want of people, do prostitute themselves unto us, like a fair and beautiful woman, in the pride and flower of desired years" (Lawrence Keymis, "A Relation of the Second Voyage to Guiard," in *Principal Navigations,* Hakluyt, 487; qtd. in Montrose, "The Work of Gender" 18).

54. It is surely no coincidence that when Dryden revisited this struggle half a century later in *Amboyna,* he did it with a partial reworking of Fletcher's story of the Indian bride.

55. Raman also notes the parallel between the "stranger" Armusia and belated English enterprise, but understands it in terms of Drake's intrusion into Portuguese colonial territory ("Imaginary Islands" 137-39).

56. See, for example, Thomas Spurway's letter of 1617 reporting English negotiations at Poolaroon, where they assure the Bandanese that "we desired not to usurp, and bring them in subjection, or bondage, as the Hollanders, and other Nations have formerly" (*Pilgrimes* 4: pt. 1, bk. 5, ch. 3, p. 511).

57. This confusion is referred to in a succession of *Pilgrimes*'s documents—see, e.g., 5: pt. 1,

bk. 5, ch. 12, "An Answere to the Hollanders Declaration," where the company pamphleteer claims that "the Hollanders robbed and spoyled other nations under the English colours, pretending (to disgrace the English) that they were Englishmen, counterfeiting the Coyne of other Nations, charging the English with the same" (161). The issue is treated at length in Edmund Scott's pamphlet—see my "Putting History to the Question: An Episode of Torture at Bantam in Java, 1604," *ELR* 25 (1995): 45-75.

58. Edmund Scott, *An Exact Discourse of the Subtleties, Fashions, Religion and Ceremonies of the East Indians* (1606), H3.

59. "The Journall of Master Nathaniel Courthop" (1616-20) in *Pilgrimes* 5: pt. 1, bk. 5, ch. 9, p. 108.

60. *A True Relation* (cited in note 40 above), A3v-A4. Cf. also the claims of Thomas Spurway, quoted above (note 25). *Pilgrimes*'s material on "The Dutch Navigations to the East Indies" (5: pt. 1, bk. 5, ch. 15) quotes the Portuguese warning to the rulers of Java and Bantam that the Dutch "were not merchants but pirates, and if they had access now in ten or twelve years they would return and subdue their country: and this spark, if now unquenched would set the whole East on fire" (197).

61. Raman discusses the significance of Armusia's merchant guise in similar terms, but relates it to tensions inside the East India Company between the dominant merchant faction and resentful gentry: in the interests of reconciling these groups, Armusia reveals that "the merchant is really a knight in disguises. . . . In so doing [he] redefines . . . the notion of nobility, which he presents as an interleaving of mercantile and military" ("Imaginary Islands" 144-45).

62. The Governor's disguise may have been suggested by a historical detail (preserved in the 1617 edition of Purchas's *Pilgrimage*) from Achen in Sumatra where "They had one Prophet, disguised in his apparrell, whom they much honoured" (695).

63. For the important, but ambiguous role played by "toys" and "trifles" in the English discourse of trade, see Knapp, *An Empire Nowhere* 3, 76, 120-21. The Governor's disdain may also reflect the fact that (not surprisingly) the English experienced particular difficulty in the vending of their principal export, woollen cloth, in the tropical East Indies.

64. See also 4.2.155-59.

65. Dryden employs a similar device in *Amboyna,* where the suspicion that English motives are all too like those of the Dutch (whose "religion . . . is only made up of interest" [2.1 p. 38]) is disarmed by being put into the mouth of the villainous Harman Senior: "interest is their god as well as ours. To that almighty will they sacrifice a thousand English lives, and break a hundred thousand oaths" (1.1. p. 16).

66. Letter to James I, cited in note 34 above.

67. See my "Mulattos, Blacks, and Indian Moors: *Othello* and Early Modern Constructions of Racial Difference," *Shakespeare Quarterly* 49 (1998).

68. De Bellan 338; trans. mine. Cf. Thomas Candish [Cavendish] in *Pilgrimes* 2: pt. 1, bk. 2, ch. 2, p. 181.

69. Compare Ysabinda's fear that the pollution of her "black and fatal" rape will turn her into "A black adulteress" in Towerson's eyes (4.3 p. 65).

70. *Pilgrimes* 1: pt. 1, bk. 1, ch. 1, p. 55. In *Amboyna* Towerson dissociates himself from

the "endless jars of trading nations" and implicitly identifies his nation with "those who can be pleased with moderate gain" (1.1 p. 22).

71. De Bellan 339; trans. mine.

72. Writing of this episode, McMullan discovers a "scene of highly inflammable native houses succumbing to fire ignited by Europeans [that] rehearse familiar colonists' narratives," and he cites the wanton burning of a West African village in one of Hakluyt's narratives (*Politics of Unease* 231, 309n64); but once again this is a detail that seems to invite a more local reading.

73. See my "Putting History to the Question."

74. Compare Anthony Nixon's account of Robert Sherley's triumphal display of the heads of thirty captured Turkish captains "according to the custom of Persia," in which (as Anthony Parr writes) "the implication is not that Robert has 'turned Turk' in a savage land but that he has legitimized Persian custom by making it a tool of Christian retribution"—see Anthony Parr, "The Sherley Brothers and the 'Voyage of Persia,' " in Jean-Pierre Maquerlot and Michele Willems, eds., *Travel and Drama in Shakespeare's Time* (Cambridge: Cambridge UP, 1996), 14–31 (25).

75. The Citizen's taste for huge quantities of drink and for smoked herrings sounds like a piece of incidental anti-Dutch satire, like the naming of Dryden's Dutch merchant, Van Herring.

76. The direction in *Tamburlaine, Part 2* for a display of "The town burning" during Zenocrate's funeral at the beginning of 3.2 suggests that such displays were part of the theater's standard repertory of effects. As *Tamburlaine*'s editor comments: "Perhaps fireworks were used to simulate flames or to produce realistic smoke (as they had been in medieval drama), perhaps a symbolic backdrop was hoisted up or fiery streamers hung from the tiring house wall, or perhaps, if it could be managed, an emblematic structure of some kind representing a city . . . was actually burned. Such spectacular effects were not unknown during the sixteenth and seventeenth centuries"—see Christopher Marlowe, *Tamburlaine, Parts One and Two,* ed. Anthony B. Dawson (London: Black, 1996), 124.

77. Scott, *Exact Discourse,* siq. F2v; see my "Putting History to the Question" 55.

78. Cf. Boon: "Whitehall rhetorically courted Indic realms as trading partners, all the while desiring commercial concubines" (*Other Tribes, Other Scribes* 177).

"My Body Bestow upon My Women": The Space of the Feminine in The Duchess of Malfi

JUDITH HABER

The issue is not one of elaborating a new theory of which woman would be the *subject* or the *object*, but of jamming the theoretical machinery itself, of suspending its pretension to the production of a truth and of a meaning that are excessively univocal. . . .

What a feminine syntax might be is not simple nor easy to state, because in that "syntax" there would no longer be either subject or object, "oneness" would no longer be privileged, there would no be proper meanings, proper names, "proper" attributes.

—Luce Irigaray, *This Sex Which Is Not One*[1]

BOTH OF John Webster's most famous plays manifest a clear interest in the problems involved in constructing a female subject. *The White Devil* and *The Duchess of Malfi* approach those problems, however, from contrasting perspectives. *The White Devil* presents us with two opposite, mirroring images of woman, Isabella and Vittoria—both of whom are explicitly portrayed as speaking the language of men. Isabella, who can express her unconscious rage only in the process of repeating her husband's words and sacrificing herself for him (2.1), effectively self-immolates; and although Vittoria claims to be "too true a woman" (5.6.220), her characteristic activity is "personat[ing] masculine virtue to the point" (3.2.135).

In a series of insightful analyses, Jonathan Dollimore has termed the kind of imitation that Vittoria performs "transgressive reinscription" (and, in particular, "transgressive inversion") and has argued persuasively for its extreme radical force. He posits it as the only alternative to an outworn "humanist transgression," which assumes the existence of a self prior to or outside of society.[2] From the perspective of *The White Devil*, Webster (whom I take to be a thoroughgoing materialist himself) would seem to agree. Vittoria's appropriation of masculine discourse effectively unmasks

133

gender as impersonation, and she provides us with a piercing indictment of the mystifications that structure her society. There is, moreover, no other even temporarily viable option available; Vittoria speaks the only language she has.

Yet Webster also seems to be acutely conscious of the limitations of inversion; and, as a result, *The White Devil* is a profoundly pessimistic play. It successfully anatomizes but simultaneously cedes to a social and symbolic order that provides women with no place to stand, that offers no mode of existence other than being "for-men" or "like men,"[3] that (and this is, crucially, conceived as the same problem) provides no access to a subject-position that does not implicate one in violence toward and violation of the other. "Personating masculine virtue" is, after all, a deeply ironic phrase here, since all forms of virtu(e)—the heroic *virtus* in which Vittoria intermittently believes, as well as the moral virtue that she disdains—are seen as attempts to obscure the mechanisms of aggression and power.[4] In the same place that Vittoria learned Latin, learned to speak forcefully against her oppressors, she learned to murder, manipulate, and (metaphorically) rape (see 3.2.274-75). Furthermore, as Dollimore notes, Vittoria's positioning as a woman makes it impossible for her to enact aggression as effectively as those she imitates (*Radical Tragedy* 235). Webster provides us with a brilliant emblem of her impotence when, in the only direct action she undertakes in the play, she attempts to shoot Flamineo: the gun she uses is given to her by a man—and it is loaded with blanks. From the point of view of those in power, she functions primarily as a pawn in a political struggle. Her concluding pretensions to tragic heroism and centrality (and those of her brother) are wickedly parodied in the minor character Lodovico, who sees himself as author of all that has transpired ("I do glory yet / That I can call this act mine own. . . . here's my rest: / *I limb'd this night-piece and it was my best*" [5.6.290-91, 293-94]). And she is finally more like her opposite, Isabella, than either would care to admit. Each woman, significantly, acts the part of the other; and if Isabella is more implicated than she can acknowledge in the role she assumes to save Brachiano—the role of the "fury" who wishes she were a man (2.1.241-44)—so Vittoria, who plays the helpless victim when it suits her, is more passive and more victimized than she knows.

In *The Duchess of Malfi,* Webster adopts a different strategy; he questions whether it is possible not only to invert and decenter the structures of patriarchal power but to deploy those structures themselves to (provisionally) imagine oneself out of them. He engages in a self-consciously contradictory effort to construct a subjectivity that is specifically female, to reimagine speech, sexuality, and space—most particularly, the space of the female body—in "feminine" terms. Somewhat surprisingly from our twentieth-century perspective, Webster's challenge here to the erotics of patriarchy and the structure of conventional tragedy—to the desire for a self-defining, self-defeating moment of phallic orgasm and death—is conceived in terms of reproductive sexuality; as we shall see, his play both draws upon and suggests a number of ways in which contemporary constructions of pregnancy could be threatening to the dominant order.[5]

The disruptive form of the play itself—its refusal to hold, even minimally, to the classical unities—is explicitly associated with the Duchess's pregnancy. There is an extraordinary moment at the beginning of act 3 when Antonio tells Delio, "Since you last saw [the Duchess] / She hath had two children more, a son and a daughter," and Delio replies:

> Methinks 'twas yesterday. Let me but wink
> And not behold your face, which to mine eye
> Is somewhat leaner: verily I should dream
> It were within this half hour.
>
> (3.1.6-11)

The structure that is being mocked here—the "sweet violence" of the unified classical tragedy that is "represented in one moment"[6] is inscribed within the play as Ferdinand's fantasy: "Die then, quickly," he tells his sister (3.2.71). The ideal of perfect wholeness and unity that this fantasy implies is integral (at least theoretically) to classical heroic tragedy, and is explicitly thematized in tragedies of love, which regularly end with an image of orgasmic union that Ferdinand can only wish for. Consider, for example, *Romeo and Juliet,* in which Romeo's "Thus with a kiss I die," is met by Juliet's "Then I'll be brief. O happy dagger, / This is thy sheath" (5.3.120, 168–69), or *Antony and Cleopatra,* which mocks this image but simultaneously fulfills it when Antony's excruciatingly botched suicide is made good by Cleopatra's assertion, "Husband, I come" (5.2.287);[7] and compare Ferdinand's almost wistful comment after he has effected his sister's death: "She and I were twins; / And should I die this instant, I had liv'd / Her time to a minute" (4.2.261–63).[8]

Webster's play leaves no doubt that both this image and the belief in the coherence and adequacy of the male subject that it subtends are phantasmal. Ferdinand asks early on, "When shall we leave this sportive action, and fall to action indeed?" (1.2.11–12), and the answer, from one perspective, seems to be "never." No one dies quickly here; most of the characters die very slowly indeed—one could say that they just sort of peter out. Many of the deaths—in fact many of the significant actions—occur not once but twice (like most of the characters, they are relentlessly doubled);[9] and they are often presented in such a manner that it is impossible to tell "sport" from "reality," the imitation from the thing itself. Closure is repeatedly undermined, and the most significant "end"—the Duchess's death—notoriously takes place well before the play is over. It seems appropriate that, in the final act, we find Ferdinand falling murderously upon his own shadow, and hallucinating that he is fighting on a heroic battlefield. These events themselves suggest, however, that if Ferdinand's beliefs are hallucinatory, they are also deadly. As much of Jacobean drama suggests, and *The Duchess of Malfi* makes painfully clear, the illusion of male purity, wholeness, and unity depends upon a violent appropriation of the female body, which functions simultaneously as the repository for man's abject desires, and as his necessary complement: "Damn her!" Ferdinand cries, "That body of hers, / While that my blood ran pure in't, was more worth / Than that which thou wouldst comfort, call'd a soul" (4.1.119–21).

The dynamic that is at work here appears in a strikingly similar form in *The Revenger's Tragedy*; it will therefore be useful to glance briefly at that play. As Peter Stallybrass has noted, the discussion of the rape and suicide of Antonio's wife in the first act suggests in a simple way the appropriation involved in viewing female chastity as reflective of male honor ("Reading the Body" 130).[10] Her rape is conceived as "a sight that strikes man out of [Antonio]" (1.4.5); and he rejoices in her death because it proves his adequacy (in spite of his age):

> That is my comfort gentleman, and I joy
> In this one happiness above the rest,
> That being an old man I'd a wife so chaste.
>   (1.4.75–78)

The problems evident in this exchange become even more insistent in the interaction between Vindice and his sister, Castiza. Vindice, having been metaphorically penetrated ("entered" [1.3.88, 89]) by Lussurioso, is instructed to repeat this action upon his sister, whom the Duke's son desires:

> Go thou and with smooth enchanting tongue
> Bewitch her ears and cozen her of all grace;
> Enter upon the portion of her soul,
> Her honour, which she calls her chastity.
> (1.3.113–16)

And he agrees to do so in extremely suggestive terms:

> My brain
> Shall swell with strange invention: I will move it
> Till I expire with speaking and drop down
> Without a work to save me—but I'll work—.
> (1.3.122–24)

Ostensibly, of course, Vindice hopes to prove his sister chaste, but the self-contradictory nature of this impulse is laid bare in the scene between them. Against all odds, Castiza resists his blandishments; she asserts her purity by giving "*A box o' the ear to her brother*" (2.1.30sd), and Vindice rejoices:

> It is the sweetest box that e'er my nose came nigh:
> The finest drawn-work cuff that e'er was worn:
> I'll love this blow forever, and this cheek
> Shall still henceforward take the wall of this.
> Oh I'm above my tongue!
> (2.1.40–44)

This speech as a whole, and its astonishingly filthy first line in particular,[11] unmask the desire for purity and chastity *as* desire, and make evident that the ideal of inviolability is necessarily involved in—is ultimately identical to—forced entry and violation. In the second line, the paradox of purity as artifice (which runs throughout the play) is presented as another version of the same problem; and the final comment raises the question of whether, as the creature of a language thoroughly penetrated by sexuality (and a sexuality thoroughly penetrated by language), one can ever be "above [one's] tongue." Significantly, Vindice repeatedly reconfigures Castiza's assertive action here as his passive receptacle—the container that he enters, the garment that he wears. *The Revenger's Tragedy* is itself interested in the problems and paradoxes it explores primarily from the perspective of the male speaking subject; Castiza exists—insofar as she exists at all— merely as a miniature Vindice. The play focuses throughout on the contradictions inherent in (masculine) desire, and particularly on the ways in which masculine self-assertion ("swelling") is inextricably involved with self-destruction—with detumescence and death.[12]

The Duchess of Malfi anatomizes these contradictions even more pitilessly: nowhere can one find a more damning representation of the patriarchal desire for purity[13] than in Ferdinand's incestuous impulses, crystallized in his admonition to the Duchess, "You are my sister, / This was my father's poniard: do you see, / I'll'd be loth to see't look rusty, 'cause 'twas his" (1.2.249-51). The play evidences a clear consciousness of the coincidence of conventional desire and violence, and of the intersection of the structures of erotic, familial, and social dominance.[14]

But Webster also opposes to Ferdinand's conventional (if exaggerated) phallic fantasies the Duchess's attempt to construct and control her own body, to create a circular, "feminine" space that is free from invasion—the space that is evoked in 1.2 when she declares to Antonio: "All discord, without this circumference, / Is only to be pitied, and not fear'd" (384-85). "This circumference" refers, of course, to her arms that surround Antonio and to the ring that she places on his finger; but it also suggests the circular form of her sexuality and of her pregnancies—and the circle that is formed by the Duchess and her two confidantes, Antonio and Cariola. The bedroom scene (in 3.2) in which these three characters participate represents Webster's (and the Duchess's) most sustained effort at constructing "this circumference"; I would therefore like now to examine it in some detail.

Here, the three characters engage in a playful, erotic "chaf[ing]" (3.2.56), aimed not at the phallic orgasm/death that is constitutive of conventional tragedy, but at the feminine sexual excitement that was associated with— and frequently thought necessary to ensure—pregnancy.[15] Husbands of the time were repeatedly counseled to provide sufficient heat for their colder wives through teasing and talk, to intermix "wanton kisses with wanton words," because women are not "all that quick in getting to that point."[16] It is precisely this sort of teasing—a form of "sportive action" rather than "action indeed" which we now term foreplay—that the three characters are practicing, for the purpose of "serving" the Duchess: Antonio declares, in a speech rife with double entendre, "I have divers times / Serv'd her the like, when she hath chaf'd extremely. / I love to see her angry" (55-57). It is, of course, important that there *are* three characters here, rather than the traditionally unified pair (Antonio fears several times that Cariola will betray their union, but the Duchess admonishes him, "This woman's of my counsel" [1.2.390]). And, throughout this scene, the sexual innuendo circulates freely among them; this is particularly noticeable when Cariola complains of the Duchess's sleeping habits—"She'll much disquiet you . . . / For she's the sprawling'st bedfellow" (12-13)—and when she and Antonio "play" with the judgment of Paris (33-43).

It is not, however, until Antonio and Cariola slip out and "let [the Duchess] talk to herself" (55) that the scene's climax occurs; looking at her reflection in the mirror, she muses:

> Doth not the colour of my hair 'gin to change?
> When I wax grey, I shall have all the court
> Powder their hair with arras, to be like me:
> You have cause to love me, I ent'red you into my heart
>   [enter Ferdinand unseen][17]
> Before you would vouchsafe to call for the keys.
> We shall one day have my brothers take you napping.
> Methinks his presence, being now in court,
> Should make you keep your own bed: but you'll say
> Love mix'd with fear is sweetest. I'll assure you
> You shall get no more children till my brothers
> Consent to be your gossips. Have you lost your tongue?
>   (3.2.58-68)

At the center of this speech is the Duchess's assertion, "I ent'red you into my heart before you would vouchsafe to call for the keys." The emphasis on female agency that is evident here and throughout the play has led Catherine Belsey to characterize *The Duchess of Malfi* as "a perfect fable of emergent liberalism," which "valorizes woman's equality" (197). I would suggest, however, that Webster's constructions are more radical than Belsey allows: the play is not simply asking that women be treated as equals; it is implicitly posing Irigaray's question—"equal to whom?"[18] The Duchess is, of course, implying here that her integrity as subject consists not in remaining impenetrable but in choosing who may "enter" her; and such a claim necessarily revises the notions of "integrity" (which both etymologically and logically depends precisely upon remaining single, intact, and whole) and "subjectivity" themselves. It is important that her assertion contains the ghost sentence, "I entered you," which reverses the conventional positions of male and female, placing woman on top, as active subject: while inverting the normal power relations of patriarchy, this sentence still operates according to their logic (and, indeed, it is the power that the Duchess derives from conventional social hierarchies that enables her actions). As she continues, however, the Duchess significantly complicates this formulation: she effectively positions herself (and Antonio) both as subject and as object, both as penetrator and as penetrated. And in so doing, she unsettles the logic upon which conventional (male) subjectivity depends—which, as Ferdinand's entry at precisely this moment suggests, is the logic of uninvited penetration, the logic of rape. This sequence simultaneously crystallizes and calls into question the cultural equations that are apparent in Vindice's assertion in *The Revenger's Tragedy*: "That woman is all male that none can enter" (2.1.111);[19] but unlike *The Revenger's Tragedy*— and many other self-consciously subversive early modern texts—it also attempts, provisionally, to rewrite them.

By removing woman from her position as "universal predicate" (Irigaray, *Amante* 97; trans. Whitford 45), the Duchess revises—instead of merely reversing—the fundamental syntax of gender and power. And a similar revision is evident in her explicit presentation of the dynamics of speech. On the simplest level her claim to voice depends upon Antonio's silence, upon a seizing of the phallic tongue ("Before you would vouchsafe to call for the keys"). And in fact, earlier in the bedroom scene, she had playfully "stopp[ed] his mouth" with kisses (as Brachiano had been counseled—less playfully—to silence Vittoria in *The White Devil* [4.2.188-89]). But again, the Duchess's presentation of the discourse of power complicates it. Her description of Antonio as silent simultaneously endows him with will and voice—both of which he exercises plentifully in this scene (giving as good as he gets); and her formulations during the proposal that she is recalling here function similarly: although Antonio complains, "These words should be mine," she asserts, "You speak in me in this," again invoking—and unsettling—the logistics of penetration (1.2.387, 410).

The above analysis suggests that by privileging female desire (even a comparatively "orthodox" form of that desire), one necessarily changes the terms in which desire is understood. Indeed, as Ferdinand's tragic fantasies (which present themselves as reality) are isomorphic with the form of the male body and the rhythms of male sexuality,[20] so the Duchess's self-presentation here seems to accord with—and perhaps to be constructed out of—contemporary understandings of female sexual pleasure. While opinion is by no means univocal on this subject, one of the most frequently repeated distinctions between male and female orgasm is that man's pleasure is "single," "undivided," and therefore more intense, whereas a woman's pleasure is "double" or "multiple": she takes pleasure both in emitting her own seed and receiving that of her partner; her pleasure occurs at multiple sites, consists of a succession of events, and takes place over a longer period of time (Cadden 150–65; Laqueur 50–51, 64; Eccles 35). Usually, of course, this distinction is made for the purpose of asserting the superiority of the male: thus, Gerard of Brolio declares, "The single mode of delectation which exists in the man is greater than the double which exists in the woman" (trans. Cadden 158). But at least one woman writer made a more ambivalently valenced distinction that seems relevant here: Hildegard of Bingen declared that "a man's *delectatio* is like a fire which alternately flares up and dies down; a woman's is like the sun, gentle and productive of fruit" (Cadden 85).[21] And a similar understanding seems to underlie many of the Duchess's constructions in the rest of her speech.

The lines surrounding the Duchess's self-assertion spin out the implications of her central statement. She begins by pointing to her aging body, and imagining herself growing old: "When I wax grey, I shall have all the court / Powder their hair with arras, to be like me." One should note, first of all, that this image presupposes an arena in which it is *possible* to grow old; it depends upon a different sense of time (and of sexuality) than Ferdinand's. The Duchess's playful image is clearly indebted to more conventional constructions. It both recalls and revises the disgust for old women that Bosola voices in the play—a disgust that brings together the traditional associations of woman both with the body (and therefore ultimately with the grotesque body) and with the deceptively artificial; in an earlier scene, for example, his excoriations of the Old Lady's "painting" (her "scurvy face physic") and of her "closet" (2.1.23–48)[22] had seemed to lead naturally to a meditation on the corrupt "outward form of man" (48–49), ending with a *contemptus mundi*:

> And though continually we bear about us
> A rotten and dead body, we delight
> To hide it in rich tissue: all our fear,
> Nay all our terror, is lest our physician
> Should put us in ground, to be made sweet.
>   (2.1.66–70)[23]

The Duchess's comic solution to the problem of her aging further recalls Ferdinand's attempt to have those he controls reflect (and complete) him—an attempt that already verges on the absurd in its original form: "Methinks you that are courtiers should be my touchwood, take fire when I give fire: that is, laugh when I laugh, were the subject never so witty" (1.2.43–46). In her own witty vision, the Duchess is, of course, playing with conventional notions of power (and of women) by putting her power to explicitly frivolous ends; but in so doing, she paradoxically confirms the validity of the image she creates. For as she sits, in classically "feminine" fashion, before her looking glass, she is, in effect, stepping through that looking glass to remake the world in her own image (by troping on the patriarchal constructions out of which that image is made), all the while self-consciously acknowledging (and this is part of her project) that she is engaging in "sportive action," rather than "action indeed."

This process is even more evident in the lines that end her speech. Here, the Duchess continues to envision her situation as remediable and comic. She begins by transforming her brothers' threat into the material of erotic teasing ("Methinks his presence, being now in court,/ Should make you keep your own bed: but you'll say / Love mix'd with fear is sweetest")—teasing that inevitably gestures toward the fear and violence of the phallic construction that it simultaneously depends upon and mocks ("You are my sister, / This was my father's poniard . . . / I'll'd be loath to see't look rusty, 'cause 'twas his"). She goes on to reimagine Antonio's sexuality specifically in terms of pregnancy, and, even more extraordinarily, to reimagine her brothers (in a playfully conceived contrary-to-fact condition)[24] as his "gossips." Although this word is usually glossed simply as "godparents" (which was, indeed, its original meaning), it has resonances in this context that are difficult to ignore. As Adrian Wilson and others have noted, by the seventeenth century, the term "had acquired a wider meaning that referred specifically to women" ("Ceremony" 71): a woman's gossips were her close female friends, and, especially, those friends who were invited to a pregnant woman's lying-in (*OED* 2b). In his fascinating discussion, Wilson shows how the ceremony of childbirth, of which the gossips were an essential part, was associated with the creation of a collective female space, from which men were excluded; during the lying-in, conventional roles were reversed, female agency was privileged, and women were placed "on top" (Davis).[25]

One sees this reversal occurring during the Duchess's first pregnancy, when (for reasons other than the usual) all the officers are locked in their rooms, and she is given their keys, reversing the traditional enclosure of the woman that Ferdinand eventually literalizes in this play. Wilson also points out that "the immersion of the mother in a female collectivity elegantly inverted the central feature of patriarchy, namely its basis in individual male property" ("Ceremony" 87).[26] Finally, of course, one must note that "gossip" is associated with speech—and with a particular kind of speech, both feared and disdained by men: a chattering, frivolous, "sportive" speech, rather than "speech indeed."[27] In early modern contexts, even more clearly than now, "to gossip" seems to imply "to speak as a woman"; loosely flowing like women's bodies, similarly lacking in control and closure, "gossiping" was the activity of all-female gatherings, and was often connected with explicit hostility to males (Wilson, "Ceremony"; Paster 45–47; Woodbridge). Most of the suggestions that I have been outlining here are brought together in the satirical defense of childbirth customs in a 1683 pamphlet, *Fifteen Real Comforts of Matrimony*. This pamphlet, which was purportedly authored by a woman and which ends with a manifesto for government by women, was written in response to an earlier, explicitly misogynist piece that detailed the woes of marriage (*XV Comforts of Rash and Inconsiderate Marriage*); the author replies to the earlier writer's complaints about the gathering of a woman's friends during her pregnancy:

Then for Gossips to meet, nay to meet at a lying in, and not to talk, you may as well dam up the Arches of *London*-Bridge, as stop their mouths at such a time. 'Tis a time of freedom, when women, like Parliament-men, have a priviledge to talk Petty Treason. (*Fifteen Real Comforts* 24)[28]

In the pamphlet, the lying-in is seen as a form of carnival, a "time of [allowed] freedom": the topsy-turvy misrule of the gossips is but licensed sport, which is ultimately not threatening to the dominant order. In *The Duchess of Malfi*, however, the sportiveness of the Duchess's circle is inseparable from its subversiveness. When Ferdinand enters (with a visual pun on "enter"), holding up his phallic poniard to relocate the scene's climax, reassert the terms of patriarchy, and remind the Duchess whose image she "properly" is, he seems at first not only terrifying, but also ridiculous—as if he had wandered in from another, more melodramatic play. We have briefly glimpsed another possibility, which, if it cannot permanently displace the governing structures of social power and tragic form, does effectively question their positioning as "inevitable" and "true"—and perhaps further suggests that the notions of "inevitability" and "truth" are themselves contingent constructions.

The Duchess's counterfactual transformation of her brothers into gossips may be taken as emblematic of the scene as a whole. The mode of the scene is, after all, gossip as well as foreplay—or, more accurately, these are constructed as forms of the same thing. Throughout the scene, the Duchess and her companions take the language of patriarchy (the only language they have) and use it to create a playful, women-centered chatter—a kind of Renaissance *parler-femme*. Thus, they play repeatedly with the language of class and power (e.g., Antonio's references to "labouring-men," and "service"), the terms of heroism (the inverted judgment of Paris),[29] and, of course, the language of penetration and entry: Ferdinand's efforts to "gain access to private lodgings" (1.2.202; cf. 4.2.2–4) are specifically reimagined in the opening lines of the scene, when the Duchess declares, "You'll get no lodging here to-night, my lord," and "I hope in time 'twill grow a custom / That nobleman shall come with cap and knee, / To purchase a night's lodging of their wives"(3.2.2, 4–6). The Duchess and her circle self-consciously acknowledge the inversions that are occurring ("You are a lord of mis-rule" [8]), and their double-edged self-consciousness about the roles they play guarantees that they are not merely inversions. Indeed, the whole scene seems, from one perspective, to be a rethinking of the traditional feminine images with which it began—the "casket" and the "glass" (1)—out of which the Duchess "sportively" constructs her female space.[30] When Ferdinand enters that space, uninvited and "unseen," he forcibly reappropriates her body/room/stage and defines it as his container—the empty, passive receptacle that is the ground of his existence—and he revisualizes the reflection in the mirror as his own. At this point, understandably, the Duchess's speech undergoes a radical change. She attempts to defend against invasion by presenting herself as impenetrable, "personating masculine virtue to the point"; she once more adopts a public, aristocratic persona and asserts her power in conventional heroic terms: "For know, whether I am doom'd to live, or die, / I can do both as a prince" (70-71).[31]

The transformations that the Duchess both constructs and undergoes in the bedroom scene are characteristic of the play. Several critics have pointed to her heroic resolution in earlier scenes. In 1.2, for example, she declares after her threatening brothers have left the stage:

> Shall this move me? If all my royal kindred
> Lay in my way unto this marriage:
> I'll'd make them my low foot-steps. And even now,
> Even in this hate (as men in some great battles
> By apprehending danger, have achiev'd
> Almost impossible actions: I have heard soldiers say so)
> So I, through frights and threat'nings, will assay
> This dangerous venture. Let old wives report
> I wink'd, and chose a husband.
>
> (1.2.260-68)

Frank Whigham comments on this passage: "The apostrophe, the amplification of the hostile odds, the abjection of the enemy, the martial comparison, the imperative call for historical (if female) witness—all are heroic topoi, Tamburlaine's trumpet vigorously displacing the impoverished trope of the 'lustful widow' " (*Seizures* 204).[32] While Whigham's description of the first part of the passage seems quite accurate, he glosses over the shift that occurs toward the end. The "female witness" that he notes only parenthetically is crucial here: the heroic materials of the soldiers' speech (the only means through which the Duchess has access to battle) are being transformed, not into chronicles of Amazonian feats, but into old wives' tales—which are precisely *not* the "historical" truths that Whigham invokes. The Duchess's phrase has resonances similar to those of "gossip": old wives are despised because of class, gender, age, and lack of education (all of which are conflated here), and their frivolous, fabulous tales are conventionally opposed to the knowledge of learned men[33]—in fact, the implication is that their speech is fabulous precisely *because* it is female. The Duchess's transformation of speech here further parallels the transformation within her speech; although Whigham does not note it, the effect of juxtaposing the heroic lines that build to a crescendo in the description of "this dangerous venture" with the blunt statement that follows ("Let old wives report / I wink'd, and chose a husband") seems inescapably comic. If, as Mary Beth Rose asserts, the Duchess's marriage project is imbued with the values of more conventional heroism (155-77), it is equally true that her appropriation of heroic values effectively mocks and changes them. The Duchess is, of course, in deadly danger, a fact of which she is clearly aware, but here and elsewhere, she "winks"[34]—and transforms that danger into something else.

   Throughout this early scene, she shifts repeatedly from evaluating, in heroic terms, the threat that she faces, to constructing a space— identified with romances, with frivolous old fables, and with fantasies of the feminine—where the heroic stance is no longer necessary and one is protected from invasion.[35] Most obviously, in her proposal to Antonio, she moves from speaking like a "tyrant" who must "fearfully equivocate," to "put[ting] off all vain ceremony" and "only appear[ing]" as "a young widow / That claims [him] for her husband" (1.2.359-60, 372-74); and it is at this point that she reassures him about her brothers:

> Do not think of them:
> All discord without this circumference,
> Is only to be pitied, and not fear'd.
> Yet should they know it, time will easily
> Scatter the tempest.
>   (1.2.383-87)

The Duchess's professed confidence in the healing powers of time here seems to go hand in hand with her evocation of contemporary romances. Later in the scene, she similarly appeals to an "old tale" when she describes their marriage bed:[36]

> We'll only lie, and talk together, and plot
> T'appease my humorous kindred; and if you please,
> Like the old tale, in Alexander and Lodowick,
> Lay a naked sword between us, keep us chaste.
>   (411-14)

Here, she reconfigures not only Ferdinand's central image of violently (and phallicly) enforced chastity, but also his ideal of perfect twinship: according to the New Mermaids editor, "The friends Alexander and Lodowick were so alike that they could change places without anyone noticing" (*Duchess* 31). In all of these speeches, the safe "feminine" space that the Duchess constructs is clearly marked as fictional; and it is created and defended only by deploying the materials of the masculine, the tragic, and the "real." Yet from the perspective of that fiction, "all discord without" seems pitiable indeed.

The Duchess's efforts are not, of course, completely successful, and one could argue that they founder (at least in part) on the self-contradictions in which Webster is necessarily involved. Nevertheless, the play does effectively subvert orthodox constructions and suggest alternative ones, and it points, moreover, to its own inadequacies. If, for example, the Duchess's death ultimately allows her to be transformed into the artifact the men desire, into the "bearer" rather than the "maker of meaning" (Mulvey 7, qtd. in Rose 171), it also robs the play of meaning and signals the emptiness of that masculine construction; the fifth act seems but the disembodied, confused echo of the Duchess's death.

As she is about to die, the Duchess assumes all of the conflicting postures I have been outlining, and she gives us, typically, not one but a series of "dying lines." In the most famous of these—"I am the Duchess of Malfi still" (4.2.139)—she once more assumes her impenetrable public persona. This line is frequently quoted (quite appropriately, considering its stance); it is not usually noted, however, that it is uttered as a (characteristic) defense against Bosola's (characteristic) attempts to identify her once again with the despised—and necessarily grotesque—body (which must be cast off to free the soul, 4.2.123-32); in a speech that, significantly, reappropriates and redemonizes the terms of the bedroom scene, Bosola declares:

Thou art some great woman sure; for riot begins to sit on thy forehead (clad in *grey hairs*) twenty years sooner than on a merry milkmaid's. Thou sleep'st worse than if a mouse should be forced to take up her *lodging* in a cat's ear. A little infant, that breeds his teeth, should it lie with thee, would cry out, as if thou wert the more *unquiet bedfellow.* (4.2.133-38; emphasis added)[37]

And the Duchess responds as she always does to the rape that this appropriation entails. Later, she appears as a mother as well as a prince:

> I pray thee look thou giv'st my little boy,
> Some syrup for his cold, and let the girl
> Say her prayers ere she sleep.
> (4.2.200-02)

While these lines have also been frequently discussed, they are, I believe, usually viewed as more conventional than they in fact are—or, more precisely, not enough attention is given to the disruptive force of their extraordinary ordinariness.[38] For it is surely remarkable for a "tragic hero-ine" to die neither attempting wholly to "personate masculine virtue," nor wholly focused on her male partner (declaring, in one form or another, "O happy dagger, this is thy sheath," "Husband, I come"), but concerned instead with the mundane comforts of her children; and it necessarily unsettles our notions of "tragedy" and of "heroism" when she does so. Finally, of course (the second time she "dies"), the Duchess does cry out "Antonio" (although he is, significantly, not present to die in an "instant" with her)[39] and "Mercy" (4.2.344, 347). But perhaps most striking, from the perspective I have been exploring, are the lines she utters after she vows to "put off [her] last woman's fault / . . . [and] not be tedious with you" (4.2.223–24). She, in effect, answers Ferdinand's need (which is presented as the general male need) for "that body of hers" and points simultaneously to her own absence and to the disembodied emptiness at the end of play by instructing her executioners, "Dispose my breath how please you, but my body / Bestow upon my women, will you" (4.2.227–28).[40]

* * *

Many of the problems that *The Duchess of Malfi* confronts and analyzes are, in their most general form, the long-standing legacy of Western culture. The logic of penetration and entry in the play, in particular, resonates not only with contemporary texts like *The Revenger's Tragedy*, but with important cultural documents from Plato to the present. Judith Butler writes, for example, of the foundational spatial dynamics of Plato's *Timaeus:*

For he is the impenetrable penetrator, and she, the invariably penetrated. And "he" would not be differentiated from her were it not for this prohibition on resemblance which establishes their positions as mutually exclusive and yet complementary. In fact, if she were to penetrate in return or penetrate elsewhere, it is unclear whether she could remain a "she" and whether "he" could preserve his own differentially established identity. (50)

And Lee Edelman discusses in somewhat similar terms the "conceptual paradigm" of " 'active vs. passive, insertive vs. receptive, . . . man vs. woman' "[41] that "is, regrettably, our enduring heritage"; he notes:

In a phrase that registers the persistence not merely of a sexual but also of an erotic politics in the fantasmatics of subjectivity, [Leo] Bersani, commenting on the

Athenian belief in a "legal and moral incompatibility between sexual passivity and civic authority," draws the inevitable conclusion: *"To be penetrated is to abdicate power."* (98)

I have been suggesting that *The Duchess of Malfi* attempts to unsettle early modern formulations of this paradigm by reconsidering the fundamental syntax of subjectivity itself, by positing a subject that is also an object and that therefore does not depend on the objectification of another. As we have seen, the play does not simply call our attention to the constructedness of gender definitions or try to reverse them: it attempts to open up a space of sexual difference, a space in which "woman" can exist—not as container, a box, a body for man, but for herself. This, as the masculinist logic of penetration and entry suggests, is centrally a question of territory. It means reclaiming the female body for women (both socially and symbolically). And it means simultaneously interrogating the cultural association of "female" with the body *and* questioning the devaluation of the body (and of "analogous" terms) that this association implies. As Margaret Whitford notes, thinking sexual difference means "seeking to define . . . the topology of the female subject, of *her* reflection, . . . of *her* space-time, of *her* dwelling, of *her* espacement" (155).[42] Of course, these definitions can only be formulated in a masculine language that already excludes them; and Webster's play is acutely aware of this fact: it constructs its notion of the "feminine" out of contemporary ideas of the conventionally masculine *and* (perhaps more surprisingly) out of ideas of the conventionally feminine, which its Duchess plays with and sportively mimes;[43] and it carefully marks the space that emerges from the interplay of the two as "sportive" and "fictional." In so doing, it simultaneously acknowledges its own embeddedness in the constructions of its society *and* (again, more surprisingly) suggests that "truth" and its privileged reflections are themselves constructed. In Butler's felicitous phrase, it "inhabits—indeed, penetrates, occupies, and redeploys—the paternal language itself" (45).

This is, of course, a risky strategy, one that takes the chance of simply reproducing conventional ideas of femininity or of being reassimilated to them;[44] and the play, in fact, shows us this reassimilation occurring (albeit incompletely) after the Duchess's death. To return to my initial discussion of *The White Devil*, it would seem that the risks run in that play—which consistently foregrounds the constructedness of gender but accedes to the structure of a universal (male) subject—are complementary to those taken here, in an effort to construct a space of sexual difference.[45] And it may be that the two plays together describe a kind of Heisenberg Uncertainty Principle of gender—both providing us with important perspectives that it is difficult (impossible?) to assume fully at the same time.[46]

As much of the above suggests, if the larger problems that Webster confronts are part of "our enduring cultural heritage," the particular forms in which he conceives those problems are often more historically specific. The play's constructions of female sexuality and pregnancy are clear examples of this—and it is perhaps worth reemphasizing that (however disturbing Webster's conflation of the two may be) the association of pregnancy here with sexual pleasure and bodily excess on the one hand and with female sociality on the other make it potentially threatening to a patriarchal order in ways that have been lost or muted in its current desexualized and medicalized form.[47]

A different sort of example—which I would like to mention briefly before I exit—is afforded by the play's presentation of the idea of "entry" itself. "To enter" quite obviously has here, and in other plays of the period, a specifically theatrical dimension that is absent from both classical and twentieth-century invocations of the term—a dimension that is forced upon us when Ferdinand intrudes upon his sister and the stage. This dimension (like so much else here) is two-edged: it once again alerts us to the artificiality of gender positions; but it also presses upon us the gender-inflected nature of theatrical space, positioning, and modes of acting. It points, perhaps, to the necessity of reconsidering (and interrogating) in gendered terms such useful concepts as *platea* and *locus, mimesis* and "sporte" (Weimann). And, as I have already suggested, it asks us to think further about the gendering of theatrical genres, not simply from the perspective of their major characters, but with an eye to dramatic form, space, and time. Early modern theories of genre such as Sidney's in the *Apology for Poetry* make us acutely aware how notions of decorum, naturalness, truth, and value are traditionally identified with what one might term a masculine morphology. By making explicit the assumptions underlying such judgments, and by examining contemporary challenges to them, we can better understand—and perhaps reshape—the spaces that we still inhabit.

Notes

Earlier versions of this essay were presented to a seminar organized by Valerie Wayne and Akiko Kusunoki at the World Shakespeare Conference in 1996, and in panels at the annual meetings of the Renaissance Society of America and the Modern Language Association; I am grateful to colleagues at these conferences for their helpful comments. I would like particularly to thank Richard Burt, Cristina Malcolmson, Valerie Traub, and Deborah Willis for their careful readings and their questions, criticism, and suggestions.

1. Irigaray's work has helped me to formulate many of the larger problems involved in attempting to conceptualize sexual difference within the framework of Western culture (although the particular forms these problems take in the texts I examine are often specific to the early modern period). For the larger problems involved in thinking about Irigaray (including the now generally discredited charge of "essentialism"), I found especially useful Whitford; all the essays in Burke, Schor, and Whitford (esp. Schor, "This Essentialism Which Is Not One," and Burke); Butler (esp. ch. 1, printed also in Burke, Schor, and Whitford); and Grosz. I have also been helped by Schor and Weed; Fuss; Gallop; and Chanter.

2. Dollimore develops this idea at length in "Subjectivity" (reworked slightly in *Sexual Dissidence* 284-306); see also his illuminating discussion of *The White Devil* in *Radical Tragedy* (231-46). Despite my divergence from Dollimore, I have found his analyses extremely helpful; the strategy that I outline in *The Duchess of Malfi* could, in fact, be viewed as another form of "transgressive reinscription."

3. See Irigaray, *This Sex* 83-85, *Speculum* 133, "Poverty"; cf. Whitford 151-52.

4. Thus, the nominally "good" characters in the play, Marcello and Cornelia, revere those above them (as Lodovico comments, "The violent thunder is adored by those / Are pash'd in pieces by it" [1.1.11-12]) and displace their aggression downwards—kicking and striking the black maid Zanche (who, when given the chance, plots to rob Vittoria). The only character who does not attempt to violate another is Isabella, who self-destructs.

5. I by no means wish to conflate female sexual desire with reproductive sexuality (although I think it is arguable that the play does); I do, however, want to note that such a perspective—which we tend to think of as conventional—can be potentially subversive. Cf. Patricia Parker's examinations of female "dilations" in *Literary Fat Ladies* and *Shakespeare from the Margins*. For a commentary on the dangers of collapsing sexuality and gender (as well as an acute analysis of the subversive potential of pregnancy), see Traub, *Desire and Anxiety* 91-116, 50-70.

6. Sidney 46, 78; see also Callaghan 50.

7. The strong possibility that Cleopatra is only "faking it" here reinforces as well as undermines the strength of this assertion.

8. This image is not confined to tragedy (which simply presents it in one of its most powerful forms); it is endemic to Western ideas of romantic love. One thinks, for example, of the central verses of Dibbe's "The Canonization":

> The Phoenix riddle hath more wit
> By us: we two being one, are it.
> So, to one neutral think both sexes fit.
> We die and rise the same.
>
> (23-26)

Despite—in fact because of—the pretence of prefect "neutral" union here, there is no question whose orgasm is being described, whose "I" is behind the "we."

9. For different accounts of the insistent doubling in the play, see Enterline 242–303, and Wilkinson.

10. Stallybrass comments that "the *hortus conclusus* of a deathly chastity reasserts the *hortus conclusus* of male honor. The silencing of the women's voice reaffirms the differentiation between possessor and desirer. More than that, within this sexual economy the possessor is freed by the lady's death from the challenge of the desirer" ("Reading the Body" 130). See also Stallybrass's extremely influential discussion of the sexual politics of enclosure in "Patriarchal Territories."

11. On the bawdy use of "box" in Shakespeare's plays, see Partridge 70, 130; on noses in early modern texts, see Stallybrass, "Patriarchal Territories" 138.

12. The play is littered with images of (mindless) swelling and deflation; it could be said of all the characters as it is of Lussurioso, "How strangely does he work to undo himself" (4.1.61; cf. 2.2.173: "He may show violence to cross himself"). Vindice is, of course, hired to kill himself, and in a sense he finally does: having constructed his masterpiece, he is unable to resist signing his name to it, saying in effect, "'Tis I, 'tis Vindice, 'tis I" (3.5.166); as a result, he is killed. Castiza, who lies to her mother in order to be "honest" (4.4.150–51), repeats her brother's paradoxical actions on another level.

13. This desire is, as I conceive it, continuous with but not confined to the impulse toward aristocratic exclusivity that Frank Whigham outlines in his seminal article, "Sexual and Social Mobility in *The Duchess of Malfi*," and his more recent book, *Seizures of the Will* (188–225); it is a particularly intense expression not only of aristocratic self-preservation and of heroic self-definition but of conventionally constructed romantic love. For acute criticisms of Whigham's perspective, see Rose 157–62; Malcolmson 52–53; and Enterline 252–54.

14. As numerous critics have noted, the lines following Ferdinand's threat, with their invocation of the "tongue" and puns on "tale" (1.2.157–580) explicitly bring speech into this nexus.

15. See Laqueur 98–103; Cadden, esp. 105–65; Eccles 33–42; see also Greenblatt 66–93. Laqueur and Eccles argue for the near-universality of this belief; Laqueur uses it to substantiate his argument for the dominance of the "one-sex model." Cadden, however, shows authoritatively that the multitude of questions and debates concerning sexuality and conception at the time are not easily reducible to Laqueur's model (3); the arguments she recounts, however, offer abundant evidence for the currency of the belief in the necessity of female orgasm, and it is regularly assumed in English midwifery manuals (including those that call the one-sex model into question). See, e.g., Sharp 99; Sadler 108–09, 118; and Culpepper 70, in addition to the works cited below. For other important criticisms of Laqueur's historical and theoretical model, see Park and Nye; Paster 16–17; Parker, "Gender Ideology"; and Traub, "Psychomorphology."

16. Paré 889; Paré, *Oeuvres* (Paris, 1579), trans. Laqueur 102.

17. This and the stage direction following line 68 ("She sees Ferdinand holding a poniard") are, of course, editorial additions; but they are generally accepted and appear to accord with the logic of the text.

18. That is, it is not simply demanding that women be treated or valued like men but questioning the structures upon which valuation depends, not simply asserting the identity or equality of the sexes but trying to open up a space of difference between them—a space that will allow "woman" to exist (Irigaray, "Equal to Whom?"). See also "Equal or

Different": "Demanding equality, as women, seems to me to be an erroneous expression of a real issue. Demanding to be equal presupposes a term of comparison. Equal to what? What do women want to be equal to? Men? A wage? A public position? Equal to what? Why not to themselves?" (32).

19. As I have suggested, *The Revenger's Tragedy* itself implies that the image of the male as impenetrable (and what is the same thing, as a unified subject) is a fantasy that depends on the construction of "woman" as penetrable object: Vindice has himself been repeatedly "entered" before he makes this assertion; it occurs after his paradoxical attempt to displace his permeability onto Castiza and his more straightforwardly successful corruption of his mother.

20. I am appealing here to culturally constructed ideas of bodily form and capacities, rather than to biological determinism. I have been influenced by the lucid discussions of Irigaray's distinction between "morphology" and "anatomy" in Grosz (112-19) and Whitford (58-59, 150-52). For a criticism of this kind of argument, see Traub, "Psychomorphology."

21. Although both Gerard and Hildegard are medieval writers, the arguments in which they are involved and the distinctions they are making persist into later periods. See, for example, Crooke (1615): "But whether the pleasure of the man or of the woman be the greater, it would be a vaine and fruitlesse disquisition to enquire. Indeede the woman conceiuethe pleasure more waies, that is in the auoyding of her owne seede and also in the attraction of the mans: for which cause the *Tyresian* Priest who had experience of both sexes preferred the woman in this kinde: but the pleasure of the man is more intense, partly because his seede is more hot and sprituous, & partly also because it yssueth with a kinde of Almaine leape or subsultation" (288).

22. He describes this with relish: "One would suspect it for a shop of witchcraft, to find in it the fat of serpents, spawn of snakes, Jews' spittle, and their young children's ordure, and all these for the face. I would sooner eat a dead pigeon, taken from the soles of feet of one sick of the plague, than kiss one of you fasting" (37-43). There seems to be a suggestion here—and in Bosola's spying in general—of the horrified fascination with peering into women's "secret" parts that Patricia Parker outlines in "*Othello* and *Hamlet*" (revised in *Shakespeare from the Margins* 229-72). See also Paster 187-88, and Maus.

23. If the Old Lady bears the brunt of Bosola's conventionalized disgust with rotting flesh, Julia is similarly made the focus for his sexual nausea. And both forms of disgust are conflated in his queasy descriptions of the Duchess's pregnancy:

> I observe our Duchess
> Is sick a-days, she pukes, her stomach seethes,
> The fins of her eyelids look most teeming blue,
> She wanes i'th'cheek, and waxes fat i'th'flank;
> And contrary to our Italian fashion,
> Wears a loose-bodied gown.
>
> (2.1.66-71)

See also Callaghan 107-08, 143-45; Jankowski 174-75; and Lifson 47-59.

24. Not only does the Duchess's teasing proviso ("till my brothers / Consent to be your gossips") constitute a condition contrary to fact, it is, within the world of the play, perhaps

the ultimate condition contrary to fact (and it is important that it is marked as such); but like all such conditions, it necessarily involves imagining what "can't happen."

25. Gail Kern Paster criticizes this reading as overly optimistic; she argues that "whereas pregnancy and childbirth *were* instances of female empowerment, that empowerment was constrained by a whole host of stratagems, both real and symbolic, designed to counter an understanding of the maternal body as polluted and polluting" (165). See also Stanton. I would suggest that both Wilson's optimistic and Paster's more pessimistic readings are clearly inscribed in Webster's play—and it is further implied that the former is necessarily created out of (and is therefore, in Paster's words, "hard to distinguish from" [189]) the latter.

26. He notes elsewhere that the network of gossips both "partly mirrored the male hierarchy . . . [and] partly cut across that hierarchy" ("Ceremony" 96-97).

27. *OED* "gossip," noun 3 ("A person, mostly a woman, of light and trifling character, esp. one who delights in idle talk"), and verb 3.

28. Another interesting example, which simultaneously valorizes and undercuts female speech, appears in the 1612 translation of Jacques Guillemeau's treatise on pregnancy, *Childbirth:* "Some do obserue, that the Navell must be tyed longer, or shorter, according to the difference of the sexe, allowing more measure to the males: because this length doth make their tongue, and priuie membres the longer: whereby they may both speake the plainer, and be more seruiceable to Ladies. And that by tying it short, and almost close to the belly in females, their tongue is lesse free, and their naturall part more straite: And to speake the truth, the Gossips commonly say merrily to the Midwife; if it be a boy, *Make him good measure;* but if it be a wench, *Tye it short*" (99).

29. Cf. the earlier (ambiguous) reference to the Trojan War:
FERDINAND. You are a good horseman, Antonio; you have excellent riders in France, what do you think of good horsemanship?
ANTONIO. Nobly, my lord: as out of the Grecian horse issued many famous princes: so out of brave horsemanship, arise the first sparks of growing resolution, that raise the mind to noble action. (1.2.64-67)

30. On caskets, see Freud; cf. Castiza's "box" in *The Revenger's Tragedy.*

31. This shift and similar ones (including some of those I consider below) are discussed in somewhat different terms by Whigham (*Seizures* 201-10), Rose (155-72), and Jankowski (163-79).

32. The limitations of Whigham's perspective are more evident in his earlier essay, in which his description of this passage concluded: "The tones are martial, not erotic" ("Social and Sexual Mobility" 172). But while he has clearly attempted to modify his stance in response to the criticisms of Mary Beth Rose and others, his revised version reintroduces, in my view, the difficulties it tries to suppress. Webster, he maintains, creates sympathy for his heroine by "split[ting] gender and sexuality, masculinizing the duchess while diverting specifically erotic heterodoxy onto other characters." He persists in viewing the Duchess's defiance as uttered in the "the unmistakably masculine voice of the Renaissance hero"; and he concludes: "Going knowingly to colonize a new social realm of privacy, she arrogates to herself a defiance that here speaks essentially of gender, and only incidentally of sexuality. 'As men . . . so I' " (*Seizures* 204).

33. Cf. *Faustus,* 2.1.135. The phrase frequently appears in male doctors' and writers' descriptions of the beliefs and practices of midwives, which are dismissed as "Old *Wifes* Frivolous *Clatters,* or Crafty *Fictions* some *Midwifes* uses to amuse silly Credulous *People*" (Eccles 93). For discussions of the invasion of the midwives' province by male practitioners during the seventeenth century and of the rivalry that existed between the two groups, see Adrian Wilson, *The Making of Man-Midwifery;* Richard Wilson; and Harvey 79–92.

34. The primary meaning of "wink" in the Duchess's speech is, of course, "to close ones eyes" (*OED* 1); the meaning, "to 'shut one's eyes' to something faulty, wrong or improper" (*OED* 5) is clearly also present. The *OED* further records another (possibly relevant) contemporary meaning, "to give a significant glance, as of command, direction, or invitation" (7, gives examples of sexual invitation).

35. For an extended discussion of the early modern association of gossips, pregnancy, old wives' tales, and romances (with particular reference to Shakespeare's plays), see Richard Wilson.

36. Cf. the repeated phrase in *The Winter's Tale,* "like an old tale" (5.2.29, 61; 5.3.117); see also Ben Jonson's scornful assessment in *Bartholmew Fair* of the unnatural, topsy-turvy form of "Tales, Tempests, and such like drolleries" (Ind. 124–26).

37. The evocations of pregnancy, breeding, and child-rearing here are, of course, also significant.

38. But see Rose 162, 169, and Jankowski 177–79.

39. Cf. Ferdinand, 4.2.261–63.

40. These lines—carefully poised between a command and a request—pick up and alter the "rhetoric of will-making" that the Duchess employs in her marriage proposal (Wall 307–09).

41. These binaries are from a longer list of hierarchical distinctions outlined by David Halperin and cited by Edelman that helped to constitute a "cultural poetics of manhood in ancient Athens" (Halperin 102); Halperin's list also includes "master vs. slave, free vs. unfree. dominant vs. submissive . . . customer vs. prostitute, citizen vs. non-citizen" (102–03).

42. Whitford (155) quotes Irigaray: "In order for [sexual] difference to be thought and lived, we have to reconsider the whole problematic of *space* and *time*. . . . A change of epoch requires a mutation in the perception and conception of *space-time*, the *inhabitation of place,* and the *envelopes of identity*" (*Ethique de la Différence Sexuelle* 15; her trans.; cf. *Ethics* 9). See also Grosz 173–76, and Best.

43. Cf. Irigaray: "One must assume the feminine role deliberately. Which means already to convert a form of subordination into an affirmation, and thus to begin to thwart it. . . . To play with mimesis is thus, for a woman, to try to recover the place of her exploitation by discourse, without allowing herself to be simply reduced to it. It means to resubmit herself— inasmuch as she is on the side of the 'perceptible,' of 'matter'—to 'ideas,' in particular to ideas about herself, that are elaborated in/by a masculine logic, but so as to make 'visible,' by an effect of playful repetition, what was supposed to remain invisible: the cover-up of a possible operation of the feminine in language. It also means 'to unveil' the fact that, if women are such good mimics, it is because they are not simply resorbed in this function. *They also remain elsewhere*" (*This Sex* 76). See also Bartels for an argument that the Duchess uses submission as a strategy.

44. See Belsey for an argument that the "affective ideal" that is at the heart of the play's "liberalism" has been assimilated by patriarchy over time (199–200).

45. Webster's own gender, of course, makes his stance more self-contradictory here than in *The White Devil,* and one could argue that his use of the Duchess is (must be) yet another example of the appropriation of women's voices by men. But I believe that it is important to emphasize the radical (and unusual) nature of the strategy he deploys. Cf. Carol Neely's exhortation to focus on "the possibility of human (especially female) gendered subjectivity" in early modern texts (15).

46. Cf. Naomi Schor's analysis of two exemplary, diametrically opposed, feminist positions, held by Beauvoir and Irigaray: "Just as Beauvoir lays bare the mechanisms of othering, Irigaray exposes those of what we might call by analogy, 'saming.' If othering involves attributing to the objectified other a difference that serves to legitimate her oppression, saming denies to the objectified other the right to her difference, submitting the other to the laws of phallic specularity. . . . If exposing the logic of othering . . . is a necessary step in achieving equality, exposing the logic of saming is a necessary step in toppling the universal from his/(her) pedestal" ("This Essentialism" 65). Each position, Schor suggests, "has its own inescapable logic" (65), and each inevitably risks falling victim to what the other exposes. See also Fuss on the strategic value of "risking" essentialism.

47. It is also, of course, significant that the play's conception of the Duchess's sexuality does not seem to involve the kinds of mutually exclusive choices that characterize modern sexual identities; indeed, it is deployed *against* an image of all-consuming exclusivity.

Works Cited

Bartels, Emily. "Strategies of Submission: Desdemona, the Duchess, and the Assertion of Desire." *Studies in English Literature, 1500–1900* 36 (1996): 417–33.

Belsey, Catherine. *The Subject of Tragedy: Identity and Difference in Renaissance Drama.* London: Methuen, 1985.

Best, Sue. "Sexualizing Space." *Sexy Bodies: The Strange Carnalities of Feminism.* Eds. Elizabeth Grosz and Elspeth Probyn. New York: Routledge, 1995. 181–94.

Burke, Carolyn. "Irigaray through the Looking Glass." Burke, Schor, and Whitford 37–56.

Burke, Carolyn, Naomi Schor, and Margaret Whitford, eds. *Engaging with Irigaray: Feminist Philosophy and Modern European Thought.* New York: Columbia UP, 1994.

Butler, Judith. *Bodies That Matter: On the Discursive Limits of Sex.* New York: Routledge, 1993.

Cadden, Joan. *Meanings of Sex Difference in the Middle Ages: Medicine, Science, and Culture.* Cambridge: Cambridge UP, 1993.

Callaghan, Dympna. *Woman and Gender in Renaissance Tragedy: A Study of* King Lear, Othello, The Duchess of Malfi *and* The White Devil. Atlantic Highlands, NJ: Humanities, 1989.

Chanter, Tina. *Ethics of Eros: Irigaray's Rewriting of the Philosophers.* New York: Routledge, 1995.

Crooke, Helikiah. *Microcosmographia: A Description of the Body of Man.* London, 1615.

Culpepper, Nicholas. *A Directory for Midwives.* London, 1656.

Davis, Natalie Zemon. "Women on Top." *Society and Culture in Early Modern France.* Stanford: Stanford UP, 1975. 124-51.

Dollimore, Jonathan. *Radical Tragedy: Religion, Ideology and Power in the Drama of Shakespeare and His Contemporaries.* 2nd ed. Durham: Duke UP, 1993.

———. *Sexual Dissidence: Augustine to Wilde, Freud to Foucault.* Oxford: Clarendon, 1991.

———. "Subjectivity, Sexuality, and Transgression: The Jacobean Connection." *Renaissance Drama as Cultural History: Essays from Renaissance Drama, 1977-1987.* Ed. Mary Beth Rose. Evanston: Northwestern UP, 1990. 335-63.

Donne, John. *The Complete English Poems.* Ed. A. J. Smith. London: Penguin, 1971.

Eccles, Audrey. *Obstetrics and Gynaecology in Tudor and Stuart England.* Kent: Kent State UP, 1982.

Edelman, Lee. *Homographesis: Essays in Gay Literary and Cultural Theory.* New York: Routledge, 1994.

Enterline, Lynn. *The Tears of Narcissus: Melancholia and Masculinity in Early Modern Writing.* Stanford: Stanford UP, 1995.

The XV Comforts of Rash and Inconsiderate Marriage. London, 1682.

Fifteen Real Comforts of Matrimony. London, 1683.

Freud, Sigmund. "The Theme of the Three Caskets." London: Hogarth, 1958. Vol. 12 of *The Standard Edition of the Complete Psychological Works of Sigmund Freud.* Ed. James Strachey. 23 vols. 1957-66. 291-301.

Fuss, Diana. *Essentially Speaking: Feminism, Nature and Difference.* New York: Routledge, 1989.

Gallop, Jane. *Thinking through the Body.* New York: Columbia UP, 1988.

Greenblatt, Stephen. "Fiction and Friction." *Shakespearean Negotiations: The Circulation of Social Energy in Renaissance England.* Berkeley: U of California P, 1988. 66-93.

Grosz, Elizabeth. *Sexual Subversions: Three French Feminists.* Sydney: Allen & Unwin, 1989.

Guillemeau, Jacques. *Child-birth, or, The Happy Deliverie of Women.* London, 1612.

Halperin, David. *One Hundred Years of Homosexuality and Other Essays on Greek Love.* New York: Routledge, 1990.

Harvey, Elizabeth D. *Ventriloquized Voices: Feminist Theory and English Renaissance Texts.* London: Routledge, 1992.

Irigaray, Luce. *Amante marine. De Friedrich Nietzsche.* Paris: Minuit, 1980.

———. "Equal or Different." Trans. David Macey. *The Irigaray Reader* 30-33.

———. "Equal to Whom?" Trans. Robert L. Mazzola. Schor and Weed 63-81.

———. *An Ethics of Sexual Difference.* Trans. Carolyn Burke and Gillian C. Gill. Ithaca: Cornell UP, 1993.

———. *The Irigaray Reader.* Ed. Margaret Whitford. Oxford: Blackwell, 1991.

———. "The Poverty of Psychoanalysis." Trans. David Macey. *The Irigaray Reader* 79-104.

———. *Speculum of the Other Woman.* Trans. Gillian C. Gill. Ithaca: Cornell UP, 1985.

———. *This Sex Which Is Not One.* Trans. Catherine Porter. Ithaca: Cornell UP, 1985.

Jankowski, Theodora A. *Women in Power in the Early Modern Drama.* Urbana: U of Illinois P, 1992.

Jonson, Ben. *Bartholmew Fair.* Ed. G. R. Hibbard. New Mermaids. New York: Norton, 1991.

Laqueur, Thomas. *Making Sex: Body and Gender from the Greeks to Freud.* Cambridge: Harvard UP, 1990.

Lifson, Martha Ronk. "Embodied Mortality in *The Duchess of Malfi.*" *Pacific Coast Philology* 23 (1988): 47-59.

Malcolmson, Cristina. " 'What You Will': Social Mobility and Gender in *Twelfth Night.*" *The Matter of Difference: Feminist Materialist Criticism of Shakespeare.* Ed. Valerie Wayne. Ithaca: Cornell UP, 1991. 29-57.

Marlowe, Christopher. *Doctor Faustus. Drama of the English Renaissance.* Ed. Russell A. Fraser and Norman Rabkin. Vol 1. New York: Macmillan, 1976. 2 vols.

Maus, Katherine Eisaman. "A Womb of His Own: Male Renaissance Poets in the Female Body." *Inwardness and Theater in the English Renaissance.* Chicago: U of Chicago P, 1995. 182-209.

Mulvey, Laura. "Visual Pleasure and Narrative Cinema." *Screen* 16 (1975): 6-18.

Neely, Carol Thomas. "Constructing the Subject: Feminist Practice and the New Renaissance Discourses." *English Literary Renaissance* 18 (1988): 5-18.

Paré, Ambroise. *The Works of the Famous Chirurgion.* Trans. Thomas Johnson. London, 1634.

Park, Katharine, and Robert A. Nye. "Destiny Is Anatomy." *New Republic* 18 Feb. 1991: 53-57.

Parker, Patricia. "Gender Ideology, Gender Change: The Case of Marie Germain." *Critical Inquiry* 19 (1993): 337-64.

———. *Literary Fat Ladies: Rhetoric, Gender, Property.* London: Methuen, 1987.

———. "*Othello* and *Hamlet*: Dilation, Spying, and the Secret Place of Woman." *Representations* 44 (1993): 60-95.

———. *Shakespeare from the Margins: Language, Culture, Context.* Chicago: U of Chicago P, 1996.

Partridge, Eric. *Shakespeare's Bawdy.* Rev. ed. New York: Dutton, 1969.

Paster, Gail Kern. *The Body Embarrassed: Drama and the Disciplines of Shame in Early Modern England.* Ithaca: Cornell UP, 1993.

The Revenger's Tragedy. Ed. Brian Gibbons. 2nd ed. New Mermaids. New York: Norton, 1991.

Rose, Mary Beth. *The Expense of Spirit: Love and Sexuality in Renaissance Drama.* Ithaca: Cornell UP, 1988.

Sadler, John. *The Sicke Womans Private Looking-Glasse.* London, 1636.

Schor, Naomi. "This Essentialism Which Is Not One: Coming to Grips with Irigaray." Burke, Schor, and Whitford 57-78.

Schor, Naomi, and Elizabeth Weed, eds. *The Essential Difference.* Bloomington: Indiana UP, 1994.

Shakespeare, William. *The Riverside Shakespeare.* Ed. G. Blakemore Evans. Boston: Houghton Mifflin, 1974.

Sharp, Jane. *The Midwives Book.* 1671. New York: Garland, 1985.

Sidney, Sir Philip. *An Apology for Poetry.* Ed. Forrest G. Robinson. New York: Macmillan, 1970.

Stallybrass, Peter. "Patriarchal Territories: The Body Enclosed." *Rewriting the Renaissance: The Discourses of Sexual Difference in Early Modern Europe.* Eds. Margaret W. Ferguson, Maureen Quilligan, and Nancy J. Vickers. Chicago: U of Chicago P, 1986. 123-44.

————. "Reading the Body: *The Revenger's Tragedy* and the Jacobean Theater of Consumption." *Renaissance Drama* ns 18 (1987): 121–48.

Stanton, Domna C. "Recuperating Women and the Man behind the Screen." *Sexuality and Gender in Early Modern Europe: Institutions, Texts, Images.* Ed. James Grantham Turner. Cambridge: Cambridge UP, 1993. 247–65.

Traub, Valerie. *Desire and Anxiety: Circulations of Sexuality in Shakespearean Drama.* London: Routledge, 1992.

————. "The Psychomorphology of the Clitoris." *GLQ* 2 (1995): 81–113.

Wall, Wendy. *The Imprint of Gender: Authorship and Publication in the English Renaissance.* Ithaca: Cornell UP, 1993.

Webster, John. *The Duchess of Malfi.* Ed. Elizabeth M. Brennan. 3rd ed. New Mermaids. New York: Norton, 1993.

————. *The White Devil.* Ed. Elizabeth M. Brennan. New Mermaids. New York: Norton, 1993.

Weimann, Robert. *Shakespeare and the Popular Tradition in the Theater: Studies in the Social Dimension of Dramatic Form and Function.* Ed. Robert Schwartz. Baltimore: Johns Hopkins UP, 1978.

Whigham, Frank. *Seizures of the Will in Early Modern English Drama.* Cambridge: Cambridge UP, 1996.

————. "Sexual and Social Mobility in *The Duchess of Malfi.*" *PMLA* 100 (1985): 167–86.

Whitford, Margaret. *Luce Irigaray: Philosophy in the Feminine.* London: Routledge, 1991.

Wilkinson, Charles. "Twin Structure in John Webster's *The Duchess of Malfi.*" *Literature and Psychology* 31 (1984): 52–65.

Wilson, Adrian. "The Ceremony of Childbirth and Its Interpretation." *Women as Mothers in Pre-Industrial England: Essays in Memory of Dorothy McLaren.* Ed. Valerie Fildes. London: Routledge, 1990. 68–107.

————. *The Making of Man-Midwifery: Childbirth in England, 1660–1770.* Cambridge: Harvard UP, 1995.

Wilson, Richard. "Observations on English Bodies: Licensing Maternity in Shakespeare's Late Plays." *Will Power: Essays on Shakespearean Authority.* Detroit: Wayne State UP, 1993. 158–83.

Woodbridge, Linda. "The Gossips' Meeting." *Women and the English Renaissance: Literature and the Nature of Womankind, 1540.* Urbana: U of Illinois P, 1986. 224–43.

King Lear *Without: The Heath*

HENRY S. TURNER

Mais enfin le drame? S'il a, chez l'auteur, sa fulgurante origine, c'est à lui de capter cette foudre et d'organiser, à partir de l'illumination qui montre le vide, une architecture verbale—c'est-à-dire grammaticale et cérémoniale—indiquant sournoisement que de ce vide s'arrache une apparence qui montre le vide.

But the drama? If it has its dazzling origin in the author, it is up to him to capture this thunder and to organize, out of the illumination that shows the void, a verbal architecture—one that is grammatical and ceremonial—indicating, craftily, that from this void is torn an appearance that shows the void.

—Jean Genet, "L'Etrange mot de . . ."

IMAGINE KING LEAR without the Heath.

Perhaps the imperative with which I begin my essay will prove impossible for a critical tradition that has become accustomed to the conventions of the modern printed text, accustomed both to the presence of a particular location "in" the world of that text and to the presence of a particular character "in" that particular location—a character, moreover, who has become emblematic of subjectivity in its most acute, most essential form. This is a critical tradition for whom concepts of "space" and discrete location function as inseparable dialectical poles, and for whom the most basic analytic categories and gestures have become imbued with a spatial imaginary that has become inseparable from the idea of subjectivity itself.

Writing in 1904, A. C. Bradley already articulated in another vocabulary and sensibility the problem that I will be discussing here, saying of *King Lear* that the "very vagueness in the sense of locality . . . give[s] the feeling of vastness, the feeling not of a scene or particular place, but of a world; or, to speak more accurately, of a particular place which is also a world" (261). If Bradley prefers this immediate re-formulation of his own statement, it is because the phrase not only describes with greater precision a sense of space that he perceives almost intuitively in the play, a space that seems to exceed the stage, filling it with a looming and unrepresentable significance, but because it does so by fixing the "overwhelming" (244) space of the stage into a convenient and predictable dialectical relation. I will quote

161

Bradley at some length below, both because his comments formulate a long-standing set of critical objections to the play and because the categories and oppositions he introduces are central to the analysis that I will be proposing:

The stage is the test of strictly dramatic quality, and *King Lear* is too huge for the stage. Of course I am not denying that it is a great stage-play. It has scenes immensely effective in the theater. . . . But . . . that which makes the *peculiar* greatness of *King Lear*—the immense scope of the work; the mass and variety of intense experience which it contains; the interpenetration of sublime imagination, piercing pathos; the vastness of the convulsion both of nature and of human passion; the vagueness of the scene where the action takes place, and of the movements of the figures which cross this scene; the strange atmosphere, cold and dark, which strikes on us as we enter this scene, enfolding these figures and magnifying their dim outlines like a winter mist; the half-realized suggestions of vast universal working in the world of individual fates and passions—all this interferes with dramatic clearness even when the play is read, and in the theater not only refuses to reveal itself fully through the senses but seems to be almost in contradiction with their reports. . . . *King Lear,* as a whole, is imperfectly dramatic, and there is something in its very essence which is at war with the senses, and demands a purely imaginative realisation. (247–48)

"A purely imaginative realisation": these are Bradley's terms for a *reader* who already seems to participate in the cruel world of the play and to "enter this scene." If we are to recover the true magnitude of the play, Bradley argues, it is only as readers that we will be able to do so. The power of poetry, even of language itself, is at stake:

The influence of all this on imagination as we read *King Lear* is very great; and it combines with other influences to convey to us, not in the form of distinct ideas but in the manner proper to poetry, the wider or universal significance of the spectacle presented to the inward eye. But the effect of theatrical representation is precisely the reverse. There the poetic atmosphere is dissipated; the meaning of the very words which create it passes half-realized; in obedience to the tyranny of the eye we conceive the characters as mere particular men and women; and all that mass of vague suggestion, if it enters the mind at all, appears in the shape of an allegory which we immediately reject. (269)

The two passages suggest, somewhat paradoxically, that *King Lear*'s "peculiar greatness" derives from its pre-eminent spatial qualities—its "immense scope," "huge" action, and "vagueness of scene" (all 261)—but that the open stage, arguably the most fully spatialized mode of representation, can finally only obscure the play's total achievement. The stage "over-powers" (261) the viewer, disrupting the operation of linguistic meaning and even the effect essential to tragedy: that which strikes us as "revolting or shocking" in performance "is otherwise in reading," where "imagina-tion . . . can do its duty as a stimulus to pity" (251) and make possible a recognition of the characters' terror and grief. The stage's insufficiency derives from its particularity, its rootedness in a precise time and place. The "tyranny" (269) of the sensory eye, riveted in the particular and the mundane, must give way to the "spectacle of the inward eye" (269) pos-sessed by the reader who contemplates the "vastness" (256) of the drama from a "wider point of view" (253). Elements that appear inconsistent, implausible, superfluous, or excessively graphic on the stage are resolved on the page into the majesty of "one of the world's greatest poems" (277). Bradley's analysis transforms the lived space of the stage and body into the idealized and metaphorical space of perspective, "intellect," and "speculation" (264); this space is in turn aligned with aesthetic judgment, and, through "imagination," with consciousness itself.

By adopting a critical attitude that imagines "a particular place which is also a world" (261), Bradley thus gives spatial form to the larger allegorizing movement from individual to universal—and from stage to page—that allows him to secure the play's ultimate moral and aesthetic relevance. But it is striking that even as Bradley turns to the page as a tool of hermeneutic authority, he finds that the conventions of the open stage are too persistent to be overlooked and finally intrude to disrupt his gesture. *King Lear,* he observes, presents unusual difficulties by virtue of its very *placelessness,* a placelessness that is typical of the Elizabethan theater. Although in *Hamlet, Macbeth,* and *Othello* "the imagination is . . . untroubled" by lack of precise locations, in *Lear* "the indications are so scanty that the reader's mind is left not seldom both vague and bewildered."[1] This is the problem of the entire play, and he singles out several scenes in particular as exemplary instances of the confusing effects of early modern stage practice and the necessity of overcoming them with the printed text:

A similar conflict between imagination and sense will be found if we consider the dramatic centre of the whole tragedy, the Storm scenes. . . . The Storm-scenes in *King Lear* gain nothing and their very essence is destroyed. . . . [It is] such poetry as cannot be transferred to the space behind the foot-lights, but has its being only in imagination. (269-70)

Bradley's reluctance to locate these scenes is notable: even in imagination, they unfold in a "place" that remains as undesignated as the scenes that unfold on the open stage. His hesitation is perhaps all the more surprising in that for nearly two hundred years Shakespeare's editors had proposed a location for these scenes that had come to seem self-evident: this place is the "heath."[2]

But the moment is also a testament to Bradley's critical perceptiveness: the so-called "heath," in fact, appears nowhere in either the 1608 Quarto or the 1623 Folio editions of Shakespeare's play. No single line in any of the early texts records any such place; only Lear's tirade and a brief direction— "storm still"—that appears silently but insistently six times in the Folio, and *not* in the Quarto, provide any indication of a specific placement for the scene.[3] Not until Rowe's 1709 edition of Shakespeare's works does a stage direction appear specifying "A Heath." No doubt the entire weight of a later tradition intrudes on this moment—that of the Restoration stage with its perspective scenery and careful attention to the unities of time, place, and action—filling with a simple, single word a textual moment that Rowe's retrospective eyes could perceive only as absence or error.[4]

In spite of warnings by recent editors and scholars as to the anachronism of using location directions in modern editions of Renaissance plays, I suspect that like Rowe and his successors many of us find it difficult *not* to map the action of a play onto an imaginary topography.[5] The habit says a great deal about our own understanding of space and illuminates, somewhat surprisingly perhaps, how dependent it is on the printed book. But the tendency is not always as illegitimate as it might seem. Some genres positively require spatial precision: domestic tragedy and city comedy, for instance, tend to specify locations in much more detail than comedies or tragedies attributed to Shakespeare. Moreover, as Bradley himself observed, in any single play the places of the action may emerge more or less distinctly at different points, and in some respects his characterization of *Lear* is perhaps too categorical: we do, after all, glimpse the "casement" of Edmund's "closet" (1.2.58); the action seems at one point to be outside a "hovel"; we overhear occasional references to France; and some characters travel to "Dover," where the imaginative detail of a particular place is magnificently realized.

Nevertheless, to presume location at *all* points in the case of *Lear,* as Rowe does, is to take as self-evident a set of logical and imaginative relationships that the play itself seeks to examine in all their complexity and to hold in tension, rather than to resolve. I have examined Bradley's reading in such detail because, at bottom, his analysis is centrally concerned with this aspect of the play, even if his appeal to universal categories finally prevents a full elaboration of the representational problems involved and forecloses some of their more radical implications. Stated simply, these are the relationships between the categories of "place" and "space" during dramatic performance, "place" being understood, provisionally, as any discrete, bounded location with finite dimensions, and "space" as the larger, seemingly limitless dimension that would contain it.[6] An extended consideration of *King Lear*'s treatment of these categories leads directly to one of the most difficult aspects of the play and to the topic of this special issue: before we can open a discussion of "the space of the stage" we must ask first how we understand the phrase, what the characteristics of this "space" might prove to be, and how this "space"— the very medium that makes all dramatic representation possible—could ever "itself" appear as an object of representation, and thus as an object of analysis. These questions raise a set of concerns that are simultaneously formal (they concern a particular mode of representation), philosophical (and have been treated as such both in the early modern period and in our own), historical (how we think about them has changed over time), and ideological (they are not discursively neutral).

I will argue that no play more than *King Lear* so self-consciously engages the power of the early modern open stage to take up and transform, in the process of its fiction and for the duration of that fiction only, the spatial medium in which a dramatic action took place. Explicit verbal reference to the stage's mimetic capacity is largely absent from the play—with one important exception, as we shall see—and yet the sheer scope of its action, with its wanderings, displacements, and geopolitical subplot, ensures that the stage's spatial potential remains fully felt throughout. In some scenes, moreover, the space of the stage would appear to move beyond tacit convention to become the subject of direct theoretical and formal inquiry, and this not always in an overtly "poetic" or rhetorical manner. Indeed, one of the central questions the play forces us to confront is finally this: how might the open stage allow the exploration of a series of spatial concepts in a way that is *beyond* print or words, even beyond the language of poetry?

The analytic categories that Bradley favored—stage and page, viewer and reader—remain fundamental to critical discussion of early modern drama, but their relationship must be further elaborated and their separate spatial sensibilities specified in more detail. To this end I have divided my argument into two sections. The first reads several key scenes from the play in the context of early modern performance practice and argues that they can be fully understood only when the specific epistemological protocols of the open stage are taken into account. The second section then examines how the categories of "place" and "space" are modified when the play is translated into print and become essential components of an emerging notion of dramatic "form." When printed according to certain techniques and in certain formats, the play on the page has a conceptual integrity that differs from the play in performance. Contained within the physical confines of a bound page that may be held, contemplated, analyzed, and moved through at varying rates, the printed text prepares the way for our more modern spatial conception. Each section thus delineates several modes of understanding and representing space and then situates them within a larger argument about how ideas of space changed in England during the sixteenth and seventeenth centuries. Each section also depends on a heuristic distinction between *fictional* and *historical* space: the space of the story, or "diegetic" space, as opposed to the space of the theater, page, or society that supports it.[7]

I. Stage

I will approach *King Lear* first as if it were a technical exercise in spatial representation, a demonstration piece that deliberately sets out to explore the mimetic possibilities and limitations of the open stage. Like all such demonstration pieces, the play exhibits virtuosity by adopting techniques that expose the limits of its representational medium and that, as a consequence, are calculated to impress; it also incorporates a level of self-awareness into its *praxis* by comparing stage technology to other possible modes of representation over which it asserts itself. This approach to the play is not itself unusual; others have approached it as a self-reflexive project.[8] However, the play's specific concern with *spatial* representation has not received the attention it might. In a sense, the idea that *Lear* is a "demonstration piece" is itself misleading, since it suggests a deliberate and authorial display of skill, but by beginning with this claim I mean to shift the focus from the putative "hand behind the work" to the "work" itself, so that the play is understood as making explicit its own participation in a set of representational problems which are larger than any particular author and which are, quite simply, part of the enabling conditions of the drama itself.

Surely the most obvious example in the play of the virtuosity and mimetic self-awareness I am describing is the scene at Dover Cliff, and several scholars have commented both on its obvious references to perspective painting and on the cleverness of its stage business.[9] The journey toward Dover, by both Gloucester and Edgar and by Lear and his party *simultaneously* (and I will return to the importance of this simultaneity below), already foregrounds the flexibility of the open stage to represent distant locations, but the trip itself would in fact be unremarkable in spatial terms—simply one more instance of that freedom that first Sidney and later Jonson derided—without the vertiginous scene at Dover Cliff "itself." The striking thing about the scene, however, is less its self-conscious *debt* to perspective painting than the way it strives to trump a two-dimensional technique. The sheer knowingness of the scene is so blatant that it nearly becomes a cruel joke, as witnessed by the way in which Edgar's sudden aside to the audience—"Why I do trifle thus with his despair / Is done to cure it" (4.5.33–34)—registers a niggling need to justify the entire conceit. As Edgar stands at the supposed edge of the cliff, his lines invoke the structure of monocular point-of-view only to undermine it, first by substituting a *verbal* description for the geometrical forms and mathematically-derived proportions typical of perspective painting, and then, additionally, by turning this illusion into a second-party narration for a blind man who, after all, *cannot see anything*:

> Come on sir, here's the place. Stand still. How fearful
> And dizzy 'tis to cast one's eyes so low!
> The crows and choughs that wing the midway air
> Show scarce so gross as beetles. Halfway down
> Hangs one that gathers samphire, the dreadful trade!
> Methinks he seems no bigger than his head.
> The fishermen that walk upon the beach
> Appear like mice, and yon tall anchoring barque
> Diminished to her cock, her cock a buoy
> Almost too small for sight. The murmuring surge
> That on th'unnumbered idle pebble chafes
> Cannot be heard so high. I'll look no more,
> Lest my brain turn and the deficient sight
> Topple down headlong.
>
> (4.5.11–24)

At the very moment that the ocular illusion should be at its most breath-taking and convincing, the audience is caught up short by the grotesque reality of Gloucester's gaping eye-sockets; it is as though Edgar finds himself carried away by his own verbal skill and is unable to resist luxuriating in the ecstasy of vision, even as he stands next to a man who will never see again.

In the second place, the scene departs from the usual horizontal view of two-dimensional perspectival exercises by unfolding along a precipitous *vertical* axis. Imogen's imagining of Posthumus's departure in *Cymbeline* or Aspatia's mournful stare in Beaumont and Fletcher's *The Maid's Tragedy* are more conventional in this respect; the clear association between look-ing, perspectival space, and subjectivity in these scenes is also striking.[10] In *Lear,* however, the scene's elaborate technique draws our attention *as much to the devices used to represent the space as to the final effect of that space itself*—so much so that Samuel Johnson is said by Boswell to have complained about Shakespeare's execution of the scene, remarking that "the crows impede your fall" (cited in Levin, 97). This is an important point, since it serves as a corrective to some readings of the scene which rely on Albertian perspective theory. As James Elkins has convincingly argued (esp. 45–80), the conventional notion that Renaissance painters, artisans, engineers, architects, natural scientists, and mathematicians deployed a single perspective "theory" is a modern misconception, as the sheer variety of practitioners just listed might well indicate. So-called "perspective" (Albertian or otherwise) in fact consisted more of a loosely related series of *practices* and methods than a formal, codified, and unified theory; as a consequence, Elkins argues, multiple perspectives were used to represent particular *objects* in paintings and *not* to achieve a homogenized, rational-ized, or mathematically derived "picture space," a space of extension that preceded those objects.[11]

Edgar's lines thus establish a direct relationship between the technique of perspective in this scene and techniques as practiced in fifteenth- and sixteenth-century paintings, and they even make evident a paradox in how "space" itself is conceived. The focus of Edgar's lines is not space but *smallness*: his use of multiple and shifting metaphors creates an illusion of diminution—crows mutate into beetles, the body of a beachcomber shrinks (or expands) to the size of his head, fishermen scramble like mice— of which "space" could only be an aftereffect. The persistent details of crows and samphire gatherers make evident the fact that the eye can never fully apprehend pure, expansive "space" but only individual places and objects. As William Ivens has argued, the simplest experiment is enough to demonstrate that our view can perceive only objects in a spatial field and not the spatial field itself, unless that field is understood as the *effect* of particular objects grouped in a particular way and especially if those objects are grouped according to principles that emphasize interrelatedness—and proportion, in whatever guise, is first and foremost such a principle.[12] The closest analogy I can think of to a visual perception of pure "space" might be the experience of looking out an airplane window during flight, as the plane enters a cloud: in this moment we see "nothing." In the history of spatial concepts (which is not, after all, the same as artistic technique), single-point perspective is significant less because it offers a method for *representing* space to the eye than because it marks the emergence of an analytical, abstract space of *mathematical* principles that is strictly "invisible" (it is impossible to "see" the space described by an equation) and which is itself conceptually distinct from the idea of the visual geometry of the picture plane or the "window" illusion.

But Edgar's narration of space in this scene is, after all, much more than a reference to perspective technique: as Stephen Orgel has noted, it is paradigmatic for all dramatic treatment of space on the open stage. In a theater that used no perspective backdrops, a minimum of stage properties, and rudimentary sound and lighting effects, the primary illusionistic tool for designating location *was* spoken dialogue, and the final power of the scene depends on this awareness of stage convention.[13] When Edgar and Gloucester re-enter the stage space after the exchange between Regan and Oswald, and Gloucester asks, "When shall we come to th' top of that same hill?" (4.5.1), the audience is prepared to believe that they *are* in fact climbing a hill—after all, the characters' disappearance into the off-stage space has readily been accommodated into the fictional space of the "journey." It is only when Gloucester begins to question the topography ("Methinks the ground is even" [4.5.3]) that the illusion opens or bifurcates, such that the originary fictional space of the play is supplemented by the additional spatial conceit of the approach to Dover Cliff, and the audience is now faced with the tension of either identifying with Gloucester and entering this secondary layer of illusion or identifying with Edgar and recognizing the illusion as such—which immediately forces an awareness of the larger enabling illusion taking place on the stage before them. To recognize the well-intentioned nature of Edgar's deception, therefore, is to recognize the limitations of performative language and thus to question the very possibility of stage representation itself; and just when the audience has been led, like Gloucester, to this point of dizzying mimetic complexity, Gloucester jumps—and flops down onto the bare playing space before them. The resounding impact caps the scene by asserting, once more, the representational potential of the open stage, as Gloucester crawls about on the "beach" and believes he has survived the fall.

The final irony, however, is that even as Gloucester's blindness makes it impossible for him to perceive the specific location of the "cliff" (requiring Edgar's designation: "here's the place" [4.5.11]), this same blindness is precisely what will allow him to perceive "space" while Edgar cannot. A comment by Ivens makes clear that Gloucester's difficulty is simultaneously perceptual, representational, and logical:

Tactically, things exist in a series of *heres* in space, but where there are no things, space, even though "empty," continues to exist, because the exploring hand knows that it is in space even when it is in contact with nothing. The eye, contrariwise, can only see *things,* and where there are no things there is nothing, not even empty space, for that cannot be seen. There is no sense of contact in vision, but tactile awareness exists only as conscious contact. The hand, moving among the things it feels, is always literally "here," and while it has three dimensional coördinates it has no point of view and in consequence no vanishing point; the eye, having two dimensional coördinates, has a point of view and a vanishing point, and it sees "there," where it is not. The result is that visually things are not located in an independently existing space, but that space, rather, is a quality or relationship of things and has no existence without them. (5)

Just as later the blind Gloucester will reply to the mad Lear, "I see it feelingly" (4.5.141), at Dover Cliff Gloucester can only be said to "see nothing," and in his tentative, groping progress toward the audience and the subsequent silence of his leap the stage offers a momentary apprehension of what perspective could never represent: a fissure in the fictional location through which we "grasp" a larger "spatial" dimension. It is a moment for which there is no easy conventional language, given the pervasiveness of the perspective metaphor that is already beginning to take hold in these scenes—is it a "representation" of space? An "image"? A "view"? It is both a scene enacted *in* space and a scene *of* space.

Consider now another scene, equally obvious in its citation of a specific early modern mode of spatial representation: the infamous "division" scene. In contrast to the mimetic ambiguities of the scene at Dover Cliff,

Lear's peremptory "Give me the map there" (F 1.1.35) at the opening of the play would seem to promise a precise and measured spatial sensibility for the action that follows. Even more, the appearance of the map confirms the royal power to administrate and allocate space, not least because the map itself seems to function, initially, less as a *necessary* instrument of power than simply as a convenience, a way for Lear to illustrate and reenact for those gathered before him the content of a royal act which has already been completed and which did not require the map to do so ("Know that we *have divided* / In three our kingdom" [1.2.35–36; emphasis added]. Of course the map is more than a simple prop, since it demonstrates in an unspoken (but for that no less blatant) way Lear's power not simply to distribute space but to control its very representation, and then to treat this representation as a casual attribute of power. In this way the map becomes a metonym, in spatial form, for the burden of power itself ("rule / Interest of territory, cares of state" [1.1.47–48]), and the ease with which Lear wields both device and the property it encompasses would seem, at first glance, to be beyond question.

Already, however, the Quarto's shorter and more ambivalent "The map there" (Q sc. 1.35) casts the relationship between authority and spatial representation in another light. Does Lear *command* the map? Or simply gesture weakly in its direction? And where is "there," except already at a *distance* from the king and his authority? Lear's demonstrative pronoun hovers indistinctly over a referential point that refuses to materialize, and seems suddenly not to capture a location but to resist any correspondence; as readers we are, like the Quarto Lear, suddenly confronted by a representational surface that promises some kind of spatial order but also insists resolutely on its distance and inscrutability. The Quarto's "shake all cares and business from our *state*" (sc. 1.37; emphasis added) would seem to underscore the link between political authority and spatial representation, but in this context "shake" suggests not the infirmity and "age" of the Folio (1.1.37) but a trembling fear of cartography and its ability to make Lear's decision irrevocable by permanently inscribing it. Does Lear shrink from the map, an instrument whose power he recognizes but which he does not fully understand? These are precisely the questions that the printed text, in its two distinct versions, forces upon us.

In the terms of Henri Lefebvre, the map is, moreover, both a "representational space" and a "representation of space," which we might rephrase by saying that it is both a "place" and a "space."[14]

On the one hand the map represents the "territory," presumably "Britain," and more specifically a land "With shadowy forests and with champaigns riched, / With plenteous rivers and wide-skirted meads" (F 1.1.62-63). Even more specifically, however, this is the *Folio*'s gift of place to Goneril; the Quarto gives her less. But on the other hand the map also represents what we might call a "modern" idea of space as a quantifiable and measurable geometric abstraction—"all these bounds even from this line to this" (1.1.61)—and this initial abstraction becomes more and more salient in the subsequent exchanges between Regan and Lear and finally between Lear and Cordelia, as the "spatial" qualities of the map assert themselves over the form of the bequest. Regan gets "this ample third of our fair kingdom, / No less in space, validity and pleasure" (1.1.79): hers is exactly a space and not a place, a gift of equivalence more than content, and what content it does have ("validity and pleasure") is also abstract. The latent unfairness of Lear's division now emerges precisely in the precision with which he uses the quantitative language of space to describe the gifts, since they are equal *only* in the abstract; each daughter gets "a third," but Cordelia's is already "a third more opulent" (1.1.84). In preferring one daughter over the others, Lear has already opted for the particularity of place and property over the equalizing commensurability of geometrical and mathematical space that makes cartographic representation itself possible.

As one may begin to suspect, Lear's strategic use of spatial rhetoric is, in short, duplicitous, and it is not surprising to find the same language of insincerity in the mouths of Goneril and Regan. The first avows her love in the language of spatial abstraction ("Dearer than eyesight, space, and liberty" [1.1.54]); the second in arithmetic figure, commercial value, and geometric form ("prize me at her worth . . . which the most precious square of sense possesses" [1.1.68-72]). This association between the language of space, geometry, and betrayal is in keeping not only with other plays attributed to Shakespeare but with a more pervasive mistrust of specialized figures and symbols in early modern Europe, a knowledge associated with magic and the supernatural as well as with a lack of formal education, "craft," and the lower-class *ingenium* typical of the mason, the carpenter, and the engineer.[15] When the archbishop of York, Mowbray, Bardolph, and Hastings, for example, plot to overthrow the king in *2 Henry IV,* they invoke surveying and building metaphors for their treacherous action. More obviously, Lear's language is in keeping with that other Shakespearean "division scene" between Hotspur, Glendower,

Mortimer, and Worcester in *1 Henry IV* as they anticipate dominion and seek to redirect the natural course of rivers through dams and waterworks.

Lear's mistake is to uncouple the power of kingship from the instruments and attributes which made that power appear self-legitimating. Since Goneril and Regan understand the power of the map to convert space into property—so well that they glibly speak in the cartographic register—they understand also that Lear's use of the map has rendered him powerless by assisting him in his distribution of his kingdom, and it is no wonder that they follow his action to its logical conclusion by forcing him to renounce his knights in the later scenes. Cordelia, however, uses a different language: her "nothing" obviously speaks volumes—or, to be more precise, it *enacts* its meaning. The elaborate rhetoric of both Goneril and Regan can only belie their gestures toward the inadequacy of speech; Cordelia, recognizing here the duplicity of language, actualizes her meaning by saying "nothing" and thus reduces the conceptual and emotional content of her response to the absolute minimum of verbal expression. Lear's enraged retort—"Nothing will come of nothing. Speak again" (1.1.88)—focuses her response into a paradox: as Rosalie Colie, Paul Jorgensen, and Edward Grant have discussed, in very different contexts, the crucial epistemological dilemma turns on whether or not the concept of "nothing" is in fact "something."[16] What would it mean for Cordelia—or Lear, for that matter—to "possess nothing"?

The frequent recurrence of the term "nothing" throughout the play has sponsored no small amount of critical commentary, but its connection to the notions of attribute, property (in both the material and the philosophical or scientific senses), and space requires further elaboration. The problem is formulated most concisely by France, when he reassures Cordelia that "thou losest here, a better where to find" (1.1.259): is "here" the location in which Cordelia suffers the act of losing (property)? Or is "here" exactly what she loses, her proper portion of her father's realm (as the syntax of "where" would suggest)? Both readings seem possible; as queen of France, after all, Cordelia could be said simply to lose one place only immediately to gain another. But Lear is in a more difficult position, since he now moves uneasily through the space that he once ruled; indeed, given the close association between "space," property, and authority in the division scene, the term "space" would seem inappropriate to describe the medium of his dispossessed state.

Which brings us to the "storm scenes." For when Lear wanders out into the storm he is wandering out into a place over which he once exercised dominion, but does no longer; indeed, that place and his dominion over it were recognizable to him only on the map and in the spatial terms it made available, in which this location was simply a smaller part within the larger whole that contained it—"a particular place which is also a world," to use Bradley's phrase. Once this representation of space has been removed, once "space" itself, as a property of kingship, is no longer something Lear can in any way lay claim to, this "containing" relationship is also removed, and Lear begins to move in a dimension that is probably best described in the terms that the play uses: "nothing." Certainly the play explores these problems at the linguistic level, especially in the repeated use of the term "nothing" and the variations of the *ex nihilo* phrasing that recur in both plot and subplot and the many associations among "place," property, and power scattered throughout the early scenes. But these resonances are simply the verbal expression of a theoretical problem that is *enacted* non-verbally during the storm. To understand this we must consider the space of the stage during performance in more detail.

A comment by Sir Walter Greg illustrates some of its paradoxical qualities. Greg has made a brief excursus into the use of stage directions in manuscript copy, and to illustrate the documents' "bewildering . . . diversity" adduces the example of the term "within":

The use of "within" for off the stage is sometimes cited as belonging to the theatre. Logically this is doubtless so, though in fact the use is common to nearly all writers. But there is no consistency even in the playhouse. A character leaving the stage goes "within" from the point of view of the actors, and goes "out" from that of the spectators. . . . Any writer, whether actually writing for the stage or not, will use "within"—it is the only word available.[17]

The passage leaves us with many points to consider, not the least of which is the phrase "point of view," which Greg introduces as casually as Bradley does but to a somewhat different effect. When perspective, ostensibly the most rational mode of spatial representation, becomes Greg's paradigm for thinking about the space of the stage, it marks the *limits* of bibliographic and literary analysis and only multiplies the potential confusion of theatrical performance.

I would like to focus on another aspect, however: the initial dualism that animates the term "within" conceals an additional set of interrelated meanings that are central to understanding stage space. First, regardless of point of view, the terms designate some kind of *location*, a place that the actor goes "to," even if this place remains elusive: perhaps it is "offstage," and thus in the theater; perhaps it is "elsewhere," and thus in the fiction. The terms are difficult to situate outside of a purely reciprocal relation to one another; Greg attempts to resolve the potential ambiguity by invoking a larger conceptual abstraction (the "theatre," the "fiction") to surround and thus to provide a measure of precision and definition to the places that the terms would seem to designate.

The Prologue's evocation of the "Wooden 'O' " in *Henry V* neatly captures this sense of space: the phrase describes a static, transparent medium contained by the theater building, the "air" through which the actor moves and "in" which a series of scenes will be represented. We soon realize, however, that the Prologue's lines, as well as those of the Chorus in subsequent scenes, do not reveal space but rather conceal it. At the very moment that the empty space of the stage would seem to appear most clearly, the audience is urged to fill this space with a dazzling sequence of fictional *places*: "the vasty fields of France" (Pro.13), "the perilous narrow ocean" (Pro. 22), from London to Southampton to France and then back again to "Dover pier" (3.0.4). Wardrobes, pastures, ship-boys climbing in the tackle—the stage is not a blank platform but a tableau of almost cinematic proportions, in which "space" is obscured by all the bustling detail. If space "itself" is to emerge onto the stage, it must be in a different mode, and more indirectly.

It is evident from Greg's comment that the terms "within" and "out" also have another meaning: they are words that signify a *direction*, or a vector of movement. The stage "platts" studied by Greg in such detail indicate that during performance the space of the stage was parcellized into a series of entrances and exits from offstage to on, and *vice versa*.[18] The documents describe a space of practice, flux, and process constituted out of a performative movement across an invisible threshold: it is an act that creates, in its movement, the very fictional location that will give that act coherence and significance. Here too, however, the true *spatial* capacity of the open stage would be apprehensible only momentarily— at the instant the performance begins or ends, or in the slight break between scenes, if at all—since these fleeting appearances are simultaneously moments of dissolution and disappearance, as the "space" of the stage is instantaneously converted into the specific "places" of the fiction that the performance brings to life. This is a space of *potential* more than transparent substance.

But if an actor were to enter the stage as a character recognizable from the play and fail to designate a new location; as a character, moreover, who has been excluded first from one fictional place and then another; if this actor were to occupy the stage and gesticulate wildly, gratuitously, even to run about the playing area, as other characters entered to him from the world of the play and urged him to depart with them to other places in that world; and if, despite their entreaties, this actor were to remain stubbornly on stage and refuse to recognize the presence of these characters or the locations they spoke of: "where" exactly would this actor be? And how would a superstitious world describe such a character, except as mad? In such a moment the places of the theater and of the fiction would coincide with equal vividness—and if this "moment" was one of any duration, it might even qualify as a "scene." The resolute *negation* of place by one character, surrounded by the equally persistent affirmations of place by others, would result in a glimpse of the stage's *potential* to produce these places, and thus of its *space*.

The storm marks such a moment. All the peculiar qualities of the open stage, usually subordinate to the fiction unfolding upon it, begin to crowd in through a rift in this fiction and suddenly become visible with unusual vividness. The text records only attributes or qualities, but no location: the "storm and tempest" marked by the Folio at 2.2.449.1, "the night," "high winds" (2.2.464), the "wild night" (2.2.472), and a deranged old man, whose hair "the impetuous blasts make nothing of" (Q sc. 8.8). Like Gloucester at Dover Cliff, Lear has been "blinded" by his madness, floundering in the "eyeless rage" of the storm (Q sc. 8.7); like the madman Poor Tom, Lear will "embrace" the "unsubstantial air" (4.1.7), allow the storm to "Invade us to the skin" (3.4.7), and, if he is to speak at all, will adopt the language of the storm: "I will say nothing" (3.2.37).

Intriguingly, this is Lear's response to Kent, who enters in disguise as Caius (and like an actor) and who struggles repeatedly, in the face of Lear's "madness," to *re-localize* the scene and to draw it back firmly into either the world of the fiction or onto the space of the stage: "Alas, sir, are you here?" (3.2.41); "hard by here is a hovel" (3.2.60); "Here is the place, my lord. Good my lord, enter. / The tyranny of the open night's too rough" (3.4.1–2); "Good my lord, enter here" (3.4.4); "Good my lord, enter" (3.4.5); "Good my lord, enter here" (3.4.22). The phrase becomes incantatory, frustrated and desperate in its attempts to manage the spatial disorder that surrounds the feeble party, but the technical language of the actor goes unrecognized and the cue ignored. When Lear suddenly decides to enter ("but I'll go in" [3.4.25]), the scene would presumably snap into focus, except that he never actually *does* enter and the inconsistent exit markings in both Quarto and Folio make it unclear whether the scene takes place inside or outside the hovel (which seems to be offstage). The silent stage direction, "storm still," offers no indication of location but only of turbulence and dim outlines.

Greg has maintained that "within" is the "only word available" to describe the relation between onstage and offstage space, but he has already provided another: I will combine them to form a third term that describes this spatial "crux." This term is "without." Lear refuses to leave the stage, declines to move either "within" or "out" and instead wanders "without" into a breach in fictional space to flail in the *potentia* that surrounds him, a point somewhere *between* a coherent location and the open stage: he is not in one, nor is he entirely in the other. He has, in these moments, become the full impersonation of the Fool's earlier witticism, "Now thou art an O without a figure" (1.4.158). The phrase concisely articulates, in numerical terms, the paradox of "nothing" that is also "something," designating the "placeholder" that carves out a space for an imagined content (the figure) even as it simultaneously negates that content by occupying the space reserved for it. It is a sudden emblem not only for the spatial capacity of the empty open stage but for Lear's own displaced position during the storm, in which his mere presence on stage simultaneously invites the audience to imagine a fictional location and then prevents that location from becoming fully realized.

An analogy from another discursive field may help make this "space" more readily comprehensible: if the Dover Cliff scene, through its invocation of perspective, gestures toward the mathematical and spatial concept of infinity, the "nothing" of the storm could be said to perform the quasi-scientific space of the "vacuum" or "void," concepts debated in both natural philosophy and in the newer Stoicism and neo-Platonism of Campanella, Bruno, Francesco Patrizi, and many others. The "nothing" of the open stage would thus seem to frame in a different discursive context—and above all in a different *praxis*—a moment of transition in spatial thinking that we can also see operating at the most rarified levels of Renaissance academic argument, between a neo-Aristotelian scholastic philosophy that could conceive *only* of container or "place" and the emergence of a distinct notion of "space" understood as a homogeneous, extended medium that precedes and receives all bodies and their movements.[19] This distinction is, of course, only a heuristic one, since the conceptual history is more complicated than my schematic comments can do justice to here. But Lear's peculiar epithet for Poor Tom as he insists on remaining "without"—"let me talk with this philosopher" (3.4.137, 155, 158); "this same learned Theban" (3.4.140); this "good Athenian" (3.4.162)—suggests, however ironically, a philosophical context for the scene. As Edward Grant has demonstrated, scholastic arguments over vacuum and void space during the sixteenth and seventeenth centuries were in fact regularly posed as problems of "nothing" (*nullam, nihil*); even more significantly, these debates took place through recourse to a concept of "imaginary space" (*spatium imaginarium*): that quality of space which the mind is able to conceive of and project beyond itself, whether as fiction or even as "nothing" at all.[20]

II. Page

To reimagine "nothing" as the expanse of space itself, and to contain the power of the storm in a familiar location: if this is a task well suited to the philosophers of the seventeenth century, it will be accomplished in another register by the readers of the centuries that follow. In his preference for the printed page, Bradley is in many ways elaborating a judgment made nearly a century earlier by Charles Lamb, who objected even more strongly to the pretensions of performance and declared Lear "essentially impossible to be represented on a stage," because "on the stage we see nothing but corporal infirmities and weakness, the impotence of rage: while we read it, we see not Lear, but we are Lear" (1: 107). In order to chart the differences between the "nothing" of the open stage and the mental space of the modern reader, it will be useful to consider briefly how the relationship between "place" and "space" is reconfigured by the translation of a play into print and how a location direction comes to be regarded as indispensable to the editorial and critical apparatus.

Both the Quarto and the Folio *Lears* have been variously linked to the conditions of the early modern playhouse and to performance.[21] The predominant interest in bibliographical discussion of performance has been, understandably, to establish the status of *copy* and by extension the authority of the text on which it is based. In what follows, however, I would like to direct critical attention away from debates over copy and to focus instead on the effects of performance practice on print *format,* or the space of the page, and through this on the reader. In this respect, also, the Folio and Quarto *Lears* differ remarkably from one another, and two aspects in particular contribute significantly to the sense of "space" that each offers: the markings of act and scene divisions and the use of stage directions.

The question of act and scene division in early modern drama is a difficult one, and if the evidence for actual practice were not already confusing and elusive enough, discussion is often made even more complicated by a failure to distinguish four separate aspects of the problem: acts and scenes in composition, in literary theory, in performance, and in the printing house. The first two aspects are often treated as being virtually identical to one another, but they are not necessarily so; acts in performance are properly speaking act-*intervals* and not units of action. Aside from a few entries in Henslowe's diary, most of which concern a single author, there is scant evidence to suggest that early modern plays intended for performance in the so-called public theaters were composed according to a five-act structure before the second decade of the seventeenth century. With the exception of Jonson and a few other university-educated and classically conscious playwrights, English writers almost certainly composed plays in a series of scenes that were meant to be played continuously in the theater, and not in five acts.[22] Henry Snuggs makes the remarkable observation (49–50) that even Thomas Heywood, whose *Apology for Actors* clearly shows familiarity with the major statements of dramatic theory as early as 1607 (and perhaps before), does not seem *in practice* to have composed his plays according to these principles until after 1610.

Even here, however, the evidence concerns primarily the *printed* text, which immediately introduces conventions and habits which should be kept distinct from the use of divisions in composition, literary theory, or performance, even if finally all four categories tend to converge. We might assume that act and scene divisions in a printed text often indicate copy that has been modified in some way for use in the theater; Greg, Snuggs, and Chambers all agree that divisions in manuscript documents prior to c. 1610 are very likely to be the product of a later hand and that authors seem to have added divisions to their playscripts gradually in deference to stage practice.[23] But these later divisions, as well as those in printed play texts, may equally be the classicizing gestures of a professional scribe and thus similar to other scribal conventions (such as the massed entrances attributed to Ralph Crane) that sought to emulate the printing—or page— conventions of Roman comedy; in both cases, furthermore, the divisions are often arbitrary, and it is hard to say how much "literary" or "structural" role they actually play.

To argue in this way is again, however, to resort to the categories of author and copy, but it is important to remember that "structural" theories of act and scene divisions are in some respects possible only from the position of the *reader,* who has the capacity to arrest the flow of the action temporarily, to pause over scenes, flip through pages, carefully weigh one moment with another, and gradually distinguish the architecture of the composition.[24] *On the page,* act and scene divisions do not simply reproduce a break in performance: they contribute a conceptual unity to the play by subdividing its action into discrete parts, and these parts are then presumed by the reader to fit together into a coherent structural whole. Redistributed across the page in deliberately segmented units of action, the newly unified "work" makes possible a completely different sense of space from that which predominates on the stage: it allows the reader to project across the play *in its entirety* a homogeneous, unbroken, "containing" space that is imagined to link or underlie the various "places" of the fiction, whether these be onstage or off, "within" or "without." The Folio *Lear,* with its full use of act and scene divisions, obscures the specific performative tension between "space" and "place"—the dynamic whereby space, as potential, "solidifies," as it were, into a specific location, which in turn redissolves into "emptiness" and another potential location—and moves gradually toward a notion more similar to "setting" which inserts the action into a preexisting spatial dimension. A stage direction such as "Storm still" (in F but *not* in Q) is significant not least because it implies a concern for spatial continuity in the fiction best characterized as a space of *simultaneity,* in which separate subjects and their actions are understood as taking place *at the same time* and are thus linked to one another within a homogeneous, extended space: the imagined "world" of the play that contains both Gloucester's castle and Dover, both Britain and France.[25]

But for the critics of the eighteenth century the act and scene divisions did more than provide a sense of structural unity: the divisions sutured this "literary" structure to a concept of "place," which rendered the play's action comprehensible and made possible a final aesthetic judgment. We

can see this subsequent development quite vividly as early as Pope's edition of the plays. In keeping with the Continental critics, Pope correlates scene division with the "removal of place" in the name of consistency and clarity:

The Scenes are mark'd so distinctly that every removal of place is specified; which is more necessary in this Author than in any other, since he shifts them more frequently: and sometimes without attending to this particular, the reader would have met with obscurities. (xxii)

Moreover, the entire work is conceptualized in a striking architectural metaphor such that all the action is given a continuous spatial structure and coherence:

I will conclude by saying of *Shakespear,* that with all his faults, and with all the irregularity of his *Drama,* one may look upon his works, in comparison of those that are more finish'd and regular, as upon an ancient majestick piece of *Gothick* Architecture, compar'd with a neat Modern building: The latter is more elegant and glaring, but the former is more strong and more solemn. It must be allow'd that in one of these there are materials enough to make many of the other. It has much the greater variety, and much the nobler apartments; tho' we are often conducted to them by dark, odd, and uncouth passages. (xxiii–xxiv)

Fifteen years later, Lewis Theobald picks up the image but dilates it to encapsulate the architectural within the perspectival, and both within a much more expansive world or city:

The attempt to write upon SHAKESPEARE is like going into a large, a spacious, and a splendid Dome thro' the Conveyance of a narrow and obscure Entry. A Glare of Light suddenly breaks upon you, beyond what the Avenue at first promis'd: and a thousand Beauties of Genius and Character, like so many gaudy Apartments pouring at once upon the Eye, diffuse and throw themselves out to the Mind. The Prospect is too wide to come within the Compass of a single View: 'tis a gay Confusion of pleasing Objects, too various to be enjoyed but in a general Admiration; and they must be separated, and ey'd distinctly, in order to give the proper Entertainment.[26]

The passage marks the emergence of a "metaphorics" of perspective as pluralism and cultured selection, a refinement that depends on distance and separation. By the time of Edward Capell's 1767 edition, the space of the Shakespearean text has been thoroughly redistributed: noting that he has derived a principle of scene division (the removal of location) from those plays in the Folio which have already been divided "as of the Author's own settling," Capell proceeds to locate the action with stage directions that further subdivide an *interior* space: virtually all the scenes are assigned to "*A State-room in King* Lear's *Palace*"; "*A Hall in the Earl of* Gloster's *Castle*"; "*A Room in the Duke of* Albany's *Palace*" ; "*An outer Hall in the same,*" such that Pope's metaphor of linked apartments has been literalized into a world of intimacy and domestic realism.[27]

If we now return to compare the format of the Folio *Lear* to that of the first Quarto, we notice that the earlier text lacks all act and scene divisions and unfolds in a space that we might characterize as *linear* or *sequential*. Here the Quarto format preserves, to some degree, a sense of stage and performance space that is "Elizabethan," typical of public theaters, and disappearing from historical view: stage directions are few, exits and entrances are omitted, and the organizational "unit" (to import spatial and structural terms that are better suited to the page) is more closely linked to character groupings and their movements—but these movements are *not* correlated with any sense of "place," and the relation between onstage and offstage space remains as elusive as ever. Here any dramatic pause between scenes would lack *by definition* the conceptual substance of a break between acts: true neoclassical "Acts" and "Scenes" are meaningful only in the context of the conceptual integrity that the larger "work" provides, and *vice versa*; this dependency derives from the more general dialectic between any part and its whole. In any case, distinctions of this sort inevitably beg the textual question, since the action of *Lear* as it is printed in the Quarto advances with no clear division whatsoever and consequently does not offer the same spatial or structural skeleton to the reader.

It has often been remarked that the Folio was a text printed specifically for a reading market and for readers of some affluence. Many aspects of the collection suggest this, among them the size and quality of the book and its elaborate prefatory materials, not the least of which are the dedicatory poem "To the Reader" by "B. I." and Heminge and Condell's own direct address "To the great Variety of Readers." I have thus aligned the format of each version of *Lear* with one of the distinct spatial sensibilities I have been discussing: the Folio with what I will call a "readerly" space of quantifiable, measured extension and the Quarto with a "performative" space of movement that produces more of itself.[28] But early modern printing-house practice offers a technical distinction that also serves as a convenient metaphor for the spatial modes materialized on their pages. This is the difference between composing and printing by casting-off,

and composing and printing *seriatim*. The former technique, whereby
a compositor estimated the total number of printed pages required for a
given portion of the control text at hand (whether print or manuscript),
and only then set his type into formes accordingly, necessitated a *spatial
grasp of an entire segment of text*—either a page, a forme, a sheet, or
the complete work—that was subsequently "translated" by the compositor
into the blank expanse of the page. Composing *seriatim,* in contrast, meant
that the compositor set his type sequentially, in a linear spatial fashion and
with no necessary same regard for the total dimensions of the text before
him, and worked from the beginning of the copy through to the end. As
historical coincidence would have it, Nicholas Okes set the Quarto *Lear
seriatim,* while the compositors in Isaac Jaggard's print shop set the Folio
according to the more conventional process of casting-off.[29]

III

Perhaps it will be impossible for us to imagine *King Lear* "without the
heath," especially when, as readers, the idea of imagination itself so quickly
assumes a spatial dimension and when the very conventions of literary
analysis—citation by act and scene, for instance—make it difficult to
separate a modern idea of space and location from the idea of dramatic
structure. The title of my essay is meant, of course, to describe the state of
the early play-texts. But it is intended also to evoke a fanciful early modern
stage direction, in which the flexibility of the colon suggests a syntax of
elaboration or further specification. Read in this way, the "Heath," which is
properly Rowe's term and the familiar signifier for these crucial "scenes,"
appears reinscribed as the phrase "King Lear Without." By this substitution
I mean first to recall Lear's liminal dramatic situation "in the world of the
play": he is a king and father, excluded from the castles of his daughters,
who has been deprived of all authority, property, and "position" in the
social sense. But he also lacks a proper "position" in the locational and
dramatic sense: he is "outside" or "without" a fictional place that is itself
barely visible and defined only negatively or by attributes. This moment,
peculiar to the open stage, appears in the early texts only through a silent
absence; by designating it with a term that is meant to recall stage *practice*
rather than readerly imagination or editorial convention, I mean to mark
the moment when *King Lear* turns on itself and begins to explore its own
conditions of possibility as a dramatic performance.

It will now be useful to consider by way of a conclusion several points that have emerged in the preceding discussion and which are pertinent to any study of "the space of the stage" or to the history of spatial concepts more generally. We may begin by stating a now-familiar lesson: that to speak of the "drama" it is necessary to consider both stage and page simultaneously and to admit all the potential difficulties, both theoretical and practical, that this implies for the scholar and editor.[30] As much as my argument is committed to recognizing the enduring qualities of the play *text,* in other words—its language and the interpretive potential of its "materiality," as Margreta de Grazia and Peter Stallybrass have described it in a seminal essay—I am equally concerned with the limitations of this text, with what it can only gesture at but never reveal. If the transfer from stage to print ultimately makes possible a more familiar and more modern spatial sensibility, moments in the early modern play-text such as that of the storm also produce spatial confusion, rupture, tensions, faultlines: seams in the spatial fabric which are accentuated because the conventional stage solutions are no longer present. Editorial attempts to defuse the undecidability of these moments—whether through the use of location directions (which hypostatize the space of fiction) or a reconstructed *refusal* to use them (which hypostatize the space of the stage)—inevitably foreclose the capacity of these scenes to make available to us a moment in which concepts of "space" and "place" were becoming dialectically inseparable from one another but still retained a measure of independence. They offer a space of process and linear movement more than property or reified and measurable entity, of potential more than extension and boundary.

Considering the play from the axis of both page and stage thus forces us to make finer conceptual distinctions in our discussions about space and to recognize a more precise and varied range of space*s* operating in the drama's different modes of existence. Here the question of "form" emerges as one that is indispensable to a literary, theoretical, or historical analysis of space but one that is nevertheless in desperate need of redefinition. This is because the principle of "form" is always both a principle of specificity and a mode of historical appearance. In a literal way the "form" of a play is not the ideal object of New Criticism but the physical shape of the play when printed and extended across the page, with its title bars, rules, margins, and binding. The "form" of a performance is more difficult: it is a series of forces and movements that coalesce into a recognizable thing; in this it is a *dialectical* "form" more like Marx's use of the term in *Capital,* for instance, or for that matter Aristotle's. How do the particular exigencies and material conditions of a theater performance differ from a play-book, and what different understandings of space do these contingencies—these "forms"—make possible? How are we to describe or explain a historical change in any single spatial domain if we do not observe some principle of form—indeed, inasmuch as "form" itself is a spatial concept, if we do not confront it directly?

Finally, *King Lear* suggests the importance of distinguishing between our use of "space" as an abstract category for analysis—a usage that tends to bracket, temporarily, the question of historical development—and the historically specific meanings that such words and their concepts might have had in other periods and cultures. The former usage allows us to move beyond the largely formal concerns I have been exploring in this essay and directly to a broader cultural investigation; the latter ensures that the object of this investigation will remain specific to the sixteenth and seventeenth centuries.[31] It would be intriguing to consider, for instance, how the spatial distinctions operating on the early modern open stage could themselves be aligned with a variety of current theoretical paradigms: in this view onstage and offstage space might be correlated with (for example) conscious and unconscious, or discursive and non- or extra-discursive, and thus might begin to operate as a conceptual model for thinking through how some strands of early modern culture become explicit while others remain occluded or structurally "invisible." It is surely significant, for instance, that the heterogeneous, unfamiliar "space" that appears in the storm scenes is also the point of articulation for a radical critique of power, justice, kingship, normative sexual systems, and other early modern conventions.[32] Assimilating the "nothing" of these scenes to a later, post-Newtonian "absolute space" or Kantian *a priori* is at the very least anachronistic; perhaps the term "space" itself even becomes insufficient in these cases, in that it inevitably implies these subsequent ideas. But to reimagine the scenes according to these later notions is also to foreclose the radical potential of their "nothing" and to appropriate it for more conventional ideological uses, reconceiving it as "emptiness" that can be owned or bequeathed (space as property), invaded (the space of the nation and the threat of France), or filled with subjective content (the space of humanism and literary history as it has traditionally been understood). To imagine *King Lear* "without the heath" is to begin to displace, in a small way, this subsequent conceptual history and to delineate the analytic potential of the stage that lies beneath it.

Notes

I would like to thank Jeffrey Masten and Wendy Wall for their interest in this essay and for their thoughtful suggestions for revision, as well as the two anonymous readers for the journal who helped to clarify its argument. I am delighted to have the opportunity to thank Jean E. Howard, David Scott Kastan, Douglas Pfeiffer, and Rebecca L. Walkowitz for their many comments, readings, and conversations. Portions of the essay were presented at the 1997 Shakespeare Association of America meeting, and I am grateful to Lauren Shohet and Julian Yates for their efforts in organizing the seminar and to its members, especially Mary Thomas Crane and Graham Hammill, for their stimulating discussion and responses.

1. Bradley, 259. "In Shakespeare's dramas, owing to the absence of scenery from the Elizabethan stage, the question, so vexatious to editors, of the exact locality of a particular scene is usually unimportant and often unanswerable; but, as a rule, we know, broadly speaking, where the persons live and what their journeys are. The text makes this plain, for example, almost throughout *Hamlet, Othello* and *Macbeth*; and the imagination is therefore untroubled. But in *King Lear* the indications are so scanty that the reader's mind is left not seldom both vague and bewildered."

2. Compare L. C. Knights's discussion of the scene: "*Lear* . . . is a universal allegory. . . . In the scenes on the heath, for example, we do not merely listen to exchanges between persons whom, in the course of the play, we have got to know; we are caught up in a great and almost impersonal poem in which we hear certain voices which echo and counterpoint each other; all that they say is part of the tormented consciousness of Lear; and the consciousness of Lear is part of the consciousness of human kind" (92).

3. For all citations to Shakespeare I have decided to follow the *Norton Shakespeare: Based on the Oxford Edition,* for several reasons. To my mind the Norton's primary advantage is that it makes facing-page Folio and Quarto versions of the play easily accessible and thus facilitates comparison between them; it also reprints the ground-breaking Oxford text. I have thus chosen the Norton for ease of reference, since the other parallel text editions of *King Lear* edited by René Weis and Michael Warren, while indispensable, are not widely available. I have followed the Norton Folio (F) version as my copy-text, but provide separate citations for the Quarto (Q) where relevant. Citation from facsimile seems to me to promise more authenticity than it actually delivers: even Warren's meticulous facsimile, or Charlton Hinman's facsimile of the First Folio for Norton are ideal texts assembled from separate copies and thus seem to undercut the very gesture that would appeal to them. In cases where the difference between the Oxford text and Q or F seems particularly significant I have consulted Helge Kökeritz's facsimile edition of the Folio, since it reproduces a single copy, and the 1608 Quarto in the Huntington Library that Michael Allen and Kenneth Muir reproduce in their facsimile edition. The direction in question appears first at 3.1.0.1, then at 3.2.0.1, 3.4.3.1, 3.4.55.4, 3.4.90.1, and 3.4.145.1. The direction "Storm and tempest" has already appeared at 2.2.449.1. I will return to the significance of this recurrence in more detail in the argument that follows.

4. Frederick Flahiff has also noted the absence of any place designations in the play, including the "heath," and points out that Rowe's direction derives from Nahum Tate's seventeenth-century adaptation, where the location appears as "A Desert Heath." Flahiff goes on to read the play in terms of biblical flood imagery, comparing Lear's division of the kingdom to Noah's three-part division of the world in the Apocrypha. I have chosen to focus on Rowe's stage direction here because I think that it carries more significance than Tate's, not least because of the former's foundational role in the formation of an editorial apparatus for the Shakespeare canon.

5. Cf. Alan Dessen, who notes that "editors have imposed upon many, most, or all Elizabethan scenes a later sense of 'place' or locale . . . . Thanks to generations of editing and typography, modern readers have thereby been conditioned to expect placement of a given scene ('where' does it occur?), regardless of the fluidity or placelessness of the original context or the potential distortion in the question 'where?' " (84). See also G. E. Bentley's concise discussion of the "placeless" stage and eighteenth-century editorial convention (53–63).

6. These terms are already modern, but *some* categories must be used to open the discussion. Theoretical and critical work on the concepts of "place" and "space" is growing by the day, and I have limited myself here to those works which have been of immediate influence on my own argument. The disciplinary specificity of each should by no means be overlooked, since often a series of seemingly analogous statements are in fact speaking to a particular set of questions, terms, assumptions, and problems. Perhaps the most influential statement has been that of Michel de Certeau, from a poststructural anthropological standpoint (esp. 117); Yi-Fu Tuan also approaches the terms from within anthropology, with a particular emphasis on cognitive psychology and phenomenology. David Harvey organizes an entire section around the distinction; see 207–326, esp. 291–326. Although he does not formulate the opposition in these precise terms, James Elkins's discussion of the relation between object (or body) and space is relevant and includes a discussion of concepts of "space," which is admirable for its subtlety, breadth, and clarity; see esp. 22–29. The problem is one of the central concerns of Hubert Damisch, particularly in the way that he conceives of the relation between perspective and architectural forms; it is also crucial to William Ivens's distinction between the "eye" and the "hand," which I consider in more detail later in my essay. I draw also on Henri Lefebvre's seminal analysis of space, which I discuss further in note 14 below.

7. I draw this distinction for the purposes of argument and am setting aside the fact that our own historical accounts of the "early modern stage" must themselves always be in some sense fictions: they are a different type of fiction, and while the point is an important one it leads away from the specific analysis I am pursuing here. See Mullaney for an account of how the "historical" early modern theater was itself subject to complex discursive determinations; for the theater's "place" in our narratives of periodization see de Grazia, "World Pictures," esp. 13–21.

8. Most famously Granville-Barker; see also the studies cited in note 13 below.

9. My discussion of the scene is indebted to the articles by Stephen Orgel and Jonathan Goldberg, although the emphasis of their arguments is on the specific problem of *linguistic* representation and not on the representation of space per se; see also the two articles by Philip Armstrong. Sensitive readings of the scenes "stagey" qualities are provided by Janet Adelman, esp. 1–2, and Harry Levin, esp. 96–99. I draw also on Guillén.

10. "I would have broke mine eye-strings, cracked them, but / To look upon him till the diminution / Of space had pointed him sharp as my needle; / Nay, followed him till he had melted from / The smallness of a gnat to air, and then / Have turned mine eye and wept" (*Cymbeline* 13.17-22); "Sit down, and let us / Upon that point fix all our eyes, that point there. / Make a dumb silence till you fell a sudden sadness / Give us new souls" (Beaumont and Fletcher, *The Maid's Tragedy* 2.2.79-82).

11. "[T]he phrase 'perspective space' is a Janus figure, half Renaissance and half modern. The Renaissance artists had no conceptual equivalent for our term *space,* and when they juxtaposed *prospettiva* and *spazio* (or *perspectiva* and *spatium*), they usually had something decidedly scholastic or humanistic in mind. The Renaissance painters made perspective pictures without the benefit of a concept of space . . . . artists and writers thought first of objects and second of what we call perspective space or fictive space" (Elkins 14-15).

12. Ivens 5; see also Wittkower, "Brunelleschi" 127: "Now the term *proporzionale* used by Alberti in connection with similar triangles is the adjective of *proporzionalità* ('proportion-ality') which, in Renaissance usage, is the most comprehensive notion expressing relations. Ratio involves the comparison of one magnitude with another, proportion that of one ratio with another and *proporzionalità* that of one proportion with another."

13. Orgel 556-57; Goldberg, *passim*. On the conventions of the open stage, see Dessen; Bentley; Styan; Beckerman; and Gurr 172-211.

14. Lefebvre's distinctions admit of a certain co-implication and even confusion, and they are best approached, I think, as suggestive general outlines rather than exact analytic categories. A "representation of space" may be understood as a graphic form, of which maps and plans are examples, that takes "space" in all its abstraction as the object of representation. "Representational spaces" are those specific spaces that are encountered in imaginative forms such as drama, narrative, or painting but also those spaces that take on symbolic or ideological qualities in discourses of all types (the stocks, the "heath," the "hollow of a tree" [2.2.159], the hovel, might be examples from *King Lear*); these may be thought of as equivalent to "place." Lefebvre uses "spatial practice" (the third category in this particular triad) to describe the material, historical set of behaviors and patterns by which space is used, created, and destroyed in daily life. Of more immediate relevance are his comments on the space of the theater: "To the question of whether such a space is a representation of space or a representational space, the answer must be neither—and both. Theatrical space certainly implies a *representation of space*—scenic space—corresponding to a particular *conception* of space (that of the classical drama, say—or the Elizabethan, or the Italian.) The *representational space,* mediated yet directly experienced, which infuses the work and the moment, is established as such through the dramatic action itself" (188).

15. Cf. Vérin, esp. 19-42; also Parker, esp. 43-48.

16. See Colie 220-72, who discusses the paradox of "nothing" and "something" in rela-tion to debates over Creation and the existence of a vacuum; Colie deals specifically with *Lear* on 461-81 (esp. 470-75). Her focus on Traherne and Milton gives her discussion a firm theological and seventeenth-century emphasis and thus operates with a conception of space later than that which emerges in *King Lear.* Grant's "Place and Space" provides an accessible discussion of the larger philosophical context; this article includes informa-tion that is more fully developed in his 1981 book. Max Jammer also offers a detailed

philosophical and scientific overview of spatial thinking. On Shakespeare's use of "nothing" in particular see Tayler, whose interest lies in the significance of the verbal patterns which are organized around the term and in the relationship between negation and epistemology in a quasi-psychoanalytic framework; he does not consider the term's associations with early modern physics or scientific theory. Jorgensen cites a wide range of references to the term; readers may also wish to consult Kastan 117-119, and the essays by Burckhardt and Wilburn.

17. Greg, *Dramatic Documents* 1: 208; cf. Stone 111: "It is well known that in Elizabethan theatrical parlance the stage was 'out' or 'without' and the tiring-house 'in' or 'within,' though a spectator would most naturally take the opposite view."

18. Greg, *Dramatic Documents* 1: 1-11, 70-171; the seven surviving platts are reproduced in facsimile in vol 2.

19. Aristotle, in contrast to the Greek atomists, rejected any notion of a "void" and offered no concept of "space" in the familiar, modern sense as a homogeneous, extended medium unoccupied by a body: such a concept was inconceivable for him, since he maintained that the dimensions of a body and the "place" that contained that body were identical. For Aristotle, who could conceptualize only a series of ever-larger, containing "places," the notion of an extended, empty "space" of pure dimension would be absurd, since this space would itself by definition be a body and collide or "interpenetrate" with the other bodies that putatively occupied it. See Grant, *Much Ado* 5-8 and *passim*; Jammer, *passim*.

20. Grant, *Much Ado, passim*, esp. 11-13, 117-21, 182-255.

21. Q2, printed in the shop of William Jaggard in 1619 (one of the so-called "Pavier Quartos" and perhaps part of an early attempt at a volume of collected works) essentially reproduces Q1 and for this reason I have omitted it from my discussion. For the text of Q1 scholars have proposed memorial reconstruction, either by two actors (typically those playing Goneril and Regan) or by the entire group on provincial tour; shorthand transmissions by a member of the audience; surreptitious glances at a prompt-book; and, more recently, autograph foul papers. F, traced through copies of either Q1 or, as is now thought, Q2 annotated with any number of prompt-books or other manuscript copies, departs from Q1 in ways that have been taken to suggest either deliberate theatrical or authorial revision or a combination of both. Jay L. Halio provides a concise discussion of the major points in his introduction to his edition of the play, esp. 58-81 and 265-89; see also the essays surveying the debates on this subject, along with a bibliography of its major statements, collected in Taylor and Warren.

22. See the discussions of the problem in Greg, *Shakespeare First Folio* 143-45, and Greg, *Dramatic Documents* 1: 79-81, 206-07, 210-13; Chambers 1: 118, 123-24, 199-201; Snuggs, esp. 35-51; and Jewkes. The work of T. W. Baldwin, while indispensable, should be used carefully.

23. Inter-act music was a convention of the hall theaters as early as 1604 (as evidenced by Marston's *Malcontent*), and after the occupancy of the Blackfriars theater by the King's Men in 1609 the practice seems to have spread to the Globe and the other amphitheaters. See Chambers 1: 200; Snuggs 37-45.

24. This is true even of skillful dramatic analyses such as that by Mark Rose, which includes an exposition of *King Lear*'s "scenic" or emblematic staging but argues finally that an awareness of theatrical convention alone is insufficient to account for Shakespeare's approach

to dramatic structure. Rose describes a space of symmetry and stasis somewhat different from the unfolding, performative space I am concerned with here.

25. Cf. Anderson.

26. Theobald, "Preface," in Smith 59.

27. Capell 1: 25; stage directions from 9: 3, 14, 19, 20.

28. I should perhaps emphasize again that I am making this distinction on the basis of the formatting characteristics contributed by act and scene divisions (the space of the page) and not on the basis of copy, since recent discussion of F's copy has emphasized its proximity to performance, and some have even preferred it on that account as a later, revised version of the play. See Jewkes 185–86, and Stone 100–112.

29. See Blayney, esp. 89–150, and Hinman, *Printing and Proofreading* 1, 47–51 and *passim*. Both of the spatial sensibilities I am describing obviously operated simultaneously during the period of 1608 to 1623, even if the overall historical movement during the seventeenth century and beyond is toward the "readerly" space of the Folio. Several features of both texts suggest that the period was in fact one of *transition* in spatial thinking. We see this first in the Folio's very inconsistency in dividing plays into acts and scenes (nineteen plays fully divided, including *Lear* [three imperfectly]; eleven into acts alone [two imperfectly]; and six not at all [they indicate *Actus primus Scena* (or *Scœna*) *prima* only]). Even more intriguingly, while Okes actually *printed* the Quarto using *seriatim* methods, an analysis of type and watermarks by Peter Blayney (96–100) indicates that Okes knew in advance exactly how much paper the entire job would require. Considered from the bibliographic unit of the sheet or page, therefore, Q reflects a *seriatim* spatial practice, but when considered *as a total book* it reflects a spatial understanding more typical of casting-off.

30. Dessen (22–27) has pointed out that the needs of theatrical historians and conventional editors are the inverse of one another: for the study of performance, texts that bear evidence of staging—the more revisions the better—are of primary importance, while texts with no direct connection to the stage are of no particular interest. When the critical goal is not composition but the conditions of play production, the entire range of texts produced in this process— so-called "foul papers," scribal copy, plot summaries, prompt-books, and all printed Quartos, "bad" or otherwise, in addition to the Folio—serve as potentially authoritative sources.

31. See, for instance, the recent works by Orlin, Ziegler, and Wilson.

32. Cf. Halpern's recent reading of the play in terms of property and an economics of *dépense,* and de Grazia, "Ideology of Superfluous Things."

Works Cited

Adelman, Janet. "Introduction." *Twentieth-Century Interpretations of* King Lear: *A Collection of Critical Essays.* Ed. Janet Adelman. Englewood Cliffs, NJ: Prentice-Hall, 1978. 1–21.

Anderson, Benedict. *Imagined Communities.* New York: Verso, 1991.

Armstrong, Philip. "Spheres of Influence: Cartography and the Gaze in Shakespearean Tragedy and History." *Shakespeare Studies* 23 (1995): 39–70.

———. "Uncanny Spectacles: Psychoanalysis and the Texts of *King Lear.*" *Textual Practice* 8 (1994): 414–34.

Baldwin, T. W. *On Act and Scene Division in the Shakespeare First Folio.* Carbondale: Southern Illinois, UP, 1965.

————. *Shakespeare's Five-Act Structure.* Urbana: U of Illinois P, 1947.

Beaumont, Francis, and John Fletcher. *The Maid's Tragedy.* Ed. Howard B. Norland. Lincoln: U of Nebraska P, 1968.

Beckerman, Bernard. *Shakespeare at the Globe, 1599-1609.* New York: Macmillan, 1962.

Bentley, Gerald Eades. *Shakespeare and His Theatre.* Lincoln: U of Nebraska P, 1964.

Blayney, Peter W. M. *The Texts of* King Lear *and Their Origins,* Vol. 1. Cambridge: Cambridge UP, 1982.

Bradley, A. C. *Shakespearean Tragedy.* New York: St. Martin's, 1960.

Burckhardt, Sigurd. *Shakespearean Meanings.* Princeton: Princeton UP, 1966. 237-59.

Certeau, Michel de. *The Practice of Everyday Life.* Trans. Steven Rendall. Berkeley: U of California P, 1984.

Chambers, E. K. *William Shakespeare.* 2 vols. Oxford: Clarendon, 1930.

Colie, Rosalie. *Paradoxia Epidemica: The Renaissance Tradition of Paradox.* Princeton: Princeton UP, 1966.

Damisch, Hubert. *The Origin of Perspective.* Trans. John Goodman. Cambridge: MIT P, 1995.

de Grazia, Margreta. "The Ideology of Superfluous Things: *King Lear* as Period Piece." De Grazia et al. 17-42.

————. "World Pictures, Modern Periods, and the Early Stage." *A New History of Early English Drama.* Eds. John D. Cox and David Scott Kastan. New York: Columbia UP, 1997. 1-21.

de Grazia, Margreta, and Peter Stallybrass. "The Materiality of the Shakespearean Text." *Shakespeare Quarterly* 44 (1993): 255-83.

de Grazia, Margreta, Maureen Quilligan, and Peter Stallybrass, eds. *Subject and Object in Renaissance Culture.* Cambridge: Cambridge UP, 1996.

Dessen, Alan. *Elizabethan Stage Directions and Modern Interpreters.* Cambridge: Cambridge UP, 1984.

Elkins, James. *The Poetics of Perspective.* Ithaca: Cornell UP, 1994.

Flahiff, Frederick. "Lear's Map." *Cahiers Elisabethains* 30 (1986): 17-33.

Goldberg, Jonathan. "Perspectives: Dover Cliff and the Conditions of Representation." *Poetics Today* 5 (1984): 537-48.

Grant, Edward. *Much Ado about Nothing: Theories of Space and Vacuum from the Middle Ages to the Scientific Revolution.* Cambridge: Cambridge UP, 1981.

————. "Place and Space in Medieval Physical Thought." *Motion and Time, Space and Matter.* Eds. Peter K. Machamer and Robert G. Turnbull. Columbus: Ohio State UP, 1976. 137-67.

Granville-Barker, Harley. *Prefaces to Shakespeare.* London: Batsford, 1930. Repr. 1978.

Greg, W. W. *Dramatic Documents from the Elizabethan Playhouses: Stage Plots, Actors Parts, Prompt Books.* 2 vols. Oxford: Clarendon, 1931. Vol. 1 (Commentary) and 2 (Facsimiles).

————. *The Shakespeare First Folio.* Oxford: Clarendon, 1955.

Guillén, Claudio. *Literature as System: Essays toward the Theory of Literary History.* Princeton: Princeton UP, 1971. 283-371.

Gurr, Andrew. *The Shakespearean Stage, 1574-1642.* Cambridge: Cambridge UP, 1992. 172-211.

Halpern, Richard. "*Historica Passio: King Lear*'s Fall into Feudalism." *The Poetics of Primitive Accumulation: English Renaissance Culture and the Genealogy of Capital.* Ithaca: Cornell UP, 1991. 215–69.

Harvey, David. *Justice, Nature and the Geography of Difference.* Cambridge: Blackwell, 1996.

Hinman, Charlton. *The Printing and the Proofreading of the First Folio of Shakespeare.* 2 vols. Oxford: Clarendon, 1963.

Ivens, William M., Jr. *Art and Geometry: A Study in Space Intuitions.* New York: Dover, 1946.

Jammer, Max. *Concepts of Space.* Cambridge: Harvard UP, 1954.

Jewkes, Wilfred T. *Act Division in Elizabethan and Jacobean Plays, 1583–1616.* Hamden, CT: Shoe String, 1958.

Jorgensen, Paul A. *Redeeming Shakespeare's Words.* Berkeley: U of California P, 1962. 22–42.

Kastan, David Scott. *Shakespeare and the Shapes of Time.* Hanover: UP of New England, 1982.

Knights, L. C. *Some Shakespearean Themes.* Stanford: Stanford UP, 1959.

Lamb, Charles. "On the Tragedies of Shakespeare, Considered with Reference to Their Fitness for Stage Representation." 1811. *The Works of Charles and Mary Lamb.* Ed. E. V. Lucas. 7 vols. London: Methuen, 1903.

Lefebvre, Henri. *The Production of Space.* Trans. Donald Nicholson-Smith. Cambridge: Blackwell, 1991.

Levin, Harry. "The Heights and the Depths." *More Talking about Shakespeare.* Ed. John Garrett. London: Longmans, 1959. 87–103.

Mullaney, Steven. *The Place of the Stage: License, Play and Power in Renaissance England.* Chicago: U of Chicago P, 1988.

Orgel, Stephen. "Shakespeare Imagines a Theater." *Poetics Today* 5 (1984): 549–61.

Orlin, Lena Cowen. " 'The Causes and Reasons' of all Artificial Things' in the Elizabethan Domestic Environment." *Medieval and Renaissance Drama in England* 7 (1995): 19–75.

———. *Private Matters in Public Culture in Post-Reformation England.* Ithaca: Cornell UP, 1994.

Parker, Patricia. "Rude Mechanicals." De Grazia et al. 43–82.

Rose, Mark. *Shakespearean Design.* Cambridge: Harvard UP, 1972.

Shakespeare, William. *The Complete King Lear, 1608–1623.* Ed. Michael Warren. Berkeley: U of California P, 1989.

———. *King Lear.* Ed. René Weis. London: Longman, 1993.

———. *Mr. William Shakespeare His Comedies, Histories and Tragedies.* Ed. Edward Capell. 10 vols. London, 1767–68. New York: AMS, 1968.

———. *Mr. William Shakespeare's Comedies, Histories, & Tragedies.* Ed. Helge Kökeritz. New Haven: Yale UP, 1954.

———. *The Norton Facsimile: The First Folio of Shakespeare.* Ed. Charlton Hinman. New York: Norton, 1968.

———. *The Norton Shakespeare: Based on the Oxford Edition.* Eds. Stephen Greenblatt, Walter Cohen, Jean E. Howard, and Katherine Eisaman Maus. New York: Norton, 1997.

———. *The Parallel King Lear, 1608–1623.* Ed. Michael Warren. Berkeley: U of California P, 1989.

————. *Shakespeare's Plays in Quarto.* Eds. Michael J. B. Allen and Kenneth Muir. Berkeley: U of California P, 1981.

————. *The Tragedy of King Lear.* Ed. Jay L. Halio. Cambridge: Cambridge UP, 1992.

————. *The Works of Shakespear.* Ed. Alexander Pope. London, 1725.

————. *The Works of Shakespeare.* Ed. Lewis Theobald. London, 1740.

Smith, E. Nichol, ed. *Eighteenth-Century Essays on Shakespeare.* Oxford: Clarendon, 1963.

Snuggs, Henry L. *Shakespeare and Five Acts: Studies in a Dramatic Convention.* New York: Vantage, 1960.

Stone, P. W. K. *The Textual History of* King Lear. London: Scolar, 1980.

Styan, J. L. *Shakespeare's Stagecraft.* Cambridge: Cambridge UP, 1967.

Tayler, Edward W. "*King Lear* and Negation." *ELR* 20 (1990): 17-39.

Taylor, Gary, and Michael Warren, eds. *The Division of the Kingdoms: Shakespeare's Two Versions of* King Lear. Oxford: Clarendon, 1983.

Tuan, Yi-Fu. *Space and Place: The Perspective of Experience.* Minneapolis: U of Minnesota P, 1977.

Vérin, Hélène. *La gloire des ingénieurs: L'intelligence technique du XVIe au XVIIIe siècle.* Paris: Albin Michel, 1993.

Wilburn, David. "Shakespeare's Nothing." *Representing Shakespeare: New Psychoanalytic Essays.* Eds. Murray M. Schwartz and Coppélia Kahn. Baltimore: Johns Hopkins UP, 1980. 244-63.

Wilson, Eric. "Plagues, Fairs, and Street Cries: Sounding Out Society and Space in Early Modern London." *Modern Language Studies* 25 (1995): 1-42.

Wittkower, Rudolf. "Brunelleschi and 'Proportion in Perspective.'" *Idea and Image: Studies in the Italian Renaissance.* London: Thames & Hudson, 1978. 125-35.

Ziegler, Georgianna. "My Lady's Chamber: Female Space, Female Chastity in Shakespeare." *Textual Practice* 4 (1990): 73-90.

Gynocentric London Spaces: (Re)Locating Masterless Women in Early Stuart Drama

FIONA MCNEILL

I. Staging the Masterless Woman: Looking Away from *The Roaring Girl*

MIDDLETON AND Dekker's *The Roaring Girl* brings to center stage an unusual female character: the single unmastered woman. Moll Cutpurse, the play's protagonist, has aroused much critical inquiry into her status as both a crossdresser and a permanently unmarried woman.[1] Moll does indeed challenge the marital strictures of mastery: she refuses to be governed by a husband; masters any man who tries to rule her; claims the state of permanent "maidenhood";[2] and performs no mastered labor yet has easy access to money. We may thus be tempted to think of Moll as self-mastered, but we can do so only if we forget that the movements of permanently unmarried women in early modern England were extremely circumscribed by the law. Self-mastery might suggest sexual and economic independence, but it does not describe the legal status of a woman repeatedly pursued by the law both in the play and in real life. Not just a crossdresser and a maid, Moll is also a pickpocket who is further suspected as a prostitute, bawd, and vagrant. More than an appealing literary trope,[3] mastery is a legally binding status that affords protection to servants, employees, and wives; it cannot define women living outside the mastered household economy. A criminally active unmastered woman, Moll might instead be considered, like her male counterparts, master*less*.

But who exactly were masterless women and where else might we find them? Some have found more Molls than one in the play; there is her namesake, Mary, who is soon to be mastered in marriage.[4] The play's characters themselves, however, offer a very different estimate: "Forseek all London from one end to t'ther, / More whores of that name than of any ten other" (2.2.154–55).[5] Moll's chief antagonist, a justice of the peace, reckons London's population of Marys—a common term for prostitute—at more than the sum of ten other names.[6] Worrying about one Moll prompts this judge to envision London as densely populated by many, and his fears are not unfounded; Moll's presence in the action signifies exponentially to generate a whole imaginary population of masterless women. The play's characters recite a litany of names: "common whore" (4.2.151); "whore i'th' suburbs" (2.1.304); "whore of clients all" (3.3.32-33); "whores in small ruffs" (5.1.344-45); "trug" (2.2.438);[7] "ramp" (3.3.7, 5.2.12);[8] "punk" (4.2.29); "drab" (3.3.61); "stale" (4.2.153);[9] "stale mutton" (3.2.183); "strumpet" (4.2.154); "oyster wench" (3.3.11); "old bawd" (4.2.171); "baggage" (3.3.56); and "sisters" (4.1.104). Living below the economic level necessary for marriageability, and not legally bound to a husband or marital household as a servant or wife, prostitutes were distinctly unmastered. Moreover, besides being the most common sexual insult of the period, "whore" labeled sexual deviation from marriage and activity outside the legitimate monetary economy of the household as criminal behavior. Like the term "masterless man," "whore" was a criminal category.[10] Unlike male masterlessness, however, prostitution was invariably figured as both economic and sexual deviation. The play's insistent whore-calling identifies the economic crimes of women with sexually deviant behavior, and female sexual deviance with economic criminality.

The play defines another population of profoundly unmastered women. Moll's demand to hear about a vagrant soldier's "doxy" elicits a catalogue of terms for female vagrants. The soldier tells her: "I have, by the solomon, a doxy that carries a kinchin mort in her slate at her back, besides my dell and my dainty wild dell" (5.1.161-63). Outnumbered by female companions four to one, this masterless man draws on four of the seven discrete categories of female vagrant defined by Thomas Harman's *Caveat . . . for Commen Cursetors,* an encyclopedic guide to vagrancy.[11] While most historians now use the term, "masterless men" to define the vagrants of early modern England, Moll conjures up a more feminine "commonwealth of rogues"(131-32).[12]

The criminal language of cant does seem uniquely designed to detect masterless women. Trapdoor uses Harman's terms to make fine distinctions between his companions. A "doxy" is an unmarried but sexually active female vagrant.[13] Tied to the doxy's back in a sheet is another generation of homeless female: a "kinchin mort" (161-62).[14] Accompanying the doxy and her child are two "dells"—which Harman (*Caveat* 107, 105) describes as a "young wench, able for generation, and not yet known or broken." At least two of these four females—the kinchin mort, and the "wild" dell—were even born into vagrancy (162-63).[15] As Valerie Traub has said of the terms "Maid, Wife, Widow, and Whore," Harman's categories define female vagrants "not merely by their biological sex, but by their sexual activity."[16] With their propensity to procreate outside the household, female vagrants constitute a threat to the future of mastery. Harman thus alerts his fellow justices to the possibility of streets and highways perpetually repopulated by masterless women. Female vagrants and prostitutes may remain entirely absent from the stage, (with the ambiguous exception of Moll) but they people its linguistic imaginary, making London into a "fantasmatic" cityscape filled with masterless women.[17] Reproduced at the imaginary peripheries of the stage by the relentless repetition of names, this mob of masterless women threatens at any moment to surface in the action. Echoing Harman's *Caveat,* this play generates a veritable "plague of fantasies" about masterless women.[18]

While marriageable "maids" are everywhere in plays, Frances Dolan suggests that persistently unmarried women are harder to find: "Representations of this threatening space outside the patriarchal household are especially infrequent in the drama, which rarely focuses on women who are neither married nor to be married."[19] *The Roaring Girl,* Dolan suggests, counts only among the "remarkable exceptions." A female cutpurse is an unusual choice of protagonist, but even within the play Moll is less of an exception than a hyperbolically composite signifier; the action of *The Roaring Girl* may revolve around a very patriarchal household—the home of a justice of the peace—but Moll's movements repeatedly distract our attention away from the marital center of the city household toward the much more marginal urban spaces where unmarried characters reside. Few plays outside *The Roaring Girl* may make such women their central characters—although I suspect that outside of Shakespearean and more canonical plays we might find otherwise—but this play reminds us that we may find them in significant numbers, if we look in the right ways.

Locating the many female types from the lower orders that made it onto the stage in the first two decades of the seventeenth century requires a revision of class-bound readings that look only for marriageability. Turning from *The Roaring Girl* to the other, virtually unexamined, Moll Cutpurse play of the same year—Nathan Field's *Amends for Ladies*—we immediately notice that, like *The Roaring Girl,* Field's play is ostensibly concerned with securing a marriage. It begins with three characters known simply as Maid, Wife, and Widow debating the happiest "state" for a woman to inhabit (1.1.1), and ends in a spectacularly satirical marriage scene that leaves all three as wives. Yet most of Field's characters occupy a different "state" entirely. Even after the triple wedding of the final scene, at least fourteen of the twenty-four characters that actually appear remain unmarried. While most of the unmarried characters in *The Roaring Girl* remain imaginary, *Amends for Ladies* populates its action with real, persistently unmarried city residents—a page, a male servant, a maidservant, a wine-drawer, a boy, four roaring boys, a gallant, a poor cousin, and a seducer of wives. Moll's appearance suspends the main plot to focus much of the action on minor characters, forcing us to ask what we mean when we say that city comedy is always about "money and marriage."[20] If we stop worrying about those situated fully within the marriage economy and instead locate the many characters with limited access to marriage and money, we find that unmarriageability abounds.

The persistence of minor and imaginary unmarried women in the plays questions our own ideas about where women might fit into early modern households; sometimes they just don't fit. Early modern drama does with some regularity position women in the threatening space outside the patri- archal household. Street and threshold scenes make up much of the drama, especially of "city" plays, where the abstract and empty space of the stage is translated into specific London places, and the dialogue names many city streets, buildings, parishes, and institutions.[21] The rapidly expanding city at this time comprised a very new kind of urban space in England, a space where people, houses, sewers, and new kinds of industry and household were tightly packed together, creating much insecurity for city households and a more urgent need to maintain order in the streets.[22] Poor women often spilled over into the nooks and crannies between city households or inhabited new kinds of household entirely. These two city comedies construct an imaginary map of early Stuart London's "complex city geog- raphy,"[23] figuring overpopulation, dense urbanization, underemployment, criminal activity, and unmarriageability as distinctly female problems.

Looking for more single women in these ways, we begin to notice a multitude of women who until recently have remained at the peripheries of our critical consciousness. Far from conforming to the ideal of the marital household governed by a properly sexed husband and wife, the volatile thresholds, chambers, streets, households, and suburbs inhabited by unmarried women in these plays vividly emblematize governmental anxieties about the failure of mastery in securing erotic and economic order in both the household and the city. I find no neat taxonomic divisions between mastery and masterlessness, between the inside and outside of the household, between private and public space, between the City and suburbs, or between master- and subplot; such critical conventions solidify borders that in the drama remain distinctly blurred. Instead, I find everywhere in these plays a fascination with femininity at the margins.

I begin at the center of the patriarchal household and proceed, through a range of city households and streets, to the extreme peripheries of the City. But before we can understand how poor women fit into the outer limits of the city economy, we need to examine how they might fit into the urban household. Most women in early modern England lived not at the center of households as wives, Dolan reminds us, but "on the margins of households" as unmarried women.[24] This reminder leads me to interrogate more closely the margins of early modern drama. I place my focus squarely on persistently unmarried women, as they serve urban households, cross the social and geographic margins of the City, appear as relatively minor characters, feature in short and apparently incidental scenes, and figure as fantasmatic inhabitants of spaces imagined or gestured toward but not depicted; the marginal spaces of early modern drama are precisely where we might find unmarried, unmastered, and masterless women.

II. Unmastered Maids at the Threshold

The Roaring Girl begins by defining the margins of a patriarchal household. In what E. K. Chambers calls a "threshold scene," a footman greets a sempster at the axis between the interior of the Justice's house and the exterior city street.[25] This exchange between two minor characters on the doorstep of a key city household may seem incidental, yet this moment establishes from the outset the precarious margins between mastered service and unmastered labor. Here we see a mastered servant welcome into the household a woman who is apparently (she is really a marriageable maid in disguise) from outside of mastery. Spinsters and sempsters, as Merry Wiesner has shown, were the product of a "process of removing women from the workplace" in urban industrialization.[26] Like London spinsters, who spun wool on a piecework basis, sempsters were predominantly unmarried outworkers living not in mastered households, but in low-income tenement lodgings.[27] Performing piecework in order to avoid becoming dangerously "idle," a category used in proclamations and trials to distinguish the criminal poor, spinsters and sempsters thus embodied the lowest level of legitimate unmastered employment for a poor "maid" in London before she became criminally masterless.

This sempster has to negotiate her potential shift between lawful industry and criminal idleness. Spinsters appear frequently in the Middlesex Sessions Rolls, as they shifted into criminality. Moll herself reminds us of the provisional identity of "sempster," when she corrects a gallant that she is not, like "distressed needlewomen and trade-fallen wives," to be mistaken for a prostitute (3.1.95). Shifting between selling sewing and selling sexual services door to door, sempsters oscillated between legal employment and criminal activity. Poor unmarried and economically unmarriageable women shifted between jobs and residences at the very bottom of London's labor market, sometimes upwardly mobile into marital households as maidservants, sometimes subsisting outside the marital household entirely as outworkers, and sometimes downwardly mobile into the illegitimate city economy to become vagrants, prostitutes, or thieves.

Neatfoot the footman, himself a mastered servant concerned with meeting his young master's needs, misrecognizes the sempster as a prostitute. Interpreting her discussion of "falling bands" as a disguised offer of sexual service for sale, he congratulates himself that he can now serve his master "a daintier bit or modicum than any lay upon his trencher at dinner" (1.1.13–14).

He offers the sempster plenty of such work, inviting her to join the servants in their quarters before moving on to the young master:

If you please to venture your modesty in the hall amongst a curl-pated company of rude serving-men, and take such as they can set before you, you shall be most seriously and ingeniously welcome. (1.1.17–21)

Undaunted by the sempster's refusal of his sexual innuendo, Neatfoot presumes she may wish a different kind of sexual venture: "Or will you vouchsafe to kiss the lip of a cup of rich Orleans in the buttery amongst our waiting-women?" (23–24). Suggesting that both the men and maidservants in their respective single-sex parts of the household would welcome the sexual services of a prostitute, this footman gives us a very different impression of an orderly city household; the Justice's servants may be legally mastered, but they are sexually active outside of marriage.

The footman construes the buttery as a sexualized female chamber laden with gynoerotic possibilities. Inviting verbal puns on "butt" and "butter," the buttery was a place for servants' recreation in poetry and plays. Perhaps prompted by the idea of unmarried but sexually mature maids secluded in all-female activity, the conjunction of the term "maid" with the activity of "making butter" formed a common euphemism for specifically female masturbation. In *Gesta Grayorum,* a wanton dairymaid is caught "makinge butter with her tayle,"[28] and later in *The Roaring Girl,* the image comes up again, when Trapdoor, imagining sexual intercourse with Moll, threatens to serve her "as country wenches beat cream, till butter comes" (1.2.228). These maidservants, however, are not making butter, but "kissing the lip of a cup." Still imagining the buttery as a gynoerotic chamber, the footman offers a clever euphemism for cunnilingus. He compounds several images for female anatomy into one; "cup" was a frequent euphemism for the vagina or its fluids,[29] so to "kiss" the "lip" of such a "cup" requires little deciphering. Even the syrupy liquor that the maidservants sip—a rich Orleans—is made of plums, a popular image for the ripe pudenda.[30] In this first scene, the footman compels the audience to imagine a house that holds a buttery where maidservants are sexually active among themselves.

The Justice's buttery here is a gynocentric space populated by poor but mastered maids who are engaged in erotic communion. Precariously close to the sexual and economic situation of the sempster, maidservants were hired and fired, particularly in early Stuart London, with great frequency. A pregnant maidservant lost her status as both maid and servant, and parish records show pregnant former maidservants as vagrants in their numbers.[31] For mastered maids and sempsters alike, heterosexual activity meant downward mobility. Gynoerotic activity thus provided a safe form of sex for poor women. This particular buttery is figured as a distinctly gyno*erotic* enclosure where maidservants "make butter"—or masturbate among themselves—in eroticized industry that avoids reproductive sexuality while reproducing the patriarchal household.

I call the buttery a gynocentric space in order to insist on the presence of exclusively female enclosures in the ideological work done by early Stuart drama, as Valerie Traub has done with early modern travel narratives.[32] These spaces are gynocentric not simply because they involve only women, but because they invariably enclose erotic behavior, economic activity, and dangerous conversation among women. Imaginary spaces, as Julia Kristeva says of the production of abjected space, are the focus of great cultural anxiety and production: "It is thus not lack of cleanliness or health that causes abjection but what disturbs identity, system, order. What does not respect borders, positions, rules. The in-between, the ambiguous, the composite."[33] Far from idealized spaces where women are fully autonomous and independent, the gynocentric gaps inhabited by unmarried women in these plays are figured as the locus of deformation of identity, disruption of systems of gender meaning, and deviation from erotic order in which borders, positions, and rules are disregarded.

The "threshold" scene serves as an ideal prompt for the linguistic config-uration of fantasmatic chambers located further within the house. The play may open with a marital household, but rather than representing the center of this household—a husband and wife—it uses the threshold to gesture toward the borders of the household occupied by the eroticized labor of servants. While all theatrical space is fantasmatic in its representation of imagined, not real, action and events, the dialogue can vividly evoke characters, spaces, and action situated offstage. Indeed, the fantasmatic dimension is a powerful and necessary device of early modern drama. Like the buttery, few of the female spaces I consider are depicted; instead, gynocentric scenes more often constitute the imaginary borders of the action. The absence of such talked-about gynocentric spaces and behaviors on stage only more effectively prompts speculations about what such scenes might look like. Fantasmatic space is evoked by vividly graphic dialogue that arouses the speculative work of the spectator's fantasy. Such powerfully hallucinatory spaces, as Kristeva and Slavoj Žižek suggest, tell us much about the productive work of ideology. Each space is differently gynocentric, but a certain pattern emerges: the household walls and City walls are imagined as possible sites of dissolution. Imbued with female incontinence, gynocentric gaps in the City are imagined as a threat to mastery, the organizing principle behind the household, the City, and social control.

I examine the in-between, ambiguous, and composite female interstices of city plays, and the particular configurations of gender, sexual, and eco-nomic status represented as occupying each space. Eve Sedgwick's work on the closet as an enclosed imaginary space has prompted much inter-rogation of sexualized spaces,[34] eliciting queer cartographies and anthro-pologies of the disposition of sexuality in urban, geographic, architectural, and (anti)domestic space.[35] Lee Edelman's interrogation of the discursive configuration of the "tearoom"—or public urinal—by the U.S. government, law, and media as a "notorious hangout for deviates" leads us to consider the reciprocal process by which certain sexual behaviors are figured as deviant or safe because of the kind of places they inhabit, and certain spaces are imagined as always enclosing criminalized sexuality.[36] Esther Newton's crucial demographic microanalysis of the distinctions between female spaces on a small, particularized geographic scale authorizes and even demands a critical attentiveness to the micro-organization of sexual space.[37] Rather than encouraging an ability to categorize neatly the spaces inhabited by early modern female homoeroticism as either always "relatively unthreatening" or always a "frightening specter,"[38] Newton teaches us a valuable lesson about the social organization of space and the assimilation, or not, of specific "lesbian" identities in different early modern spaces. Recent work has insisted on the centrality of homoeroticism to the structures of the early modern household. While Valerie Traub detects an "absence" of concern with female homoeroticism in the period, Mario DiGangi proposes that some female homoeroticism was construed as threatening. I find places in these plays both where female homoeroticism is figured as relatively safe, and where it constitutes a hallucinatory fantasm; safe or dangerous, these gynocentric gaps always contain women at the margins of mastery.

III. Mastering Maidservants: The Widow's Closet

More than *The Roaring Girl, Amends for Ladies* pursues the sexual habits of the unmarriageable in and around the household. Many of Field's characters are maids, since they are unmarried; however, as their names suggest—Whorebang, Botts, Well-tri'd, Bould, Subtle, Ingen (suggestive of "ingle"), and Princox—they demonstrate extensive sexual knowledge. Being a "maid," male or female, was not so much about virginity or lack of sexual experience as it was an economic signifier of marital eligibility.[39] Field's unmarried characters know a lot about sex, and Field concerns himself most with what unmarried women know. Moll appears only once in the play, but she generates an extraordinary exchange of female sexual knowledge outside of marriage that is only further intensified in the all-female scene at the exact center of the play.[40]

Amends for Ladies actually stages an eroticized all-female chamber. In the Widow's closet, two unmarried women—the Widow and her newly hired maidservant, Princox—prepare for bed. This scene realizes the kind of unmastered erotic conversation and action between two unmarried women in an enclosed chamber that is more usually restricted to fantas-matic scenes. While the house has no master, this chamber too is still part of a relatively secure patriarchal household; the status of "widow" was secured by ecclesiastical laws concerned with preserving wills and matrimonial property, and in city spaces widows were far more likely to be the sole executrix of their husband's property.[41] Under the protection of a permanently absent master, both women remain unmastered. No longer a wife, the Widow now masters her own house. She is not married, hires her own maid, and is economically and erotically independent of a husband. The maidservant, too, has no master; instead, she is newly mastered by a mistress. A widow's household thus represents a very distinct economic and erotic space in early modern London.[42]

In this vision of gynocentric closet talk, when women are left unmastered and with free time to themselves, they seem to talk dirty. When Princox tells the Widow it is "Bed-time an't please you Madame" (3.3.2), the mention of bed prompts the Widow to urge her maid, "Come, undress me, would God had made me / a man" (4-5).[43] The Widow's wish, in the context of the maid's physical act of unlacing her clothing, suggests that she wants to be a man because she is being undressed by a woman. When pressed, however, the Widow coyly offers a more mundane gloss: "Because I would have beene in bed as soone / as they, wee are so long unpinning and unlacing" (7-8). She playfully offers and then denies erotic suggestions in her conversation, seeming to test her new maid's skill in serving her.

With this first mention of "unpinning and unlacing," the only modern editor of the play, William Peery, is in no doubt of the eroticism in this chamber scene. He comments tersely: "The entire scene seems quite salacious. I do not attempt to gloss all the puns."[44] Later in the same scene, however, he interjects once more when the maid handles her mistress's clothing. The Widow expresses surprise at the excessive groping necessary to undo her: "Ha'st not done yet? Thou art an old fumbler / I perceive" (46-47). Sensing that she is being handled unusually, she says, "me thinkes thou doest not do things like a woman" (47). Peery refrains from explaining "fumbling," a fairly obvious euphemism for sexual groping;[45] yet just in case the reader misses the gynoerotic humor here, he cannot resist adding an "explanatory" note to remind us that "the theatrical effectiveness of this scene is understood to be great when we remember that Bould's being a man has not necessarily yet been revealed to the audience."[46] While we discover only later that Princox is a man in disguise, Peery proposes that we see the maidservant as a woman throughout this scene. Surprisingly, this 1950s editor publishing at the height of McCarthyism risks pointing out that the humor of this scene relies on the recognition of female homosexuality.[47]

Playing a maidservant is a difficult task for a man to perform without being discovered. The job of a "chamber" maid employed to work in the mistress's closet was a position of intimate bodily service,[48] in which she dressed and bathed the mistress as well as handling her mistress's chamberpot. Such a position, like that of the more widely discussed gentleman of the stool, made the chambermaid "privy" to the mistress's intimate conversation.

Princox is quick to pick up on the intimacies of her new job and to insist on the erotic girls' talk: "Yet many of us Madame are quickly undone / sometime, but heerein we have the advantage of men, / though they can be a bed sooner than we, i'ts[*sic*] / a great while when they are a bed e're they can get up" (9-12). Princox counters her mistress's wish to be a man by asserting that women can be "quickly undone." Understanding "unpinning" and "unlacing" as metaphors for female orgasm, Princox reminds her mistress that "we" women can be quickly "undone"—accomplish sexual satisfaction—while men take a while to get an erection. This maidservant lives up to the sexual maturity implicit in her name, which suggests "too soon ripe."[49]

As the two women saturate their conversation with the exchange of contemporary erotic information, the maidservant worries about her "maiden" status. When the Widow welcomes Princox's suggestion as a critique of male sexual prowess, Princox plays innocent: "Oh God Madame, how meane you that" (15). She proclaims her reluctance to talk about sexual subjects: "I hope / you know, ill things taken into a Gentlewoman's eares, are the quick corrupters of maiden modesty" (15-17). As an unmarried "maiden" in service, her future marriageability depends on her erotic status: "I would be / loath to continue in any service unfit for my virgin / estate" (17-19). Keen to maintain her marriageability, Princox claims a "virgin" ignorance of sexual knowledge; she cannot continue in employment that impugns her virgin status. Talk of being "undone" raises for her the dangers of bastardy, the crime of unmarried pregnancy.[50] Playing the role of a maidservant, Bould seems well aware of the precarious "estate" he occupies.

Princox worries about the lack of mastery in this chamber: "though wit be a wanton Madame: yet / I beseech your Lady-ship for your owne

credit and mine, / let the bridle of judgement be alwaies in the chaps
of / it to give it head, or restraine it, according as time and / place shall be
convenient" (24–28). Echoing strictures on bridling the female tongue for
fear of not only scolding but also lustful talk, Princox does not, however,
refuse the Widow's terms; she merely reminds her mistress to talk like this
only in a conveniently enclosed space at an appropriately idle moment like
bedtime.[51] Lustful tongues can be unbridled among unmarried women in
the safety of an all-female closet; they are not so fit for women on the market
as "maids" to unleash in the company of men. Secure that the hemmed-in
space of the Widow's closet is safe for sexual talk, this maid warns her
mistress that the status of Widow and Maid are not so secure.

The Widow asserts herself as master of this house by testing her new
maid's erotic intelligence: "Precise and learned *Princox,* dost not thou / goe
to *Black-fryers*" (29–30). Maids do not come away sexually ignorant from
Blackfriars, the playhouse that stages Field's own plays, where the dialogue
provides a more than adequate erotic education for women. Princox does
attend Blackfriars, "Most frequently madame, unworthy vessell / that I am
to partake or retaine any of the delicious dew, / that is there distilled" (31–
33). Parodying strictures on virginity, this maid claims to be an "unworthy
vessell" eager to be filled with the "delicious" liquid knowledge of erotic
plays.[52] The Widow and her maid engage in precisely the kind of unruly
erotic dialogue staged by playhouses for the consumption of ladies and
their maids.

Seeking to establish her maid's competence in erotic dialogue, the
Widow challenges Princox's maidenhood: "But why shouldst thou aske
me what I meant / e'ne now, I tell thee there's nothing utter'd that carries
a / double sence, one good, one bad" (34–36). Both women show off a
formidable facility for erotic euphemism. Complimenting the Widow with
"You speake most intelligently Madame," the maid reassures her mistress
of her mastery over her in sexual conversation.

Having established her erotic mastery, the mistress proposes a sexual
act. Hearing Princox's offer to "let my good will stand for the action," she
interprets "stand" as suggesting an erect sexual organ (54), and responds
dexterously as if to an offer to satisfy her sexually:

Let thy good will stand for the action? If good will would doe it, there's many a
Ladie in this Land would be content with her old Lord, and thou canst not be a
burthen to me, without thou lie upon me, and that were preposterous in thy sexe.
(55–59)

The Widow teases Princox about whether she can or cannot satisfy her mistress sexually: "and thou canst not / be a burthen to me, without thou lie upon me." She suggests both that her maid cannot satisfy her, and that she can satisfy her only if she lies on top of her. Yet the Widow tells Princox that such an act "were preposterous in thy sexe"; she asserts the feasibility of a sexual act, but labels it as deviant or preposterous—literally backwards or inverted—behavior.

Undeterred by the "preposterousness" of her maid lying *on top of* her, the Widow asks Princox to lie *with* her: "Prin- / cox, I would have you lie with me, I doe not love to lie / alone" (113–15). Asking, "Are you cleane skind?" she interrogates Princox about venereal diseases, and then hurries her into bed: "Well, well, come to bed, and wee'le talke / further of all these matters" (117, 125). The verbal foreplay of this entire scene gestures toward the shared bed, but still defers the action in the bed to the fantasmatic space beyond the end of the scene. The spectator can only imagine the kind of erotic acts that might ensue once they get there.

The space of the lady's closet is more usually interpreted as a sacrosanct private female space, an enclosed chamber secure from prying eyes and away from the business of the household.[53] Yet here the "private" space of the closet emerges as the site of intimate industry performed by the maid for her mistress. Indeed, this maid's trial employment comes to an abrupt termination when the Widow discovers in bed that her maid is a man in disguise. Such a maid would not serve for the intimacies of her mistress's bed.

Displacing the bed offstage into fantasmatic space, this scene nevertheless leaves us in no less doubt that even the early modern bed was not a "private" space outside of service and mastery; rather, it too was inhabited by relations of economic reproduction.[54] Here the Widow's closet is the subject of a very publicly inscribed—or staged—spectacle of female homoeroticism.

IV. "Disorderly" Households: Taverns, Tenements, Brothels, and Playhouses

Field maps the Widow's house as a distinct city space that redefines mastery from the inside, then he turns to a cluster of households defined by their departure from mastery. Courts defined many London households as criminally deviant spaces, as did the London ecclesiastical court that charged Moll Cutpurse with frequenting "all or most of the disorderly and licentious places in this Cittie as namely she hath usually in the habite of a man resorted to alehowses Tavernes (Tobacco shops) and also to play howses there to see plaies and pryses."[55] Such households deviated sharply from the hierarchized heteroerotic structure prescribed by marriage manuals, law, and custom. The term "household" alone did not always mean order.

The action shifts to one such disorderly household. At a tavern, a raucous company of "roaring boies" arrives and orders tobacco from the wine-drawer who works there (3.4). Rather than seeing unmarried men here, we are encouraged to see the tavern as a single-sex space populated by boys. The roarers are all specifically "boys," not men, and are renowned for their evasion of mastered labor. Even the wine-drawer himself is a boy employed in a tavern that is also a tobacco shop, one of early Stuart London's controversial "new industries."[56] A new kind of disorderly city household, this tavern attracts unmastered and masterless boys in their numbers.

But is the tavern an enclosed household, or does it spill out onto the street? Worrying over the location of this scene, the play's editor designates it as a chamber—not a threshold or street—scene. Yet, urging the roarers to hush, the wine-drawer suggests that this is a more borderline city space: "I beseech you consider where you / are, *Turne-bole* streete, a civil place; do not disturbe a / number a poore Gentlewomen, Master *Whoore-bang,* / Ma: *Bots,* Ma: *Teare-chops,* and Ma: *Spill-bloud,* the / Watch are abroad" (11–15). Calling Turnbull Street "a civil place," the drawer points out they inhabit a very publicly policed street. Any unmastered boys found in this particular street, a notorious criminal sanctuary aggressively patrolled by armed men, would be of great interest to the Watch.[57] On Turnbull Street seventy-five taverns inhabit a kind of permeable or intermediate household; here there can be no illusion of private space.

Not just in any tavern scene, these boys occupy a "definite and familiar" city space.[58] More than just a topical reference, Turnbull—also known as Turnmill—Street and its most notorious tavern, Pict-hatch, appear frequently in plays and poetry as a means of mapping London's sexual and criminal demography.[59] Far from an expansively open street, Turnmill was rapidly urbanized with densely packed makeshift tenements between 1550 and 1676 (see figs. 1 and 2). By 1610, Turnmill was already a very enclosed criminal sanctuary whose "internal topography" consisted of "labyrinths

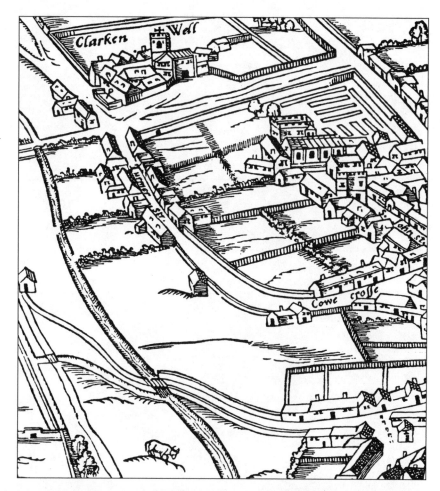

FIGURE 1.   Section of the map *Civitas Londinum* produced between 1561 and 1570, showing Turnmill Street as surrounded by fields in Tudor London. Anonymous (attributed to Ralph Agas). By permission of the Guildhall Library.

of tightly packed hidden lanes and alleys with buildings that provided 'double, triple, even quadruple entrances and exits.' "[60] Its tightly packed tenements housed a warren of taverns, brothels, and inns. The Middlesex Sessions Rolls paint a lively demographic of this disorderly street; Turnmill seems to be a predominantly female street whose women—spinsters, widows, prostitutes, and thieves—often used married aliases to escape the

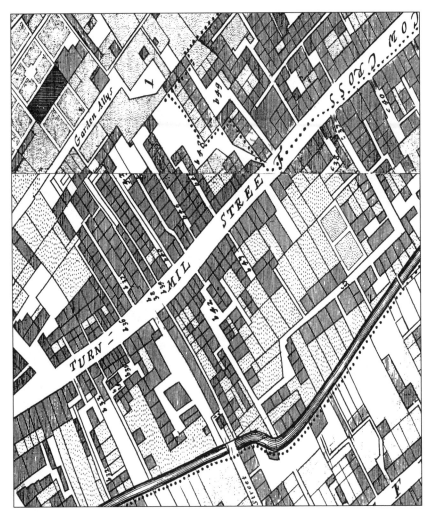

FIGURE 2. This section from John Ogilby and William Morgan's 1676 *New and Accurate Map of the City of London* shows the rapid and dense urbanization of Turnmill Street. By permission of the Guildhall Library.

law.[61] This may be a street, but its hemmed-in maze of buildings brought unmarried bodies dangerously together. Field represents this notorious tavern street as a distinctly gender-disorderly trouble-spot in London.

Turnmill's intricate internal topography represents a notoriously masterless enclosure. Its closely built tenements not only attracted the unmarriageable, but also housed them. Tenement households, erected or converted outside the City walls to evade City building restrictions, satisfied London's rapidly growing market in low-income single housing. Teeming with masterless servants, transient laborers, outworkers, poor families, children, thieves, and prostitutes, tenements were distinctly decentered from the City's marital economy.

Such an innovation in masterless housing was a constant source of governmental insecurity.[62] A 1603 royal proclamation "against Inmates and multitudes of dwellers in strait Roomes and places in and about the Citie of London" condemned tenement developments.[63] Prohibiting the translation of orderly, hierarchized households into disordered clusters of chambers, this proclamation was concerned not with the production of too much city housing, but with "the great confluence and accesse of excessive numbers of idle, indigent, dissolute and dangerous persons, And the pestering of many of them in small and strait roomes and inhabitations." Not just unmarriageable, the persons crammed into tenements were considered dangerously "idle," a term that appears everywhere in early modern legislation on poverty, vagrancy, and criminality, to signal criminalized poverty. Unlike mastered households that operated according to a hierarchical schematization of unmarried labor and spaces, tenements housed a confluence of idle bodies in a non-hierarchical confusion of narrow rooms. Distinctly masterless households, tenements were imagined by this royal proclamation as "pestered" with sexually and economically diseased bodies that may invade the City walls.

Field situates this tavern against the fantasmatic background of an excessive number of sexually deviant chambers. When the wine-drawer warns the boys not to disturb "a number a poor Gentle-women," the roarers are quick to understand what kind of women he means, adding "And a whoore" to their order (3.4.22). The action may be restricted to a tavern, but this all-male space is walled in by brothels. The brothel chamber is imagined as an exotic sexual destination. When the roarers order a whore along with their wine, the wine-drawer exclaims, "Why what d'ee thinke of me, am I an Infidell, / a Turke, a Pagan, a Sarazin" (23–24). Alluding to contemporary descriptions of Islamic seraglios or harems, the drawer claims that he is not master of a house of women. As Valerie Traub suggests of the "all-female" space of the seraglio in early modern travel narratives, the London brothel here represents a hallucinatory enclosure inhabited by desire between women.[64] Indeed, for Londoners "seraglio" was synonymous with "brothel."[65] The London seraglio, however, relocated the fantasm of female homoerotic desire from a distant uncharted territory to the uncharted borders of the city, figuring the brothel household as an "infidel" or deviant structure.

The law imagined the brothel as an archetypally deviant household; in fact, in the Middlesex Sessions "disorderly household" and "house of incontinencie" were used exclusively as synonyms for "brothel."[66] Understanding such houses as harboring disorderly and excessive bodily exchange, the Middlesex Sessions indicted a gentleman found in "a house of incontinencie with one Mary Harrison a woman of verie lewd conversation."[67] Like the Widow's closet, brothel chambers enclosed erotic exchange or "conversation," in the sense that the "conversation" signified in this period both sexual intercourse and an intimate proximity of habitation.[68] Associated with idleness, brothels nevertheless enclosed the industry of masterless "conversation."

Even more than the Widow's house, Bess Turnup's is a very particular female-owned and female-centered city space. Owned by a woman, this building houses "tenement prostitutes who led a group existence centered around a landlady's pennyrent lodging."[69] The erotic and economic center of this household is unequivocally all female. However, far from being an ideal situation, this gynocentric household is still masterless; it houses poor women who barely subsist on their criminal activity. Turnmill's prostitutes were among the poorest—and cheapest—in the city, only a precarious step above the double masterlessness of vagrant prostitutes who lived and worked in the streets.[70] The Widow's house and Bess Turnup's house offer enticing images of gynocentric households, both of which are extremely inscribed by the law; but widows' households were protected by the law, while brothels were imagined as criminal enclosures.

Demonstrating a thorough familiarity with London's deviant demography, the wine-drawer refers to yet another new kind of city household: "I have been at Besse Turn- / ups, and she sweares all the Gentlewomen went to see a / Play at the Fortune, and are not come in yet, and she / beleeves they sup with the Players" (25). The prostitutes move through the city

FIGURE 3. Vagrants being carted through the streets. A woodcut from the title page of Thomas Harman's *A caveat for commen cursetors vulgarely called vagabones* (1567, STC 12787). By permission of the Bodleian Library.

streets from the gynocentric economy of a tenement brothel to the homosocial economy of a playhouse. Even naming the playhouse where *The Roaring Girl* was performed in 1610, simultaneously with *Amends for Ladies,* the drawer implies that the women are gone to a Moll Cutpurse play, but have chosen the competition. Prostitute playgoers would certainly appreciate a play about a masterless woman pursued by the law who escapes punishment; but prostitutes were as likely to visit a playhouse for business as for pleasure. Indeed, staying on to "sup" with the all-male company of players, these women seem to solicit business not only from playgoers, but also from the players. Field reminds us that the playhouse was not just a theater; it was a new kind of suburban household where players worked and lived in a predominantly homosocial economy.

Amends for Ladies brings tavern, brothel, tenement, and players' households into close association. The Fortune playhouse, which catered to the lowest orders, was a distinctly "disorderly" city house. In the same year as the performance of these two female cutpurse plays, the Fortune attracted "great multitudes" of prostitutes and cutpurses, according to the Middlesex Sessions.[71] Not entirely masterless households, playhouses had "housekeepers" who ran the predominantly male household economy. Indeed, the extremely recent phenomenon of the play-*house* afforded to the traveling "company" of players greater legal and financial protection from masterlessness—a term often leveled at players. Nonetheless, playhouses entertained "men and women mixt together, / fair ones with foul" (*Roaring Girl* 1.2.17–18), each occupying a different position of criminality or mastery—players, prostitutes, cutpurses, apprentices, maidservants, and gentle men and women. At the volatile threshold of the City, where tenements and brothels often comprised part of players' shareholdings as well as the playhouse itself, players and prostitutes "converse" closely with one another at the margins between mastery and masterlessness.[72] Playhouses and brothels were dangerous not simply because they were single-sex households; unlike the patriarchal households reproduced by single-sex industry, the playhouse and brothel industries housed idleness.

The lure of the brothel suburbs beyond the City walls is a powerful force; both *The Roaring Girl* and *Amends for Ladies* threaten permanently to displace their action into a suburban brothel, the ultimate site of female masterlessness. The dialogue in *The Roaring Girl* gestures repeatedly to the outlying suburbs as a sexually disorderly destination. At Lincoln's Inn Fields, a criminally disorderly open space just outside the City's jurisdiction, a coachman beckons a gallant further into the suburbs with the temptation that "all your famous whores have gone to Ware" (3.1.18–19), a brothel suburb where the sexual adventurers go in *Northward Ho!* The gallant, himself familiar with where to find criminally deviant women, tells Moll that she will fit right in where they are going: at Brentford's Three Pigeons inn, a suburb destination in *Westward Ho!,* he expects to find other masterless women in men's clothes (3.1.56–57).[73] Pointing to all points northward, westward, eastward, and southward,[74] the dialogue devotes incredible energy to surrounding the City walls with brothel suburbs.

For such detailed attention to the space outside the City walls and jurisdiction, we might call these plays "suburb" rather than "city" comedies. Field, Middleton, and Dekker map the City's suburbs as sites of dissolution—the threshold between proper city space and the outlying developments where sexual and social order threaten to dissolve entirely. *The Roaring Girl* not only mapped criminal spaces; it was performed in a criminal territory. Conveniently located for criminal playgoers, the Fortune stood in a notorious refuge just beyond the City walls; St. Giles in Cripplegate Without was a vagrant parish covered with "spotted tents, huts and hovels and portable accommodation."[75] The vagrants and criminals who lived there inhabited structures that were, like playhouses themselves, precariously temporary.[76] Having lost their prestigious hall playhouse within the City, the downwardly mobile Blackfriars "boys" were now performing *Amends for Ladies* in a tattered and leaky hall in Whitefriars,[77] an outlying area dangerously filled with tenements.[78] The tavern, brothel, tenement, and theater were extremely permeable household structures where masterlessness was most likely to invade the city street. Staged inside very real masterless enclosures, both plays demonstrate a comprehensive erudition in London's criminal spaces.

Defining the shifting threshold of the City, tenement streets were a threatening new urban space outside the household. In labyrinthine streets like Turnmill, household "conversation" often shifted into street-roaring, and roaring easily escalated into riot.[79] Turnmill did have a reputation for riot; just five years before this play, over two hundred "unknown disturbers of the peace" had "assembled riotously and in warlike array, and armed with stones and clubbes," wrecked houses in Turnmill, then moved on to do the same in nearby Cowcross Lane. In such a profusion of secret alleys and exits, it is not surprising that only five men were apprehended and "whipt at a cartes tayle,"[80] a punishment often assigned to the masterless (see

fig. 3). Culminating in a swordfight, Field [...] of "the Humor of Roaring" as beginning [...] street fight.[81] More dangerous than Lon[...] were its increasingly masterless streets. [...]

Field imagines the rioters in Turnmi[...] considered Turnmill as a distinctly fe[...] on prostitution, the Middlesex Sessions [...] lewd and loose percons dwelling nee[...] London within the County of Midd. in [...] who keepe common and notorious b[...] entertaine divers impudent and infamo[...] as a suburban brothel street encroachi[...] the Middlesex Sessions inadvertently cr[...] female sexuality besieging the skirts of [...]

V. The Breach: A C[...]

So what would happen if the many m[...] begin to roar and spill into London's st[...] possibility was already imaginable. In [...] it is poor unmarried women, not appr[...] and give the call to arms.[83] Neither *[...] Girl* goes as far as staging crowds of [...] Fletcher's play of the same year, a plag[...] the City of London. More usually kn[...] *The Taming of the Shrew,* Fletcher's [...] ways I suggest; the dialogue insists [...] of unmastered women, and then a f[...] characters stages a whole insurrecti[...]

Fletcher envisions London as a city [...] riageability, where poor women no [...] but declare war on the institution [...] by no means presents a fantastical [...] rural poor had long been rioting ov[...] and women were heavily involved [...] women's shift into criminal "idlene[...] tion, and from there to "roaring" a[...] bellion. At least thirteen anti-enclo[...]

women, and several were "entirely feminine protests." On Shrove Tuesday 1604, sixteen women rioted on a manor in Lancashire, and in a 1607 riot in Derby organized around the watchwords "arise and take a poke-pudding in thy hand," a woman called "Captain Dorothy" led thirty-seven women wielding knives and stones against men who were putting up fences. There were more all-female enclosure riots in 1609; in 1630 too, a poor widow planned a riot against a grain dealer, and "poor ragged women" elsewhere congregated to riot over grain.[86] The large population of poor unmarried women in London had not yet begun to organize, but if "entirely feminine" protest was already happening in rural areas, it was more than likely to occur in London.[87]

In this extraordinarily satirical inversion of *The Taming of the Shrew,* unmarried maids master men in a war, or "prize" fight, between the sexes. Abandoning Shakespeare's displacement of the action to distant Padua, Fletcher places what Lynda Boose calls the "single woman in a married culture" squarely in the heart of the city of London.[88] By depicting a London where "women are in Insurrection" (2.1.52), however, Fletcher compels his audience to envisage what might happen if single women, like apprentices, rioted against their "abjected position in the social order."[89]

Petruchio's second wife, Maria, resists the heteroerotic mastery of marriage far more efficiently than Shakespeare's Kate. Before Petruchio can consummate the marriage, she expels him from his home and walls herself up with two other maids. Together, the three mis-gendered women—Maria and Livia, Petronius's "masculine daughters," and their cousin, Bianca, plan a maiden insurrection. Like "Captain Dorothy" of the Derbyshire riot, Bianca is "Commander-in-Chief" of this female rebellion. Recruiting other maids to the rebellion, Maria urges: "Adieu all tendernesse, I dare continue; Maides that are made of feares and modest blushes, view me, and love example" (1.2.76–78). Agreeing to "weare breeches," the symbols of masculine mastery (146), these maids use this watchword to turn Petruchio's mastered home into a rebelliously unconquered maiden household.

The male householders immediately assume a siege mentality. Like Shakespeare's Henry V at Harfleur, they see the "barricadoed" household as a virgin fortress: "She's fortified for ever" (1.3.71). Identifying Petruchio's persistently maiden wife with the permanently fortified household, Petruchio and his friend Sophocles follow the erotic convention of warfare in which a fortress is imagined as a virgin female body to be besieged and ultimately conquered (1.3.48).[90] Assuming the role of English soldiers, they call the women "the most authentique Rebels, next *Tyrone,* / I ever read of" (212–13).[91] Using the language of colonial warfare familiar to English military strategists, the men compare the women to the Irish chief Tyrone.[92] Next to Irish rebellion, these maids pose the most real threat to established English authority.

Calling this fortified maid "an Anagram of an ill wife" (1.3.123), Petruchio and Sophocles proceed to anatomize a mirror-inversion of the chastity, silence, and obedience of an idealized female anatomy. The fortress is far from silent. Petruchio, "the first breaker of wilde women" of Shakespeare's play, can now only exclaim: "What are they mad? have we another Bedlam?" (1.3.75). He imagines the female fortress as a second Bedlam, a London house of detention for the insane, and peoples this new Bedlam with wild women. When he asks, "She doth not talke I hope?" Sophocles asserts, "Oh terribly, extreamly fearfull, the noise at London- / bridge is nothing neere her" (1.3.75–78). This woman is as wild as Bedlam, and rowdier than a crowd at London Bridge. Bemused, Petruchio asks himself, "How got she tongue?" Instead of allowing her tongue to be bridled, Maria has taken charge of it.

Female tongues master this fortress, but the men seem to fear the roaring of another female member.[93] Surveying the opening—or breach—into this fortress, Jacques, a servant, notices "two as / desparate tongues planted behind it as ere yet battered: they stand / upon their honours, and will not give up without strange com- / position Ile assure you; marching away with their Pieces cockt, / and Bullets in their mouthes will not satisfie them" (1.3.56–60). Not just fearing the female tongue as a "symbolic relocation of the male organ," Jacques imagines yet another erect female member "standing" in for phallic mastery.[94] He figures the "breach" of this fortress as policed by tribade maids with their "Pieces cockt."

Yet another orifice of this female body is violently unmastered. Sophocles reports that he approached the door and "would have broke in by force; when suddenly / a water-worke flew from the window with such violence that had / I not duck'd quickly like a Fryer, *coetera quis nescit*?" (86–88). More than a little leaky, this virgin fortress literally expels urine in outright revolt. Like his namesake, the Greek philosopher whose wife, Xantippe, was "a favorite *exemplum* of the formal misogynist" in the early modern controversy over women, this Sophocles gets female urine on his head.[95] Any man who tests the threshold of this house will be "beaten off with shame" (84).

In a masculinized version of the leaky female body, the maids' urine is made to follow a distinct arc that can be aimed at a target. Indeed, some contemporary anatomists believed, as Gail Paster has noted, that virgins could urinate like men: "The virgin's pissing is more unfettered and clear than any other women, because her womb pipe is still tight and narrow, all the way to the outside end, which makes her piss straight and far, in rather the same manner as a man."[96] This maiden fortress, like its maiden soldiers, pisses like a man.

Even the female chamberpot is feared as a powerful substitute for the male organ: "The chamber's / nothing but a meere *Ostend,* in every window Pewter cannons / mounted, you'l quickly finde with what they are charg'd sir" (86-90). The women have mounted "Pewter cannons"—or chamberpots—at every window of this gynocentric interior. The female chamber is a "discursive site" where feminine unruliness is often staged; however, as Paster reminds us, the female chamberpot too can signify gendered dissolution.[97]

Surveying the fortress's openings, Petruchio grows increasingly concerned about the insecurity of the men's position in this street scene. Like the contemporary anatomists who mapped women's internal pipes, Petruchio is anxious to contain the labyrinth of secret female passages that lead through the city: "Ile see all passages stopt, but those about 'em: if the / good women of the Towne dare succour 'em, we shall have warres / indeed" (282-84). Fearing that the "good"—a common appellation for poor women—city women will support the female fortress, he orders London's complex internal confusion of alleys and passageways to be blocked.[98]

To implement this starvation strategy, a messenger is "sent to lay / an imposition upon Sowse and Puddings, / Pasties and Penny Custards, that the women / May not releeve yon Rebels" (1.4.14-17). Imposing sanctions against the women in London's "housewife trades" of baking and victualling,[99] Petruchio worries about the poor women who performed such labor making their way through the city. Adding yet a new twist to his siege strategy, Petruchio promises to punish his wife by stopping up her own leaky passages: "She shall not know a stoole in ten moneths Gentlemen." He imagines feeding her "hard egges, till they brace her like a Drum" (30-32), and then beating her: "I would tabor her, / Till all the Legions that are crept into her, / Flew out with fire i'th tailes" (2.4.21-23). Petruchio will wage war on his wife's body until he has stopped up her incontinence.

In spite of the measures to blockade women's passageways, "newes" and "rumour" about this fortress of warlike maids travel swiftly through the city (1.4.31, 2.1.53). As the men prevaricate, they discover that female intelligence networks have already spread the news of a maiden war throughout the kingdom, and that a female countersiege is headed their way. Jacques warns them, "There are more women, marching hitherward, / In rescue of my Mistris, then ere turn'd taile / At Sturbridge Faire" (2.4.39-41). The male householders are urged to imagine an unimaginable multitude of women coming their way. This servant creates a vivid fantasmatic army of women, describing it as a plague or pestilence to be stamped out: "Arme, arme, out with your weapons, / For all the women in the Kingdom' on ye; / They swarm like waspes, and nothing can destroy 'em, / But stopping of their hive, and smothering of 'em." (2.4.34-37). In a re-schematization of the popular humanist emblem of the beehive as a perfectly hierarchized "feminine monarchie" supported by the compliant industry of its workers, these upstart women "swarm" idly and dangerously through the streets with a sting in their tails (see fig. 4).[100]

Reporting on these offstage women, Jacques vividly describes the army's leader as embodying deviant government. Heading the army is a tanner's wife who used her craft to flay her husband and make reins from his skin, thus violently bridling her husband and taking the reins in marriage. The industry of tanning, with dangerous chemicals that tanned the skin and polluted the water supply to the City, was banished to the suburbs.[101] Jacques imagines that dangerous industry has translated this suburban female anatomy into a monstrously unmastered wife: "her plackett / Lookes like the straights of Gibralter, still wider / Downe to the gulphe, all sunburnt Barbary / Lyes in her breech" (2.4.45-47). Using the pornographic rhetoric of discovery, Jacques applies a common trope of blackness—sunburn—to depict this woman's nether anatomy as tanned black. He describes her "breech"—here used to mean vagina—as a huge gulf that encompasses the entire region of Barbary, a geographically distant place habitually associated with monstrously "unnatural" sexual practices.[102] Jacques makes this Barbarous suburban "breech" represent, in Patricia Parker's term, an "ob-scene," or offstage, fantasy of a black tribade penetrating the female city of London.[103] In strikingly pejorative language Jacques describes this fantasmatically "obscene" woman as emblematic of the gendered threat to

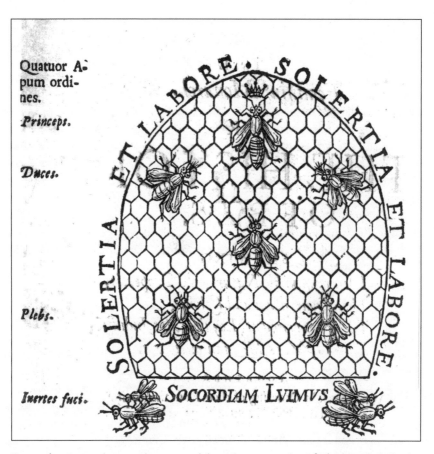

Quatuor A-
pum ordi-
nes.

Princeps.

Duces.

Plebs.

Inertes fuci.

SOLERTIA ET LABORE. SOLERTIA ET LABORE ET LABORE

SOCORDIAM LVIMVS

FIGURE 4. A woodcut on the verso of the title page to the 1634 edition of Charles Butler's *The Feminin' Monarchi', Or The Histori of Bee's*. This 1609 treatise on both beekeeping and feminine government depicts the beehive as a highly schematized emblem of the orderly segmentation of social classes (1634 edition, STC 4194). By permission of Columbia University Rare Book and Manuscript Library.

City government; the Barbarous black tribade here stands in for the English masterless woman who must somehow be "marked as 'other.' "[104]

Outside the fortress, the men can only imagine what government by such women might look like. Fortunately, they have Jacques to feed their imaginations: "They have got a stick of Fiddles, and they firke it / In wondrous waies" (2.6.36–37). Jacques is quick to imply that the women are celebrating their autonomy by "firking"—or "fiddling"—without men.[105] A popular euphemism for specifically female masturbation, "fiddling" was exploited to its full potential in *The Roaring Girl*'s puns about Moll fiddling with her instrument.[106] Like Moll, the women here usurp the masculine role of playing upon the fiddle. "Firke," too implies sexual activity; originally meaning a sword-thrust, it was a euphemism for penis and for thrusting sexual activity. Here referred to women, "firke" implies that the sexual activity in the fortress is not just masturbation, but phallic sexual acts between women. Jacques's assertion that they "have got a stick" and "firke it / In wondrous ways" suggests that the women have invented new and remarkable ways of thrusting a stick—possibly a dildo— across their instruments.[107] This maiden fortress houses an orgy of female masturbation and sexual congress. Jacques offers his masters a compelling orgiastic image of a whole army of women masturbating in an exclusively gynocentric space, a far more powerfully hallucinatory and negatively valenced eroticization of gynocentric space than those real or imagined in *The Roaring Girl* or *Amends for Ladies*. By painting a highly sexualized picture of rebelliously unmastered female space, Jacques makes female homoeroticism into an emblem of bad government.

Jacques's hallucinatory description of the all-female festivities makes female genitalia signify social and political disorder. Inverting Thomas Elyot's image of the man and woman dancing as a paradigm of both marital harmony and ideal government, Jacques imagines the tanner's wife dancing with a bawd inside the fortress: "the two grand Capitanos, / (They brought the Auxiliary Regiments) / Daunce with their coats tuckt up to their bare breeches, / And bid the Kingdom kisse 'em" (2.6.37–40). In a gesture of mastery, these women offer up their "bare breeches" to be kissed by the Kingdom. Refusing to define which breeches he means, Jacques exploits the productive confusion between "breach," a term for vagina, "breech," a name for the buttocks, "breach" as a vulnerable opening to the female fortress, and the plural "breeches," a kind of male clothing.[108] With this one word, he figures the tanner's wife and the bawd as displaying the

streets from the gynocentric economy of a tenement brothel to the homosocial economy of a playhouse. Even naming the playhouse where *The
Roaring Girl* was performed in 1610, simultaneously with *Amends for
Ladies,* the drawer implies that the women are gone to a Moll Cutpurse
play, but have chosen the competition. Prostitute playgoers would certainly
appreciate a play about a masterless woman pursued by the law who
escapes punishment; but prostitutes were as likely to visit a playhouse
for business as for pleasure. Indeed, staying on to "sup" with the all-male
company of players, these women seem to solicit business not only from
playgoers, but also from the players. Field reminds us that the playhouse
was not just a theater; it was a new kind of suburban household where
players worked and lived in a predominantly homosocial economy.

Amends for Ladies brings tavern, brothel, tenement, and players' households into close association. The Fortune playhouse, which catered to
the lowest orders, was a distinctly "disorderly" city house. In the same
year as the performance of these two female cutpurse plays, the Fortune
attracted "great multitudes" of prostitutes and cutpurses, according to the
Middlesex Sessions.[71] Not entirely masterless households, playhouses had
"housekeepers" who ran the predominantly male household economy.
Indeed, the extremely recent phenomenon of the play-*house* afforded to
the traveling "company" of players greater legal and financial protection
from masterlessness—a term often leveled at players. Nonetheless, playhouses entertained "men and women mixt together, / fair ones with foul"
(*Roaring Girl* 1.2.17–18), each occupying a different position of criminality or mastery—players, prostitutes, cutpurses, apprentices, maidservants,
and gentle men and women. At the volatile threshold of the City, where
tenements and brothels often comprised part of players' shareholdings
as well as the playhouse itself, players and prostitutes "converse" closely
with one another at the margins between mastery and masterlessness.[72]
Playhouses and brothels were dangerous not simply because they were
single-sex households; unlike the patriarchal households reproduced by
single-sex industry, the playhouse and brothel industries housed idleness.

The lure of the brothel suburbs beyond the City walls is a powerful force;
both *The Roaring Girl* and *Amends for Ladies* threaten permanently to
displace their action into a suburban brothel, the ultimate site of female
masterlessness. The dialogue in *The Roaring Girl* gestures repeatedly to
the outlying suburbs as a sexually disorderly destination. At Lincoln's Inn
Fields, a criminally disorderly open space just outside the City's jurisdiction,

a coachman beckons a gallant further into the suburbs with the temptation that "all your famous whores have gone to Ware" (3.1.18–19), a brothel suburb where the sexual adventurers go in *Northward Ho!* The gallant, himself familiar with where to find criminally deviant women, tells Moll that she will fit right in where they are going: at Brentford's Three Pigeons inn, a suburb destination in *Westward Ho!,* he expects to find other masterless women in men's clothes (3.1.56–57).[73] Pointing to all points northward, westward, eastward, and southward,[74] the dialogue devotes incredible energy to surrounding the City walls with brothel suburbs.

For such detailed attention to the space outside the City walls and jurisdiction, we might call these plays "suburb" rather than "city" comedies. Field, Middleton, and Dekker map the City's suburbs as sites of dissolution—the threshold between proper city space and the outlying developments where sexual and social order threaten to dissolve entirely. *The Roaring Girl* not only mapped criminal spaces; it was performed in a criminal territory. Conveniently located for criminal playgoers, the Fortune stood in a notorious refuge just beyond the City walls; St. Giles in Cripple-gate Without was a vagrant parish covered with "spotted tents, huts and hovels and portable accommodation."[75] The vagrants and criminals who lived there inhabited structures that were, like playhouses themselves, precariously temporary.[76] Having lost their prestigious hall playhouse within the City, the downwardly mobile Blackfriars "boys" were now performing *Amends for Ladies* in a tattered and leaky hall in Whitefriars,[77] an outlying area dangerously filled with tenements.[78] The tavern, brothel, tenement, and theater were extremely permeable household structures where masterlessness was most likely to invade the city street. Staged inside very real masterless enclosures, both plays demonstrate a comprehensive erudition in London's criminal spaces.

Defining the shifting threshold of the City, tenement streets were a threatening new urban space outside the household. In labyrinthine streets like Turnmill, household "conversation" often shifted into street-roaring, and roaring easily escalated into riot.[79] Turnmill did have a reputation for riot; just five years before this play, over two hundred "unknown disturbers of the peace" had "assembled riotously and in warlike array, and armed with stones and clubbes," wrecked houses in Turnmill, then moved on to do the same in nearby Cowcross Lane. In such a profusion of secret alleys and exits, it is not surprising that only five men were apprehended and "whipt at a cartes tayle,"[80] a punishment often assigned to the masterless (see fig. 3). Culminating in a swordfight, Field's tavern scene offers a definition of "the Humor of Roaring" as beginning with swaggering and ending in a street fight.[81] More dangerous than London's new masterless households were its increasingly masterless streets.

Field imagines the rioters in Turnmill Street as all male, but the law considered Turnmill as a distinctly feminine street. In a general ruling on prostitution, the Middlesex Sessions attempted to regulate "the many lewd and loose percons dwelling neere unto the skirts of the city of London within the County of Midd. in Turnemill Street and other places, who keepe common and notorious brothell houses and harboure and entertaine divers impudent and infamous queanes."[82] Singling out Turnmill as a suburban brothel street encroaching on the "skirts" of the City walls, the Middlesex Sessions inadvertently create a powerful image of disorderly female sexuality besieging the skirts of the City's maiden modesty.

V. The Breach: A Contested Border

So what would happen if the many masterless women in the suburbs did begin to roar and spill into London's streets in warlike array? In 1610 such a possibility was already imaginable. In John Fletcher's *The Woman's Prize,* it is poor unmarried women, not apprentices, who assemble in the streets and give the call to arms.[83] Neither *Amends for Ladies* nor *The Roaring Girl* goes as far as staging crowds of poor women in the cityscape, but in Fletcher's play of the same year, a plague of masterless women overwhelms the City of London. More usually known as a reworking of Shakespeare's *The Taming of the Shrew,* Fletcher's play stages masterless women in the ways I suggest; the dialogue insists on the imaginary presence of armies of unmastered women, and then a fleeting street scene with three minor characters stages a whole insurrection of masterless maids into London.

Fletcher envisions London as a city invaded by distinctly feminine unmarriageability, where poor women not only remain outside the household, but declare war on the institution of the mastered household itself. He by no means presents a fantastical vision of female riot in London.[84] The rural poor had long been rioting over land enclosure and grain shortage, and women were heavily involved in these riots.[85] In the country, poor women's shift into criminal "idleness" regularly led to disorderly conversation, and from there to "roaring" assemblies where women organized rebellion. At least thirteen anti-enclosure riots during James's reign involved

FIGURE 3. Vagrants being carted through the streets. A woodcut from the title page of Thomas Harman's *A caveat for commen cursetors vulgarely called vagabones* (1567, STC 12787). By permission of the Bodleian Library.

women, and several were "entirely feminine protests." On Shrove Tuesday 1604, sixteen women rioted on a manor in Lancashire, and in a 1607 riot in Derby organized around the watchwords "arise and take a poke-pudding in thy hand," a woman called "Captain Dorothy" led thirty-seven women wielding knives and stones against men who were putting up fences. There were more all-female enclosure riots in 1609; in 1630 too, a poor widow planned a riot against a grain dealer, and "poor ragged women" elsewhere congregated to riot over grain.[86] The large population of poor unmarried women in London had not yet begun to organize, but if "entirely feminine" protest was already happening in rural areas, it was more than likely to occur in London.[87]

In this extraordinarily satirical inversion of *The Taming of the Shrew,* unmarried maids master men in a war, or "prize" fight, between the sexes. Abandoning Shakespeare's displacement of the action to distant Padua, Fletcher places what Lynda Boose calls the "single woman in a married culture" squarely in the heart of the city of London.[88] By depicting a London where "women are in Insurrection" (2.1.52), however, Fletcher compels his audience to envisage what might happen if single women, like apprentices, rioted against their "abjected position in the social order."[89]

Petruchio's second wife, Maria, resists the heteroerotic mastery of marriage far more efficiently than Shakespeare's Kate. Before Petruchio can consummate the marriage, she expels him from his home and walls herself up with two other maids. Together, the three mis-gendered women—Maria and Livia, Petronius's "masculine daughters," and their cousin, Bianca, plan a maiden insurrection. Like "Captain Dorothy" of the Derbyshire riot, Bianca is "Commander-in-Chief" of this female rebellion. Recruiting other maids to the rebellion, Maria urges: "Adieu all tendernesse, I dare continue; Maides that are made of feares and modest blushes, view me, and love example" (1.2.76–78). Agreeing to "weare breeches," the symbols of masculine mastery (146), these maids use this watchword to turn Petruchio's mastered home into a rebelliously unconquered maiden household.

The male householders immediately assume a siege mentality. Like Shakespeare's Henry V at Harfleur, they see the "barricadoed" household as a virgin fortress: "She's fortified for ever" (1.3.71). Identifying Petruchio's persistently maiden wife with the permanently fortified household, Petruchio and his friend Sophocles follow the erotic convention of warfare in which a fortress is imagined as a virgin female body to be besieged and ultimately conquered (1.3.48).[90] Assuming the role of English soldiers, they call the women "the most authentique Rebels, next *Tyrone,* / I ever read of" (212–13).[91] Using the language of colonial warfare familiar to English military strategists, the men compare the women to the Irish chief Tyrone.[92] Next to Irish rebellion, these maids pose the most real threat to established English authority.

Calling this fortified maid "an Anagram of an ill wife" (1.3.123), Petruchio and Sophocles proceed to anatomize a mirror-inversion of the chastity, silence, and obedience of an idealized female anatomy. The fortress is far from silent. Petruchio, "the first breaker of wilde women" of Shakespeare's play, can now only exclaim: "What are they mad? have we another Bedlam?" (1.3.75). He imagines the female fortress as a second Bedlam, a London house of detention for the insane, and peoples this new Bedlam with wild women. When he asks, "She doth not talke I hope?" Sophocles asserts, "Oh terribly, extreamly fearfull, the noise at London- / bridge is nothing neere her" (1.3.75-78). This woman is as wild as Bedlam, and rowdier than a crowd at London Bridge. Bemused, Petruchio asks himself, "How got she tongue?" Instead of allowing her tongue to be bridled, Maria has taken charge of it.

Female tongues master this fortress, but the men seem to fear the roaring of another female member.[93] Surveying the opening—or breach—into this fortress, Jacques, a servant, notices "two as / desparate tongues planted behind it as ere yet battered: they stand / upon their honours, and will not give up without strange com- / position Ile assure you; marching away with their Pieces cockt, / and Bullets in their mouthes will not satisfie them" (1.3.56-60). Not just fearing the female tongue as a "symbolic relocation of the male organ," Jacques imagines yet another erect female member "standing" in for phallic mastery.[94] He figures the "breach" of this fortress as policed by tribade maids with their "Pieces cockt."

Yet another orifice of this female body is violently unmastered. Sophocles reports that he approached the door and "would have broke in by force; when suddenly / a water-worke flew from the window with such violence that had / I not duck'd quickly like a Fryer, *coetera quis nescit*?" (86-88). More than a little leaky, this virgin fortress literally expels urine in outright revolt. Like his namesake, the Greek philosopher whose wife, Xantippe, was "a favorite *exemplum* of the formal misogynist" in the early modern controversy over women, this Sophocles gets female urine on his head.[95] Any man who tests the threshold of this house will be "beaten off with shame" (84).

In a masculinized version of the leaky female body, the maids' urine is made to follow a distinct arc that can be aimed at a target. Indeed, some contemporary anatomists believed, as Gail Paster has noted, that virgins could urinate like men: "The virgin's pissing is more unfettered and clear than any other women, because her womb pipe is still tight and narrow, all the way to the outside end, which makes her piss straight and far, in rather the same manner as a man."[96] This maiden fortress, like its maiden soldiers, pisses like a man.

Even the female chamberpot is feared as a powerful substitute for the male organ: "The chamber's / nothing but a meere *Ostend,* in every window Pewter cannons / mounted, you'l quickly finde with what they are charg'd sir" (86-90). The women have mounted "Pewter cannons"—or chamberpots—at every window of this gynocentric interior. The female chamber is a "discursive site" where feminine unruliness is often staged; however, as Paster reminds us, the female chamberpot too can signify gendered dissolution.[97]

Surveying the fortress's openings, Petruchio grows increasingly concerned about the insecurity of the men's position in this street scene. Like the contemporary anatomists who mapped women's internal pipes, Petruchio is anxious to contain the labyrinth of secret female passages that lead through the city: "Ile see all passages stopt, but those about 'em: if the / good women of the Towne dare succour 'em, we shall have warres / indeed" (282-84). Fearing that the "good"—a common appellation for poor women—city women will support the female fortress, he orders London's complex internal confusion of alleys and passageways to be blocked.[98]

To implement this starvation strategy, a messenger is "sent to lay / an imposition upon Sowse and Puddings, / Pasties and Penny Custards, that the women / May not releeve yon Rebels" (1.4.14-17). Imposing sanctions against the women in London's "housewife trades" of baking and victualling,[99] Petruchio worries about the poor women who performed such labor making their way through the city. Adding yet a new twist to his siege strategy, Petruchio promises to punish his wife by stopping up her own leaky passages: "She shall not know a stoole in ten moneths Gentlemen." He imagines feeding her "hard egges, till they brace her like a Drum" (30-32), and then beating her: "I would tabor her, / Till all the Legions that are crept into her, / Flew out with fire i'th tailes" (2.4.21-23). Petruchio will wage war on his wife's body until he has stopped up her incontinence.

In spite of the measures to blockade women's passageways, "newes" and "rumour" about this fortress of warlike maids travel swiftly through the city (1.4.31, 2.1.53). As the men prevaricate, they discover that female intelligence networks have already spread the news of a maiden war throughout the kingdom, and that a female countersiege is headed their way. Jacques warns them, "There are more women, marching hitherward, / In rescue of my Mistris, then ere turn'd taile / At Sturbridge Faire" (2.4.39-41). The male householders are urged to imagine an unimaginable multitude of women coming their way. This servant creates a vivid fantasmatic army of women, describing it as a plague or pestilence to be stamped out: "Arme, arme, out with your weapons, / For all the women in the Kingdom' on ye; / They swarm like waspes, and nothing can destroy 'em, / But stopping of their hive, and smothering of 'em." (2.4.34-37). In a re-schematization of the popular humanist emblem of the beehive as a perfectly hierarchized "feminine monarchie" supported by the compliant industry of its workers, these upstart women "swarm" idly and dangerously through the streets with a sting in their tails (see fig. 4).[100]

Reporting on these offstage women, Jacques vividly describes the army's leader as embodying deviant government. Heading the army is a tanner's wife who used her craft to flay her husband and make reins from his skin, thus violently bridling her husband and taking the reins in marriage. The industry of tanning, with dangerous chemicals that tanned the skin and polluted the water supply to the City, was banished to the suburbs.[101] Jacques imagines that dangerous industry has translated this suburban female anatomy into a monstrously unmastered wife: "her plackett / Lookes like the straights of Gibralter, still wider / Downe to the gulphe, all sunburnt Barbary / Lyes in her breech" (2.4.45-47). Using the pornographic rhetoric of discovery, Jacques applies a common trope of blackness—sunburn—to depict this woman's nether anatomy as tanned black. He describes her "breech"—here used to mean vagina—as a huge gulf that encompasses the entire region of Barbary, a geographically distant place habitually associated with monstrously "unnatural" sexual practices.[102] Jacques makes this Barbarous suburban "breech" represent, in Patricia Parker's term, an "ob-scene," or offstage, fantasy of a black tribade penetrating the female city of London.[103] In strikingly pejorative language Jacques describes this fantasmatically "obscene" woman as emblematic of the gendered threat to

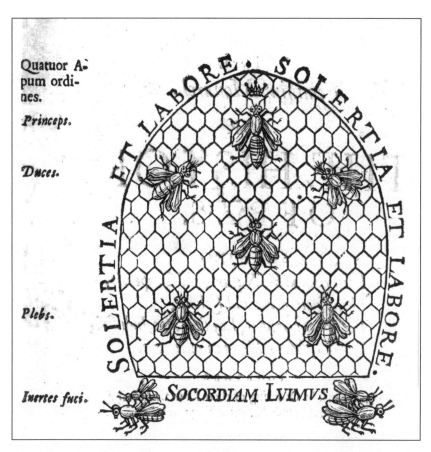

FIGURE 4.   A woodcut on the verso of the title page to the 1634 edition of Charles Butler's *The Feminin' Monarchi', Or The Histori of Bee's.* This 1609 treatise on both beekeeping and feminine government depicts the beehive as a highly schematized emblem of the orderly segmentation of social classes (1634 edition, STC 4194). By permission of Columbia University Rare Book and Manuscript Library.

City government; the Barbarous black tribade here stands in for the English masterless woman who must somehow be "marked as 'other.' "[104]

Outside the fortress, the men can only imagine what government by such women might look like. Fortunately, they have Jacques to feed their imaginations: "They have got a stick of Fiddles, and they firke it / In wondrous waies" (2.6.36–37). Jacques is quick to imply that the women are celebrating their autonomy by "firking"—or "fiddling"—without men.[105] A popular euphemism for specifically female masturbation, "fiddling" was exploited to its full potential in *The Roaring Girl*'s puns about Moll fiddling with her instrument.[106] Like Moll, the women here usurp the masculine role of playing upon the fiddle. "Firke," too implies sexual activity; originally meaning a sword-thrust, it was a euphemism for penis and for thrusting sexual activity. Here referred to women, "firke" implies that the sexual activity in the fortress is not just masturbation, but phallic sexual acts between women. Jacques's assertion that they "have got a stick" and "firke it / In wondrous ways" suggests that the women have invented new and remarkable ways of thrusting a stick—possibly a dildo— across their instruments.[107] This maiden fortress houses an orgy of female masturbation and sexual congress. Jacques offers his masters a compelling orgiastic image of a whole army of women masturbating in an exclusively gynocentric space, a far more powerfully hallucinatory and negatively valenced eroticization of gynocentric space than those real or imagined in *The Roaring Girl* or *Amends for Ladies*. By painting a highly sexualized picture of rebelliously unmastered female space, Jacques makes female homoeroticism into an emblem of bad government.

Jacques's hallucinatory description of the all-female festivities makes female genitalia signify social and political disorder. Inverting Thomas Elyot's image of the man and woman dancing as a paradigm of both marital harmony and ideal government, Jacques imagines the tanner's wife dancing with a bawd inside the fortress: "the two grand Capitanos, / (They brought the Auxiliary Regiments) / Daunce with their coats tuckt up to their bare breeches, / And bid the Kingdom kisse 'em" (2.6.37–40). In a gesture of mastery, these women offer up their "bare breeches" to be kissed by the Kingdom. Refusing to define which breeches he means, Jacques exploits the productive confusion between "breach," a term for vagina, "breech," a name for the buttocks, "breach" as a vulnerable opening to the female fortress, and the plural "breeches," a kind of male clothing.[108] With this one word, he figures the tanner's wife and the bawd as displaying the breeches they had sworn to wear, baring their genitalia, and flaunting the impenetrability of the fortress's breach. Using metaphor and euphemism, Jacques compels his masters to imagine two monstrously unmastered female pudenda displayed in a flagrant inversion of the "shamefastness" valued by early modern marriage manuals.[109] The fantasm of two masterless breeches dancing together represents for Jacques an emblem of tyranny, invoking the horrifying prospect of female genitalia forcing men into submission.

We never get to see the much-inscribed interior of this fortress, but there does seem to be a striking disparity between Jacques's imaginary scenes of dissolution and unruly female bodies and the moments when we do see women congregating. Immediately after Jacques's warning, we get a fleeting glimpse of this imaginary female army: "Enter three Maides, at severall doors" (2.5). Converging on this street from different directions like envoys from several regiments are three unnamed maids known simply as Maids 1, 2, and 3. These women have a more practical idea than Jacques of political subversion. When the first asks, "How goes your business Girles?" the second urges her to rejoin her regiment and prepare for battle: "away to your strength, the Country Forces are ariv'd, be gone. We are discover'd else." These city maids who have been awaiting the arrival of rural women converge only briefly in a secret street space; to avoid detection, they exchange a few crucial words of conspiracy and quickly disperse.

While only three foot soldiers enter the action, they function by synecdoche to represent a whole army of unmarried women. There is indeed a surplus of maids in London, as Petruchio himself is aware: "there are more Maides then *Maudlin,* that's my / comfort" (1.3.221–22), but these numbers provide little reassurance; the inner areas of Stuart London increasingly formed a predominantly female city, but most of these women were poor and unmarried.[110] Many London maids would never marry and would instead join the unruly city population. Such maids present a threat to the household. Indeed, these three maids plot a countersiege against male householders. The first urges the other two to "Arme, and be valiant"; the second reminds the others to "Think of our cause"; and the third urges her sisters to visualize "Our Justice." These London maids agree that they have a common cause in the war against mastery.

This war is about monogamy as an embattled institution, as Kathleen McLuskie has suggested, not so much because women demand greater sexual freedom within marriage, but because a large population of women remains outside marriage entirely.[111] We find in this play permanent maids arming themselves in a street and threatening to overwhelm the institution of the mastered household from which they are excluded. In this drama Fletcher stages London's maze of alleys and backstreets as feminine passages that crosscut the mastered structures of the City.

VI. "Severed Roomes": Mastering Synglewoemen in the Correctional Household

None of the plays that I discuss here simply celebrates female disorder; rather, while naming the criminal spaces of London, each play catalogues many of the correctional technologies applied to disorderly women in the city space. Petronius, the father of the two "masculine maids," prescribes whipping as a good antidote for female disorder: "I have a medicine clapt to her back will cure her," and offers carting, only a more effective mode of street punishment than whipping at a post, as another possible measure (2.1.8, 2.6.2); tied to the back of a cart, the convict was whipped from the courthouse door all through the city streets to conclude with a whipping on her own doorstep (see fig. 3).[112] These were both common punishments for prostitutes and vagrants; whether she is a maid, a whore, or a scold, Petronius wants his daughter punished in the open street as a "marginal member of the community."[113] He envisages the kinds of public punishment appropriate for women who incontinently inhabit the street. We find unmastered, masterless, and marginalized women moving through the city streets in this play, but we also find them in references to street punishments like whippings, cartings, cuckings, and the stocks.[114] Lynda Boose reminds us that "brank" or "scold's bridle" "is an artifact that exists in *Shrew*'s offstage margins."[115] In *The Woman's Prize*, whipping, carting, and the stocks punctuate the imaginary borders of the action.

Recent critical examinations of street punishments force us to reevaluate how women inhabited the very public space of the street in early modern England, giving us a far more contextual understanding of these two plays.[116] Such work also encourages us to apply historical scrutiny to the citation of other punitive technologies in early modern drama. Street punishments were an effective means of advertising the punishability of unruly women by disciplining them back to their own threshold, but they were still public punishments; carting and whipping did not discipline women back into the household. This job was left to the London prison and poor hospital, which were designed to reorder the masterless into a strictly mastered household schema.

I began by locating masterless women in particular city households and progressively moved out into city streets. Now I want to bring us to a particular London household in order to consider how poor women were imagined as inhabiting the disciplinary city household. While studies of street punishments have provoked a more sophisticated understanding of how the law was staged in early modern drama, little attention has been paid to the prison household.[117] Yet just these three plays point to prisons everywhere in and around the City,[118] and talk of policing and the burgeoning legal bureaucracy by which people are imprisoned—the sessions courts, sergeants, catchpolls, clerks, scriveners, and justices—everywhere gestures toward the courtroom and the prison household as fantasmatic sites of punishment.

As they map real London spaces, city comedies draw us to particular buildings, often using them not just as a convenient imaginary backdrop for the action, but to map the structures of authority within the play. When Moll enters a shop in *The Roaring Girl,* the shopkeeper's wife merely expels her with scolding, but when Moll does the same in *Amends for Ladies,* a shopkeeper's wife warns her: "Bawd, take your letter with you and begone, / When next you come (my Husband's Constable) / And *Bridewell* is hard by" (2.1.50-52). Expelling Moll from her shop with every sexual insult she can muster, this shopkeeper's wife finishes with an ominous hallucinatory image of punishment for women like Moll. She reminds Moll that constables keep the streets under surveillance to arrest disorderly women, and that she may end up in Bridewell, London's first house of correction. Field vividly reminds his audience, just as the shopkeeper's wife reminds Moll, that for masterless women the possibility of correction is never far. In all three of these plays, Bridewell House of Correction persists as a fantasmatic structure for reordering disorderly women.

Just as *The Honest Whore* has led Jean Howard to historicize the place of the prostitute in the play's Bridewell scenes,[119] *Amends for Ladies* leads me to scrutinize this relatively recent disciplinary technology of the house of correction. Both plays document a crucial moment in the evolution of early modern techniques of social control. With the establishment of Bridewell, early humanist proposals for correcting the willfully "idle" poor—thieves, vagrants, and prostitutes—by forcing them to work were put into social practice. In late-eighteenth-century France, Michel Foucault has argued, the prison quickly replaced torture as a technique of punishment, as imprisonment satisfied a developing humanist impulse not only to punish, but to reform criminals.[120] In early modern England, however, torture and reform coexisted in the humanist-inspired Bridewell House of Correction.[121]

Even the term *house of correction* originated in early humanist appropriations of this classical term. Already current in the bureaucratic vernacular of court records and royal proclamations as a legal formula indicating the prescribed corporal punishment—such as whipping, carting, or branding—"correction" is a term often found in court indictments of women. In his 1531 *The Instruction of a Christen Woman,* Juan Luis Vives, humanist and friend of Thomas More, applied the term to women outside the courtroom: "in all kyndes of beastis the femals obey the males, and wayten upon them, and fawne upon them, and suffre them selfe to be corrected of them."[122] He instructs men to use correction to govern women, and women to let themselves be governed by a man's correction. Always implying both gentle government and physical violence, "correction" encompassed two seemingly contradictory impulses—to rule or govern the subject, and to teach the subject how to rule itself.[123] It was an expeditious term for humanists who, like Vives, were concerned with discipline in both marriage and government.

Vives had a direct role in innovating the house of correction as a technology of mastery. His 1525 report on poor-relief in the Low Countries proposed confining the poor to hospitals and setting them to work, and his proposal was implemented there in 1551 with establishment of the first house of correction.[124] Showing great interest in this new city household, the Corporation of London published Vives's report the following year, and five years later in 1557 composed its own *Ordinances* outlining Bridewell House of Correction.[125] In the technology of the house of "correction," the humanist project for both household and civil government combined the seemingly contradictory impulses to punish the bodies of criminals— especially women—for their bad conduct and to reform their behavior by setting them to work. A refinement of the prison, Bridewell was intended as a correctional and not just punitive household.

Projected as a perfectly hierarchized schematization of mastery, Bridewell imitated Utopian models of top-down household surveillance.[126] At the top of Bridewell's carefully structured system of governance was the

City itself. Head of the Corporation of London, the Lord Mayor was supreme master of this city household. Below him were the City Aldermen, several of whom administered Bridewell as treasurers and even presided as judges in Bridewell's own court of corrections. Beneath these humanist-inspired "Governors"[127] extended several branches of household government. There were bureaucratic servants like the secretary to the treasurer and the clerks and scriveners who served the Court Room.[128] With a Whipping Room adjoining the Court Room (see fig. 5), Bridewell was not short on torture either, and must have employed jailers and torturers to administer the more traditional disciplinary measures. Outside Bridewell stood a whipping post, a cage, and a cucking-stool; and inside were the manacles and the rack.[129] After being whipped, new convicts were set to work in the various sub-workhouses within Bridewell, where they were observed by lesser household "governors"—or wardens.[130]

From its inception Bridewell was projected as a carceral technology suited to the correction of criminally idle women. Like the plans for schools, poorhouses, and prisons that Foucault analyzes, Bridewell's *Ordinances* indicate great energy spent on specifying the division of space within the correctional household and restricting the forms of activity that were to take place inside each chamber. Women were to occupy "severed Roomes" and even then they were appointed "a Matrone to governe the synglewoemen which were in nomber at that tyme."[131] In plotting the separation of the sexes, Bridewell's projectors anticipated the confinement of many single women, appointing matrons to govern—or master—them.

The *Ordinances* even created an all-female workhouse within Bridewell's walls; in the clothworking rooms, criminally masterless single women were imagined finally to become profitable to the City. In his *Instruction of a Christen Woman,* Vives prescribed the "women's crafts" of spinning and working wool as a means of preventing women's idleness, which he believed led to incontinent erotic thoughts and activities.[132] Bridewell's *Ordinances* enforced this proposal too; prostitutes and female vagrants—sexually and economically aberrant single women—were to be reformed through the womanly industry of spinning.[133]

However, spinning was not just an idealized feminine occupation; as women were pushed out of the increasingly masculinized division of labor in the clothworking guilds, spinning and working wool were all that was left to women as the lowest class of labor. Spinning was not even a guild sanctioned "craft," as the records of the Norwich textileworkers' guild

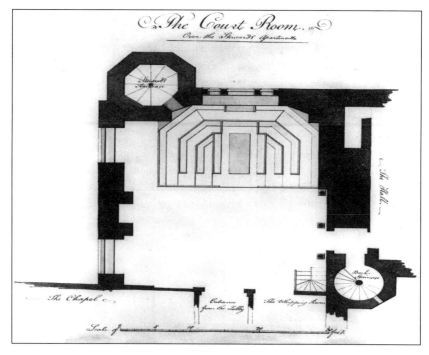

FIGURE 5.   "The Court Room" from the detailed room-by-room survey of
Bridewell Hospital made in 1791. Bridewell had its own courtroom, with an
adjoining whipping room for swift movement of prisoners from conviction to
punishment. This section of Bridewell survived the 1666 Fire of London. By
permission of the Guildhall Library.

show. From 1525 to 1569 the guild increased its categorization of cloth-
workers according to minute separation of tools and work surfaces within
the workshop from sixteen to twenty-two different categories; spinning
and wool-combing, however, remained unclassified since it was subsis-
tence labor.[134] Assigning female prostitutes and vagrants to the lowest class
of feminized labor, Bridewell mirrored the gendered division of labor in the
guild-ruled City, where masters, apprentices, and even journeymen pushed
women out of skilled labor into the lowest end of the clothmaking industry,
ultimately forcing them out of the mastered workspace into tenement
lodgings. Rather than enforcing upward mobility, Bridewell's governors
ordained that masterless women would be confined to the gynocentric
gaps at the very bottom of the labor market.

At the same time as poor women were being forced out of the household, the formation of poor women's spheres aroused anxiety about what women who were engaged in both the gendered industry of spinning and the gendered idleness of female vagrancy and prostitution might do in these spaces. Even within the house of correction such spaces were suspect. In the clothworking rooms women were to be "employed in spinning or carding, and the whole under the supervision of the chief workmaster, who was to correct anything that might be unseemly."[135] Even as they proposed the separation of women, the city masters saw the clothworking rooms as a fantasmatic space where—they hoped—women would be corrected, but where—they feared—women would resort to all kinds of disorderly and incontinent activities. In spite of—or perhaps because of—all this surveillance anxiety, the Corporation of London envisaged the clothworking rooms as the problem area in Bridewell's correctional schema.

Strikingly resonant of Thomas More's Utopian city with its ideally hierarchized households, and obviously imitative of Vives's proposals on poor reform and women's conduct, the City *Ordinances* for Bridewell read like a program for a perfectly schematized division of labor and sexes. Bridewell failed, however, to live up to its Utopian projection, becoming dangerously proximate in its internal demography to the masterless households of brothels and tenements. But Bridewell was not a failure, as A. L. Beier believes; rather, there was an intrinsic conflict in this project.[136] While it failed as a humanist reform, it satisfied the corporate needs of London's Guildhall; Bridewell was supposed to reform masterless women, but the training it provided them with ensured that they would remain unskilled in unstable employment at the volatile margins of mastery. While City masters planned total mastery for London, city plays represented a far more chaotic and disordered picture of London's labor and marriage markets.

Conclusion: Synglewoemen at the Margins

In 1602 it was estimated that there were thirty thousand "idle persons and masterless men" in London.[137] If women outnumbered men by about thirteen to ten in early modern London, and city women were mostly poor, this ratio suggests that almost seventeen thousand of London's masterless were women.[138] Between 1600 and 1620, when female-gendered poverty and criminality became an even greater concern in London courts and royal proclamations, many city plays depicted poor and unmarriageable women at the margins of social structures. The year 1610 does seem to mark a striking moment in the "continual crises around gender and gender relations" that were so often replayed on the city stage;[139] these three plays elaborate a plague of *fantasies* about the real presence of poor women in London.

While providing crucial sources on female poverty and vagrancy, A.L. Beier's *Masterless Men: The Vagrancy Problem in England,* and Carl Bridenbaugh's *Vexed and Troubled Englishmen* have represented the problems of vagrancy and criminalized poverty as *about men.*[140] "Masterless man," the contemporary legal term used in courts and royal proclamations, may seem useful to classify an indeterminate population that shifted between migratory and transient labor, unemployment, and criminal activity. Yet court records and proclamations did not use the term "masterless woman"; women were often convicted as "vagrant," but never as "masterless." Extending the legal formula "masterless *man*" to define an entire social class serves only to re-occlude the significant population of masterless women in early modern England and London, thus enabling Beier, in his first study of masterlessness, to ask, "Who were the vagrants of Elizabethan London?" and confidently respond, "They were mainly young and male."[141]

Nonetheless, living in streets and highways, and in disorderly households like tenements and brothels, women unattached to a proper master, household, or husband were those most subject to correction. County sessions, ecclesiastical and parish courts, Bridewell's own Court of Corrections, and even the Privy Council's own Star Chamber court registered acute awareness of a shifting underclass of unmarried and economically unmarriageable women.[142] Women were less likely to be convicted for vagrancy; more usually, the law found ways to label itinerant and unattached women as sexually or gender deviant. Court records show poor women coming frequently before courts for prostitution, bastardy, cutting purses, theft, or the murder of newly born babies, but in these cases many historians have been reluctant to identify them as vagrant or masterless. Faced with a profusion of female felonies, historians like Beier fail to define these women as criminally masterless.

Literary work on the feminization of poverty and the criminalization of impoverished femininity has until very recently been hindered by this kind of statistical inability to taxonomize a shifting female underclass neatly under one convenient contemporary term as can be done with "masterless man." Only with recent feminist historical work on women's encounters with the law have we begun to notice this marginal class of women in early modern drama.[143] Feminist historical scholarship, Lynda Boose suggests, has spent much energy studying women in power; now she enjoins us to study women's position in the structures of authority "from the bottom up."[144] As we acknowledge the persistent citation of women in historical and judicial documents on poverty and vagrancy, we must rethink the categories we have been using to discuss women in early modern drama.[145] A perusal of the list of characters for most plays of this period will render at least one marginal female character. Sempsters, maidservants, rural milkmaids, women working in fairs, shops, and in the "housewife trades" selling food, unmarried pregnant maidservants, women who—like Julietta in *Measure for Measure*—are accused of bastardy, female vagrants, prostitutes, and witches all represent the potential eruption of unmarried women into that "threatening space" outside the marital order. Most of these characters play peripheral or bit-part roles, but many plays do indeed place the feminization of poverty and criminality in the foreground; any play with "whore" or "witch" in its title can be said to focus precisely on criminalized poor women.[146]

Living on the borders of the political economy, many poor single women were legally definable as "maids," since they were unmarried; yet economically they were unmarriageable. As long as they could be defined as maids or widows, women could always be translated into wives and contained within the household. Prostitutes, vagrant women, itinerant maidservants, pregnant former maidservants, and female cutpurses and thieves, however, could not. They instead belonged to a vast female underclass comprising persistently single criminally masterless women. John McMullan can neatly taxonomize the City's lower orders into five tiers, ranging from the master craftsmen and their skilled journeymen and apprentices, down through the common workers like cooks, servants, and tanners, to transient laborers, and finally vagrants.[147] I cannot conclude with an easy re-hierarchization of women at the bottom of the social scale; indeed, such a taxonomy has limited our understanding of how women occupied their extremely compromised situations. We need to stop thinking about prostitute, witch, and vagrant as female archetypes, and start thinking about them as terms for the different "states" that could be occupied by any poor woman. Maidservants were often also spinsters spinning wool as part of a cloth-working household or regular household duties, and many maidservants

joined the thirteen percent of the City's poor comprised of unemployed
servants; neither was the state of maidservant mutually exclusive with that
of prostitute or vagrant. It was not unlikely for a woman to be a spinster, an
unemployed maidservant, a vagrant, and convicted of bastardy all at once.
The state of maidservant, as mastered labor, may seem to fit conveniently at
the top of this female underclass, but it is a highly unstable and provisional
identification.

The City's problem, and the problem of the courts, was not a lack of
ways to name poor women, but the plethora of crimes, occupations,
and available terms for women; how were such women to be assigned a
single fixed identity when they had no stable profession and no permanent
sexual identity? I want to draw on the term "spinster-clustering" to describe
this confused taxonomic situation. Poor women did not occupy discrete
economic, marital, or sexual identities; instead, they clustered together
at the bottom of the social scale.[148] The terms maidservant, spinster,
witch, prostitute, vagrant, bastardy, and infanticide were by no means
mutually exclusive identifications; more usually, one woman "improvized"
an income, occupying several of these positions at once or in quick
succession.[149] Sempsters were not either seamstresses or prostitutes or
thieves; prostitute was not a permanent profession; and a vagrant could be
a spinster, a maidservant, and a prostitute. Thus domestic service, spinning,
shopkeeping, prostitution, bastardy, theft, adultery, witchcraft, virginity,
and vagrancy cannot usefully be defined as discrete social, economic, and
sexual identities for women; rather, they comprise a cluster of extremely
provisional identities for poor women in early modern England. Women
inhabiting multiple identifications at one time cannot be neatly mapped
into just one city space. Clustering represents the diametric opposite of
the neatly hierarchized and subdivided beehive mimicked in Bridewell's
top-down model of governance. The further removed women are from
the ruling authorities, the more confused their social categories.

To avoid the rigidity of the categories of whore, vagrant, spinster, and
maidservant, we must be more flexible in our taxonomies—by thinking
of masterlessness as a condition of potentiality rather than a permanent
state for poor and especially unmarried women. Masterlessness was a
real threat for all poor women, and the term does suggest the particular
vulnerabilities of unmarried women to the law. I want to think of masterless
women—by which I mean poor women who were not mastered by a
husband or master, those who were legally convicted as vagrants, and all

unmarried women who came before the law—as comprising a distinct "workless" class, a class of women who occupied the border between employment, unemployment, and criminality, often in multiple ways. I borrow the term "workless" not from early modern legislators, but from Tony Blair's Britain, where the New Labour government innovated this term to define an unemployed underclass comprised predominantly of unmarried mothers.[150] New Labour's welfare policy is itself modeled on U.S. Democrat methods of counting unemployment, and we might also notice a striking continuity between early modern indictments requiring an unmarried mother to confess the name of her bastard child's father and recent U.S. legislation enforcing unmarried mothers to contact the father of the child and demand financial support.[151] The feminization of poverty is clearly an enduring process, important enough to warrant much legislative attention in both early and late modern English-speaking countries. In order to think of the women in various positions at the borders between the legitimate and illegitimate economies of England as masterless, we have to expand the term beyond its juridical use and think of it as signaling the presence of an until recently invisible female workless class in early modern England—a class of women who were not always unemployed, but who always risked unemployment, who because unmarried, were not subject to the government of a husband and were vulnerable to the law.

Rather than celebrating the successful operation of a marital economy, these three plays indicate the potential failure of heteroerotic mastery as an organizing civic principle. The capitalization of industry was a crucial process that impoverished female labor, gendering poverty as significantly female. This is by no means a new proposition;[152] recent work on early modern drama has begun to examine this capitalizing process that feminized poverty and created a population of persistently single women. What remains to be considered is the process by which poverty is gendered female, poor single women are criminalized, and female masterlessness is figured as a kind of sexual deviance. Moll is not a "remarkable exception" in the London represented by early modern drama; instead, she draws our attention to a shifting—and until recently invisible—population of sexually and socially deviant single women in early modern London, who, always clustered at the bottom socioeconomic layer, inhabited the legitimate and illegitimate categories of servant, spinster, vagrant, thief, and prostitute.

Having located these provisional feminine identifications in early modern drama, we must now situate them in the cultural landscape of each play. Rather than conclusively distinguishing between public and private spaces or between the early modern household and the dangerous space outside, we must attend to the blurred and permeable boundaries of the household, to unusual and new kinds of city space, and to the offstage streets and enclosures that map the margins of the action. Reading in their specificity the spaces charted by these three plays—the shop, the widow's house, the justice's threshold and parlor, service rooms like the buttery, the courtroom, whipping room, the cloth-working room of the house of correction, and the labyrinthine back-alleys and passageways of the city streets—leads us repeatedly to the improvisational identities of the masterless woman.

Notes

For inspiration, guidance, and example, I am grateful to Jean Howard, Anne Prescott, David Kastan, John Archer, RL Widmann, Gordon McMullan, to my fellow seminar members in the Shakespeare Association of America, and to the editors and readers behind *Renaissance Drama.* I would not have been able even to begin this work without the Folger Shakespeare Library, Columbia University's Rare Book and Manuscript Library, and the Rare Book Collection of New York Public Library.

1. For critical examinations of the play, see Simon Shepherd, *Amazons and Warrior Women: Varieties of Feminism in Seventeenth-Century Drama* (New York: St. Martin's, 1981), 67–92; Patrick Cheney, "Moll Cutpurse as Hermaphrodite in Dekker and Middleton's *The Roaring Girl," Renaissance and Reformation* 19.2 (1983): 120–34; Mary Beth Rose, "Women in Men's Clothing: Apparel and Social Stability in *The Roaring Girl," ELR* 14.3 (1984): 367–91; Viviana Comensoli, "Play-Making, Domestic Conduct, and the Multiple Plot in *The Roaring Girl," Studies in English Literature, 1500–1900* 27.2 (1987): 249–66; Marjorie Garber, "The Logic of the Transvestite: *The Roaring Girl,*" in *Staging the Renaissance: Reinterpretations of Elizabethan and Jacobean Drama,* eds. David Scott Kastan and Peter Stallybrass (New York: Routledge, 1991), 221–34; Deborah Jacobs, "Critical Imperialism and Renaissance Drama: The Case of *The Roaring Girl,*" in *Feminism, Bakhtin, and the Dialogic,* eds. Dale M. Bauer and Susan Jaret McKinstry (Albany: State U of New York P, 1991), 73–84; Jo E. Miller, "Women and the Market in *The Roaring Girl," Renaissance and Reformation* 14.1 (1991): 11–23; Jean Howard, "Sex and Social Conflict: *The Roaring Girl," Erotic Politics: Desire on the Renaissance Stage,* (London: Routledge, 1992); Stephen Orgel, "The Subtexts of *The Roaring Girl,*" in *Erotic Politics,* ed. Susan Zimmerman (London: Routledge, 1993), 12–26; Jean Howard, *The Stage and Social Struggle in Early Modern England* (London: Routledge, 1994), 121–28; Jodi Mikalachki, "Gender, Cant, and Cross-Talking in *The Roaring Girl," Renaissance Drama and the Law* 25 (1994): 119–43; Susan E. Krantz, "The Sexual Identities of Moll Cutpurse in Dekker and Middleton's *The Roaring Girl* and in London," *Renaissance and Reformation* 19.1 (1995): 5–20; and Nicole Roman, "Issues of Gender and Sexuality in Middleton and Dekker's *The Roaring Girl," Bridges: A Senegalese Journal of English Studies* 6 (1995): 67–78.

2. In her recent work in progress, "Queer(y)ing Virginity in Early Modern Drama," Theodora Jankowski examines Moll's virgin status.

3. With his examination of mastery in eroticized master-servant relationships, Mario DiGangi has usefully reminded us of this in *The Homoerotics of Early Modern Drama* (Cambridge: Cambridge UP, 1997), 64–99.

4. Jean Howard discusses Moll's counterpart, Mary, at length in "Sex and Social Conflict: The Erotics of *The Roaring Girl.*"

5. Quotations and act and scene numbers are from *The Roaring Girl,* ed. Paul Mulholland (Manchester: Manchester UP, 1987).

6. In *Homosexuality in Renaissance England,* Alan Bray argues that Moll is a name for prostitutes only in late seventeenth century (London: Gay Men's, 1982), 81–114. However, in his *Dictionary of the Sexual Language and Imagery in Shakespearean and Stuart Literature* (London: Atlantic Highlands, 1994), Gordon Williams notes that "mention of 'common Molls' is found as early as Middleton" (2: 898–99).

7. Andor Gomme, ed., *The Roaring Girl* (New York: Norton, 1976), 344n62.

8. "A bold, vulgar, ill-behaved woman or girl" (*Roaring Girl* 158n7).

9. Gordon Williams defines "oyster-wench" as a term for a "low prostitute" in *Dictionary* (3: 1303–04).

10. On whore as a criminal category, see Valerie Traub, *Desire and Anxiety: Circulations of Sexuality in Shakespearean Drama* (London: Routledge, 1992), 110, and Laura Gowing's work on whore-calling in *Domestic Dangers: Women, Words, and Sex in Early Modern London* (Oxford: Clarendon, 1996).

11. Thomas Harman, *A Caveat or Warening for Commen Cursetors vulgarely called Vagabones, set forth by Thomas Harman* (London, 1566), in *The Elizabethan Underworld,* ed. A. V. Judges (London: Routledge, 1930), 94–107.

12. Jodi Mikalachki examines Moll's knowledge of cant, but prefers to see Moll's familiarity with this language as "canting entertainment" rather than "real criminality." I suspect that both aspects come into play in Moll's use of cant, and serve to support the productive confusion in the play about whether Moll is indeed a "real" criminal— "Gender, Cant and Cross-talking in *The Roaring Girl.*"

13. "These doxies be broken and spoiled of their maidenhead by the upright-men, and they have their name of doxies, not afore" (Harman, *Caveat* 105).

14. "A kinchin mort is a little girl. The morts their mothers carries them at their backs in their slates, which is their sheets, and brings them up savagely, till they grow to be ripe" (Harman, *Caveat* 107).

15. Of dells, Harman says, "These go abroad young, either by the death of their parents and nobody to look unto them, or else by some sharp mistress that they serve do run away out of service; either she is a naturally born one, and then she is a wild dell" (*Caveat* 107).

16. Traub, *Desire* 26.

17. Slavoj Žižek, *The Plague of Fantasies* (London: Verso, 1997), 1.

18. Žižek uses these terms to offer a detailed elaboration of the fantasmatic production of hallucinatory sexual fears in *Plague* 1–44.

19. Dolan, *Dangerous Familiars: Representations of Domestic Crime in England, 1550–1790* (Ithaca: Cornell UP, 1994), 14–15.

20. Andrew Gurr provides this succinct definition in *Playgoing in Shakespeare's London* (Cambridge: Cambridge UP, 1987), 160.

21. In her forthcoming book, *Theater of a City,* Jean Howard examines how the city plays *Edward IV, Westward Ho!* and *The Honest Whore* draw our attention to particular city places.

22. On the rapid urbanization, market expansion, population explosion, and housing pressures of early Stuart London, see C. G. A. Clay, *Economic Expansion and Social Change: England 1500–1700,* vol. 1 (Cambridge: Cambridge UP, 1984), 197–213.

23. So much that both the Revels and New Mermaids/Norton edition of *The Roaring Girl* provide maps of some but by no means all of the city locations named in the play. Mulholland, *Roaring Girl* xiv, and Gomme, *Roaring Girl* xxxix–xl.

24. Dolan, *Dangerous Familiars* 14.

25. E. K. Chambers defines the threshold scene in *The Elizabethan Stage,* vol. 3 (Oxford: Clarendon, 1923), 60.

26. Wiesner, "Spinsters and Seamstresses: Women in Cloth and Clothing Production," *Rewriting the Renaissance: The Discourses of Sexual Difference in Early Modern Europe,* eds. Margaret W. Ferguson, Maureen Quilligan, and Nancy J. Vickers (Chicago: U of Chicago P, 1986), 191–205 (203).

27. On the economic circumstances of English spinsters and sempsters, see Alice Clark, *The Working Life of Women in the Seventeenth Century,* 1919 (London: Routledge, 1992), 113, 155, 175, 202, 221.

28. Williams gives further examples of the erotic associations of the conjunction of the term "butter" with the feminine signifiers, "maid," "wife," and "whore" (*Dictionary* 1: 181).

29. Williams, *Dictionary* 1: 353–54.

30. Williams again provides useful bibliographic information. On the usage of "plum" as a euphemism for the female genitals, he notes that this is a popular image with Thomas Middleton (*Dictionary* 2: 1060–62).

31. J. A. Sharpe examines the frequent appearance of vagrant pregnant maidservants in parish records in "Crime and Delinquency in an Essex Parish, 1600–1640," *Crime in England, 1500–1800,* ed. J. S. Cockburn (Princeton: Princeton UP), 90, 109.

32. Valerie Traub, "The Psychomorphology of the Clitoris," *Gay and Lesbian Quarterly* 2 (1995): 86.

33. Julia Kristeva, *Powers of Horror: An Essay on Abjection,* trans. Leon S. Roudiez (New York: Columbia UP, 1982), 4.

34. Eve Kosofsky Sedgwick, *The Epistemology of the Closet* (Berkeley: U of California P, 1990).

35. We have only to look at the essays comprising *The Lesbian and Gay Studies Reader,* eds. Henry Abelove, Michele Aina Barale, and David M. Halperin (New York: Routledge, 1993) to notice how much of queer theory is about the discursive construction of sexualized space.

36. Lee Edelman, "Tearooms and Sympathy, or, The Epistemology of the Water Closet," *Lesbian and Gay Studies Reader* (cited in note 34) 554.

37. Esther Newton's crucial anthropological study of female space in Fire Island's Cherry Grove informs my own understanding of the gynocentric borders that these plays depict. In a micro-anthropology of the spaces occupied by the various sexual identities that comprise Fire Island's historically gay demography, Newton distinguishes between two lesbian immigrations

into the "in-between" space of Cherry Grove—the rich "ladies" who in the 1920s and 1930s bought houses and assimilated unostensibly into the gay male community; and the much more visibly "lesbian" working-class women who rented houses in the 1960s and 1970s and insisted on a more public presence. "Just One of the Boys: Lesbians in Cherry Grove, 1960–1988," *Lesbian and Gay Studies Reader* 528-41; and *Cherry Grove, Fire Island: Sixty Years in America's First Gay and Lesbian Town* (Boston: Beacon, 1993).

38. DiGangi, *Homoerotics* 92-93; Traub, "The (In)Significance of 'Lesbian' Desire in Early Modern England," *Erotic Politics: Desire on the Renaissance Stage,* ed. Susan Zimmerman (New York: Routledge, 1992), 164.

39. Theodora Jankowski's work on demystifying the sexual status of virginity in early modern English allows me to further qualify the term "maid" in economic terms; see " 'The scorne of Savage People': Virginity as 'Forbidden Sexuality' in John Lyly's *Love's Metamorphosis,*" *Renaissance Drama* ns 24 (1993): 123-53; " 'Where there Can Be No Cause of Affection': Redefining Virgins, Their Desires, and Their Pleasures in John Lyly's *Gallathea,*" *Feminist Readings of Early Modern Culture: Emerging Subjects,* eds. Dympna Callaghan, M. Lindsay Kaplan, and Valerie Traub (Cambridge: Cambridge UP, 1996), 253-74; and "Pure Resistance" (forthcoming).

40. In the only critical evaluation of *Amends for Ladies,* Anthony Dawson concludes that Moll's function is similar to that in *The Roaring Girl*—simultaneously to undermine and to promote the practices of marriage. Dawson, however, ignores how this play is different from *The Roaring Girl* and how Moll's single appearance frames our understanding of the subsequent action, especially of the conversation in the Widow's closet. Dawson, "Mistris Hic & Haec: Representations of Moll Frith," *Studies in English Literature, 1500-1900* 3 (1993): 385-404.

41. Loreen Giese notes the significant "number of women that were appointed the executrixes of their husbands' estates" in the testamentary dealings of London's Consistory Court in *London Consistory Court Depositions, 1586-1611* (London: London Record Soc., 1995), xxv.

42. On the economic and legal situation of London widows' households, see Amy Louise Erickson, *Women and Property in Early Modern England* (London: Routledge, 1993), 158-59.

43. Quotations and scene numbers are from *Plays,* ed. William Peery (Austin: U of Texas P, 1950).

44. Peery 280n11.

45. Gordon Williams provides a convenient bibliography of contemporary dramatic usage of "fumbling" as a euphemism for lively erotic encounters in which the fumbler makes awkward attempts at coitus (*Dictionary* 1: 565).

46. Peery 281n46.

47. Senator Joseph McCarthy had become a real threat to academic publishing in this year, 1950, when he accused members of literary communities of membership in the Communist Party—*Encyclopedia of American Political History,* ed. Jack P. Greene (New York: Scribner, 1984), 1: 367. On the troubled relationship between McCarthyism and homosexuality, see Warren Johansson and William A. Percy, *Outing: Shattering the Conspiracy of Silence* (New York: Haworth Press, 1994).

48. Theodora Jankowski ("Pure Resistance") has most usefully engaged my understanding of the relationship between widow and maidservant by offering the term "service," used by DiGangi, to describe the eroticized labor of master-servant relationships.

49. Peery 272n307.

50. Frances Dolan points out that from the Elizabethan to the Stuart period, statutes on illegitimacy focused more on punishing "the *mothers* of bastards" than on the illegitimacy rates (*Dangerous Familiars* 128).

51. For critical discussions of early modern texts on unbridled and lustful female tongues, see Linda Woodbridge, *Women and the English Renaissance: Literature and the Nature of Womankind, 1540-1620* (Urbana: U of Illinois P, 1984), 207-10; Ann Rosalind Jones, "Nets and Bridles: Early Modern Conduct Books and Sixteenth-Century Women's Lyrics," *The Ideology of Conduct,* eds. Nancy Armstrong and Leonard Tennenhouse (New York: Methuen, 1987). On scolding as a punishable crime, see Gowing, *Domestic Dangers* (cited in note 10); Lynda Boose's "Scolding Brides and Bridling Scolds," *Shakespeare Quarterly* 42 (1991): 179-213; and Martin Ingram's "Scolding Women Cucked or Washed," *Women, Crime and the Courts in Early Modern England,* eds. Jennifer Kermode and Garthine Walker (Chapel Hill: U of North Carolina, 1994), 48-80.

52. Gail Kern Paster discusses "leaky vessel" ideas of the female body in *The Body Embarrassed: Drama and the Disciplines of Shame in Early Modern England* (Ithaca: Cornell UP, 1993), 23-63.

53. Thanks to the leaders and members of the Shakespeare Association of America seminar for our extremely useful discussions of "Public and Private Spaces in Early Modern England."

54. See Jeffrey Masten, "My Two Dads: Collaboration and the Reproduction of Beaumont and Fletcher," *Queering the Renaissance,* ed. Jonathan Goldberg (Durham: Duke UP, 1994), 280-309.

55. Transcribed in Paul Mulholland, "The Date of *The Roaring Girl,*" *Review of English Studies* 28 (1977): 31.

56. Clay defines tobacco as one of the "new consumer goods industries" enabled by a rapidly expanding consumer market in London (*Economic Expansion* 2: 38-42).

57. John McMullan points this out in *The Canting Crew: London's Criminal Underworld* (New Brunswick, NJ: Rutgers UP, 1984), 62, 124.

58. Chambers, *Elizabethan Stage* 3: 56-57.

59. Thomas Nashe's fictional masterless man, Pierce Pennilesse, thinks of "oure unclean sisters in Shoreditch, the Spital, Southwark, Westminster, and Turnbull Street" as his counterparts at the bottom of the social scale: "Pierce Pennilesse his Supplication to the Devil," *The Unfortunate Traveller and Other Works,* ed. J. B. Steane (London: Penguin, 1972), 118. Pict-hatch is referred to in Shakespeare's *Merry Wives of Windsor* (2.2.19), Ben Jonson's *The Alchemist* (2.1.62), and in Field's other known play, *A Woman is a Weather-Cocke* (1.2.67). For further citations of Turnmill, see E. J. Burford, *London: The Synfulle Citie* (London: Hale, 1990), 102.

60. McMullan, *Canting Crew* 56. For a colorful if not entirely reliable map illustration of Turnmill Street's tightly packed taverns, see Burford, *London,* 126.

61. When the Middlesex Sessions convicted residents of Turnmill Street for not attending church, women outnumbered men thirty-nine to seventeen, and of these women, spinsters and widows outnumbered wives (25 June, 13 James I)—J. C. Jeaffreson, ed., *Middlesex*

County Records, 2 vols. (London: Middlesex County Records Soc., 1886–92), 1: 114–15. The men in Turnmill Street were involved in stealing, forgery, and unlawful operation of trades; and the women were convicted for prostitution, slander, and theft (Jeaffreson 1: 262, 141, 192; and 2: 165, 186). The Sessions also document the common practice of unmarried women using married aliases in an attempt to protect themselves from the law. Convicted women often used the same surname for two different aliases—one as a spinster and one as a wife (see 4 January, James I, "True Bill that, at Turmilstreete co. Midd. on a day not discoverable, Frances Davies spinster *alias* Frances Davies wife of William Davies stole. . . .")—Jeaffreson 2: 25.

62. McMullan, *Canting Crew* 56, 58, 60.

63. James F. Larkin and Paul L. Hughes, eds., *Stuart Royal Proclamations,* vol. 1 (Oxford: Oxford UP, 1973), 47. King James issued this proclamation shortly after assuming English rule, and the Middlesex Sessions Rolls for his reign document several convictions of landlords for dividing houses into tenements (Jeaffreson, *Middlesex County Records* 2: 44, 86, 166, 183, 184).

64. Traub, "Psychomorphology" 86.

65. Williams, *Dictionary* 3: 1217–18.

66. Jeaffreson, *Middlesex County Records* 2: 9, 85, 96.

67. 5 March, 11 James I (Jeaffreson, *Middlesex County Records* 2: 96).

68. Jeffrey Masten reminds us of this usage in *Textual Intercourse: Collaboration, Authorship, and Sexualities in Renaissance Drama* (Cambridge: Cambridge UP, 1997), 179n32.

69. McMullan, *Canting Crew* 124.

70. Ibid.

71. Chambers, *Elizabethan Stage* 4: 341.

72. Andrew Gurr points out the ideological proximity between playing and the sex industry in *The Shakespearean Playing Companies* (Oxford: Oxford UP, 1996), 14. Philip Henslowe aggressively acquired tenement brothels on Bankside, which ultimately became the property of his son-in-law, Edward Alleyn (Chambers, *Elizabethan Stage* 1: 359).

73. Thanks to Jean Howard for pointing out these destinations in *Westward Ho!* and *Eastward Ho!*

74. St. Katherine's lies to the east (4.1.107); Moll and Sebastian are apprehended eloping in a boat on their way to the Sluice, on the south embankment of the Thames (5.2.8–9).

75. For the location of the Fortune see Gurr, *Shakespearean Playing Companies* 136–39. On St. Giles in Cripplegate Without, see McMullan, *Canting Crew* 61.

76. Gurr describes how the Globe itself was constructed from the timbers of the Theatre, a playhouse literally moved from the northern suburb of Shoreditch to the Bankside suburb of Southwark (*Shakespearean Playing Companies* 45–46, 136).

77. In 1616 a contemporary observer wrote of this playhouse: "It hath little or no furniture for a playhouse saving an old tattered curten, some decayed benches, and a few worn out properties and pieces of Arras for hangings and the stage and tire house. The rain hath made its way in"—qtd. in Ben Weinreb and Christopher Hibbert, eds., *The London Encyclopedia* (London: Macmillan, 1983), 985.

78. Gurr, *Shakespearean Stage* 54–55. On Whitefriars as a criminal sanctuary, see McMullan, *Canting Crew* 58. For some historical background, see Weinreb and Hibbert, *London Encyclopedia* 985.

79. McMullan, *Canting Crew* 53-55.

80. 17 February, 4 James I (Jeaffreson, *Middlesex County Records* 2: 26).

81. The cancel title-page to the 1618 edition of *Amends for Ladies* adds the subtitle, "The Humor of Roring" to the play. STC 10851 (Huntington copy).

82. 13 January, 21 James I (Jeaffreson, *Middlesex County Records* 2: 176-77).

83. Fredson Bowers, ed., *Beaumont and Fletcher: Dramatic Works,* vol. 4 (Cambridge: Cambridge UP, 1979). My thanks to Gordon McMullan for suggesting that I might find masterless women in this play.

84. Arguing that Fletcher drew his material readily from contemporary social disorder, Gordon McMullan points out that organized rioting had already been seen in the Midlands Revolt of 1607, and that Fletcher, whose patron was lord lieutenant of a Midland county, was keenly aware of the rising—*The Politics of Unease in the Plays of John Fletcher* (Amherst: U of Massachusetts P, 1994), 1-38.

85. On rural riots, see Paul Slack, *Poverty and Policy in Tudor and Stuart England* (New York: Longman, 1988), 101-02. For women's involvement in riots, see Roger B. Manning, *Village Revolts: Social Protest and Popular Disturbances in England, 1509-1640* (Oxford: Clarendon, 1988).

86. On these riots, see Manning, *Village Revolts* 96, 114-15, 280-81, and 96-101; see also Slack, *Poverty and Policy* 102.

87. In "The 'Moral Economy' of the English Crowd," John Stevenson points out that in the late seventeenth and early eighteenth century food riots were more common in urban rather than rural areas—*Order and Disorder in Early Modern England,* eds. Anthony Fletcher and John Stevenson (Cambridge: Cambridge UP, 1985), 236.

88. Boose, "Scolding Brides" 185.

89. Boose, "Scolding Brides" 179.

90. *The Four Foster-Children of Desire,* a tilting entertainment for Queen Elizabeth, provides the most extended and actualized example of this popular trope; accompanied by a considerable army of knights, Sir Philip Sidney and his allies staged an armed mock assault on Queen Elizabeth's body and Whitehall, both of which are referred to as "The Fortress of Perfect Beauty"—"The Four Foster Children of Desire," *Entertainments for Elizabeth I,* ed. Jean Wilson (Woodbridge: Boydell & Brewer, 1980), 61-85.

91. Thanks to Patricia Cahill for sharing her work on dramatic appropriations of the language of English militarism and her proposal that military manuals evidence anxiety about the sufficient masculinity of the English soldier—"Conquest without Rest: Militarism, Manly Regimes, and Marlowe's *Tamburlaine*" (work in progress).

92. See Hiram Morgan, *Tyrone's Rebellion: The Outbreak of the Nine Years War in Tudor Ireland* (London: Royal Historical Soc., 1993).

93. Boose, "Scolding Brides" 204.

94. Ibid.

95. Woodbridge, *Women and the English Renaissance* 127.

96. Laurent Joubert's 1579 *Erreurs Populaires,* cited and discussed in Paster, *Body Embarrassed* 43-44.

97. Paster, *Body Embarrassed* 23-63.

98. "Goody" was a term for a low-class woman (*Roaring Girl* 342n42).

99. Poor women often worked in the "housewife trades" in early modern London (McMullan, *Canting Crew* 33).

100. Thomas Elyot's *The Boke named the Governour* presents the beehive as an ideal example of monarchic government: "the Bee, is left to man by nature, as hit semeth, a perpetuall figure of a juste governaunce or rule: who hath amonge them one principall *Bee* for theyr governour, whiche excelleth all other in greatnes"—Donald W. Rude, ed. (New York: Garland, 1992), 21.

101. Clay, *Economic Expansion* 1: 188.

102. Kim Hall points out that "the region known as Barbary covered most of the coastline between Tripoli and the Atlantic," and goes on to examine sunburn as a "trope of blackness" that "relies on an idea of African difference" from Englishness—*Things of Darkness: Economies of Race and Gender in Early Modern England* (Ithaca: Cornell UP, 1995), 16-17, 6, 7, 92-106. Patricia Parker examines the pornographic associations of Barbary with tribadism in "Fantasies of 'Race' and 'Gender': Africa, *Othello,* and Bringing to Light," *Women, "Race," and Writing in the Early Modern Period,* eds. Margo Hendricks and Patricia Parker (New York: Routledge, 1994), 84-100 (94).

103. Parker, "Fantasies of 'Race' " 86, 94.

104. Hall, *Things of Darkness* 6-7.

105. Williams, *Dictionary* 1: 490.

106. Williams (*Dictionary* 1: 478-80) catalogues the extensive literature on both the verb and noun, "fiddle," which can only further supplement the substantial critical work already done on this scene.

107. Williams, *Dictionary* 1: 490-91.

108. Williams, *Dictionary* 1: 145, 148.

109. The most insistent on "shamefastness" is Juan Luis Vives in his much-reproduced marriage manual, *The Instruction of a Christen Woman,* ed. Ruth Lina Marie Kuschmierz (diss., U of Pittsburgh, 1961).

110. Clay, *Economic Expansion* 1: 209.

111. Kathleen McLuskie, *Renaissance Dramatists* (New York: Harvester, 1989), 216.

112. Boose examines in detail the practice of carting in "Scolding Brides."

113. Boose, "Scolding Brides" 190.

114. Ingram, "Scolding Women" 62.

115. Boose, "Scolding Brides" 200.

116. Here I am thinking of Boose and Gowing's work on the bridle, Ingram's work on scolding and cucking; David Underdown's "The Taming of the Scold: The Enforcement of Patriarchal Authority in Early Modern England," *Order and Disorder,* eds. Fletcher and Stevenson (cited in note 86), 116-36; and Jean Howard's work on the theatricality of public punishments like the skimmington ride in *The Stage and Social Struggle in Early Modern England* (New York: Routledge, 1994), 94, 102-06.

117. Very notable exceptions are Cristine Varholy's work on Bridewell, and Jean Howard's work on *The Honest Whore I* and *II,* both works in progress.

118. Always most encyclopedic in its city topography, *The Roaring Girl* cites a plethora of London correctional households. In 5.1.11-14, Moll mimics a justice sentencing a vagrant to Newgate, a debtors' prison on the inside border of the city walls (see *Roaring Girl* 208-

09nn12-13, and Weinreb and Hibbert, *London Encyclopedia* 561-62). In 4.1.116, Moll satirizes the Fleet, a prison for debtors and convicts from the Star Chamber court (see Weinreb and Hibbert 291-92). In 3.3.76-101, two characters discuss at length the two London Counters, or Compters, both courts and debtor's prisons (see *Roaring Girl* 163n77, and John Stow *A Survey of London Written in the Year 1598,* ed. Antonia Fraser [Phoenix Mill, U.K.: A. Sutton, 1994] 370). They even consider the lowest class of lodging within the Counter, the Hole (Gamini Salgado describes the three Counter prisons in and around London and the grades of accommodation within each in *The Elizabethan Underworld* [London: Dent, 1977], 165-86). Mistress Gallipot threatens her husband with her potential imprisonment in Bedlam (3.2.94), and in 2.2.109 Sebastian mentions Ludgate, an old London gate that housed a debtors' prison that literally inhabited the border between the city and suburbs (see Weinreb and Hibbert, *London Encyclopedia* 501).

119. Howard, *Theater of a City* (forthcoming).

120. Foucault discusses proposals for "humane" penality in *Discipline and Punish: The Birth of the Prison,* trans. Alan Sheridan (New York : Pantheon, 1977), 91.

121. A. L. Beier examines some of the European humanist and specifically Utopian origins of the House of Correction in *Masterless Men: The Vagrancy Problem in England, 1560-1640* (London: Methuen, 1985), 146-52.

122. Vives, *Instruction* 137.

123. "Correction" derives from the Latin verb *regere,* meaning "to rule, to guide" (*OED*).

124. Juan Luis Vives, "Concerning the Relief of the Poor, or Concerning Human Need; A Letter Addressed to the Senate of Bruges," trans. Margaret M. Sherwood, *Studies in Social Work* 11 (1917): 1-47. The Ordinances are cited extensively in Alfred James Copeland, *Bridewell Royal Hospital, Past and Present* (London: Wells, Gardner, & Darton, 1888), esp. 44-46.

125. Edward Geoffrey O'Donoghue, *Bridewell Hospital Palace, Prison, Schools from the Earliest Times to the End of the Reign of Elizabeth* (London: Lane, 1923), 1: 194-95.

126. In *Utopia,* Thomas More described the Utopian household as a miniature government with orderly hierarchies of rule and surveillance—*Utopia,* trans. Paul Turner (London: Penguin, 1965), 79-80.

127. In his 1531 *The Boke Named the Governour,* Thomas Elyot insisted on the importance of educating a generation of "governors" whose participation in the hierarchies of top-down surveillance would maintain a stable government.

128. John Howes, secretary to the treasurer of the Royal Hospitals, in 1559 provided his master with a careful audit of Bridewell's internal government, inhabitants, and accounts in *A brief note of the order and manner of the proceedings in the first erection of The Three Royal Hospitals of Christ, Bridewell, and St. Thomas the Apostle,* ed. William Lempriere (London: Septimus Vaughan Morgan, 1904), 62.

129. O'Donoghue, *Bridewell* 2: 51; Copeland, *Bridewell Royal Hospital* 56, 58; 56-57, 59.

130. The *Ordinances* assert that "governors are appointed, some for overseeing clothmaking, others to the smithy and nailhouse, and some to the millhouse and bakehouse" (Copeland, *Bridewell Royal Hospital* 45).

131. Howes, *A briefe note* 61.

132. Vives, *Instruction* 202.

133. Copeland, *Bridewell Royal Hospital* 50-51.

134. Clay, *Economic Expansion* 2: 7.

135. Copeland, *Bridewell Royal Hospital* 46.

136. Beier calls Bridewell "a proto-penal institution that failed" (*Masterless Men* 164).

137. Cited in Carl Bridenbaugh, *Vexed and Troubled Englishmen, 1590-1642* (New York: Oxford UP, 1968), 167.

138. Alfred Harbage points out the ratio of women to men in seventeenth-century London in *Shakespeare's Audience* (New York: Columbia UP, 1941), 76. Arriving in London, banned from apprenticeship, and unable to find work in domestic service or in the burgeoning but fluctuating seasonal service industries, women were often displaced into the city's illegitimate economies of vagrancy, theft, and prostitution. John McMullan describes how London's labor market fluctuated wildly with the law terms and vacations and the seasonal labor markets in wool, sugar, and tobacco, and points out that women were more likely to suffer from labor market fluctuations (*Canting Crew* 21-51).

139. Laura Gowing argues for a model of ongoing crises in early modern gender relations rather than a single moment of crisis (*Domestic Dangers,* 28).

140. For historical work, see Beier; McMullan, *Canting Crew*; and Slack, *Poverty and Policy.* For important but somewhat undocumented literary sources, see Bridenbaugh, *Vexed and Troubled Englishmen.*

141. Beier opens this first essay on masterlessness with the indictment of an unmarried woman named as a vagrant but charged with bastardy for giving birth "openly in the street." Beier's work began with the case of a female vagrant, but early on he dismissed such convicts from being counted as vagrants. Beier, "Social Problems in Elizabethan London," *Journal of Interdisciplinary History* 19.2 (Autumn 1978): 203, 209.

142. See Jeaffreson, *Middlesex County Records;* on women in London's ecclesiastical Consistory Court, see Loreen Giese's invaluable edition (cited in note 40 above); for parish convictions of unmarried women, see J. A. Sharpe, "Crime and Delinquency in an Essex Parish, 1600-1640"; on women in Bridewell's court of corrections, Cristine Varholy's work in progress, *Representing Prostitution in Tudor and Stuart England,* will provide a crucial supplement to Beier's *Masterless Men;* and on women in Star Chamber cases, see John Popham, *Reports and Cases* (London, 1656); Richard Crompton, *Star-Chamber Cases: shewing what causes properly belong to the cognizance of that court* (London, 1641); and T. G. Barnes, "A Cheshire Seductress, Precedent and a 'Sore Blow' to the Star Chamber," *On the Laws and Customs of England,* ed. Morris S. Arnold et al. (Chapel Hill: U of North Carolina P, 1981).

143. I am thinking here particularly of Erickson's *Women and Property* (cited in note 41), and Gowing's *Domestic Dangers* (cited in note 10).

144. Boose, "Scolding Brides" 194.

145. Boose eloquently insists on feminist readings of the law in "The Priest, the Slanderer, the Historian, and the Feminist," *ELR* 25.3 (1995), 320-40, and "Scolding." In addition to Dolan's work, see also Jennifer Kermode and Garthine Walker, eds., *Women, Crime, and the Courts* (cited in note 50), and Gowing's *Domestic Dangers.*

146. Maidservants are ubiquitous yet mostly invisible to the late modern eye schooled in

post-Victorian modes of class perception, and female vagrants may be less frequent, but *The Roaring Girl* is not the only play that addresses female vagrancy.

147. McMullan, *Canting Crew* 29–30.

148. Poor unmarried women often shared housing together, as Amy Erickson notes in her discussion of Olwen Hufton's examination of "spinster-clustering" in eighteenth-century British towns (*Women and Property* 191).

149. Garthine Walker illustrates Michael Roberts's notion that working women had to resort to "necessary improvisations" for survival—"Women, Theft, and the World of Stolen Goods," *Women, Crime, and the Courts,* eds. Kermode and Walker, 81–105 (91).

150. In his first speech outside Westminster since becoming British Prime Minister, Tony Blair announced welfare reforms that would get "tough on single mothers." See Patrick Wintour and Andy McSmith, "Now Blair Gets Tough on Single Mothers," *Observer* (1 June 1997): 1.

151. Gwendolyn Mink examines the contemporary feminization of poverty in the United States and new legislation forcing single mothers to locate the biological father of their children in *Welfare's End* (Ithaca: Cornell UP, 1998).

152. In 1919 Alice Clark asserted that "with the development of Capitalism" many early modern industries that used to be women's trades were being reserved for men (*The Working Life of Women* [cited in note 27] 11).

The Idea of a Theater: Humanist Ideology and the Imaginary Stage in Early Modern Europe

WILLIAM N. WEST

The philosophico-epistemological notion of space is fetishized and the mental realm comes to envelop the social and physical ones.
—Henri Lefebvre, *The Production of Space*

Great movements begin with ideas in people's heads.
—Isaiah Berlin, *The Crooked Timber of Humanity*

IN HIS *Annales* of 1629, discussing the construction of yet another circular theater building in London, John Stow paused over a curious realization: "Before the space of threescore yeares above-sayd, I neither knew, heard, nor read, of any such Theaters, set Stages, or Play-houses, as have beene purposely built within mans memory."[1] For Stow, the brevity of the theater buildings' history must have been strange indeed; the circular structures with which London was dotted made its landscape unlike that of any other city in Europe.[2] But there was also a time, not so remote, when this significant feature of London's identity was still unthought of, or at least unseen. There had long been, and there continued to be, performances of many sorts in London, but in Stow's time the theater buildings were scarcely a lifetime old; at Shakespeare's death they had been in existence for little more than forty years. Where did the idea for this relatively recent organization of space come from? What did it mean when James Burbage and John Brayne call their "purposely built" structure for plays the "Theater"?

These are questions of ideology, since they look for a causal meaning outside any material manifestation. Henri Lefebvre observes that physical space and physical objects are always at risk of being translated into ideas of themselves, mental images that bear a variety of concepts, potentials, and characteristics but which have no physical equivalent. Lefebvre assumes the priority of the physical thing over the idea of the thing, but in this paper, I want to reverse this prioritization and take the side of Isaiah Berlin. In early modern Europe the idea of the theater preceded the material theater, shaping its subsequent history even as actual theaters broke down the assumptions surrounding them.[3] The concepts that developed around the word "theater" in the late Middle Ages and early Renaissance crucially shaped the development of performance practice and of physical theater buildings in the fifteenth and sixteenth centuries.[4] As Lefebvre warns, the early humanist writers on theater substituted a mental space for a missing social and physical one. Contrary to the Marxian understanding of Lefebvre, though, this is not a misrecognition of material elements as mental ones, but the development of mental concepts in the absence of their real equivalents, so that they apply a shaping pressure to their eventual realizations.

Before a theater was a real space in which to enact plays, the theater was an idea built around a word that referred to an object that no longer existed except in texts, in which its attributes, functions, and powers changed. The idea of the "theater" during this period was kept distinct from the performance practices of popular dramatic forms; to its humanist analysts, the "theater" they read about in ancient accounts seemed to have nothing to do with contemporary cycle plays or other performances. But the theater also seemed to humanist educators to have great pedagogical potential, which later would be converted into the lucrative structure of the entrepreneurs Burbage and Brayne. A central element in the history of the theater practice, then, is the idea of a theater that developed among humanists and other, mainly learned, readers. Berlin's point becomes non-trivial taken in this context—that the force of ideas, of mental concepts and expectations, can exert a formative influence on the world. This pressure is what I here call "ideology."

Didactic theater, as was most humanist theater both practical and imaginary, is unabashedly ideological, but I want to address the ideology of theater proper—what a theater might mean or what it could be expected to do. When I speak of ideology, I refer to the basis in thought of these humanist theaters, these stages that could only be imagined as real and figured as metaphors by their devisors. First I will look at the connotations of the word "theater" before the mid-sixteenth century, when it became fully naturalized into the vernacular languages. The connotations attached to the word in turn led to a more thickly particularized ideology of theater, a set of assumptions about the relations of writer and actor, audience and stage, that put pressure on theater practices, which I will turn to next. But actual theatrical production brought with it another set of largely unarticulated pressures, and these I examine in the final section of this essay, when I look at how one humanist play thematizes the dissonance between two conceptions of theater.

Theaters

The first object since Roman antiquity called a *theatrum* was not a physical space for performance, but a large book that contained knowledge in a visual or visualizable form. We tend to think of the use of the word "theater" in book titles as a metaphor drawn from the stages outside London, but when Burbage and Brayne called the circular playhouse that they built in 1576 north of London the Theater, that use of the name too is a metaphor.[5] The structure and the book titles are differing realizations of an ideal of seeing as a model for knowing drawn from ancient and humanist texts.[6] The inevitable temporality of language and performance was replaced, conceptually, by a picture in which knowledge could be seen, still, timeless, and whole.[7] Although the Red Lion, the recently discovered performance space of 1567, had many of the architectural features of the later Theater, it lacked the metaphorical gesture of completeness, abstraction, and knowledge production that the name of the later playhouse had come to imply and that was picked up again in the name of its later incarnation, the Globe. This linking in the word *theatrum* of conceptions of vision and knowledge, of the separation of a circular space of viewing from a real world outside it, is the metaphorical basis for titles like the *Theatrum vitae humanae* and the Theater in the suburbs alike. To choose the name Theater for their second playhouse involved Burbage and Brayne in a web of assumptions and expectations about how such an object might function that had less to do with widely varied traditions of contemporary performance than with the powerful metaphorical resonance the word *theater* had picked up in the ongoing humanist revival of antiquity.

Theater first appears in English in a Wycliffite Bible manuscript of 1382, transliterating the Latin *theatrum* or, less likely, the original Greek *theatron,* and is glossed as a "comune biholdiyng place."[8] The use of the foreign word suggests two things about the translator of this passage. First,

he could think of no English equivalent to the Latin or Greek word—
"playhouse" must not have seemed adequate for the connotations of the
word—and so chose to render it phonetically into English; second, that
the word had not entered, apparently, into ordinary usage, since he felt
compelled to define it for his readers and listeners. The definition of the theater as "a common beholding place" succinctly delineates the conceptual
image of the theater that would dominate learned European and English
thought into the sixteenth century, when permanent, "purposely built"
theater buildings were actually constructed in Italy, England, and Spain.
Based on the Greek root of *theaomai,* "look," the theater was conceived
of as principally an instrument of vision, a device for "beholding." *Theater*
shares its stem with the word *theory,* meaning literally "a looking," and
thus also *theory*'s sense of abstraction and knowing. In some early texts
the words *theater* and *theory* are actually confused: an English text on
the liberal arts from the late fifteenth century substitutes the word *theoric*
for *theatric* in its discussion of the various mechanical arts.[9] Even years
after the construction of the Theater, John Rider's *Bibliotheca Scholas-
tica* (1589), which grouped words conceptually as well as alphabetically,
something like a modern thesaurus, defined *theatrum* significantly as a
"looking place" and placed it under the heading "To looke" rather than
under "Stages to see plaies."

This looking, moreover, was, as the Wycliffite Bible said, "common"; it
was not a private inspection, but a public display. This imaginary *theater*
produced, or was thought to produce, a shared experience of what was
shown rather than a private one, a vision that received part of its authority
from the fact that it could enter into public discourse. What allowed
for this public authorization was the fact that, from its first naming and
even before it was realized architecturally, the theater was conceived
of as a place differentiated in particular ways from other similar spaces
around it. In his discussion of the social cohesions that made seventeenth-
century science possible, Steven Shapin specifies in particular a faith in
the connection of place and perception, namely the belief that the same
perception of the external world is shared by those who are "attending
to the same spatiotemporal region."[10] This schema is flexible enough
to sustain variant reports of what occurs in the "same spatiotemporal
region" through the use of such concepts as perspective, and more broadly
by distinguishing between observation—which all can agree on—and
interpretation—which is prone to inflection or error by any number of

accidental causes. The idea of the theater specifies these same concepts some two hundred and fifty years earlier, not as a precursor to science but as a system for producing—displaying—a shared experience of seeing. Many medieval accounts of the theater as an imaginary object—not to be confused with the actual dramatic practices of the time—similarly suggest these emphases on commonality and vision. John Lydgate, for instance, in the *Troy Book* (2.863ff.), describes a theater with an altar in its center, beside which a poet recited "the noble dedis, that wer historial [*sic*]." Behind the poet, mimes silently acted out the poet's words.[11] In this image of the theater, language is connected indissolubly to the fixity of a text and poetic authority, while the action of the players is subordinated to it. This relation is maintained in Tudor dumbshows such as those to *Gorboduc* (1559).

The "common beholding place" implied in these early appearances of the word *theater* is codified in the texts of later writers. In his posthumous book *L'idea del Teatro* (1550), the Italian rhetorician Giulio Camillo offers an extraordinarily clear association of theatrical display with vision and knowledge. The work describes a device built on the model of a Vitruvian theater that was meant to allow its user, visualizing himself standing at the center of the stage, to organize and command all humanly available knowledge by looking out into the rows of seats.[12] Any humanist scholar would have recognized the graceful compression with which Camillo's title expresses the visual foundation of knowledge in the etymology of its two nouns, *idea* and *teatro*, each drawn from a different Greek word relating to sight. For Camillo, the double sense of his title was no mere accident of definition, but one that extended to the actual nature of things. His *Teatro* was not intended to be merely demonstrative, but actually reflective of the world's structure: not just a case of "seeing is believing," in other words, but of "looking is knowing." For Camillo, men in the world are like men in a wood, who cannot see the shape of what is around them unless they ascend a nearby hill: "to want to see these lower things well, it is necessary to climb to higher ones and, looking down below from above, we can have surer understanding of them."[13] Distance rather than immersion offers the best position for understanding something, because only then does the object of scrutiny appear as a whole. Camillo's understanding of the implications of *theatrum* develops the suggestions of the word's earlier appearances. For a culture that had experience of the *theatrum* only through texts describing it, it seemed to be an object that promised the abstraction necessary to combine external objectivity and absolute regularity.[14] Its containment of the spectacles it displayed and its detachment of them from the world were a way of reducing the confusion of phenomena into an ordered whole— literally, of seeing the wood for the trees.

The imaginary theater took vision as an ideal of authoritive knowing: what is definitive is not what is said, but what is seen, and hence, in this ideology that distinguishes observation from interpretation, what can be taken for granted. Camillo's *Teatro* and, later, Descartes's mental intuition, share equally this desire to efface or neutralize the viewer in front of an absorbing and "objective" object, mental or physical. Such an attitude separated the theater as an idea absolutely from any empirical knowledge of playing or performance that a viewer might have acquired, where the role of the actors was typically far from objective and that of the viewers hardly passive. This idea of the theater is also one reason why to humanist writers of the fifteenth, sixteenth, and seventeenth centuries the theater so often looks so powerful as a learning tool. Along with the possibility of instant and complete knowledge, visual display seems to offer the possibility of being self-authorizing, of speaking for itself, like a hieroglyph or an emblem, then thought to be a concentrated and naturally legible form of writing that could give rise to more prosaic discourse but that itself preceded it. The theater as a "place of looking" suggested the possibility of a knowledge based on a shared sensual experience, prior to any reflection or interpretation.

But this static kind of *theater,* in which the viewer was separated from the vision before him so as to enable him to grasp it whole, was substantially different from the one suggested by the theory of public performance in the newly revitalized *Poetics* of Aristotle. For Aristotle, the key term in defining performance was *drama,* "action," from the Greek word *draô,* "I do (something)," a profoundly transitive verb. A *drama* was an imitation of something being done, *mimêsis praxeos,* and there could be no action, no *drama* in Aristotle's terms, without interference in something. The human- ist idea of the theater, then, was split between its conflicting concepts of *theater* as essentially visual (and hence, in the terms of this ideology, vivid, unambiguous, mentally affecting, and completed) and *drama* as essentially imitative and active (and hence unclear, complex, unpredictable, and re- quiring a double awareness of the thing imitated and the thing imitating).[15] In short, the humanist idea of the theater was suspended between action and spectation. The inherent tension between these two different, equally theoretical, conceptions of theatrical performance found itself played out most strikingly, as I will suggest later, when humanist critics turned their attention to actual dramatic production, when the fixity of various schemas held up for contemplation is offset by a desire to divert the audience with songs, jokes, and other action.

The theater was meant to reveal a natural order of things to its observing audience, apart from the drama of human intervention. In the Renaissance, writers like Giulio Camillo envisioned this order not as the writer's arbitrary imposition, but as literally reflective of the order of the world. What brought forth this order was the looking that the place of the theater required, the proper spectatorial activity of the theater of looking— *contemplatio*.[16] What was meant by *contemplatio*, though, was not only the detached and passive observation implied by its English cognate, *contemplation*. Rather, the Latin word contains within it two discrete moments, only one of which is passive, receptive observation. Necessarily prior to this act of passive looking, in fact what makes the looking possible at all, is an active delimitation of a space in which the observation will take place and which is what will allow it to be meaningful. According to the Roman etymologist Varro, the word *contemplatio* comes from a ritual practice of demarcating a space in the world within which the ordinary rules of activity are suspended and replaced by strategies of observation and interpretation:

Whatever place the eyes had gazed on [*intuiti*] was originally called a *templum*, from "to gaze" [*tueri*]. . . . On the earth, *templum* is the name given to a place delimited by certain formulaic words for the purposes of augury or the taking of the auspices.

Varro then describes how the augur would specify the boundaries of his *templum*. Once these were established, a bird flying outside the boundary could be safely ignored; within the *templum*, though, anything that appeared had to be interpreted as a sign.

In making this *templum*, it is evident that the trees are set as boundaries, and that within them the regions are set where the eyes are to view, that is, we are to gaze [*tueamur*], from which was said *templum* and *contemplare* . . .[17]

In Varro's etymology, *templum* becomes a Latin calque of the Greek *theatrum*, "a place of seeing." This tradition linking the two begins to explain the frequent appearance in medieval literature of altars in descriptions of theaters and of visual displays in temples, like the fifteenth-century illustrated edition of Vergil which shows the temple of Juno in Carthage with Aeneas and Achates standing outside it. The composition echoes an image of a theater in an earlier work by the same printer (figs. 1 and 2; see also fig. 8).

What links *templum* and *theatrum,* and the act designated as *contemplatio,* is not only the centrality of vision to all three, but the importance of the viewer's prior intervention into what he will later view in order to set aside a space in which signs can appear—a space which, in fact, is precisely what allows these signs to be meaningful when they are observed passively and interpreted or understood. To *contemplate* nature is to create a restricted space within which it can reappear in order to understand its secret logic. The sensual display of exotic objects in an early modern museum or cabinet of curiosities offers the viewer what Steven Mullaney calls "things on holiday," detaching them from their context and setting them into a neutrally valent space in which any virtual context can be produced, or none.[18] Within this space of display, the real world is reproduced as a reflection, in inverted form.[19] The circular space of the public theater is a similar creation of a neutral space, a segment of the world set apart from the rest of the world. Independent of the world yet supposedly mirroring it exactly—the definition of comedy as "the mirror of life" was as old as Cicero but widely cited in the Renaissance[20]—the theater was credited with showing nature its own image undistorted and free for its spectators, as clear and as remote from them as the depths of a painting in perspective. The museum or the theater posed as an empty space in which its wonderful things, released from the contexts in which they had been produced, were free and available for the disinterested scrutiny of the viewer. But in fact it was the designation of the space as neutral that made the objects within it spectacular. As Varro's account suggests, and as the historical development of theaters in Italy and England confirms, it was construction of the space, real or mental, that made possible the show within it. Authority to make a theater must be imported from outside it rather than simply discovered within it, just as in the example of Varro the ritual that establishes the space of the *templum* does not determine what appears inside it, but designates it so that things can appear in it at all. In other words, Varro's understanding contains moments of both *theater* and *drama*; there is both passive vision and active delimitation. In early

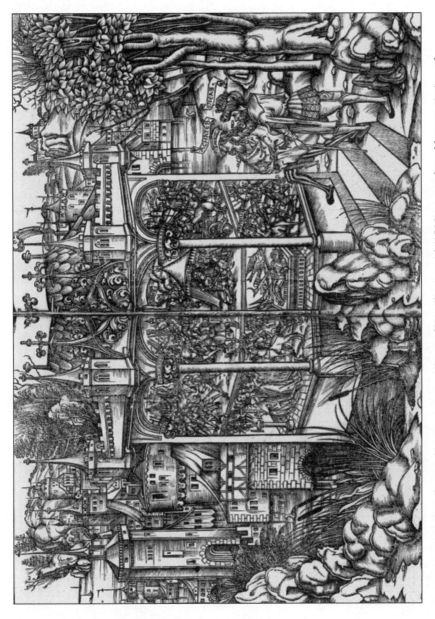

FIGURE 1. *Templum* from Sebastian Brant's edition of Vergil's *Aeneid* (1502); reproduced by permission of the Huntington Library.

THEATRVM

FIGURE 2. *Theatrum* from Sebastian Brant's edition of Terence's *Comoediae* (1496); reproduced by permission of the Huntington Library.

modern theorists like Camillo or the builders of museums described by Mullaney, though, vision serves to obscure the activity of setting aside a space within which to observe.

This blind spot is apparent in sixteenth-century accounts of imaginary theaters. In his *Universae Naturae Theatrum* (1595), the historian and political theorist Jean Bodin restages these two conflicting theorizations of the theater, the Varronian one that acknowledges human intervention in setting aside the looking place and the later, Camillan one that forgets this and sees only the objects that the space holds and reveals. Bodin's work takes the form of a dialogue between a master, Mystagogus, which means "Leader or Initiator into Mysteries," and a pupil, who in the heading of the first book is introduced as Theodorus, "Gift of God," but thereafter is Theorus, "Spectator." Theorus asks Mystagogus to educate him in the knowledge of the world. Hijacking Petrarch's famous metaphor of the humanist as an explorer in the ruined Forum of Rome,[21] he likens this to a group's journey through the ruins of an ancient city, where a guide

leads them around the city, and exposes every antiquity of the place—temples, theaters, porticoes, and what he knows to be the most beautiful and most unusual, he explains in a friendly fashion. Thus I want you to educate me, a pilgrim in this city of the world [*mundana civitate*], about everything.[22]

Theorus imagines the truth of things to occupy a space external to him, with an objective existence of its own. He also recognizes that the external objectivity of the world does not in itself make it intelligible. It is not enough to wander without guidance through the fragments and ruins of the city, which, it is worth noting, include both temples and theaters. Theorus here also revisits the influential image used by Rudolph Agricola of tracking the ancient writers by their footprints, the discrete visual marks that they have left behind them in their writing as they moved through the common places, the *loci communes,* of their works, but discovers also that these *vestigia* lead nowhere in particular.[23] Theorus requires the instruction of a knowledgeable guide able to point out what is most worthy of his attention. Thus directed, Theorus will be able, like Petrarch, to see the original wholeness of the city within the fragments that remain.

Mystagogus agrees to take Theorus on as a student, but he has a different idea of what is involved in such teaching. He will serve as Theorus's guide because we do not come into this theater of the world [*mundi theatrum*] for any other reason than that of contemplating [*contemplando*] the spectacle [*speciem*] of the universe and all the works of the highest founder of all things, and his individual workings.[24]

Mystagogus's pointed change of Theorus's "city of the world" to a "theater of the world" is critical to Bodin's understanding of the relation of man the spectator to the spectacle of things around him. For both viewers the scene before them is real; as I have been suggesting, the humanist theater is not principally one of feigning, but of seeing and knowing. Theorus, though, sees man's work as looking at leftovers, objects that do not realize that they are being looked at and only accidentally communicate their secrets to their investigator. Mystagogus, in contrast, sees the world as a theater, a complex and stylized play in which man is always participating as spectator. As a theater, the world is striving to show itself to man even as he strains to read what it says. The order that man applies to the world to make it intelligible is not, as it was for Theorus, something external to it. The world is outside man but it contains him; as Bodin notes later, he was put in its center that he might see it better. One of the many parts a man in his time plays is that of the world's spectator, and, since the world is a theater, it knows its audience and plays to him.

Mystagogus's theater of the world is a full circle from that of the external viewer proposed by Theorus, who glimpses his worldly city unawares. Bodin's theater has expanded from the limited *templum* of Varro (itself closer to Theorus's city, which he is not part of and to which he requires a guide) to encompass the whole natural world; there is no longer an outside within which things are not present for observation. For Bodin, the theatricality of an object, the way it presents itself for a spectator or spectators, is also part of its truth and must be taken into account in any complete understanding of it. How it seems, in other words, is part of how it is. For Varro, *contemplatio* was an imposition of human desire onto the world for the purpose of finding out its meaning; for Bodin, *contemplatio* is the human realization that the world intends for itself to be viewed. To look at shows in a theater is vastly different from looking at the ruins of a city. In either case, man is a spectator, but in the latter he only watches, while in the former he plays along.

The theatricality of Bodin's nature, though, is not the changefulness we would most likely associate with the theater, but predictability and order.

Although it is the product of a God who can do as he wills, Bodin's nature is nonetheless completely subject to predictable laws that belong equally to both realms; they are "divine, that is, natural [*divinae, id est naturae*]" (2v–3r, Dedication). In contrast to the changeable and fickle world of human action, poignantly evoked in the concluding sentence of the work ("The end of the Theater of Nature, which Jean Bodin compiled while all of France burned with civil war"), "in nature nothing is uncertain."[25] It is Bodin's understanding of the world as display or spectacle for its viewers that authorizes his representation of the world in a form that lays it out for a spectator—in short, as a theater. When Theorus asks Mystagogus to

spread out [*explica*, lit. "unfold"], if you will, the tablet of the universe, just as in a theater [*velut in theatro*], so that as if it were set before the eye for viewing, by the arrangement of all things the essence and faculty of each might more clearly be made out,[26]

it is because such an explicitly artificial disposition of elements most accurately reproduces their natural arrangement. We privilege the candid snapshot or the Freudian slip, the capture of an unforeseen moment, as most honest; Bodin gave the same credit to carefully controlled self-display. Nature, in this understanding, is finally always theatrical with respect to man, producing, as Pliny said, "playthings to itself, to us miracles [*ludibria sibi, nobis miracula*]," or, as Conrad Gessner put it, "These sorts of plays of nature [*Hi tanquam ludi quidem naturae*] are not set before us to judge, but to observe [*spectandi*]."[27]

What makes the representation of the world as a theater, or the theater as a vehicle for displaying worldly knowledge, possible in these seemingly unrelated instances is the construction of neutral space—for Varro, the *templum*; for Bodin, his book within the world; for the actual stage, both the physical space of the theater building and a social, legal one suspended in a web of regulations, prohibitions, and sanctions. The nuanced interlacing of the alternatively active and passive, ordering and ordered, roles of both viewer and vision, though, readily becomes much more one-dimensional in both early modern and recent critical interpretations of theater. Joel Altman has suggested that early Tudor drama became an area in which otherwise inadmissible or inexpressible ideas might find a voice and be examined through this mirroring function which simultaneously reproduced and distanced. But Altman makes a crucial omission, which echoes the omission of the public theaters themselves: the neutral space in which such examinations and re-creations can take place is not simply found, as Bodin, for instance, would have it; instead, the theater must be *made* to be a neutral space.[28]

Medieval and early Renaissance dramatic performances put stress on the construction of this space as much as did contemporary theorists. The design of the Elizabethan theater building, as the name Globe implies, had a cosmological significance, and if some critics have tended to overstate this universality, it remains an important part of the ability of that theater's plays, variously stretched by playwrights as different as Shakespeare and Jonson, to portray everything.[29] In performance, the production of space coincides with the use of the formula that begins so many early moral plays and interludes, the players' cry to the audience to "Make room!", thus allowing the space of the play to be temporarily borrowed from the space of the audience. With the construction of the Theater and the other permanent playhouses, this function was taken over by the physical boundaries of the building's circular frame. Burbage and Brayne's permanent structure of 1576 thus had a symbolic significance out of proportion to its immediate cultural impact: by being permanent, "purposely built," by refusing the ordinary schedule of worldly events, the Theater effectively created a time and space for representation that seemed to owe nothing to the world outside it.[30] What was set apart from the world in this way, though, was not merely the stage, which remained more or less open to the audience, but the circle of the theater building itself. Modern discussions of theater tend to differentiate the real world of the audience from the feigned world of the actors, but premodern ideas about the theater and performance practices tended to assimilate actors and audience to one another.[31] But such developments followed the realization that the public theater did not fulfill the humanist ideals of separation, distance, absolute vision, and instant intelligibility. Rather, the theater in execution was never merely a place of looking, but one of action, and this action, although marked as fictional, nonetheless participated in the world in a range of direct and oblique ways. The early modern theater was in fact a place of learning, but not through contemplation as humanist scholars had imagined. It taught through action, both that of its actors and its lookers. The public theater's self-authorization was perhaps its most important contribution to epistemology—that knowledge could be the creation of human action and interaction. For those who had imagined them, though, it was as a *picture* of reality—a replica that mirrored but stood apart from its object—rather than as a *part* of it that theaters, whether buildings or books, claimed their authority. And when it was no longer necessary to renew the neutral circle of the theater space by the effort of the actors because it preexisted their entrance, it became possible to forget that the circle had ever been made, that it had not simply been found like the objects within it.

Actors

At the beginning of the sixteenth century, humanists in England took to heart the idea of the theater as a perfect educational tool. In his *Image of Governaunce* (1541), a treatise on the ideal management of the state, Thomas Elyot proposes an educational system based on the mid-sixteenth-century theoretical theater of humanists. There is no suggestion in Elyot's text that he even considers contemporary popular performance as theater. Nevertheless, Elyot's imagined educational system is divided along the same lines of contemplation and performance that I have called *theater* and *drama.* The wise emperor of Elyot's text constructs

a newe lybrary, garnishying it as well with most principall warkes in every science, as also with the ymages of the authors. . . . whyche lybrarye was devyded into sundry galeryes, accordynge to dyvers sciences, all buylded round in the fourme of a cerkle, and being seperate with walles one frome an other. (*Image,* 41r)

The library's circular shape echoes that of the imaginary theater, while the clear divisions between fields of study—the quadrivium of Geometry, Astronomy, Arithmetic, and Music—show it to be firmly within the tradition of the liberal arts. The library, though, is only part of Elyot's complete educational system. It is complemented by a public theater: "Many wolde report to the commyn houses callyd *Theatres,* and purposyng some matter of philosophye, wolde there dyspute openly" (42r–v). In contrast to the private contemplation of the library, Elyot's "commyn houses callyd *Theatres*" provide a public forum for the public skills of the trivium, Grammar, Rhetoric, and Logic. Together the theater and the library form a single system for a complete humanist education in the liberal arts. For Elyot, the areas of the theater and the library are contiguous and complementary; they have different objects but the same didactic goal (41r–42v). In fact, the circularity of the library and the vivid statues and images with which it is dedicated mark it as a kind of asymptotic ideal for the theater as a kind of perfectly legible spectacle of knowledge. A reader gleans knowledge from Elyot's theater in the same way as he might from the library, like a man in a garden, collecting what is useful, leaving behind what is not, and avoiding those things that can harm him.[32] The tension between the two competing humanist conceptions of theater is erased in Elyot's version, with his theater being no more based on action than the library. Elyot's theater is a space of exposition rather than production, where disputants display their cases "openly," apparently without the mimetic possibilities of dramatic recognition or reversal.

Other humanists like Juan Luis Vives and Thomas More also approved of theater as an educational tool, but not theater that showed too much awareness of its theatricality. A passage from More's *The History of Richard III,* noting that political struggles are "Kynges games, as it were stage plays, and for the more part plaied upon scafoldes," is often quoted to show his sense of the theatricality of Renaissance statecraft,[33] but it begins with a passage less often quoted in which More insists also that the actor not show that he is acting:

And in a stage play all the people know right well, that he that playeth the sowdayne [sultan] is percase a sowter [shoemaker]. Yet if one should can so lyttle good, to showe out of seasonne what acquaintance he hath with him, and calle him by his owne name whyle he standeth in his magestie, one of his tormenters might hap to break his head, and worthy for marring of the play. (80–81)

The audience member who is so ignorant ("can so lyttle good") that he focuses on the actor instead of on what he plays is deservedly ("and worthy") beaten by the other spectators around him for drawing attention away from the portrayed role. The actor must be just as careful as the audience not to recall what is outside the role, that space which Robert Weimann has discussed as the presentational space of the *platea,* where the actor is himself, rather than the mimetic space of the *locus,* where his acting self is subordinated to his role (*Shakespeare*). "They act plays so as to seem to act," complained Vives of some theatrical productions, "which is an indecorum: for a play refers not to itself, but to what is done, or whatever deed is feigned, as a picture [refers] to a thing, not to itself."[34] This is a rejection of most contemporary performance practices, which rarely attempted to conceal the fact that what was being looked at was a performance. The anxiety over theatrical self-consciousness shown by Vives and More stems from a desire to objectify what is placed on the stage, to strip it of consciousness for its viewers so that it can be observed as a simple spectacle. It is remedied not by a presentation that is less self-aware, however, but by one that consciously restricts its show of self-awareness and subjectivity. As Bodin uses Mystagogus's awareness of theatricality to correct the naive realism of Theorus, More and Vives are careful to reject not the actor's awareness of performance as much as his display of that self-consciousness. In this their position resembles the later humanist doctrine of the dramatic unities, which make the theater still more picture-like, comprehensive, and immediate through their highly self-conscious restriction of consciousness to the real time and real space of the imagined stage.[35]

Similar concerns over self-conscious theatricality also appear in Donatus's commentary on Terence, which Renaissance editions frequently reprinted. Donatus repeatedly scorns any metatheatrical moves made in the script and rejects any hints of self-reflexivity as incompatible with decorum, since how can a character acknowledge that he or she is within a play being watched by an audience without dissolving the rules of propriety? Such self-awareness would destroy the straightforwardness of character that made up the idea of decorum, since any player would be torn between the character he was and the character he portrayed. From late antiquity onward Terence's works had been regarded as exemplary in their combination of theatrical diversion, useful knowledge of the human condition, and more narrowly of the polished Latinity that Terence above all other authors was supposed to excel in, and in humanist schools they were performed as well as read. But Terence was frequently treated more as a fixed storehouse of ideas and even words than as a script for performance.[36] The theater could teach, for the humanists, but only so long as it remained transparent as a vehicle for its contents, whether those are good Latin or good morality. What Vives and More object to is theater that displays its awareness of its own means of representation, that calls on the audience to acknowledge its theatricality as well as what it represents.

In spite of the resistance of humanist writers to the display of self-awareness on the stage, at the same time that the theater was becoming a real structure, the imaginary actor began to make an appearance as an agent in his own right. Embedded within the neutral space of the stage, the actor as an idea changed the relationship of the representations within the theater to the world outside it. A series of images in illustrated editions of the works of Terence shows a tendency to link the actor and the author, so that the theater is rendered as the visual equivalent of the legible, authoritative, predictable book. An eleventh-century illustrated manuscript of the works of Terence has as a frontispiece an image of Terence, equipped as an author with pen and books, at one side of an *aediculum,* the frame that in medieval art signifies an interior space (fig. 3). In the center of the *aediculum* is a man labeled Calliopius, the ancient redactor of the texts of Terence's plays, gesturing toward Terence with one hand and toward two detractors at the opposite side of the building with the other. One modern description of this image describes Calliopius as a judge, and so Calliopius describes himself in his prefatory materials as the defender of Terence against the sometimes pedantic objections that are brought against his stagecraft.[37] The illustrated printed editions of late fifteenth-century France, Italy, and Germany suggest a very different interpretation of Calliopius's role. From the first illustrated edition, printed in 1493 in Lyons, Calliopius appears not as the editor or judge of the written text, but as an actor who speaks the prologue. In the Lyons edition, his figure changes from play to play, showing that he is not to be understood as a real person who comes from outside the theater space and maintains a fixed identity over the six plays any more than any of the other traditional characters. Actor and redactor are combined here; to reproduce another's work, even in the medium of writing as Calliopius did, is pictured as giving it a voice in the theater, dramatic or philosophical (fig. 4).

The connection of the Latin word *actor* to the meaning that speakers of modern English most immediately associate with it is by no means direct. Its usual meaning in both classical and post-classical Latin is "agent" or "doer," less often "lawyer" or "advocate"; the modern sense of "actor" is usually covered by words like *histrio* or *ioculator. Actor* is a regular variant of *auctor* in medieval Latin,[38] but such variation takes on a par- ticular significance in the fifteenth and sixteenth centuries. In the early manuscript copies of Vincent of Beauvais's massive *Speculum maius,* a thirteenth-century compilation of useful knowledge,Vincent refers to his own contributions to the text under the name *Auctor*—the introduction, for instance, which Vincent specified was to precede each volume in its entirety, is called the *Apologia Auctoris.* The form *actor* seems to appear in Vincent's text with the advent of printing—and thus at about the time when the works of Terence were first being revived on classical stages by humanists in Italy and Germany.[39] In this case, *Actor* is not simply a variant spelling, because forms like *auctor* and *auctoritas* are distinguished in the same texts. Printed editions generally adopt the *lectio facilior* of *auctor*

FIGURE 3.   Terence with Calliopius and two detractors; reproduced by permission of the University of Michigan Special Collections.

FIGURE 4.   Calliopius as an actor; reproduced by permission of the University of Michigan Special Collections.

for the title to the introduction at least, but begin to spell the section subheadings, where an author's name would have appeared, as *Actor.* This implies that a distinction between the two forms continued to be made in the late fifteenth century.[40] When Vincent contributed the varied material that could not be assigned to a name *auctor,* he himself was labeled the *actor* of the information—a performer of words that did not originate with him and that he could neither authorize nor authenticate.

The actor in this conception is the vehicle by which the poet communicates his thoughts; in Varro's words, "it is possible to make something and not to act it, as a poet makes a play and does not act it, and on the other hand the actor acts it and does not make it."[41] The idea that texts were performed by an *actor* who reworked the words of others rather than original works by authors or mere reflections of some real cause external to them intensified over the course of the sixteenth century. It becomes almost a commonplace to locate works of knowledge between subjective *poiesis* and objective *mimesis.* Theodor Zwinger's definition in his *Theatrum vitae humanae* (1565) connects the actor's practice not only with Vincent's practices, but with knowledge itself. *Histrio,* he declares, is derived either from the Etruscan word for actor, *histor,* "or because researchers [ἱστορες, which can also mean "knowledgeable men"] are those who bring forth onto the scene the words and deeds of others in a kind of rebirth [*palingenesia*]."[42] Zwinger's researcher who produces (*producant*) or, in fact, reproduces (*palingenesia*), the words and deeds of another is filling the role of the actor, who likewise plays another's part by repeating his words and deeds. The sixteenth-century playwright and pamphleteer Robert Greene criticized the actor's art as "a kind of mechanical labour" and complained that too often the players mistake the work of the writer whose words they use for their own.[43] It was a common anxiety of the early modern English theatrical establishment, either that actors might mistake the writer's knowledge for their own, or that the spectators might learn to mimic a knowledge that they did not in fact possess.[44] The relationship between actor and author, though, remains curiously balanced, for without the actor, the poet falls as silent as the actor without the poet.

Because of the conflation of actor and author, mouthpiece and source, the imaginary theater of the humanists threatens to become a place of pure display, competent to show something exactly but not to allow it to be comfortably traced back to whatever can be said to authorize it. A variant of Varro's definition says that the actor both makes and acts (*agit et facit*) rather than dividing these functions between actor and poet. This is historically appropriate to the actors of early modern England, who themselves owned the scripts they played from and showed throughout the sixteenth century a tendency to play "outside the book" on their own authority.[45] But the actual practices of early modern playing, which we in the late twentieth century have found so compelling and which we have extended to the Renaissance as one of its principal modes of self-understanding, are regularly excluded from the imaginary theater of the humanists. Juan Luis Vives makes the exclusion of self-display a central principle of the theater of knowledge and contemplation. Likening the scholar to an actor—they both deal in the words of others—he associates the self-aware performer with the danger of *superbia,* pride, which occurs when a performer or researcher feels all eyes turn onto him (*ubi oculos in se reflexissent*). Enjoying the sensation for its own sake, such men become completely absorbed in displaying themselves, "as if they were dancing a play on stage before the eyes of onlookers [*oculis intentium tanquam in scena saltarent fabulam*]."[46] The actor's very awareness of his own liminal position makes that position a problem to him and his audience, whether readers or spectators, by introducing unphilosophical particularities and contingencies, of which there can be no sure knowledge, into what must be sure.[47] The investigator's sense of himself and his studies as on display threatens to make his research destructive instead of helpful, preempting its right usage: "A violent desire for display exciting greater admiration increased to such a degree that some persons neglected all the duties of life so as to devote and give up themselves entirely to investigation."[48] The idea of the theater required a vision that was both distanced from action and absolutely simple—the possibility of self-reflexive feedback was not included in it, in spite of the long tradition of such self-awareness in traditional performance practices.

Calliopius in Renaissance editions of Terence takes the same intermediate space as does the *Actor* of Vincent of Beauvais, half dependent on another's words, half free to alter them in delivery, as necessary to the source of the words as the words are necessary to him—but with no sign of Vives's anxiety. The blurring of the difference between actor and author is clearest in the double image from the prefatory matter of an edition of the comedies published in Venice in 1497, an Italian response to the northern editions of Lyons and Strassburg. Terence himself is pictured in the guise of an author reading, like one of the images of Calliopius; he is surrounded by listeners taking notes as he reads from his own work (fig. 5). This image draws on the medieval understanding of the theater as a place where an author read his work aloud, but it also echoes the lecture hall, so that Terence, corresponding to the humanist ideal, simply makes the knowledge of his text available to his eagerly annotating listeners, including Donatus and some early modern commentators. In an edition printed later the same year, this image is reversed by an image of an actor presenting a play in the *theatrum*. Here the illustration takes the point of view of the actor, and we look out onto the audience over the performer's shoulder. But it is as if this second image simply took Terence's perspective from the first image; seen from another direction, as it were, the author of a drama becomes its actor in a theater (fig. 6). The "objectivity" of the first view of Terence as author—that is, he serves as an authoritative, non-distorting medium of his fixed text—is replaced by a peculiarly directional perspective that reveals the presence of the watching audience and the necessity of the first view having been, albeit invisibly, framed. Seen from the point of view of the audience, the author's centrality is an image of the certainty of his words. From his own standpoint, or looking over his shoulder, the author is seen to be no more than a performance of authority. In a sense these illustrations from Terence assert the same point made by More in his discussion of the bad actor; while the actor may know himself that he is only playing at what he does, he must not show this to the audience.

In the Lyons images, the authorial function—Terence's authority in every sense—is a performance by an actor repeating another's words rather than a revelation of their origin.[49] While the earliest editor of Terence's comedic *comprehensio* is transformed in the Lyons Terence into his actor, the present editor, Guido Juvenalis, appears on the text's frontispiece in the position that earlier manuscripts and many subsequent printed editions had reserved for Terence himself.[50] Guido is shown in his study, probably in the midst of editing the volume the reader holds; the books are stacked around him in jumbled heaps to show that they are in use, and two are propped open at once, as if he were comparing two passages (fig. 7). The next page shows a structure labeled *theatrum*. Although a small figure mounts into the *theatrum* from the left of the page, the book encourages its reader to see the real actor in this theater as neither the spectator entering it nor the piper on the stage, but the editor who precedes it; the theater pictured in the book is his product. Following the image of Guido in his

Figure 5. Terence, from the Venice edition of Terence's *Comoediae* (1497); reproduced by permission of the Huntington Library.

FIGURE 6.   Actor and *Theatrum* from the Venice edition of Terence's
Comoediae (1497); reproduced by permission of the Chapin Library.

FIGURE 7.   Guido Juvenalis, the editor, from the Lyons edition of Terence's
Comoediae (1502); reproduced by permission of the Newberry Library.

study with his books, the *theatrum* shows not a mimetic rendering of
Terence's theater, but, as the anachronistic costumes of the spectators
suggest, an imaginary one that has been drawn together out of Guido's old
books. In place of an actorly author, we are given an authorly editor, so that
the authority that is merely unsettled in the Venice edition is in the earlier
Lyons edition actually shifted from Terence to his textual reconstructor.
The haphazard disorder of the redactor's study is resolved into the orderly
space of the actor framed by the proscenium; Guido's figurative *silva* of
references is reduced to the literal *theatrum* represented on the next page,
a common beholding place that displays actor, audience, and real world
with equal ease (fig. 8).

Erasmus and Vives are in agreement that one of the effects of theater is to
present what is written as if in a picture; the illustrated editions of Terence

FIGURE 8. *Theatrum* from the Lyons edition of Terence (1493); reproduced by permission of the Newberry Library.

make it clear just how literally this must be understood.[51] The proscenium of the stage that the reader sees only partially and from an oblique angle in the woodcut of the *theatrum* in the Lyons edition is reproduced over and over in the woodcuts to the *Andria,* the first play of the book.[52] In these illustrations of the play, however, the theater around the stage and the other spectators are invisible, and the stage itself is viewed frontally. The reader is thus to realize that she or he is an audience member looking on, as it were, from inside the theater of the book. The tiny figure entering the theater in the earlier image is a figure for the reader poised at the edge of the imaginary space of the theater. The common beholding place of the theater is not the actual stage, but the book, or more accurately the stage conceived on the model of its picture in a book. Once inside this printed theater, the reader's vantage changes. The image of the *theatrum* provides a bridge between the work of the editor Guido that makes order out of disorder, but itself only performs the text of Terence, and the experience of the spectator-reader. The activity that frames each scene reverts back not to Terence, but to Guido as its source, not to the *auctor* as the authoritative origin of the text, but to the *actor* as the one who reproduces those words for an audience—both the dramatic actor on stage and the bookish one in his study. Such emphasis on the role of the actor, however figured, tended to bring out the self-consciousness of performance that More and Vives had sought to exclude. The humanist idea of the theater remained a contradictory one, maintainable only so long as it remained imaginary. When the plays of the humanists were actually performed, inevitably the seams in the imaginary theater began to come to light.

Performances

At the same time that the printed editions of Terence were circulating an ideology of the theater as a neutral space of ideal representation and simultaneously critiquing the grounds for seeing it as representational, humanist theater practice was working through a similarly dialectical path. Humanists in England and elsewhere tried to put into practice their theories about the didactic potential of the theater. Although after the building of the public theaters many opponents of the theater, including the writers of the best-known antitheatrical tracts, based their criticism on religious principles, Henrician writers like John Bale, Nicholas Udall, and John Rastell seized on the imagined potency of the theater as a vehicle for Protestant propaganda, believing, it seems, that its message could be controlled and put to good use.[53] The courtly audiences for these performances, set up to counter the popular mystery cycles in a variety of towns with a Protestant, nationalist alternative, were far more homogeneous and under closer supervision than the crowds in the public theaters would later be. This may well have contributed to the bookish faith of such writers that they were using a lively, memorable technology to stamp an ideology of their own design (Protestant, nationalist) onto the *tabula rasa* of their audience. The real *tabula rasa,* though, was the place of the stage, cleared of all signification in preparation for the entrance of the players. More accurately, it existed in the imagination of playwrights, who first designated a neutral space of a theater and then acted as if it had always been there for the benefit of showing their ideas to their audiences.

The early Tudor court and the courts of its important members seem to have followed this line linking vision, learning, acting, and theater in the vernacular interludes they commissioned. Much early Tudor theater was explicitly didactic or propagandistic, but often of the blandest sort. Whether interlude or pageant, it tended to restate accepted *mores* rather than to question their justification.[54] With a relatively unquestioned reliance upon accepted truths—although in religious speculation truth was a very conflicted terrain, it tended to be relatively clear from the context of the performance on whose side truth was going to be found—and a general avoidance of irony except as ghettoized in Vice figures, all performed signs remained safely determinate, and the theater could be treated as a tool for the promulgation of its sponsors' ideas, political, metaphysical, or natural-historical.

But humanist plays are distinctly different from the moralities that they share so much with—even characters and plots—in their secularity. They show a resolute interest in worldly things considered in themselves. As M. E. Moeslein has pointed out, Henry Medwall's *Nature* excludes two of the usual evil trinity of the moralities, the Flesh and the Devil, because "for Medwall, The World is enemy enough."[55] To counter such worldly recalcitrance, interludes like Medwall's *Nature,* John Rastell's *The Nature of the Four Elements,* and John Heywood's *The Play of the Weather* combined moral and ethical instruction with straightforward natural history, geography, and cosmology, seeking to capitalize on the attributes of visibility and objectivity associated with the theater so as to produce an educational device that could teach anyone anything quickly and without distortion.

Rastell's *Four Elements* is committed to an exhaustive knowledge of things in the world and not only those in heaven:

> . . . it semyth nothynge convenyent
> A man to study and his tyme to be stowe
> Furst for the knowledge of hye thynges excellent
> And of lyght matters beneth nothynge to know[.][56]

Underlying this claim is the humanist idea of the theater as a display of information, whether of "hye thynges excellent" or more worldly "lyght matters beneth," apart from action. At the same time, though, dramatic action could not in practice be avoided, and humanist productions like Medwall's or Rastell's tended to include elements of dramatic complexity that their theories could not account for.

The title page of Rastell's *The Nature of the Four Elements,* printed between 1510 and 1520, advertises not a plot or an argument, like a Terentian drama might have, but its contents, the raw data of which it is composed. These in turn are not narrative elements or even allegorical figures, but the elements of knowledge:

Of the sytuacyon of the .iiii. elements that is to sey the yerth the water the ayre and fyre & of theyr qualytese and propertese and of the generacyon & corrupcyon of thyngs made of *th*e commyxton of them ¶Of certeyn conclusions provynge *that* the yerth must nedes be rounde. . . . ¶Of certeyn conclusions provynge that the see lyeth rounde uppon the yerth. . . . ¶Of certeyn poyntes of cosmography. . . . ¶Of the generacyon and cause of stone & metall and of plants and herbys

as well as numerous other topics, such as tides, weather, springs, and lightning (n.p.). The interlude concerns the education of Humanyte by Natura Naturata. Early in the interlude Natura Naturata reveals a visual "fygure," apparently a *mappamundi* or diagram of the elemental spheres:

> Marke well now how I have shewyd & told
> Of every element the very sytuacyon
> And qualyte, wherfore this fygure beholde
> For a more manifest demonstracyon.

Knowledge is acquired through a static and organized visual display rather than through any narrative development. The "fygure" remains visible throughout the play and is repeatedly referred to by various characters, who define themselves upon entering by their relation to it. In this Rastell's play can be said to be fully within the humanist idea of the theater—its center is literally the instantaneous, complete display of knowledge in the space of the *theatrum*. The *drama* of the play, though, such as it is, does not present the learning that the play offers as its subject, but rather provides an allegory of the role of information and curiosity in an education, and thus calls into question the applicability of its own theatrical form to learning. In a sense, then, in Rastell's play the practice of the *drama* is set self-consciously at odds with the pedagogical and epistemological theory of the *theater*.

Natura Naturata sets up his diagram and departs, leaving Humanyte with a companion, Studyous Desire. What Natura Naturata merely demonstrated with a figure, Studyous Desire takes more time to explain to Humanyte, without, however, changing the fundamentally objective form which that knowledge seems to have. The presence of Studyous Desire implies that the knowledge of the world is a kind of commodity that Humanyte can and should possess; as Natura Naturata reminds him, "For the more *that* thou desyrest to know any thynge / Therin thou semyst the more a man to be." Studyous Desire then calls for Experyence, who can give firsthand corroboration of the material that has been shown and explained, to prove to Humanyte what Studyous Desire can only expound. Before Experyence can enter, though, Sensuall Apetyte comes in through the crowd, asking them to make room. Studyous Desire urges Humanyte to have nothing to do with Sensuall Apetyte, but Sensuall Apetyte responds that no creature can live without him. As Humanyte observes, Sensuall Apetyte is "for me full necessary / And ryght convenyent," the appropriate first step toward knowledge and, as an unrelated benefit, also a source of "pleasure" and "refresshynge." Studyous Desire protests that Sensuall Apetyte alone affords "no conynge," but Humanyte insists he will only make "a pastyme of recreacyon / With this man for a while." He abandons Studyous Desire, Experyence, and Nature's figure and leaves the stage to explore the world with Sensuall Apetyte.

The rest of the extant playscript (the end is lost) proves Studyous Desire right to be skeptical. Sensuall Apetyte leads Humanyte to a tavern, introduces him to Yngnorance, who encourages him to give up "folysh-elosophy" (E.iii), and finally leads in a troupe of singers and dancers to entertain at the party. After the disguisers go out, Nature returns and explains Humanyte's error. Although Sensuall Apetyte is indeed

> full necessary
> For thy comfort somtyme to satysfy
>
> . . . .
>
> yet it is not convenyent for the[e]
> To put therin thy felycyte
> And all thy hole delyte
> ¶For if thou wylt lerne no sciens
> Neither by study nor experiens
> I shall the[e] never avaunce.

If he refuses the knowledge on the visual figure, Humanyte will be no better than a "be[a]st" like Yngnorance.

At first glance, the interlude presents a thoroughly normative educational system. It of course remains possible for a viewer to misunderstand what he or she is being taught, and many early Tudor plays took this into account. Rastell's play in particular puts special emphasis on the importance of the visual figure in educating the audience; the *mappamundi* remains constantly on stage once Natura Naturata produces it, a kind of set for a theater of the world that will be more subtly, but no less surely, mapped into the "heavens" and "hell" of the Elizabethan public stage. Its significance, however, lies in its visibility; in spite of the varying attitudes and interpretations the characters express, it remains unchanged, a spectacle that both requires and resists interpretation into language. Verified by Experyence, it rises to the status of a *fact*—an incontrovertible presence that must be reckoned with but which, in its silent visibility, holds a true picture of the world, if it can only be understood.

As in Vives's text on the danger of performative *superbia,* though, the play shows an excess beyond the norms of usefulness that can only disappoint as a source of one's "hole delyte." Humanyte errs in following Sensuall Apetyte, who answers when Experyence is called for and is desirable like Studyous Desire, but can finally be no more than a "pastyme." Sensuall Apetyte combines features of both Experyence and Studyous Desire, promoting an active and pleasurable examination of the world that is not, however, directed toward any final, fixed state of knowledge. Except through the two authorized channels of study and experience, the play seems to conclude, there can be no learning. Sensuall Apetyte experiences and desires, but continuously. There is no way to subordinate his drive to a picture of reality. He is the figure of play out of control, unlimited by any higher purpose or authority. Appetite is necessary to both study and experience, but in itself is too haphazard to advance the knowledge of Nature securely toward its fulfillment in the *mappamundi* figure without the structural frameworks provided by Studyous Desire and Experyence. Although the play has a harder time admitting it, Studyous Desire and Experyence are not sufficient for learning either. They remain limited in their action to explaining the figure left for them by Nature— that is, they seem to be incapable of actually advancing knowledge in any way, although they can verify and account for it. Their commitment to this preexisting model, which they expound (as Studyous Desire does) and verify (Experyence explains his knowledge tautologically when he declares, "I know by experyens"), also serves as a limit to their interpretations. Sensuall Apetyte, on the other hand, is wedded to mere appearance, to "pastymes" and "pleasures" that do not yield real knowledge. But these diversions also represent the only possibility for action in the play. Without Sensuall Apetyte there is literally no *drama* in the play, only *theater*— only contemplation of the diagram left by Nature, with no ability to act on it or use it. Sensuall Apetyte is, both in the play's representation of knowledge and its practical dramaturgy, the motive force of the plot. Without it, one could speculate, there would be no play at all, only the still and silent display of Nature's figure. But *The Four Elements* does not simply reconfirm the humanist idea of the theater as pure vision. If what Sensuall Apetyte produces is not truth, it is nonetheless real, and of all the characters he is the only one to be able to organize anything.[57] Because the medium of the presentation of this knowledge is neither traditional study nor actual experience, the relations among study, experience, and desire become still more complicated. What allows these differing positions to be represented—in the actual production of the interlude, not in its representations of pedagogy—is not the static spectacle of Studyous Desire or Experyence, but the dramatic activity of Sensuall Apetyte.

The interlude also acknowledges the double position of the audience, nominally present for edification but hoping for amusement. Before Sensuall Apetyte brings in the disguising, Yngnorance boasts that

> ¶For they that be nowe in this hall
> They be the most parte my servants all
> And love pryncypally
> Disportis as daunsynge syngynge
> Toys tryfuls laughynge gestynge
> For connynge they set not by.
>
> (n.p.)

Yngnorance's evaluation seems to be an accurate assessment of the audience's taste and not mere sportive mockery. As if to reinforce the importance of sensual appetite to the interlude, the printed text of the play, in contrast to Nature's and Humanyte's representation of these playful and theatrical displays as subordinate to real knowledge, advises potential producers that the interlude can be shortened by judicious cutting, but (in spite of what the play's argument values) not of the hijinks of Sensuall Apetyte's crew: "yf ye lyst ye may leve out muche of the sad mater as the messengers parte, and some of naturys parte and some of experyens parte & yet the matter wyl depend convenyently."[58] The core of the play's production, in other words, is the *drama* of Sensuall Apetyte and Yngnorance, not the imaginary humanist idea of the *theater* that displays the knowledge of the still world promised on the title page and in the *mappamundi*. The interlude's real audience enjoys the singers and dancers and other expressly theatrical fare as much as Humanyte—indeed, in exactly the same way as Humanyte—and then has the added pleasure of being able to dismiss them as empty shows opposed to the authorized knowledge of Studyous Desire and Experyence. In one sense, then, the experience of the audience parallels that of Humanyte in the interlude, passing from learning to unchecked play to learning again, and delimiting the proper place of pleasure in learning. More accurately, though, the pastime of the interlude presents both learning and play, containing them equally within the theater's neutral space. Studyous Desire and Experyence, and Nature himself, are no different qualitatively than the disguised singers and dancers who satisfy Sensuall Apetyte. They are only actors differently disguised. Play and pastime are condemned, but play and pastime are what condemn them. Taking the means of representation into account, playfulness proves not to be the excess of learning over its allotted limits, but the ground within which such limits can be established and the source of the procedures which establish them. The practice of drama is revealed as the precondition of the theater, and the social activity that had been meant to disappear in the construction of the theater revealed itself again within it.

Rastell's play shows how in practice the humanist idea of the theater is necessarily in contradiction with the real theater it can produce. The idea of the theater requires the activity of drama, so that the idea is undercut by the very medium that its promulgation required. While we must look to the *ideology* of the theater to explain its uniquely central role in sixteenth-century thought and culture, we must also acknowledge the ways in which *realizing* this idea changed it. Understanding this theater ultimately neither depends on a sheer materialism nor accepts unexamined the early viewers' declarations of the theater's spectacle. What Rastell's play and other humanist theaters, bookish and dramatic both, suggest is the impossibility in them of distinguishing ideal from material, Desire from Apetyte. When the theaters that Stow wrote about were pulled down, it was because it was recognized—rightly—that the idea of the theater as a common beholding place of visual comprehension that safely and constructively educated its passive audience was possible only so long as it was confined to the imagination.

Notes

This paper on common beholding places has left me uncommonly beholden. My thanks to Stephen Hartnett, Kathy McCarthy, and especially Lisa Manter, who all read over earlier versions, and to the two readers for *Renaissance Drama,* whose suggestions have strengthened this paper immeasurably. Much of the research for this essay was done while I was a Keck Fellow at the Huntington Library, and it is by their kind permission, and with the invaluable help of Lisa Libby of their Rare Book Department, that I reproduce figures 1, 2, and 5. I am indebted to the Chapin Library for figure 6, the Newberry Library generously allowed me to reproduce figures 7 and 8, and figures 3 and 4 are included by permission of the University of Michigan Special Collections.

1. Quoted from Chambers 2: 373, and cited and discussed by Gurr 121.

2. Claes Visscher's panoramic *View of London* of 1616, for instance, points out the theaters as unusual landmarks, and they are frequently commented on in the accounts of foreign visitors to London. On the Visscher drawing and its representation of the theaters, see Orrell.

3. For a careful working out of the material circumstances surrounding the building of public theaters in England, see Bruster 1–28.

4. The concepts I will examine here are not identical to the metaphor of *theatrum mundi,* which had a related but distinguishable development described by Ernst Curtius. The *theatrum mundi* expresses the insignificance of the present world beside the superior reality of the perspective of eternity outside it. This aspect of the metaphor has been extensively treated. Brian Vickers's article is a more narrowly focused collection of citations than Curtius's, but perhaps even more useful for the study of this period, since he discusses the various uses of theatrical metaphors in general in addition to organizing Bacon's references to them. Jean-Christophe Agnew (57-100) traces the social changes that he argues led to the dominance of the *theatrum mundi* motif over images with similar meanings like the Dance of Death and the Ship of Fools. My point is that these readings do not exhaust the uses of the *theatrum* image in the late medieval and early Renaissance periods. See also Blair, ch. 5, "Theatrical Metaphors" (153-79), which makes a similar point—there are a number of metaphorical theaters in operation in sixteenth-century Europe.

5. The physical Theater of 1576 was built—to cite only a few examples—six years after the publication of Ortelius's *Theatrum orbis terrarum,* a decade after Theodor Zwinger's

Theatrum vitae humanae, fifteen years after Pierre Boaistuau's *Theatrum mundi*, a quarter century after Giulio Camillo's *L'idea del Teatro* was published, and forty years—a generation—after the Teatro described in it was designed. The first "Theater" is thus nearly as distant from Camillo's ideal Teatro as Stow's well-theatered London is from the time when there were no theaters. Van der Noot's *Theater for Voluptuous Worldlings* (1569), which contains Spenser's first published poems, is likewise a conceptual sibling of these titles.

6. For example, on the educational potential of the theater and its universality, "Poetry comes onto the stage, with the people gathered to watch, and there just as the painter displays a picture to the crowd to be seen, so the poet [displays] a kind of image of life; . . . thus the teacher of the people is both a painter and a poet [Venit in scenam poesis, populo ad spectandum congregato, et ibi sicut pictor tabulam proponit multitudini spectandam, ita poeta imaginem quandam vitae; . . . ita magister est populi, et pictor, et poeta]" (Vives, *De causis corruptiarum artium* [1531], qtd. in Chambers 4: 186); "And though in modern states play-acting is esteemed but as a toy . . . among the ancients it was used as a means of educating men's minds to virtue. Nay, it has been regarded by learned men and great philosophers as a kind of musician's bow by which men's minds may be played upon" (Bacon, *De augmentis* 2.13.440). Ann Blair (166–79) provides a useful survey of the meaning of *theater* when used as a book title, and many of her conclusions agree with mine on what I am calling the humanist "ideology" of the theater.

7. Theaters are frequently likened to pictures; see previous note and also notes 26 and 51 on the theater as *tabula*. See also Flemming 35, on the imagistic emphasis of early printed plays.

8. For this and the Lydgate citation of the word *theater* in Middle English, I am indebted to the editors of the *Middle English Dictionary* at the University of Michigan for allowing me to use their unpublished slips.

9. In the tradition of Hugh of St. Victor's *Didascalion*, theater was one of the mechanical, i.e., non-liberal, arts; see Mooney for the English text in which the confusion occurs.

10. Shapin 31, whose account is actually more nuanced than my shortened explanation. Properly speaking, these are not beliefs, but practices that make beliefs and disbeliefs possible (29–31).

11. For other selections of primary materials that show this misunderstanding, see Marshall.

12. For the text of *L'idea del Teatro*, Camillo 59–124; for background and interpretations, Yates, *Art of Memory* 129–59; Margolin; Secret; Radcliff-Umstead. Camillo seems actually to have built a model large enough to walk into in the 1530s, although Radcliff-Umstead also mentions the possibility that it was never more than a large filing system (47).

13. "Et a voler bene intender queste cose inferiori è necessario di ascendere alle superiori e, di alto in giù guardando, di queste potremo più certa cognizione" (Camillo 62–63).

14. E.g., Samuel Quicchelberg's *Inscriptiones vel Tituli Theatri amplissimi* (1565), a work on arranging collections: "Monere hoc oportet Iulii Camilli museum semicirculo suom recte quoque theatrum dici potuisse: alii vero hoc nomine usi sunt metaphorice ut Christophorus Mylaeus, Conradus Lycosthenes, Theodorus Zwingger, Guilelmus de la Perrière et forte etiam alii, quando sic conditiones vitae humanae et scribendae historiae doctrinam et caeteras res tractandi et memorandi, non autem spectandi aedificii, et rei, quae in eo agatur, aut proponatur amplitudinem, libros pulchre tamen, inscripserunt" (D.iii.v–D.iv.r; qtd. in Hajòs 208n1).

15. As far as I know, the difference I am marking here is not made in the sixteenth century using these two terms. That is to say, while the term *theater* is a significant one, it is not systematically or even regularly contrasted to *drama*. Instead, I will use these terms as a kind of shorthand for the historically important contrast between a neo-Aristotelian view of performance and the ideology of theater that I am exploring.

16. *Contemplatio* as the appropriate reaction to the theater of the world is a commonplace from Pliny the Elder onward. Cf. the complete title of Jean Bodin's work, *Universae Naturae Theatrum in quo Rerum Omnium effectrices causae, & fines **contemplantur** . . .* , or Skalich de Lika's insistence on the importance of "ocium *contemplandi*" (my emphases). Its roots go back to Plato's Cave and Aristotle's contemplative life, but in this case the use of the Latin word has a particular importance.

17. Varro, *De lingua latina* VII.7-9, Roland Kent's translation, slightly modified: "Quaqua in<tu>iti era<n>t oculi, a tuendo primo templum dictum. . . . In terris dictum templum locus augurii aut auspicii causa quibusdam conceptis verbis finitus. . . . In hoc templo faciundo arbores constitui fines apparet et intra eas regiones qua oculi conspiciant, id est tueamur, a quo templum dictum, et contemplare . . ."

18. Mullaney 62; cf. also the observations on museum objects in Harbison 144-45 and ch. 8, *passim,* to which I am indebted for his concept of "neutral space." Walter Benjamin's discussion of collecting offers a more optimistic view of this decontextualization, seeing the objects as rescued from the circuit of commodity fetishism. But in early modern London it is much easier to see such decontextualized objects as made available for commodification— although they *were* lifted out of the circuit of aristocratic prestige that had a dominant role similar to that of capitalism in Benjamin's time and our own.

19. Cf. Harbison on the display of the Elgin marbles, which literally turns the architecture of the Parthenon inside out in order to show the metopes to their best advantage (147-48). Cf. also Ophir 165, on Montaigne's library as reproducing the network of relations that constitute the social world in inverted form; and Gillies 8-9, on the logics of inversion in mapping and history, which locate extreme forms of human behavior at the ends of the earth and find that opposite sides of the world are culturally opposite as well. Encyclopedic space is an inversion of Gillies's inversion; it sets the world's reflection at the world's center as the thing that both gives the measure of the world and can never be made commensurable with it.

20. See Norland (70-71), for the influence of this tag, quoted by Donatus, in Renaissance dramatic theory. Donatus's larger answer to the question "What is comedy?" was: "Comedy according to the Greeks is the epitome [*comprehensio*] of public and private fortune without peril of life. According to Cicero it is the imitation of life, the mirror of custom, and the image of truth."

21. In letter 2 of bk. VI of the *Rerum familiarum,* Petrarch and Giovanni Colonna visit the ruins of Rome. See Barkan (10-19), for the importance of the image of the ruined city as a place of discovery in the Renaissance.

22. Bodin 10: "eosque per civitatem circunducat, omnemque loci antiquitatem aperiat, templa, theatra, porticus, quaéque pulcherrima ac rarissima sciat, comiter explicet: ita me quoque in hac mundana civitate peregrinantem, de rebus omnibus abs te erudiri . . ."

23. Crane 19-26; for more on Agricola and his logic, see Ong 92-130, Schmidt-Biggemann 2-15; on the metaphor of following a track for imitation, see Pigman.

24. Bodin 10: "quia non aliam ob causam in hoc mundi theatrum venimus, quam ut speciem universi, omniaque summi rerum omnium conditoris opera ac singula opificia contemplando."

25. The first quotation ends the volume, Bodin 633: "Finis Theatri Natura [sic], quod IOAN. BODINUS Gallia tota bello civili flagrante conscripsit." The second virtually begins it, Bodin 3r (pages before the regular numberings): "At in natura nihil est incertum."

26. Bodin 129: "explica, si placet universitatis tabulam, velut in teatro: ut quasi ob oculus [sic] rerum omnium distributione ad intuendum proposita, essentia cuiusque ac facultas planius intelligatur." A *tabula* could be a tablet for writing, a picture, or a game board; s.v. *OLD.* Bodin repeats the image from his Dedication, 3v: "Et quidem Naturae Theatrum aliud nihil est, quam rerum ab immortali Deo conditarum quasi tabula quaedeam sub uniuscuiusque oculos subiecta."

27. *Historiae Animalium,* "Epistola Nuncupatoria," 1: a3v: "Hi tanquam ludi quidem naturae non contemnendi nobis sed spectandi proponuntur."

28. See, for instance, Mullaney on the pronounced a-neutrality of the space in which the neutral theater spaces developed.

29. Here again we stand on well-traveled ground. On the possible cosmological and universal significance of the Elizabethan stage, see Gillies, ch. 3; Kernan 2-6; van den Berg; Yates, *Theatre.*

30. See Mullaney 10-15, on the policing of the structures of communal time and space in early modern London, and 47-55 on the stage's challenge to these orders by establishing its own, very different, boundaries at the margins of the larger communal ones.

31. In the definition he gave for the word *theatrum* in his *Thesaurus Linguae Romanae et Britannicae* (1565), Thomas Cooper specified that the word meant "Sometime the multitude that beholdeth. Sometime the sight or play set forth in that place." Ben Jonson's prologue to *Bartholomew Fair* points out to the audience that by paying "preposterously" for their seats, they have become part of the play even before it has begun. See also Weimann, *Popular Tradition,* for a discussion of stage practice and the ways in which the audience and the actor in a sense interpenetrated. A variant of this position in recent criticism is Howard, which essentially argues that the radical effectiveness of the Elizabethan theater lay in the composition and behavior of its audience more than in what was presented on stage.

32. The metaphor is a favorite of Elyot's, following Plutarch; see Elyot's *Dictionary,* Second Preface, 1; *Governour* 51v-52r.

33. More's association of the two was still remembered in Elizabethan England; Anthony Munday's much-revised *Play of Sir Thomas More* has More muse on his way to the block that "my offence to his highness makes me of a state pleader a stage player" (5.4.72-73). I am indebted to an anonymous reader from *Renaissance Drama* for bringing this to my attention.

34. Vives, *De disciplinis* 90-91: "Sic agunt fabulas, ut videantur agare, quod est indecorum: nam fabula non refert seipsam, sed rem gestam, aut quae gesta fingitur, ut rem pictura, non se." Alberti in *De pintura* and Erasmus in *Praise of Folly* likewise reject any overt theatricality in representation as crude and disturbing.

35. For the unities as a mark of artistic skill in sixteenth-century German theater, see Flemming 46-47; Lodovico Castelvetro, a translator and commentator on Aristotle's *Poetics* whose work in formulating the doctrine of unities was highly influential, concludes that unity of time, place, and plot are rules "not of necessity but to show the excellence of the poet" (comments to *Poetics* VIII. 318).

36. See Norland's section on Erasmus (84–94), for that humanist's great belief in the value of Terence's texts for study; the educational program he designed for John Colet's St. Paul's School was based on reading principally Terence and other dramatists.

37. The image is from Vaticanus Latinus 3305, reproduced in Webber and Morey as plate 10. On Calliopius as a judge, see Richmond 10–11.

38. See Chenu on the history of *actor* and *auctor.*

39. In a personal communication at the International Medieval Conference in Leeds, England, 10–13 July 1995, Dr. J. B. Voorbij of Utrecht University asserted that, to his knowledge, after examining the manuscripts of the *Speculum* from Vincent's period, the variant *actor* is not used for the author's part.

40. For a collated edition of the manuscript texts of the *Apologia Actoris,* see Van den Brincken; also see Parkes 128–29.

41. Varro, *De lingua latina* VI.77: "Potest enim aliquid facere et non agere, ut poeta facit fabulam et non agit, contra actor agit et non facit." Cf. also VI.58: "Ideo actores pronuntiare dicuntur, quod in proscaenio enuntiant poetae cogitata."

42. Zwinger 186: "vel quod ἵστορες quidam sint qui aliorum dicta factaqué quadam palingenesia in scenam producant."

43. From *Francesco's Fortunes* (1590), qtd. in Chambers 4: 236.

44. See McLuskie and Haynes on the theater as a place of knowledge. While McLuskie concentrates on theatrical pretensions to knowledge, Haynes discusses the theater as an actual source of the knowledge of fashion and social custom, fields far removed from either the ethical and philosophical verities looked for by humanists or the displays of selfhood favored by the nobility.

45. This is of course one of Hamlet's main concerns in his advice to the players. William Ingram (77–78) cites an incident in 1537, when the Duke of Suffolk complained to Thomas Cromwell that the player playing Husbandry in "A playe which playe was of a kinge how he shuld Rulle his Realm" wandered from "the boke of the playe" in order to abuse some of the gentlemen watching.

46. Trans. Watson 16; Vives, *De disciplinis* 234: "Tum quae adversus necessitatem fuerant quaesita, quibusque aliquid commoditatis accesserat, ferè vel ad delitias sunt traducta, vel ad superbiae acerbissimam tyrranidem pertracta, ut vel corpus oblectarent, vel oculis intentium tanquam in scena saltarent fabulam."

47. See Daston, esp. 258–63, on the difficulty early science had with judging particulars, and the tendency to exclude them from the properly knowable.

48. Trans. Watson 16; Vives, *De disciplinis* 234: "quin ad maiorem admirationem sui excitandam aucta est ostentandi cupido importuna. Adeo ut quidam universa vitae officia deseruerint, ut huic se scrutationi cunctos dederunt, ac velut mancipent."

49. The representation of Calliopius is also probably influenced by the common medieval and Renaissance misunderstanding that, in the classical theater, a poet read the text while mimes performed the actions he described.

50. For instance, the Venice edition of Terence (1497), which rendered the images in a more modern Italian style than the gothicism of the Lyons or Strassburg editions (Richmond 34), and the line of manuscripts represented by Vat. Lat. 3305; on the medieval illustrations of manuscripts of Terence, see Webber and Morey; Richmond 8.

51. Erasmus, *Epistola* 31 (1489?), qtd. in Chambers 4: 194: "Haec nobis in fabulis, *perinde*

atque in tabula, proponuntur *depicta* [These are displayed to us in fables, just as if they were painted in pictures]"; Vives, *De causis* ii.4, p. 89 (incorrectly cited in Chambers as 99): "Venit in scenam poesis . . . et ibi *sicut pictor tabulam proponit* multitudini spectandam, ita poeta imaginem quandam vitae [Poetry enters the scene . . . and there just as a painter displays a picture to be viewed by the crowd, so the poet shows a kind of image of life]."

52. That the stage of *Andria* is the same stage as the one in the picture of the *Theatrum,* and not just a similar one, is confirmed by the ornaments at the corners of the stage. Flemming (39) makes this observation as well.

53. Ingram 78–82; he quotes Richard Moryson, a gentleman of the chamber who some time after 1540 praised plays as politically useful, "specyally when they declare eyther the abhominacion of the bisshop of rome and his adherenttes, or the benefittes brought to thys realme by yo[r] graces tornyng hym and hys out of it."

54. Joel Altman distinguishes two styles he calls *demonstrative* and *exploratory,* the first of which concludes an issue, while the second opens a question; Sydney Anglo (357–59) contrasts the superficiality of the advice offered in early Tudor pageants with the real and concerted appeals to Elizabeth in her coronation progress of 1558. See also Westfall 153–60, on the shift in performance style to one that emphasized the particular setting and encouraged the application of drama to the historical context rather than its reception and reproduction. I would add to these statements only that even exploratory interludes are careful to open their questions only within the frame of the drama, which is safely closed, often by the presence of the patron at the performance, and frequently end with their question securely answered as well. On the disruptive potential in popular medieval theater, by way of contrast, see Weimann, *Popular Tradition.*

55. Moeslein, introduction to *Nature,* 256–57.

56. No page; Messenger's speech.

57. For a similar relation of agency and authority, and the difference between seeing truth as adequation to a thing that already exists and as exploration which discovers and decides upon an object as author, see Weimann, "Author-ity in Signification" 87–99.

58. Title page. Weimann (*Popular Tradition* 103–05) notes the heavy investment of the interlude genre in its festive, playful form.

Works Cited

Agnew, Jean-Christophe. *Worlds Apart: The Market and the Theater in Anglo-American Thought.* Cambridge: Cambridge UP, 1986.

Altman, Joel B. *The Tudor Play of Mind: Rhetorical Inquiry and the Development of Elizabethan Drama.* Berkeley: U of California P, 1978.

Anglo, Sydney. *Spectacle, Pageantry, and Early Tudor Policy.* Oxford: Clarendon, 1969.

Bacon, Francis. *Works.* 14 vols. Eds. James Spedding, Robert Leslie Ellis, and Douglas Denon Heath. London: Longman, 1857–74. Facsimile. Stuttgart: Friedrich Fromann, 1963.

Barkan, Leonard. *Transuming Passion: Ganymede and the Erotics of Humanism.* Stanford: Stanford UP, 1991.

Benjamin, Walter. "Edward Fuchs: Collector and Historian." *The Essential Frankfurt School Reader.* Eds. Andrew Arato and Eike Gebhardt 1978. New York: Continuum, 1993. 225–53.

Blair, Ann. *The Theater of Nature: Jean Bodin and Renaissance Science.* Princeton: Princeton UP, 1997.

Bodin, Jean. *Universae Naturae Theatrum in quo Rerum Omnium effectrices causae, & fines contemplantur.* . . . Hanover: Typus Wechelianus, 1595.

Bruster, Douglas. *Drama and the Market in the Age of Shakespeare.* Cambridge: Cambridge UP, 1992.

Camillo Delminio, Giulio. *L'idea del Teatro dell'Eccelente M. Giulio Camillo.* Florence: Lorenzo Torrentino, 1550.

Castelvetro, Lodovico. "A Commentary on the Poetics of Aristotle." Sel. and trans. Allan H. Gilbert. *Literary Criticism: Plato to Dryden.* Ed. Allan H. Gilbert. Detroit: Wayne State UP, 1962. 304-57.

Chambers, E. K. *The Elizabethan Stage.* 4 vols. Oxford: Clarendon, 1923.

Chenu, M.-D. "Auctor, Actor, Autor." *Bulletin du cange—Archivium Latinitas Medii Aevi* 3 (1927): 81-86.

Cooper, Thomas. *Thesaurus Linguae Romanae et Britannicae.* 1565.

Crane, Mary Thomas. *Framing Authority: Sayings, Self, and Society in Sixteenth-Century England.* Princeton: Princeton UP, 1993.

Curtius, E. R. *European Literature and the Latin Middle Ages.* Trans. Willard Trask. Bollingen Series 36. Princeton: Princeton UP, 1953.

Daston, Lorraine. "Marvelous Facts and Miraculous Evidence in Early Modern Europe." *Questions of Evidence: Proof, Practice, and Persuasion across the Disciplines.* Chicago: U of Chicago P, 1994. 234-74.

Elyot, Thomas. *The Boke named the Governour.* London: n.p., 1546.

———. *Dictionary.* London: Thomas Berthelet, 1538. Facsimile. Menston: Scolar, 1970.

———. *The Image of Governaunce.* London: Thomas Berthelet, 1540.

Flemming, Willi. "Formen der Humanistenbühne." *Maske und Kothurn: Vierteljahrschrift für Theaterwissenschaft* 6 (1960): 33-52.

Gessner, Conrad. *Historiae Animalium.* 1551. 5 vols. in 4. Vol. 1. Frankfurt: Bibliopolium Camberiano, 1603. Vol. 2. Frankfurt: Robert Camberius, 1586. Vol. 3. Frankfurt: Robert Camberius, 1585. Vol. 4. Zurich: Christophoros Froscherus, 1558. Vol. 5. Zurich: Christophoros Froscherus, 1587.

Gillies, John. *Shakespeare and the Geography of Difference.* Cambridge: Cambridge UP, 1994.

Gurr, Andrew. *The Shakespearean Stage, 1574-1642.* Cambridge: Cambridge UP, 1992.

Hajòs, Elizabeth M. "References to Giulio Camillo in Samuel Quicchelberg's 'Inscriptiones vel Tituli Theatri Amplissimi.' " *Bibiothèque d'Humanisme et Renaissance: Travaux et Documents* 25 (1963): 207-11.

Harbison, Robert. *Eccentric Spaces.* New York: Knopf, 1977.

Haynes, Jonathan. *The Social Relations of Jonson's Theater.* Cambridge: Cambridge UP, 1992.

Howard, Jean. *The Stage and Social Struggle in Early Modern England.* New York: Routledge, 1994.

Ingram, William. *The Business of Playing: The Beginnings of the Adult Professional Theater in Elizabethan London.* Ithaca: Cornell UP, 1992.

Kernan, Alvin. "Hamlet and the Nature of Drama." *Yale Conference on the Teaching of English* (n.d.): 1-11.

Margolin, Jean-Claude. "Le *théâtre de memoire* de Giulio Camillo: Récapitulation des connaissances acquises, ou instrument heuristique de connaissances nouvelles?" *L'encyclopédisme: Actes du colloque de Caen, 12-16 janvier 1987*. Ed. Annie Becq. Paris: Amateurs des livres, 1991. 459-81.

Marshall, Mary H. "*Theatre* in the Middle Ages: Evidence from Dictionaries and Glosses." *Symposium* 4 (1950): 1-39; 366-89.

McLuskie, Kathleen E. "The Poets' Royal Exchange: Patronage and Commerce in Early Modern Drama." *Yearbook of English Studies* 21 (1991): 53-62.

Medwall, Henry. *The Plays of Henry Medwall: A Critical Edition*. Ed. M. E. Moeslein. New York: Garland, 1981.

Mooney, Linne R. "A Middle English Text on the Seven Liberal Arts." *Speculum* 68 (1993): 1027-52.

More, Thomas. *The History of King Richard III and Selections from the English and Latin Poems*. Ed. Richard Sylvester. New Haven: Yale UP, 1976.

Mullaney, Steven. *The Place of the Stage: License, Play, and Power in Renaissance England*. Chicago: U of Chicago P, 1987.

Munday, Anthony, et al. *Sir Thomas More*. Eds. Vittorio Gabrieli and Giorgio Melchiori. The Revels Plays. Manchester: Manchester UP, 1990.

Norland, Howard B. *Drama in Early Tudor Britain, 1485-1558*. Lincoln: U of Nebraska P, 1995.

Ong, Walter, S. J. *Ramus, Method, and the Decay of Dialogue: From the Art of Discourse to the Art of Reason*. Cambridge: Harvard UP, 1958.

Ophir, Adi. "A Place of Knowledge Re-Created: The Library of Michel de Montaigne." *Science in Context* 4.1 (1991): 163-89.

Orrell, John. *The Human Stage: English Theatre Design, 1567-1640*. Cambridge: Cambridge UP, 1988.

Parkes, M. B. "The Influence of the Concepts of *Ordinatio* and *Compilatio* on the Development of the Book." *Medieval Learning and Literature: Essays Presented to Richard William Hunt*. Eds. J. J. G. Alexander and M. T. Gibson. Oxford: Clarendon, 1976.

Pigman, George. "Versions of Imitation in the Renaissance." *Renaissance Quarterly* 33 (1980): 1-32.

Radcliff-Umstead, Douglas. "Giulio Camillo's Emblems of Memory." *Yale French Studies* 47 (1972): 47-56.

[Rastell, John.] *The Nature of the Four Elements*. The Tudor Facsimile Texts. Ed. John S. Farmer. London, 1908. New York: AMS, 1970.

Richmond, Mary L. *Terence Illustrated: An Exhibition in Honor of Karl Ephraim Weston*. Williamstown, MA: Chapin Library, Williams College, 1955.

Schmidt-Biggemann, Wilhelm. *Topica Universalis: Eine Modellgeschichte humanistischer und barocker Wissenschaft*. Hamburg: Felix Meiner, 1983.

Secret, François. "Les Cheminements de la Kabbala à la Renaissance: *Le Théâtre du Monde* de Giulio Camillo et son Influence." *Rivista di Storia della Filosophica* 14 (1959): 418-36.

Shapin, Steven. *A Social History of Truth: Civility and Science in Seventeenth-Century England*. Chicago: U of Chicago P, 1994.

Skalich de Lika [Scalichius, Scaliger], Paul. *Encyclopaediae, seu Orbis disciplinarum, tam sacrarum quam prophanarum Epistemon*. Basel: Ioannes Oporinus, 1559.

Terentius Afer, P. *Comoediae*. Ed. Jodocus Badius Ascensius. Lyons: [Johann] Wechsel, 1493.

————. [*Comoediae*]. Strassburg: J. Grüninger, 1496.

————. *Comoediae*. Venice: Jacobus Pentius for Lazarus de Soardis, 1497.

————. *Comoediae*. Venice: Simon de Luere for Lazarus de Soardis, 1497.

Van den Berg, Kent. *Playhouse and Cosmos: Shakespearean Theater as Metaphor.* Newark: U of Delaware P, 1985.

Van den Brincken, Anna-Dorothee. "Geschichtsbetrachtung bei Vincenz von Beauvais: Die Apologia Actoris zum Speculum Maius." *Deutsche Archiv für Erforschung des Mittelalters* 34 (1978): 410–99.

Varro, Marcus Terentius. *On the Latin Language [De lingua latina]*. Trans. Roland G. Kent. Loeb Classical Library. 1938. Cambridge: Harvard UP, 1977.

Vickers, Brian. "Bacon's Use of Theatrical Imagery." *Studies in the Literary Imagination* 4 (1971): 189–226.

Vives, Ioannes Lodovicus [Juan Luis]. *De disciplinis*. Cologne: Ioannes Gymnicus, 1536.

————. *On Education: A Translation of* De tradendis disciplinis [book II of *De disciplinis*]. Trans. Foster Watson. Cambridge: UP, 1913.

Webber, James Leslie, and C. R. Morey. *The Miniatures of the Manuscripts of Terence Prior to the Thirteenth Century.* 2 vols. Princeton: Princeton UP, 1930–31.

Weimann, Robert. "Author-ity in Signification: Rabelais and Vernacular Renaissance Prose Fiction." *Sprache und Literatur der Romania: Tradition und Wirkung: Festschrift für Horst Heintze zum 70. Geburtstag.* Eds. Irmgard Osols-Wehden, Giuliano Staccioli, and Babette Hesse. Berlin: Berlin, 1993. 87–99.

————. *Shakespeare and the Popular Tradition in Theater: Studies in the Social Dimension of Dramatic Form and Function.* Ed. Robert Schwartz. Baltimore: Johns Hopkins UP, 1978.

Westfall, Suzanne R. *Patrons and Performance: Early Tudor Household Revels.* Oxford: Clarendon, 1990.

Yates, Frances. *The Art of Memory.* Chicago: U of Chicago P, 1966.

————. *Theatre of the World.* London: Routledge, 1969.

Zwinger, Theodor. *Theatrum vitae humanae.* 1565. Basel: Frobenius, 1571.

Notes on Contributors

CRYSTAL BARTOLOVICH is an assistant professor of English at Syracuse University. She has published articles in cultural theory and early modern studies and is completing a book on spatial politics in the seventeenth century entitled *Boundary Disputes.*

JUDITH HABER is an associate professor of English at Tufts University. She is the author of *Pastoral and the Poetics of Self-Contradiction: Theocritus to Marvell* (Cambridge, 1994) and of various articles on Renaissance drama and narrative. Her chapter in this volume is part of a book-length project examining the intersections of erotic desire and dramatic form in early modern texts.

ROSEMARY KEGL is an associate professor of English and the director of the Susan B. Anthony Institute for Gender and Women's Studies at the University of Rochester. Her research and teaching interests include English Renaissance literature, feminism, and Marxism. She is the author of *The Rhetoric of Concealment: Figuring Gender and Class in Renaissance Literature* (Cornell, 1994) and is working on a book-length manuscript entitled *Inhabiting Shakespeare's "Wooden O": Theater, Intellectuals, and the Production of Knowledge.*

FIONA MCNEILL is a doctoral candidate in literature at Columbia University. She is currently completing her dissertation on single women in early modern drama.

MICHAEL NEILL is a professor of English at the University of Auckland. His recent publications include *Anthony and Cleopatra* (Oxford, 1994), *Issues of Death: Mortality and Identity in English Renaissance Drama* (Oxford, 1997), and *Putting History to the Question: Power, Politics and Society in English Renaissance Drama* (Columbia, 1999). He is currently editing *Othello* for the Oxford Shakespeare.

GARRETT A. SULLIVAN JR., assistant professor of English at Pennsylvania State University, is the author of *The Drama of Landscape: Land, Property, and Social Relations on the Early Modern Stage* (Stanford, 1998). He is currently writing a book on forgetting, memory, and English Renaissance drama, a portion of which recently appeared in *Shakespeare Quarterly.*

HENRY S. TURNER is a doctoral candidate in English at Columbia University. He is completing a dissertation entitled "Plotting Early Modernity" that examines how concepts of dramatic form, structure, and action emerged from early modern technical manuals and changes in the built environment of London. He has essays forthcoming in *ELH* and *Twentieth Century Literature.*

WILLIAM N. WEST has taught at the University of California at Berkeley and is a fellow in the humanities at Stanford University. He has published articles on the semiotics of, among other things, early modern libraries, dinner parties, and gifts. He is completing a manuscript entitled *Circles of Learning: Theaters, Encylopedias, and the Performance of Knowledge in Early Modern Europe.*